Between History and Philosophy

SUNY series in Chinese Philosophy and Culture
———————
Roger T. Ames, editor

Between History and Philosophy

Anecdotes in Early China

Edited by

Paul van Els

and

Sarah A. Queen

Cover art by Monica Klasing Chen © 2017

Published by State University of New York Press, Albany

© 2017 State University of New York

All rights reserved

Printed in the United States of America

No part of this book may be used or reproduced in any manner whatsoever without written permission. No part of this book may be stored in a retrieval system or transmitted in any form or by any means including electronic, electrostatic, magnetic tape, mechanical, photocopying, recording, or otherwise without the prior permission in writing of the publisher.

For information, contact State University of New York Press, Albany, NY
www.sunypress.edu

Production, Jenn Bennett
Marketing, Michael Campochiaro

Library of Congress Cataloging-in-Publication Data

Names: Els, Paul van, editor. | Queen, Sarah A. (Sarah Ann), editor.
Title: Between history and philosophy : anecdotes in early China / edited by Paul van Els and Sarah A. Queen.
Description: Albany : State University of New York Press, 2017. | Series: SUNY series in Chinese philosophy and culture | Includes bibliographical references and index.
Identifiers: LCCN 2016040637 (print) | LCCN 2017000322 (ebook) | ISBN 9781438466118 (hardcover : alk. paper) | ISBN 9781438466125 (pbk. : alk. paper) | ISBN 9781438466132 (ebook)
Subjects: LCSH: Anecdotes—China. | Anecdotes—China—History and criticism. | Chinese literature—Philosophy. | China—Intellectual life—To 221 B.C. | China—Intellectual life—221 B.C.–960 A.D.
Classification: LCC PN6267.C5 B48 2017 (print) | LCC PN6267.C5 (ebook) | DDC 895.18/02—dc23
LC record available at https://lccn.loc.gov/2016040637

10 9 8 7 6 5 4 3 2 1

He misses what an anecdote may say
Who thinks it voices merely jests and play.

—Elizabeth Hazelton Haight

Contents

Acknowledgments ix

Anecdotes in Early China 1
    Paul van Els and Sarah A. Queen

Part I
Anecdotes, Argumentation, and Debate

1. Non-deductive Argumentation in Early Chinese Philosophy 41
    Paul R. Goldin

2. The Frontier between Chen and Cai: Anecdote, Narrative, and Philosophical Argumentation in Early China 63
    Andrew Seth Meyer

3. Mozi as a Daoist Sage? An Intertextual Analysis of the "Gongshu" Anecdote in the *Mozi* 93
    Ting-mien Lee

4. Anecdotal Barbarians in Early China 113
    Wai-yee Li

Part II
Anecdotes and Textual Formation

5. Anecdote Collections as Argumentative Texts: The Composition of the *Shuoyuan* 147
    Christian Schwermann

6. From Villains Outwitted to Pedants Out-Wrangled: The Function of Anecdotes in the Shifting Rhetoric of the *Han Feizi*   193
   Heng Du

7. The Limits of Praise and Blame: The Rhetorical Uses of Anecdotes in the *Gongyangzhuan*   229
   Sarah A. Queen

PART III
ANECDOTES AND HISTORY

8. History without Anecdotes: Between the *Zuozhuan* and the *Xinian* Manuscript   263
   Yuri Pines

9. Cultural Memory and Excavated Anecdotes in "Documentary" Narrative: Mediating Generic Tensions in the *Baoxun* Manuscript   301
   Rens Krijgsman

10. Old Stories No Longer Told: The End of the Anecdotes Tradition of Early China   331
    Paul van Els

Contributors   357

Index   361

Acknowledgments

This book is the outcome of a delightful workshop that took place on May 31 and June 1, 2013, in the Blue Room of City Hotel Nieuw Minerva, which is located in an authentic sixteenth-century warehouse along one of the many canals in Leiden, The Netherlands. During two intensive days, more than a dozen scholars from a variety of nations and affiliations presented and discussed the various functions of anecdotes in early Chinese texts: Carine Defoort, Heng Du, Paul R. Goldin, Lisa Indraccolo, Rens Krijgsman, Ting-mien Lee, Wai-yee Li, Andrew Seth Meyer, Jens Østergård Petersen, Yuri Pines, Sarah A. Queen, Elisa Sabattini, Christian Schwermann, Newell Ann Van Auken, and Paul van Els. The audience included guests from places near and far, such as Ivana Buljan, Xi Hu, Simon Hürlimann, and Burchard Mansvelt Beck, as well as many Leiden University staff and students. We thank all those who were present for their comments and questions, which enriched the workshop and helped shape the present volume in significant ways.

We are also profoundly grateful to the Netherlands Organisation for Scientific Research (NWO) for sponsoring the workshop and some of the research that has led to this book. We are especially indebted to Nancy Lewandowski, History Department Assistant at Connecticut College, who generously contributed her time and expertise to prepare the manuscript for circulation and publication.

Finally, we are thankful to Roger T. Ames, Jenn Bennett, Michael Campochiaro, Nancy Ellegate, and other staff at SUNY Press, for their trust in our project and their help in materializing the present book, and to the anonymous reviewers who painstakingly scrutinized each chapter, as well as the book as a whole.

Anecdotes in Early China

PAUL VAN ELS AND SARAH A. QUEEN[1]

When the Duke of Xue served as chancellor of the state of Qi, the queen consort of King Wei of Qi died. There were ten young women whom the king esteemed. The Duke of Xue wished to discover whom the king desired to install, so he could implore the king to appoint that particular woman as his new queen consort. If the king heeded his advice, he would win the favor of the king and he would earn the respect of the newly appointed queen consort; but if the king did not heed his advice, he would not be graced with the king's favor and he would be disdained by the newly appointed queen consort. [Therefore] he wished to discover in advance which woman the king desired to appoint in order to encourage the king to appoint that very woman. So subsequently he crafted ten pairs of jade earrings, one of which was more beautiful than the others. He presented them to the king, who then distributed them among the ten young women as gifts. When they all sat together the next day, the duke spied out the whereabouts of the most beautiful pair of earrings and urged the king [that the woman who now wore them] be made the new queen consort.[2]

薛公相齊, 齊威王夫人死. 有十孺子, 皆貴於王, 薛公欲知王所欲立, 而請置一人以為夫人. 王聽之, 則是說行於王而重於置夫人也. 王不聽, 是說不行而輕於置夫人也. 欲先知王之所欲置以勸王置之, 於是為十玉珥而美其一而獻之, 王以賦十孺子. 明日坐, 視美珥之所在而勸王以為夫人.[3]

This colorful narrative is found in the *Han Feizi* 韓非子 (Master Han Fei), a voluminous text that lays out the politico-philosophical views of Han Fei 韓非 (ca. 280–233 BCE). An influential thinker of noble descent, he once served as advisor to the monarch who would be known to the world as the First Emperor of China. The brief narrative recounts an event that supposedly took place in the century before Han Fei's lifetime, when China was divided into various states that battled each other for hegemony. It features two historical figures: Tian Yinqi 田因齊, better known as King Wei of Qi 齊威王 (r. 356–320 BCE), who was one of the most powerful rulers of his day; and his youngest son, Tian Ying 田嬰, who was enfeoffed with Xue 薛 and is also known as Lord Jingguo 靖郭君.[4] The event involving these two men unfolds in the royal palace of the large state of Qi in the period following the passing of the queen consort. It is described succinctly and rather matter-of-factly, even when it details the duke's considerations ("If the king heeded his advice . . ."), and could be read as a factual depiction of a moment in Chinese history. However, brief as it may be, the story also teaches a valuable lesson, namely that clever strategies enable us to discover the hidden inclinations of others, even of those in power, and to use this knowledge to our advantage—a lesson Han Fei was keen to share with his readers. Most readers in his day, but even today, over two thousand years after the story was first committed to writing, would probably admire the duke's clever scheme and agree that as a piece of literature, the story is quite entertaining.

The earrings story bears all the hallmarks of what is generally dubbed an "anecdote," as we shall demonstrate below. Anecdotes similar to the one presented here are part and parcel of the literary tradition of early China, which typically refers to the period from the Zhou Dynasty 周 (ca. 1045–256 BCE), through the Qin Dynasty 秦 (221–206 BCE), to the former half of the Han Dynasty 漢 (202 BCE–220 CE). This formative period in Chinese history is marked by social, political, and economical turmoil as the monarchs of the Zhou house lost their political authority, especially after a disastrous military defeat in 771 BCE forced them to abandon most of the royal domain and move their capital eastwards. This gave rise to centuries of incessant warfare among competing states, which led gradually to the birth of the foundational dynasties of imperial China, the Qin and Han. The disintegration of a unified social order sparked fundamental questions about how to (re)create order in the world, as well as in one's personal life, and it served as a breeding ground for ideas on politics, ethics, society, military, history, and so on. Anecdotes played an important role in the fermentation, presentation, and transmission of these ideas, and as a result they can be found in a wide array of texts from this period, ranging from those often categorized as historical to works of a more philosophical nature.⁵ We find them in commentarial traditions associated with the canonical *Chunqiu* 春秋 (Spring and Autumn Annals), such as the *Zuozhuan* 左傳 (Zuo Commentary) and the *Gongyangzhuan* 公羊傳 (Gongyang Commentary); in philosophical writings such as the *Mozi* 墨子 (Master Mo), *Zhuangzi* 莊子 (Master Zhuang), *Yanzi chunqiu* 晏子春秋 (Spring and Autumn Annals of Master Yan), *Lüshi chunqiu* 呂氏春秋 (Spring and Autumn Annals of Mr. Lü), and *Huainanzi* 淮南子 (The Master of Huainan); in collections of anecdotes, such as the *Hanshi waizhuan* 韓詩外傳 (Han's Supplementary Commentary to the Odes), *Shuoyuan* 說苑 (Garden of Illustrative Examples), *Xinxu* 新序 (Newly Arranged [Anecdotes]), *Zhanguoce* 戰國策 (Stratagems of the Warring States), and *Lienüzhuan* 列女傳 (Biographies of Exemplary Women); and in historical writings such as the *Guoyu* 國語 (Discourses of the States), *Shiji* 史記 (Records of the Historian), and *Hanshu* 漢書 (History of the [Former] Han Dynasty). Judging by the sheer number of texts and the wealth of anecdotes they contain, in early China anecdotes constituted a pool of material that anyone could draw upon to ornament and illustrate a speech, a commentary, or a written treatise, and as such they served as powerful building blocks in arguments.

While anecdotes are well known to anyone with even a slight acquaintance with early Chinese literature, they have received surprisingly little scholarly attention as a distinctive form of writing.⁶ Scholars in China have been studying early Chinese anecdotes for some time now, resulting in several monographs, anthologies, and academic articles, but interest in other parts of the world only seriously coalesced in the past fifteen years or so.⁷ Since then, anecdotes have featured in the important and groundbreaking monographs by Wai-yee Li, Yuri Pines, and David Schaberg, which focus on their rhetorical functions in the *Zuozhuan* commentary to the *Chunqiu*.⁸ Anecdotes are also the subject of a handful of published academic articles by Albert Galvany, Jens Østergård Petersen, Sarah A. Queen, David Schaberg, Paul van Els, Kai Vogelsang, and others, several of which explore the relationship between anecdotal narrative and philosophical argumentation.⁹ Most recently, Jack W. Chen and David Schaberg have published an edited volume titled *Idle Talk: Gossip and Anecdote in Traditional China*, which provides a wonderful complement to the present volume as it picks up where this volume leaves off historically, to address anecdotes in Chinese history after the era we here identify as early China.¹⁰

The present volume is the first English-language book-length study to focus on the rhetorical function of anecdotal narratives across several literary genres of early China. In this volume we seek to clarify the nature and function of early Chinese anecdotes by raising the following questions: What are their characteristic features? What are their generic boundaries, that is to say, how do they relate to other types of narrative? What degree of historical authenticity do they display? How malleable were the stories? What different framing techniques did authors use to fit stock anecdotes into larger narrative contexts? What was the rhetorical power of anecdotes when used in argumentation? How does the early Chinese preference for using anecdotes in argumentation differ from modes of argumentation preferred in other eras and cultures? In addressing these and other questions, this book will advance the idea that anecdotes were an essential rhetorical tool that early Chinese writers used effectively to persuade their audience of one or another point of view.

Characteristic Features of Anecdotes

What is an anecdote? The word is used frequently and casually, for instance in utterings such as "they like to tell anecdotes about . . ." or "there is anecdotal evidence that . . . ," but a clear definition is not as evident at it may seem. Scholars have analyzed characteristic features of anecdotes for several decades now, predominantly on the basis of anecdotes in German, English, and other European languages, and their findings have made their way to dictionaries, encyclopedias of literature, and so on. This section discusses what anecdotes are, and what they are not, according to the literature. The next section will discuss how anecdotes in the Chinese tradition correspond to, and differ from, the more general understanding of anecdotes.

In their bare essence, anecdotes are brief narrations of events. They are created whenever and wherever people gather and talk—at dinner tables, in taverns, and so on.[11] Someone witnessed an event, or heard about it, and tells others about it.[12] Relating events to others is part of the human experience, which is why anecdotes have been around for the longest of times. It is therefore all the more remarkable that the term *anecdote* remains ill-defined to this day, as Lionel Gossman notes in his seminal paper on the topic.[13] The term finds its roots in the Greek word ἀνέκδοτα, meaning "things not given out," which is to say, "things unpublished." It was used as the title of a posthumous collection of unpublished writings by the historian Procopius of Caesarea (6th century), who had in his lifetime published a number of official histories in which he spoke favorably of the contemporaneous Byzantine emperor Justinian I (r. 527–565). In stark contrast, his unpublished writings reveal in great detail—and with much contempt—numerous scandalous doings of the emperor, his wife, and their entourage. Here is an example of the alleged depravity of emperor Justinian and his wife Theodora:

> There was in Constantinople a man by the name of Zeno, grandson of that Anthamius who had formerly been Emperor of the West. This man they appointed, with malice aforethought, Governor of Egypt, and commanded his immediate departure. But he delayed his voyage long enough to load his ship with his most valuable effects; for he had a countless amount of silver and gold plate inlaid with pearls, emeralds and other such precious stones. Whereupon they bribed some of his most trusted servants to remove these valuables from the ship as fast as they could carry them, set fire to the interior of the vessel, and inform Zeno that his ship had burst into flames of spontaneous combustion, with the loss of all his property. Later, when Zeno died suddenly, they took possession of his estate immediately as his legal heirs; for they produced a will, which it is whispered, he did not really make.[14]

Passages such as these would assuredly infuriate the powers that be, which was why, for fear of retribution, Procopius did not include them in his published histories, though they were eventually published after his death.[15]

During the Renaissance, following the rise of cities, a true leisure class, and the cult of the individual, anecdotes began to shake off their "association with the merely scandalous," as Clifton Fadiman notes, and they no longer remained unpublished.[16] As a result, in the centuries that followed the meaning of the term gradually broadened to amusing trivialities about people's lives, which eventually led the *Oxford English Dictionary* to define *anecdote* as "the narrative of a detached incident, or of a single event, told as being in itself interesting or striking."[17]

As accounts of single events, anecdotes are marked by brevity, or rather, by a lack of complexity, as they do not contain complex storylines, character developments, etcetera. The event related in the anecdote unfolds in a limited setting of time and space, and typically involves no more than a handful of actual persons, mostly prominent figures in society: rulers, statesmen, authors, actors, artists, athletes, and so on. Here is an example of a modern anecdote that describes a remarkable event in the life of Ansel Adams (1902–1984), the famous American landscape photographer:

> During his early years Adams studied the piano and showed marked talent. At one party (he recalls it as "*very* liquid") he played Chopin's F Major Nocturne. "In some strange way my right hand started off in F-sharp major while my left hand behaved well in F major. I could not bring them together. I went through the entire nocturne with the hands separated by a half-step." The next day a fellow guest complimented him on his performance, "You never missed a wrong note!"[18]

As can be seen from this example, anecdotes are "directly pointed towards or rooted in the real," as Joel Fineman puts it.[19] They generally relate real events involving actual people, mostly of some renown, whether from the past or still alive. This is not to say that the events actually happened as described, because anecdotes may have been "passed around by word of mouth or borrowed by one writer from another."[20] In fact, they may very well have been invented in the first place. The historicity of anecdotes is therefore often somewhat doubtful, as their veracity may be difficult to determine.[21] For example, Ansel Adams's story can only be verified by those who attended the bacchanalian party (and stayed sober enough to remember the event), and Procopius's revelations are even more doubtful. In the passage on Zeno's ship, we find it "whispered" that the imperial couple forged the governor's will, and in the same chapter it is reported that "one man said" he witnessed Justinian walking to and fro with his head detached, whereas "another" said he was there when the emperor's face all of a sudden changed into a shapeless mass of flesh. Reliable historical writings require more than just a few dubious eyewitness accounts before portraying the emperor as a headless zombie, so to speak, and it is therefore understandable that anecdotes are sometimes dismissed as mere hearsay, rumor, or gossip.[22]

These concerns hardly matter for those who produce and consume anecdotes. They value anecdotes not primarily as *historically accurate* depictions of events, but as *literary* depictions of events. Although anecdotes are somehow pointed toward or rooted in the real, they have something literary about them, Fineman notes, something that distinguishes them from other, non-literary ways to refer to the real.[23] One present-day anecdote-monger goes so far as to write that anecdotes are "not about facts," adding that "with anecdotes, story is everything."[24] As cleverly crafted stories, no matter how brief, anecdotes have a beginning (situation or exposition), middle (encounter or crisis), and end (resolution).[25] In the Ansel Adams anecdote, for example, the beginning describes the situation by mentioning the time ("his early years") and place ("at one party") of the event; the middle part describes the out-of-the-ordinary event; and the closing sentence delivers a witty punchline.

The punchline indicates that anecdotes such as this one aim for a smile on the reader's face. Indeed, humor is an important function of anecdotes, and humorous anecdotes are known to spread most widely. This is not to say that all anecdotes are humorous, as "there is plenty of room for the quieter anecdote whose value lies in the illumination of character or the inculcation of a moral lesson."[26] Whether anecdotes prompt delectation or contemplation, an important function—broadly speaking—is diversion, as anecdotes are somehow considered interesting or amusing.[27]

Although anecdotes are understood as detached and freestanding narratives, they often do not occur on their own but as part of larger narrative contexts, such as biographies, histories, speeches, and essays. Indeed, "the anecdote appears to be both sufficient to itself and yet to gesture to its incompleteness, always invoking a larger whole into which it needs to be inserted. Anecdotes are memorable, often personal narratives that open up something beyond them, and they are capable of uncovering the neglected, the strange, or the unfamiliar that lies within a more familiar narrative."[28]

In sum, anecdotes can be described as short, freestanding accounts of particular events in the lives of actual persons, most of whom are of some renown.[29] The accounts are rooted in reality, but their historicity may be doubtful. They should be seen as literary constructs, often with a tripartite structure. With a didactic message or a witty punchline, they are narrated as being somehow interesting or entertaining. They rarely stand on their own, but often form part of larger narrative structures.

Anecdotes in Early Chinese Texts

The characteristic features of anecdotes outlined in the previous section are developed by scholars who worked primarily on the European and American literary traditions, not on the literary tradition of early China. Interestingly, the brief narratives that pervade early Chinese literature share many of these features, but also diverge from them in important ways. We shall now turn our attention to the early Chinese anecdote. By defining its characteristic features, we hope to contribute to a fuller understanding of the rich potential of anecdotes as a distinct literary form.

Time, Place, and Protagonists

Early Chinese anecdotes can also be described as short, freestanding accounts of single events. The time frame of the anecdote typically corresponds to the duration of the event, possibly with brief references to the lead-up and the outcome of the event. The locales tend to fall within common stereotypes that provide a discrete context (a royal court, battlefield, gateway, riverbank, bridge), though idiosyncratic settings occasionally appear. The *dramatis personae* that participate in the event are few. In the earrings anecdote, translated above, the two main characters are the powerful king and his clever son, both clearly identified to add context and status to the anecdote, with the deceased queen consort and the court ladies as nameless supporting cast. Other anecdotes feature well-known figures from China's extensive past, such as the Duke of Zhou 周公 (r. 1042–1036 BCE), Duke Wen of Jin 晉文公 (r. 636–628 BCE), King Fuchai of Wu 吳王夫差 (r. 495–473 BCE), King Goujian of Yue 越王勾踐 (r. 496–465 BCE), Kongzi 孔子 (551–479 BCE), better known to Western readers as Confucius, and Sunzi 孫子 (ca. 545–470 BCE), also known as Sun Tzu. These actual historical persons fascinated the creators of anecdotes, as well as their readers, all of whom belonged to the literate upper echelons of society. Occasionally the main characters are clearly fictionalized, such as the Confucius character in the *Zhuangzi*, who in some passages espouses teachings that are obviously at odds with how he is portrayed in other texts. In addition to anecdotes about prominent figures, and in stark contrast to anecdotes in other traditions (outlined in the previous section), early Chinese texts also contain numerous anecdotes featuring people who remain unnamed. In most cases, the anecdotes merely characterize the unnamed protagonists and identify the state where they were from. For example, "in Chu there was someone who was skilled at being a thief" 楚有善為偷者 or "among the inhabitants of Song there was one who had obtained jade" 宋人有得玉者. In addition to unnamed people, and in even starker contrast to anecdotes in other traditions, early Chinese anecdotes occasionally portray fictional entities, such as the talking animals, trees, skulls, and personified abstractions (e.g., Bright Dazzlement 光曜 and Non-Existence 無有) made famous in the *Zhuangzi*. In form and function, anecdotes involving unnamed or even nonhuman protagonists are similar to those involving prominent historical figures. For example, the *Han Feizi* presents an anecdote about an unnamed man of wealth in the state of Song right after an anecdote involving Duke Wu of Zheng 鄭武公 (r. 771–744 BCE), and the text explicitly uses both to exemplify the dangers of speaking ones mind.[30] Similarly, the *Huainanzi* sandwiches an anecdote featuring the anthropomorphized entities Gaptooth 齧缺 and Ragbag 被衣 between anecdotes featuring well-known rulers of the state of Zhao 趙 in the fifth century BCE, and it links all three anecdotes to an enigmatic canonical scripture.[31] In other words, early Chinese authors use one and the same narrative form for short stories involving historical persons, unnamed persons, animals, objects, abstractions, and so on. Just because the main character is not a famous person, or not even a human being at all, does not seem to disqualify these short stories as anecdotes in early Chinese literature. In terms of the *dramatis personae*, early Chinese anecdotes appear to be somewhat more accommodating than their counterparts in other literary traditions, where short stories about unnamed people, animals, and so on, are more likely to be categorized as jokes, fables, and so on, than as anecdotes.

Length

As depictions of single events, depictions that are short enough to be committed to memory and recited aloud in conversation or debate, early Chinese anecdotes tend to be brief. This means that they generally contain no more than a few dozen Chinese graphs, although longer exemplars also exist. Interestingly, even different versions of the same anecdote can range widely in length. For example, the Chinese text of the earrings anecdote related above contains just over a hundred graphs. An alternative version of the same anecdote, presented below, consists of about eighty graphs, while another version presented below, runs less than forty graphs. Importantly, the main story line remains the same across the different accounts, which are clearly recognizable as distinct accounts of one and the same event.

In spite of their relative brevity, early Chinese anecdotes, much like their counterparts in other literary traditions, often have an identifiable beginning (situation or exposition); middle (encounter or crisis), and end (resolution). In the earrings anecdote, for example, the main characters and the problem of finding a new queen consort are introduced at the beginning; the duke's scheme is explained in the middle; and the final part suggests how he successfully gained influence with the king.

Some anecdotes may have been so well-known that even a brief reference was all that was necessary to call up the narrative. A simple reference to Lady Boji of Song 宋伯姬 (6th century BCE), for instance, would call to the minds of an educated audience the tale of a noble widow who chose to die in a fire rather than commit the ritual impropriety of leaving her palace without a proper escort, thus providing an opportunity to debate the deeper moral implications of her actions.[32] Should Lady Boji be remembered as a misguided matron who failed to correctly prioritize conflicting moral obligations or should she be commemorated as an exemplary martyr who was willing to die to preserve her purity? Many anecdotes similar to the one about Lady Boji achieved an almost proverbial status, and even today, numerous Chinese sayings typically consisting of four graphs each (such as "the King of Qi spared an ox" 齊王舍牛) function as a shorthand for anecdotes from early China, which truly bespeak their lasting popularity.

Historicity and Factuality

Early Chinese anecdotes typically relate historical events, but they were not necessarily intended or understood as relating events that actually occurred. The anecdotes lie on a "continuum of historicity" ranging from the generally unexceptionable historical examples to more questionable examples, to parables with no pretense of factuality.[33] It is highly unlikely that readers would have considered stories involving talking trees and skulls as real, and even when the main protagonists are historicized figures who share identities with recorded figures from the historical annals of China's hoary past, and who imbue the tale with an air of historical authenticity, it is not certain that these anecdotes were taken at face value, or even intended to be taken at face value. Authors in early China had different modes of narration at their disposal, and they opted for a different mode when presenting the reader with factual accounts of events.[34] So it seems that authors and readers expected the anecdotes to be *potentially* historically accurate, even if they did not believe them to be *actually* factually true. Consequently, anecdotes recount events that are either potentially true (such as the earrings story) or obviously false (such as the stories of talking trees and skulls in the *Zhuangzi*). In sum, similar to anecdotes in other literary traditions, historicity is not the main concern of early Chinese anecdotes, as their value resided elsewhere, for example, in their ability to persuade, instruct, or entertain.[35]

Variations and Valences

Given the appeal of anecdotes, and their rhetorical, didactic, or entertaining powers, it is not surprising that the same basic anecdote, with variations, appears across a number of texts or in some cases, even within a single text. For example, the earrings anecdote appears not only in the *Han Feizi*, but also in the *Zhanguoce*, a collection of anecdotes on warfare and political manipulation in and among the various states that divided China in the Warring States Period 戰國 (453–221 BCE). The *Zhanguoce* version reads as follows:

> The queen consort of the king of Qi died. There were seven young women who were all close to him. The Duke of Xue wished to discover whom the king desired to install, so he presented the king with seven pairs of earrings, of which one was more beautiful than the others. When he observed the whereabouts of the most beautiful pair of earrings the next day, he urged the king to install [the woman who now wore them] as the new queen consort.
>
> 齊王夫人死, 有七孺子皆近. 薛公欲知王所欲立, 乃獻七珥, 美其一, 明日視美珥所在, 勸王立為夫人.³⁶

There are notable differences with the *Han Feizi* version quoted earlier. Only about a third the length of that version, the *Zhanguoce* version is more concise and less detailed, as it does not mention the posthumous name of the king, or spell out the thought process of the duke ("If the king heeded his advice . . ."). In addition, the number of favorite court ladies is listed as seven in the *Zhanguoce*, as opposed to ten in the *Han Feizi*. It is unclear how much of this is significant. For instance, the different numbers of court ladies could be meaningful, but it could also be a textual variation of little importance, much in the same way that in our own day and age two accounts of the same event will inevitably differ in the details. Similarly, the relative brevity of this version could be meaningful, but it could also be simply due to different literary preferences, eloquently elaborate versus conveniently concise.

That said, variations in anecdotes very often were *not* simply the result of errors in transmission or mere literary preferences. Instead, they were by design quite deliberate as they enabled the various transmitters of the tale to highlight different aspects of a core story to serve different arguments. These differences—as we show below, and as several chapters in this volume demonstrate—carried significant intellectual valences. They enabled a given anecdote to speak from multiple perspectives depending on its transmitter who operates in a wider web of intellectual and cultural discourse and debate.

Framing Techniques

Framing strategies further distinguished similar anecdotes from one another and served to underscore the different purposes they served in a given text or texts. Whether entertaining, moralistic, or deployed for other rhetorical purposes, anecdotes did not stand on their own, but were part of larger structures of meaning, such as a commentary, an essay, or a debate. In these contexts, various framing techniques served to determine particular readings of the anecdote at hand. This framing worked on several levels—both implicit and explicit—and with varying degrees of narrative complexity.

The earrings anecdote from the *Han Feizi*, translated at the beginning of our essay, provides an apposite example. The anecdote occurs in a series of chapters titled "Chushuo" 儲說 (Collection of Illustrative Examples), in which several political "guidelines" (*jing* 經) are explained through "illustrative examples" (*shuo* 說). The latter mostly consist of series of anecdotes.[37] In the case of the earrings anecdote, the chapter is structured as follows:

- Opening statement
- Guideline 1 + references to illustrative examples 1
- Guideline 2 + references to illustrative examples 2
- Guideline 3 + references to illustrative examples 3
- Illustrative examples 1
- Illustrative examples 2
- Illustrative examples 3

The chapter opens with the statement that "there are three methods for a lord to maintain control over his ministers" 君所以治臣者有三. It then briefly outlines these three methods as important guidelines in governance. The second of these guidelines is outlined as follows:

The ruler of humankind is the hub of benefit and harm. The spokes are many, yet they all converge at the ruler. For this reason, if his preferences are revealed, then his subordinates will have a way to get to him, and the ruler will become befuddled; if the words he speaks are circulated widely, then his ministers will challenge his words, and the ruler will no longer be godlike.

人主者, 利害之軺轂也. 射者眾, 故人主共矣. 是以好惡見則下有因, 而人主惑矣; 辭言通則臣難言, 而主不神矣.[38]

This guiding principle warns the ruler not to let his feelings or ideas be known, for otherwise his underlings will challenge his directives, or worse, they will use this knowledge to manipulate him. A list of references to relevant anecdotes follows the description of this guiding principle. It includes the following formulation: "I will shed light on this [guideline] with [the illustrative example of] Master Jingguo's gift of ten pairs of earrings" 明之以靖郭氏之獻十珥也. Master Jingguo is another name for the Duke of Xue, and hence this formulation is an explicit reference to the anecdote that occurs below in the same chapter. The reference makes it easy for the reader to locate the illustrative anecdote further down in the chapter. In sum, in the *Han Feizi* the earrings anecdote is explicitly marked as an illustrative example in a larger argument that warns the ruler against disclosing his thoughts and feelings.

A different and implicit framing structure informs the version of the earring anecdote in the *Zhanguoce*. In that text, chapters are organized by state, and each chapter includes numerous anecdotes relevant to the history of its respective state. The earrings anecdote appears in a series of six linked chapters that tell the history of the state of Qi. The specific chapter in which it occurs focuses on the words and deeds of Lord Jingguo and his son. The earrings anecdote adds substance to the chapter by presenting one episode in the history of Qi, namely the event that followed the demise of the queen consort. The framing of the anecdote, as part of a series of historical anecdotes that focus on the two lords, suggests that the main purpose of the earrings anecdote in this text is historical, as it seeks to reveal the manipulative qualities of Lord Jingguo's character which informed the rise of this powerful courtier in the state of Qi. However, the historicity of the *Zhanguoce* has been questioned since the time of its creation, and scholars nowadays generally agree that the *Zhanguoce* is "very unreliable as a history book and was probably never intended to serve as one."[39] Instead, it is often described as a handbook of rhetoric, or a manual of persuasive speaking.⁴⁰ Still, the text lacks fundamental qualities of a textbook, as Paul R. Goldin suggests, and is perhaps best seen as a collection of anecdotes that illustrate the art of intrigue.⁴¹ The underlying idea of the *Zhanguoce*, as outlined by the Han Dynasty compiler of the text, is that enlightened rulers in times of peace transform the populace by serving as models of virtuous behavior. This was not the case in the Warring States Period, the era covered by the *Zhanguoce*, when rulers allegedly were no beacons of virtue and the slow process of transforming the population by moral education proved inefficacious in the face of the proliferating crises and emergencies. Only short-term strategies and tactics as methods of expedience would help to maintain stability in those trying times. Therein lies the role of the counselors at the courts, who used schemes and stratagems, tailored for specific crises or emergencies, to assist the benighted rulers of their day. Although no handbook in the strict sense of the word, the *Zhanguoce* contains anecdotes that illustrate to counselors what to do or to avoid for their schemes and stratagems to work. The first priority for the counselors is to gain access to the ruler. The clever trick with the earrings is instrumental in this regard, as it points Lord Jingguo to the lady that was most beloved by the king. By promoting that particular lady, he demonstrates that he truly understood the king, which increases his chances that the king would turn to him for advice in the future. Thus, in contrast to the *Han Feizi* where the anecdote serves to warn rulers not to display their likes and dislikes to their underlings, in the *Zhanguoce* it provides those underlings with the very tool to influence their ruler.

Yet another framing structure informs the version of the story that occurs in chapter 12, "Daoying" 道應 (Responses of the Way) of the *Huainanzi*, an encyclopedic politico-philosophical treatise that was written under the auspices of Liu An 劉安 (ca. 179–122 BCE), the King of Huainan 淮南王. The *Huainanzi* version reads as follows:

> The queen consort of the king of Qi died. The king wanted to appoint a new queen consort but had not yet decided who it would be, so he directed his ministers to deliberate the issue. The Duke of Xue, hoping to discover the king's choice, presented him with ten pairs of earrings, one of which was especially beautiful. The next morning he asked about the whereabouts of the most beautiful pair of earrings and urged that the woman who now had them should be appointed queen consort. The king of Qi

was delighted by this and thereafter respected and valued the Duke of Xue even more.

Thus, if the intentions and desires of the ruler of humankind are visible on the outside, he will fall subject to the control of his subjects.

Therefore the *Laozi* says, "Block the openings, shut the doors, and all your life you will not labor."[42]

齊王后死, 王欲置后而未定, 使群臣議. 薛公欲中王之意, 因獻十珥而美其一. 旦日, 因問美珥之所在, 因勸立以為王后. 齊王大說, 遂尊重薛公. 故人主之意欲見於外, 則為人臣之所制. 故《老子》曰:「塞其兌, 閉其門, 終身不勤.」[43]

Here, the earrings story is followed by a brief statement in which the meaning of the story, as understood by Liu An and his collaborators, is made explicit ("if the intentions and desires of the ruler of humankind are visible on the outside . . ."), and another brief statement quoted from the *Laozi* 老子 (Old Master), the foundational scripture of Daoism that was a major source of inspiration for those who created the *Huainanzi*. In and of itself, the *Laozi* quotation is rather enigmatic. What does it mean to "block the openings" or "shut the doors," and why would the result of these actions be that "all your life you will not labor"? By linking this quotation to the earrings anecdote, the *Huainanzi* suggests that blocking openings and shutting doors are figurative ways of encouraging people to keep their preferences to themselves, and that the phrase "all your life you will not labor" is another way of saying that as a ruler you will stay in power and have others work for you. In other words, the *Huainanzi* uses this anecdote to explain the highly enigmatic *Laozi* in a specific way, but at the same time it uses the *Laozi* to read the anecdote in a specific way. Hence, the anecdote is situated within a formal framing structure: a quotation from an authoritative text or person caps the story and suggests a particular reading of both the cautionary tale and the saying attributed to Laozi. On the one hand, the *Huainanzi* shows what particular anecdotes mean by reference to an authoritative text. On the other hand, it bolsters the authority of that authoritative text by showing that the meanings it contains are prefigured in the fabric of events described by the anecdotes. By linking the two—historical anecdote and canonical quotation—Liu An moreover displays his mastery of both Chinese history and canonical literature, thereby presenting himself as an authority to his readers, most notably the emperor to whom he presented his work in 139 BCE.[44]

In sum, anecdotes were nested in a variety of framing structures that served different rhetorical purposes. They could range from the relatively simple framings discussed above to highly elaborate narrative tapestries.[45] The significance of other framing examples will be taken up by several of the chapters included in this volume. Collectively the chapters demonstrate the fruitfulness of a methodology committed to analyzing anecdotes *in situ*, within the very significant framing structures that determine how they are to be read and understood. As we will see, not only does such a methodology reveal the rhetorical functions of anecdotes within given texts and across texts, it also promises to shed new light on the archeology of early Chinese texts, providing insights into the manner in which texts were formed.

Genre

Scholars still disagree, writes Gossman, as to "whether the anecdote can properly be considered a particular form or genre, like the novel, the maxim, or the fable."[46] Genre or not, as basic building blocks in much of the prose writing in early China, anecdotes can be seen as a distinct type of writing that is closely linked to several important forms of historical writing and philosophical argumentation. Occupying the liminal space—replete with their panoply of creative potentialities—between history and philosophy, they complement or contrast with these other types of writings in significant ways. In order to gain a better understanding of early Chinese anecdotes as a "genre," it may be helpful if we sharpen their boundaries by distinguishing them from related types of historical and philosophical writings.

Anecdotes and Historical Genres

Anecdotes in early Chinese texts often feature historical figures as they recount events in Chinese history. Even if their historicity is questionable, anecdotes may be seen as a form of historical writing, and they are clearly related to other historical genres. In this respect, early Chinese anecdotes resemble those in other traditions. For instance, Gossmann notes that anecdotes in the European tradition have "always stood in a close relation to the longer, more elaborate narratives of history, sometimes in a supportive role, as examples and illustrations, sometimes in a challenging role, as the repressed of history."[47] The longer historical narratives, preferred in the European tradition, were interspersed with anecdotes as illustrative examples to throw additional light on people or events. That the source of the anecdotes often could not be verified was part of their appeal, as they added color to the elaborate historical narratives that did meet contemporaneous fact-checking standards. Moreover, coming from unofficial sources, they could present an alternative to the "official" historical narratives that may have been stylized to meet certain (moral) standards. Still, their questionable credibility meant that they were often considered of lesser importance, and sometimes looked down upon as mere gossip or hearsay, which explains why their role in the European historiographical tradition remained ancillary to more exalted historical genres.[48]

Whereas anecdotes were considered of lesser importance in historical writings in the European tradition, they occupied a more central position in early Chinese historical writings. In several of his publications, David Schaberg has called attention to the importance of the anecdote within the Chinese historiographical enterprise, asserting that anecdotes were "the basic form of historical narrative—and therefore the basic stuff of historical knowledge itself."[49] In Chinese historiography, the anecdote was a very versatile mechanism by which the past could be rendered meaningful. That is to say, alongside other ways of deriving meaning from the past (looking for patterns in long records of events, quantifying developments and trends, etcetera), the "anecdotalization" of historical events and figures made it possible to impregnate each moment in history with discrete meaning. This had both instrumental and normative implications. It was instrumental because it made the past usable as a source of authority (important in an intellectual setting that largely lacked a body of "revealed" precepts). Normative, in that being able to show what the past meant was the chief way of demonstrating control over the past, which in itself had been a touchstone of authority in a Chinese social context since Shang 商 times (ca. 1500–1045 BCE) or before. The *Huainanzi*, as we showed earlier, is a perfect example in that Liu An asserts his authority by linking historical anecdotes to canonical quotations, thereby demonstrating his mastery of both the past and the classics.

As a text that consist mostly of anecdotes strung together without much attention to an overall structure, the *Zhanguoce* that we discussed earlier might be taken to contradict the idea that anecdotes never appear gratuitously. But we would assert that this text is another example of how anecdotes were used as primary historiographical tools in making the past meaningful. Each anecdote lends itself to generating an array of meanings for the event it encapsulates, thus taken together they provide the reader with a means to decipher what the past signified. This, we suggest, is a key norm distinguishing early Chinese historiography from classical European historicism. Early Chinese historiographers were not determined to uniquely recover the past as it was, but rather were worried that the past had not truly been redeemed from oblivion unless one could read some meaning in it. They were not horrified by the prospect that the past could be understood to have multifarious and divergent meanings, as long as it could be demonstrated to have meant *something*.

Given the historiographical significance of anecdotes, it should come as no surprise that they are closely associated with various types of historical writings. A survey of the historical writings of early China presents an interesting mix of historical forms from the *Shangshu* 尚書 (Ancient Documents) and *Chunqiu* to the *Shiji*, *Hanshu*, and later dynastic histories. With their associated anecdotes, each served a particular historical function and fueled a particular dimension of the early Chinese historical and historiographical enterprise as vehicles for historical preservation, reflection, recollection, remembrance, and imagination. As various chapters in this volume demonstrate, distinguishing the different forms and objectives of historical writings provides an important context for clarifying the boundaries between history and anecdote, as well as understanding their differing rhetorical functions.

Arguably the most famous historical treatise of early China is the *Shangshu*, also known as the *Shujing* 書經 (Book of Documents). Revered as one of the Five Classics of Chinese literature, it predominantly narrates the pronouncements of important figures from the (mythical) beginning of Chinese history up to the seventh century BCE. Tradition holds that materials that were not used in the compilation of the *Shangshu* were collected in the *Yi Zhou shu* 逸周書 (Remaining Zhou Documents), a compendium of documents on the history of the Zhou Dynasty up to the sixth century BCE.[50] These two texts were long seen as the main, if not the only, representations of what we would call a "documentary" (*shu* 書) mode of historical writing. Recently procured bamboo slip manuscripts that date from the Warring States Period, now in the collection of Qinghua (Tsinghua) University 清華大學, contain texts that present-day researchers have identified as resembling the aforementioned texts.[51] It thus appears that this "documentary mode" was not restricted to the *Shangshu* and *Yi Zhou shu*, but employed more widely in early China and may even be seen as a distinct genre of writing. In her seminal article on this topic, Sarah Allan sets out to define this genre as "any text, which claims to be a contemporaneous record of a speech of an ancient king."⁵² As a contemporaneous record of direct speech, it "demands an acceptance of historical authenticity: this is not a historical record or an interpretation. There is no intermediary: it is what kings and ministers actually said."⁵³ It is precisely in this feature of contemporaneousness that documentary narratives differ from other forms of historical writings, including anecdotes: the latter typically make no pretense of being contemporaneous records (as indicated, for instance, by the fact that protagonists in anecdotes are often referred to by their posthumous name). Although documentary and anecdotal types of writing transmit information concerning the past, they do so differently, as the former endeavor to "remember and preserve" while the latter seek to "recollect and reflect," as Rens Krijgsman observes in his contribution to this volume.

A different type of historical narrative can be found in the *Chunqiu*, another one of the Five Classics of early China. The term *chunqiu* 春秋, which literally means "spring and autumn," marks the passage of time and was used in the titles of chronicles compiled under the auspices of the rulers of the various states that divided China during the Zhou Dynasty. To date, only the *Chunqiu* from the state of Lu 魯 survives. This *Chunqiu* is a terse court chronicle of events in the state of Lu from 722 to 481 BCE. Its brief chronological entries record a very limited range of significant state events such as military actions, diplomatic meetings and treaties, deaths and funerals in the ruling family and of high officials, rituals and sacrifices, battles, invasions, and events that affected crops such as floods, frost, and pestilence, and astronomical phenomena. No attempt is made to attribute cause or motive, or describe the attitudes, thoughts, or feelings of the historical figures recorded. Moreover, historical figures are mentioned by state and title or kinship to the ruling house devoid of further description.⁵⁴ Here is a typical *Chunqiu* entry for the year 668 BCE, or the twenty-sixth year in the reign of Duke Zhuang of Lu 魯莊公 (r. 693–662 BCE) translated in accordance with the *Gongyangzhuan* commentary:

> Twenty-sixth year. Spring. The lord attacked the Rong.
>
> Summer. The lord returned from the Rong attack.
>
> Cao put to death its great officers.
>
> Autumn. The lord joined men from Song and men from Qi and attacked Xu.

Winter. Twelfth month. *Guihai* day. First day of the month. There was a solar eclipse.

二十有六年, 春, 公伐戎. 夏, 公至自伐戎. 曹殺其大夫. 秋, 公會宋人, 齊人, 伐徐. 冬, 十有二月, 癸亥, 朔, 日有食之.[55]

As this example shows, entries in the *Chunqiu* are extremely terse. Events that must have had a dramatic impact in real life, such as the invasion of another state, are here compressed into single sentences, one after the other without explanation or illustration. Such terse statements are not exclusive to the *Chunqiu* from the state of Lu. For instance, Mengzi 孟子 (Mencius) remarks that the states of Jin 晉 and Chu 楚 had texts similar to the *Chunqiu* from Lu.[56] These texts did not survive, but several early Chinese manuscripts that have recently surfaced, such as the *Biannianji* 編年記 (Record of Sequential Years) and the *Xinian* 繫年 (Sequence of Years), contain similar terse annalistic statements, which means that we can probably speak of an "annalistic" (*chunqiu* 春秋) mode of historical writing.[57] The historical aims of the dry and formulaic annalistic mode differed markedly from the documentary mode discussed above. Whereas documentary narratives purport to be contemporaneous accounts of speeches by kings, annalistic records contain no speech and do not purport to be contemporaneous. The latter also differs markedly from the anecdotal type of narrative. Annalistic histories have no identifiable didactic or literary value—salient features of anecdotes—and reading the terse chronicle entries "is no more intellectually or esthetically engaging than reading a telephone book," as Yuri Pines wittily remarks in his contribution to this volume. Although anecdotes can be sharply distinguished from annalistic records, they do play a role in the three famous commentaries associated with the *Chunqiu*, as the *Zuo*, *Gongyang*, and *Guliang* commentarial traditions all deploy anecdotes as a hermeneutic strategy to reflect upon the meaning and significance of the historical events and figures at hand. Indeed, the richly textured anecdote constituted a literary form well-adapted to fill out the terse and laconic entries of the *Chunqiu*, as Sarah A. Queen demonstrates in her contribution to this volume. In fact, these commentaries, particularly the *Zuozhuan*, which stands as the most important source of many later anecdotes, can be said to form the beginning of the Chinese anecdotal tradition.

The distinct historical aims and literary forms of writings in the documentary and annalistic modes clearly set them apart not only from each other, but also from later historical writings such as the biographies (*zhuan*

傳) of Sima Qian's *Shiji* and Ban Gu's *Hanshu*, which interweave anecdotes into their historical narratives to such an extent that the boundaries between historical and anecdotal narrative becomes indistinguishable. Indeed, these later historical productions may very well represent the Han dynasty culmination of a long historical process of experimentation beginning in the Warring States in which certain types of historical writings were combined with anecdotes while others abandoned such efforts, setting the pattern for the writing of official histories in the dynasties that followed. We will see in the chapters below, how anecdotes were incorporated into the narratives and commentaries of historical writings during the Warring States and Han periods in seemingly deliberate and self-conscious ways to further the attendant historiographical enterprises they encompassed and how during the Han their popularity waned to give rise to new stories that would vivify historical discussions of the post-Han period, as Paul van Els demonstrates in his contribution to this volume.

Anecdotes and Philosophical Genres

The "pro meaning bias" in historiography discussed above has its corollary in philosophy, which is to say that early Chinese thinkers privileged the notion that abstract, universal truths were often contingent upon and could only be known through particular actualizing contexts.[58] In other words, in the same way that early Chinese historiographers often insisted that the past must be meaningful, early Chinese philosophers sometimes insisted that meaning must be in some sense historical. Anecdotes—those compact, powerful, malleable, and often pleasurable miniature historical narratives—were ideally suited to their purposes. Hence, anecdotes almost never appear gratuitously or purely for entertainment value in early Chinese philosophical texts. Rather, they either serve to register particular meanings or are set into larger frameworks that use commentary, structure, and context to derive particular meanings from them. One could say that in early Chinese writings, anecdotes help to solve philosophical problems, as the authors come to the solution via the medium of narrative.

The intimate relationship between historical anecdote and philosophical argumentation abounds in the *Yanzi chunqiu*, *Lüshi chunqiu*, *Han Feizi*, *Hanshi waizhuan*, *Huainanzi*, and numerous other texts. Many chapters in these texts contain anecdotes, or consist entirely of collections of anecdotes, framed in various ways to yield a cohesive philosophical point. For example, the *Lüshi chunqiu*, compiled around 239 BCE under the auspices of Lü

Buwei 呂不韋 (d. 235 BCE), chancellor of the state of Qin, is a rich collection of anecdotes arranged thematically into twenty-six books that begins with a brief philosophical essay followed by a series of anecdotes that illustrate the claims of its respective opening passage. The *Lüshi chunqiu* is neither simply an anecdote collection nor a collection of philosophical essays but lies somewhere between the two genres.[59] Indeed, the distinct mix that abides in this text exhibits a salient characteristic of early Chinese philosophical argumentation more generally: it tended to be highly contextualized, moralized, and politicized, and the anecdote, moreover, provided a richly textured and multivalent medium through which to illustrate its views. Other early Chinese philosophical texts exhibit a similarly intimate relationship between anecdote and philosophical argumentation as in the *Lüshi chunqiu*.

Across early Chinese texts, anecdotes are most closely related to a form of argumentation that these texts refer to with the graph 說.[60] This graph has a number of distinct readings and meanings, two of which concern us most.[61] Read as *shuo* (OC *lhot) it broadly means "to speak, to discuss, to explain" as a verb and "explanation" as a noun.[62] Read as *shui* (OC *lhots) it broadly means "to exhort, to persuade" as a verb and "exhortation, persuasion" as a noun. We find the graph 說, with these distinct readings and related connotations as *shuo* and *shui*, in the titles of several early Chinese texts and chapters. Given the fact that the two readings are related, and both are written with the same graph, it is not always easy to determine which reading is meant in each context.

In some contexts the graph 說 is probably best read as *shui*, "persuasion," which refers to a recorded conversation or exchange in which the chief speaker tries to persuade the listener to accept a particular point of view or policy position, as Sarah A. Queen has argued in an earlier publication.[63] To persuade others obviously requires skills and tact, and early Chinese texts display full awareness of that. The *Han Feizi*, for instance, contains a chapter titled "Shuinan" 說難 (The Difficulties of Persuasion) that "discusses the principal challenges that might impede a successful persuasion," as Queen suggests.[64] The greatest difficulty, according to the *Han Feizi*, is "to know the mind of the one to be persuaded, so as to match our persuasion to it" 知所說之心, 可以吾說當之.[65] Some individuals in early China proved to be exceptionally skilled at persuasion, as can be seen from a number of outstanding persuasions collected in the "Shanshui" 善說 (Skilled at Persuasion) chapter of the *Shuoyuan*.

The graph 說 is also used in the titles of texts and chapters that consist mostly if not entirely of anecdotes, aphorisms, and other textual materials, which could be used to explain, or illustrate, certain politico-philosophical ideas. In these contexts the graph might be best read as *shuo*, and translated as "illustrations" or "illustrative examples." For instance, as we have shown above in the context of the earrings anecdote, the *Han Feizi* contains several chapters titled "Chushuo" 儲說 (Collection of Illustrative Examples), which consist of so-called "guidelines" (*jing* 經) that are illustrated by series of illustrative anecdotes (*shuo* 說). The same text also includes two chapters titled "Shuolin" 說林 (Forest of Illustrative Examples). The word forest (*lin* 林) here indicates a large number of textual materials, in other words a "collection," and when we look at the kind of textual materials contained in these collections, we find mostly anecdotes, but also a few aphoristic observations about animals or objects. For example:

> Among the various worms there is a kind of tapeworm with one body and two heads that bite at one another when fighting for food. When the one head killed the other head, it thereby killed itself as well. Ministers fighting with one another over various matters and thereby losing the state, are similar to those tapeworms.
>
> 蟲有螝者, 一身兩口, 爭食相齕, 遂相殺也. 人臣之爭事而亡其國者, 皆螝類也.[66]

One can easily imagine that someone would call up this example of self-destructing worms when arguing that ministers should focus on the state, not on their own agendas, and the *Han Feizi* clearly subsumes both historical anecdotes and aphoristic observations under the heading of 說, which probably should be read *shuo* "illustrative examples" here. The *Huainanzi* likewise contains two chapters that resemble these two *Han Feizi* chapters in title and content, except that in the *Huainanzi*, the number of aphorisms (such as "only when the boat overturns do we see who are the skilled swimmers; only when the horses bolt do we see who are the good charioteers" 舟覆乃見善游, 馬奔乃見良御) far outweigh the number of anecdotes.[67] Finally, there are the numerous anecdotes collected in Liu Xiang's work *Shuoyuan* (Garden of Illustrative Examples).[68] What the *Shuoyuan* and the various chapters in the *Han Feizi* and *Huainanzi* have in common, is that they consist mostly of brief textual narratives, ranging from aphorisms to anecdotes, which are referred to in the title with the graph 說. Thus, the graph is often read *shuo*, as these anecdotes and aphorisms themselves were not "persuasions," but they served as the main ingredient out of which persuasions could be built. In these contexts, anecdotes were deployed to encourage the audience to reflect on the validity of the argument, or adopt a particular perspective as they were most often worked into the body of longer persuasions using various techniques of contextualization and rhetorical framing. Thus, we also find that some scholars have read the graph as *shui*, yielding titles such as "Chushui," "Shuilin," and *Shuiyuan*, to emphasize this important dimension of the materials they preserve.[69]

Anecdotes in this Volume

This volume endeavors to clarify the boundaries between and relationships among anecdotes and these various forms of historical and philosophical writings from early China. As we will see, several chapters in the volume speak to this distinction while underscoring the close association between anecdotes and forms of historical writings on the one hand, and philosophical argumentation on the other by asking: What are the rhetorical functions and forms of early Chinese anecdotes? For whom were they written, and circulated? What is the importance of the anecdotes? Why are they so omnipresent in early Chinese literature? We wish to sharpen our definition of anecdotes through an analysis of their rhetorical functions, the organizing theme of the chapters described below.

Part I: Anecdotes, Argumentation, and Debate

The chapters in part I highlight the important rhetorical function of anecdotes as rich repositories for philosophical, political, historical, and cultural argumentation and debate in early China. Through intertextual analyses, these chapters show how anecdotes were created, adapted, and framed in certain ways to support specific argumentative positions. For instance, someone who wished to promote an ethic of inconspicuously achieving results, as opposed to overtly singing one's own praises, could tailor an anecdote about a well-known historical figure in such a way that this person becomes a model for the desired behavior. In this way, early Chinese philosophical writings differ from texts in the Greco-Roman philosophical tradition where—with a few notable exceptions—appeal to anecdote plays a much less significant role.[70]

In chapter 1, "Non-deductive Argumentation in Early Chinese Philosophy," Paul R. Goldin shows that early Chinese thinkers, while familiar with the principles of deductive reasoning, a kind of reasoning that was favored by their counterparts in the Greco-Roman philosophical tradition, preferred crafting non-deductive arguments instead. The strong interest in anecdotes as a "genre" of philosophical literature in early China, he argues, can be understood as a by-product of the non-deductive nature of most early Chinese philosophical reasoning. One longstanding criticism of Chinese philosophy is that it is not truly "philosophical" because it lacks viable protocols of argumentation. Confucius, for example, might provide valuable guidance, or thoughtful epigrams to ponder, but nothing in the way of formal reasoning that would permit his audience to reconstruct and reconsider his arguments in any conceivable context. Goldin argues that this criticism stands only if one accepts the premise that satisfactory argumentation must be deductive. Many famous Chinese philosophical statements, however, are patently non-deductive. Surveying different types of non-deductive argumentation commonly found in Chinese philosophy, Goldin contends that one of the most prolific types is appeal to example, and that this includes appeal to anecdote. The anecdote is intended to furnish an instructive example highlighting the particular philosophical issue under debate. The inferences gleaned from it are never deductive. One consequence is that Chinese philosophy tends to demand a high level of interpretive participation from its audience. An audience presented with a non-deductive statement must ponder it sympathetically, or else derive little, if any, benefit from it. Chinese philosophy—like literature, painting, or music—requires connoisseurship. If we lack the taste, or if we exempt ourselves from the task of developing it, we will miss most of what Chinese philosophy has to offer. Whether these observations are sufficient to rescue Chinese thought from the wilderness of "wisdom" and enshrine it in the halls of "philosophy" will be left for the reader to decide, but a conception of "philosophy" that can account for Chinese thought, Goldin argues, is more interesting than one that cannot.

In chapter 2, "The Frontier Between Chen and Cai: Anecdote, Narrative, and Philosophical Argumentation in Early China," Andrew Seth Meyer explores the philosophical use of anecdotes through the study of one particular anecdote that occurs—in different forms and with different appraisals—in a variety of early Chinese texts. Building on the insights of Goldin in the previous chapter, Meyer provides an intertextual analysis of the story of Confucius's sojourn and near-starvation between the southern states of Chen and Cai, as it appears in the *Lunyu*, *Mozi*, *Zhuangzi*, *Xunzi*, *Lüshi chunqiu*, and other transmitted texts. Meyer demonstrates that early Chinese thinkers used anecdotes to formulate logical arguments concerning ethics, politics, cosmology, and so on, in ways that differ from the logical methods and worldviews of Greco-Roman philosophy. As Meyer points out, in many versions of this story Confucius is portrayed as a sage teacher and an inspirational leader, in others he is cast as a hypocrite, a coward, or a fool. The multiple recurrences of this story across so many texts provide an excellent case for the study of the role of anecdote in early Chinese writing and thought. In this chapter, Meyer explores the intriguing recurrence and malleability of the "Chen and Cai" narrative, demonstrating that what is at stake in these appropriations and alterations is more than the mere reputation of Confucius himself. Examining the permutations of the narrative from text to text, Meyer reconstructs the parameters of a sophisticated logical debate engaging issues of politics, morality, human efficacy, and cosmology. Taken together, Meyer argues, the variant versions of the story illustrate fundamental points of contention between the latter-day disciples of Confucius and their opponents. Using these anecdotes to reconstruct debate, Meyer concludes, we can learn about the distinctive nature of early Chinese intellectual culture. Anecdotal topoi such as the sojourn between Chen and Cai were not exclusively rhetorical, but implements in an evolving discursive tradition that intensely utilized the logical potential of narrative. Properly understanding this dimension of early Chinese writing and argumentation is necessary to fully access the potential meanings encoded in early Chinese texts, and to fully appreciate the logical sophistication of early Chinese thought.

In chapter 3, "Mozi as a Daoist Sage? An Intertextual Analysis of the 'Gongshu' Anecdote in the *Mozi*," Ting-mien Lee, much like Andrew Seth Meyer in the previous chapter, explores the occurrence of a single anecdote across different textual landscapes to understand their broader rhetorical aims. In the anecdote, the main protagonist, Mozi, manages to avert a war through adroit argumentation. Given that the *Mozi*, the text in which the anecdote occurs, argues that great merit leads to fame, one would expect that the protagonist Mozi, following his incredible achievement of averting a war, would be pictured as a famous hero. Instead, the anecdote's ending curiously portrays Mozi as an unrecognized hero whose achievement went unnoticed by others. This intriguing ending, Lee argues, creates tension not only within the anecdote but also within the *Mozi* as a whole. Whereas the ending contradicts the *Mozi*'s view that great merit leads to fame, it corresponds to the view—expressed in Daoist texts such as *Laozi* and *Zhuangzi*—that a great man operates invisibly, like the spirits, and hence avoids fame. In sum, while the body of the anecdote portrays Mozi as a typical Mohist sage who detests wars and promotes caring for the people's well-being instead, the ending of the anecdote portrays Mozi as an unrecognized—perhaps even Daoist—sage who manages affairs in an inconspicuous manner (after all, he averted a war that had not yet taken place) and therefore lacks public recognition. Lee's chapter highlights the importance of an intertextual reading strategy for early Chinese anecdotes, whose true meaning sometimes can only be understood through an understanding of related passages in other texts.

In chapter 4, "Anecdotal Barbarians in Early China," Wai-yee Li discusses anecdotes that feature non-Chinese tribes, or "barbarians," in a variety of early Chinese texts. She shows how the anecdotes reveal different historical attitudes towards barbarians (for example, they can be represented as deplorably unsophisticated or admirably unadulterated), and suggests that some of the anecdotes may have even been created and transmitted as a way to engage in these debates, which could have broad political and cultural implications. In addition to revealing possible historical attitudes toward non-Chinese groups, Li also demonstrates that the anecdotes address major concerns in early Chinese thought, such as different perspectives on cultural refinement (*wen* 文) and substance (*zhi* 質), tradition and transformation, and the rhetorical contexts of policy arguments and diplomatic confrontations. Thus, Li deepens the discussion of anecdotes and argumentation by considering different anecdotes that address a shared topic across different genres of literature, some which are identified as historical and some of which are identified as philosophical. As with the preceding chapters, she emphasizes that authors used anecdotes to articulate philosophical arguments and shape cultural attitudes in conversation with others that positioned them on a spectrum in broader intellectual debates. She also shows that their rhetorical function transcends generic boundaries.

Part II: Anecdotes and Textual Formation

The chapters in part II confirm the findings of part I with regard to the rhetorical functions of anecdotes but they do so through an intratextual reading of anecdotes in the *Shuoyuan*, *Han Feizi*, and *Gongyangzhuan*, respectively. In doing so, these chapters reveal not only how such a methodology serves to highlight the defining characteristics of anecdotes and the variety of rhetorical functions they served along the broad spectrum of early Chinese literature from philosophy to history, but also how it can be utilized to understand more clearly the textual archaeology of these early Chinese texts. In other words, an analysis of multiple anecdotes within a single text helps us understand not only what a particular text is trying to say—the philosophical, historiographical, didactic messages it wishes to convey—but also how that text came to be created and the different rhetorical contexts it embodies. This is a particularly promising methodology to consider when attempting to better understand the accretional nature of early Chinese texts.

In chapter 5, "Anecdote Collections as Argumentative Texts: The Composition of the *Shuoyuan*," Christian Schwermann analyzes a Han Dynasty collection of anecdotes. Such collections were (and still are) often dismissed as mere pastiches of borrowed stories, but Schwermann convincingly shows how Liu Xiang, who is traditionally considered the editor or compiler of the *Shuoyuan*, combined the anecdotes in this collection to form an elaborate tapestry of argumentation in support of various propositions. He also demonstrates how Liu Xiang borrowed anecdotes from earlier sources and adapted them to a new argumentative context to make for a more persuasive text. More specifically, Schwermann contends that the anecdotes that constitute this collection were deliberately edited, arranged, revised, and even specifically composed in order to support a particular proposition or argument, and that this level of contribution requires us to consider Liu Xiang the author of the *Shuoyuan*, and not just its editor or compiler.

In chapter 6, "From Villains Outwitted to Pedants Out-Wrangled: The Function of Anecdotes in the Shifting Rhetoric of the *Han Feizi*," through a close reading of anecdotes within a single early Chinese text much like Christian Schwermann in the previous chapter, Heng Du discusses the creation of that text, and demonstrates that it is far more systematic than scholars previously held. Specifically, Du analyzes the numerous and contradictory anecdotal portrayals of Confucius in the *Han Feizi*, identifying systematic shifts in rhetorical situation and strategy as factors behind the apparent inconsistencies. She argues that the first half of the *Han Feizi* is a didactic, univocal presentation of its core teachings that revolve around the struggle between the ruler and ministers. Materials and ideas from competing traditions are only first introduced in the anecdote collections in the middle of the text, namely the outer "Chushuo" and "Nan" chapters. These chapters lead the transition into the intense engagement with rival teachings that characterizes the rest of the compilation. The close association between the anecdote chapters and complex polemical argumentations suggests the under-explored functions performed by anecdotal writings, beyond simple illustrations to arguments. They also contain a wealth of evidence for the emergence of intellectual identities and affiliations over the course of the *Han Feizi*'s compilation. In her chapter, Du seeks to understand how and why multiple and contradictory anecdotal narratives devoted to a single historical figure often appear together in a single text, raising our critical awareness of how context and rhetorical aim shape the manner in which anecdotes are deployed within a single text.

In chapter 7, "The Limits of Praise and Blame: The Rhetorical Uses of Anecdotes in the *Gongyangzhuan*," Sarah A. Queen draws our attention to this often overlooked collection of stories. Like Schwermann and Du in the previous chapters, Queen focuses on the creation of this one text. While it is true, she maintains, that the bulk of the *Gongyangzhuan* consists of formulaic questions and answers that parse the chronicle sentence-by-sentence, phrase-by-phrase, and word-by-word, it also deploys numerous anecdotes to lend support to the formulaic questions and terse answers concerning the formal composition and syntactical rules embedded in the *Chunqiu*, the main strategy for decoding Confucius's intentions. Queen offers several exemplary tales to consider the rhetorical uses of anecdotes as an important literary "genre" within the *Gongyangzhuan*, as distinct from other types of literary composition that comprise the commentary, most notably the judgments that are part and parcel of the *Gongyangzhuan*. Although the two are structurally distinct, they clearly work in tandem, as the anecdotes add flesh to the bones of the judgments, leaving no doubt of their didactic message. The chapter by Queen has much in common with the preceding chapters by Schwermann and Du, as all three read anecdotes within a single text as a key to understanding a particular text's rhetorical aims and how it came to exist as a textual unit. Queen's chapter also anticipates the following chapters by Pines and Krijgsman, as it contrasts anecdotes with other kinds of historical narratives—the annalistic records of the *Chunqiu*—within the context of a single text, thereby helping us to delineate more clearly the distinctive yet close relationship that abides between anecdotes and various subgenres of historical writings. Thus Queen's chapter serves as a bridge to part III.

Part III: Anecdotes and History

The chapters in part III focus on the historical aspect of anecdotes. They address intriguing questions such as: Why do some texts discuss historical events through the use of anecdotes, whereas others seem to deliberately eschew them? What is the critical difference between anecdotal histories and non-anecdotal histories? What motivated authors to bring together these two originally distinct genres of writing? How did authors overcome the generic tensions between these two modes of public memory? Why were anecdotes appealing to some historical and historiographical endeavors, and why not to others? Why did certain groups of anecdotes prevail in certain periods of Chinese history, but lose their appeal afterwards?

In chapter 8, "History without Anecdotes: Between the *Zuozhuan* and the *Xinian* Manuscript," Yuri Pines explores the tension between historical writing and anecdotal narratives through his study of the *Xinian*, a recently unearthed text from the Qinghua University collection. While Queen in the previous chapter argues implicitly that in the case of the *Gongyangzhuan*, anecdotes were instrumental in repackaging and updating the terse and laconic messages of the *Chunqiu* to broadcast the *Gongyangzhuan*'s moral agenda for a new age, Pines points out that the *Xinian* stands out as one of a handful of early historical records that lacks an identifiable moralizing agenda and the requisite anecdotes that typically relate such didactic historiographical messages. By examining this peculiar case and relating it to non-anecdotal strands of narrative in the *Zuozhuan*, Pines considers the nature, goals, and potential audience of non-anecdotal historical writings, clarifying differences between the non-moralizing strand of early Chinese historiography and the vast majority of historiographical texts that deploy anecdotes to judge historical events. Pines also explores the reasons why non-anecdotal narratives had a much shorter life span than the entertaining and philosophically engaging anecdotes.

In chapter 9, "Cultural Memory and Excavated Anecdotes in 'Documentary' Narrative: Mediating Generic Tensions in the *Baoxun* Manuscript," Rens Krijgsman distinguishes between "anecdotal" and "documentary" modes of historiography as two distinct types of narratives. Both types narrate historical events, even some of the same events in Chinese history, but in using different textual strategies they represent the past in fundamentally different ways. An important representative of the latter type, the *Shangshu* has historically been read as if it authentically preserves the actual actions and words and deeds of ancient sage kings. Providing vital information about these figures, the documentary narrative in that text is thus considered culturally important and many of them have been canonized. In his chapter, Krijgsman focuses on the *Baoxun* 保訓 (Treasured Instructions), a recently unearthed manuscript that, similar to the one studied by Pines in the previous chapter, comes from the Qinghua University collection. Krijgsman translates the *Baoxun* in full, discusses what it means for the text to be understood as a documentary narrative, and how this structures its narration of the past. This mode of narration is juxtaposed with an anecdotal mode of narration. Krijgsman argues that there is a fundamental tension between these two modes of representing the past due to the different types of claims they make in constructing cultural memory, the former predicative and the latter attributive. The *Baoxun* employs several textual strategies to mediate this tension, such as the use of formulas, framing, and structuring devices. He concludes by arguing that the incorporation of two distinct modes of narrating the past should be seen in light of changes in textual culture in the history of early China.

In chapter 10, "Old Stories No Longer Told: The End of the Anecdotes Tradition of Early China," Paul van Els brings our volume to a conclusion. He demonstrates that, although anecdotes occur across historical periods and literary genres, the specific anecdotes that were omnipresent in philosophical argumentation in early China were hardly deployed in later texts. More specifically, he shows that texts from the Zhou Dynasty to the Western Han Dynasty 西漢 (202 BCE–9 CE) use and re-use historical anecdotes, and that many of these anecdotes occur in more than one text. For example, the *Zuozhuan, Guoyu, Zhanguoce, Zhuangzi, Han Feizi, Lüshi chunqiu, Hanshi waizhuan, Huainanzi, Shuoyuan, Xinxu,* and other texts share anecdotes involving Bao Shuya, Sunshu Ao, Wang Shou, Zhao Jianzi, and other historical figures. The wording of the anecdotes may differ from text to text, and each text may use the anecdotes for a different rhetorical purpose, but the basic accounts of the events remain the same. After the Western Han Dynasty, as van Els contends, the use of these anecdotes significantly decreases. As the Western Han Dynasty came to an end, so did a long tradition of discussing and arguing through a specific corpus of historical anecdotes. At the dawn of the Eastern Han Dynasty 東漢 (25–220 CE) a new history was created, with little room for these ancient stories. This chapter analyzes the end of this distinct anecdotal tradition and the new types of stories that replaced it.

Notes

1. We would like to thank Paul R. Goldin, John Major, Andrew Seth Meyer, Yuri Pines, Gabe van Beijeren, and the anonymous reviewers for reading and critiquing earlier drafts of this Introduction. We have found their insights and criticisms to be invaluable.

2. Translation by Paul van Els and Sarah A. Queen. Translations in each chapter of this volume are by the chapter's author, unless otherwise specified.

3. *Han Feizi jijie* 韓非子集解, ed. Wang Xianshen 王先慎, Xinbian zhuzi jicheng 新編諸子集成 edition (Beijing: Zhonghua shuju, 2003), chap. 34, 319.

4. Names and titles of people in early China can be confusing. Not only are people referred to by different names, sometimes even in the same text, but some titles can also mean more than one thing. For instance, the word *gong* 公 is the designation of an official title normally translated as "duke" in English, but it is also used to refer to rulers who did not carry the title "duke," in which case "lord" would be a more appropriate translation. To avoid confusion, throughout this volume we conventionally translate *wang* 王 as "king," *gong* 公 as "duke," *hou* 侯 as "marquis," and *bo* 伯 as "earl." Note that it is not our intention to discuss the appropriateness of European aristocratic nomenclature to early China; we merely apply European ranks as a matter of heuristic convenience. For more on the problematic translation of *gong* as "duke," see C. N. Tay, "On the Interpretation of *Kung* (Duke?) in the *Tso-chuan*," *Journal of the American Oriental Society* 93, no. 4 (1973): 550–55.

5. We use the word "philosophy" (and its various forms such as "philosophical") throughout this volume, and even in its title, in full awareness that this word is not unproblematic, as demonstrated by the scholarly debate on the question as to whether or not China even had something that can be called "philosophy." Our reasoning is simple: we think that the way in which early Chinese thinkers employed the various rhetorical functions of anecdotes may enrich our understanding of the possibilities of philosophical activities. As Paul R. Goldin argues in his contribution to the volume: a conception of "philosophy" that can account for Chinese thought, is more interesting than one that cannot. For more on the thorny issue of Chinese "philosophy," see Goldin's chapter in this volume. Other relevant academic publications in English include, in chronological order: Tongqi Lin, Henry Rosemont, Jr., and Roger T. Ames, "Chinese Philosophy: A Philosophical Essay on the 'State-of-the-Art,'" *Journal of Asian Studies* 54, no. 3 (1995): 727–58, esp. 746ff; Xiao-ming Wu, "Philosophy, Philosophia, and Zhe-xue," *Philosophy East and West* 48, no. 3 (1998): 406–52; and Carine Defoort, "Is There Such a Thing as Chinese Philosophy? Arguments of an Implicit Debate," *Philosophy East and West* 51, no. 3 (2001): 393–413; idem, "Is 'Chinese Philosophy' a Proper Name?: A Response to Rein Raud," *Philosophy East and West* 56, no. 4 (2006): 625–60; Wiebke Denecke, *The Dynamics of Masters Literature: Early Chinese Thought from Confucius to Han Feizi* (Cambridge, MA: Harvard University Asia Center, 2010), esp. 11–18.

6. This also holds true for other literary traditions. Writing about the relation between anecdotes and history, and basing himself mostly on anecdotes in European languages, Lionel Gossman notes that "scholarly literature on the topic [. . .] is scattered and fairly thin, as though the anecdote were thought to be too trivial a form to deserve serious consideration." Lionel Gossman, "Anecdote and History," *History and Theory* 42 (2003): 147.

7. The Chinese language contains several terms that overlap in some respect with the English word "anecdote," such as *diangu* 典故, which denotes any kind of literary allusion, *zhanggu* 掌故, which typically refers to more colloquial stories of the past, and *yuyan* 寓言, which covers a wide range of narrative types, including those that would be called "anecdotes," "allegories," and "parables" in English. None of these terms was used consistently in any kind of premodern Chinese literary theory. In modern Chinese scholarship, the term used most often to discuss the kind of stories we would identify as "anecdotes," is *yuyan*. This term is borrowed from a chapter in the *Zhuangzi*, where it has a much broader meaning. Relevant publications on *yuyan* include, in chronological order: Wang Huanbiao 王煥鑣, *Xian-Qin yuyan yanjiu* 先秦寓言研究 (Shanghai: Gudian wenxue chubanshe, 1957); Chen Puqing 陳蒲清, *Zhongguo gudai yuyan shi* 中國古代寓言史 (Changsha: Hunan jiaoyu chubanshe, 1983); Gong Mu 公木, *Xian-Qin yuyan gailun* 先秦寓言概論 (Jinan: Qi-Lu shushe, 1984); and Bai Bensong 白本松, *Xian-Qin yuyan shi* 先秦寓言史 (Kaifeng: Henan daxue chubanshe, 2001).

8. Wai-yee Li, *The Readability of the Past in Early Chinese Historiography* (Cambridge, MA: Harvard University Press, 2008); Yuri Pines, *Foundations of Confucian Thought: Intellectual Life in the Chunqiu Period 722–453 B.C.E.* (Honolulu: University of Hawai'i Press, 2002); David Schaberg, *A Patterned Past: Form and Thought in Early Chinese Historiography* (Cambridge, MA: Harvard University Press, 2002).

9. Albert Galvany, "Philosophy, Biography, and Anecdote: On the Portrait of Sun Wu," *Philosophy East & West* 61, no. 4 (2011): 630–46; Jens Østergård Petersen, "The *Zuozhuan* Account of the Death of King Zhao of Chu and Its Sources," *Sino-Platonic Papers* 159 (2005): 1–47; idem, "The *Zuozhuan* Story about Qi Xi's Recommendations and Its Sources," *Sino-Platonic Papers* 255 (2015): 1–50; Sarah A. Queen, "The Creation and Domestication of the Techniques of Lao-Zhuang: Anecdotal Narrative and Philosophical Argumentation in *Huainanzi* 12," *Asia Major* (Third Series) 21, no. 1 (2008): 201–49; David Schaberg, "Chinese History and Philosophy," in *The Oxford History of Historical Writing, Volume 1: Beginnings to AD 600*, ed. Andrew Feldherr and Grant Hardy (Oxford: Oxford University Press, 2011), 394–414; Paul van Els, "Tilting Vessels and Collapsing Walls: On the Rhetorical Function of Anecdotes in Early Chinese Texts," *Extrême-Orient, Extrême-Occident* 34 (2012): 141–66; Kai Vogelsang, "From Anecdote to History: Observations on the Composition of the *Zuozhuan*," *Oriens Extremus* 50 (2011): 99–124.

10. Jack W. Chen and David Schaberg, eds., *Idle Talk: Gossip and Anecdote in Traditional China* (Berkeley and Los Angeles: University of California Press, 2014).

11. Richard Friedenthal, "Vom Nutzen und Wert der Anekdote," in *Sprache und Politik: Festgabe für Dolf Sternberger zum sechzigsten Geburtstag*, ed. Carl-Joachim Friedrich and Benno Reifenberg (Heidelberg: Verlag Lambert Schneider, 1968), 63.

12. Heinz Grothe, *Anekdote* (Stuttgart: J. B. Metzlersche Verlagsbuchhandlung, 1971), 14–16.

13. Gossman, "Anecdote and History," 143.

14. Translation by Richard Atwater, *Secret History of Procopius* (Chicago: P. Covici, 1927), 127–28.

15. The book containing Procopius's anecdotal writings is now popularly known as *Secret History* (after the Latin title *Historia Arcana*). For more on Procopius, his world, and his writings, see Averil Cameron, *Procopius and the Sixth Century* (London: Duckworth, 1985), particularly chapter 4, "Procopius and the Secret History."

16. Clifton Fadiman, ed., *The Little, Brown Book of Anecdotes* (Boston: Little, Brown and Company, 1985), xiii.

17. "Anecdote, n.," OED Online, accessed July 28, 2015, http://www.oed.com.

18. Fadiman, *Book of Anecdotes*, 5.

19. Joel Fineman, "The History of the Anecdote: Fiction and Fiction," in *The New Historicism*, ed. H. Aram Veeser (New York: Routledge, 1989), 57.

20. Gossman, "Anecdote and History," 159.

21. See Atwater, *Secret History*, 132–33.

22. The sense of gossip in relation to anecdotes is also noted by Schaberg ("Chinese History and Philosophy," 395), whose co-edited volume even carries the subtitle *Gossip and Anecdote in Traditional China*.

23. Fineman, "History of the Anecdote," 56–57.

24. In his collection of movie anecdotes, Peter Hay writes: "The genre is not about facts or history, [. . .] With anecdotes, story is everything, and in this respect there is a happy coincidence with the craft of the scenarist. The material of life—most of it immaterial or antithetical to drama—has to be chopped up and fashioned into something that will hold large numbers of people entertained or in suspense. Facts and research become background; characters and episodes are transposed, eliminated, or invented; key moments, especially the ending, often changed. The best screenwriters and filmmakers know that reality on the screen must be manufactured, not out of arbitrary judgment, but in order to serve the story. There is no pretense at objectivity; as with the camera, point of view creates the picture." Peter Hay, *Movie Anecdotes* (Oxford: Oxford University Press, 1990), xiv.

25. Gossman, "Anecdote and History," 149.

26. Fadiman, *Book of Anecdotes*, xvi.

27. This diversionary aspect is made explicit in many anecdote collections. For instance, in the preface to her collection of dance anecdotes, Mindy Aloff puts it as follows: "I wanted to put together the kind of collection that one might pick up in a country inn on a rainy day and while away an hour browsing through." Mindy Aloff, *Dance Anecdotes: Stories from the Worlds of Ballet, Broadway, the Ballroom, and Modern Dance* (Oxford: Oxford University Press, 2006).

28. Michael Ryan, ed., *The Encyclopedia of Literary and Cultural Theory* (Malden, MA: Wiley-Blackwell, 2011), 752.

29. Gossman, "Anecdote and History," 143.

30. For a translation of these anecdotes, see Burton Watson, trans., *Han Fei Tzu: Basic Writings* (New York and London: Columbia University Press, 1964), 77–78.

31. For Sarah A. Queen's translation of these anecdotes, see John S. Major, Sarah A. Queen, Andrew Seth Meyer, and Harold D. Roth, trans. and eds., *The Huainanzi: A Guide to the Theory and Practice of Government in Early Han China* (New York: Columbia University Press, 2010), 443–45.

32. For an in-depth study of Lady Boji and her family, as depicted in anecdotes in the *Zuozhuan*, see Anne Behnke Kinney, "A Spring and Autumn Family," *The Chinese Historical Review* 20, no. 2 (2013): 113–37. See also Sarah A. Queen, "Beyond Liu Xiang's Gaze: Debating Womanly Virtue in Early China," *Asia Major*, Third Series, 29, no. 2 (2016): 7-46.

33. See the chapter by Paul R. Goldin in this volume.

34. See the chapter by Rens Krijgsman in this volume.

35. For more on this, see Paul R. Goldin, "Appeals to History in Early Chinese Philosophy and Rhetoric," *Journal of Chinese Philosophy* 35, no. 1 (2008): 79–96.

36. *Zhanguoce* 戰國策, comp. Liu Xiang 劉向 (Shanghai: Shanghai guji chubanshe, 1985), "Qi ce" 齊冊, 3.372.

37. See the chapter by Heng Du in this volume.

38. *Han Feizi jijie*, 310.

39. Paul R. Goldin, "Rhetoric and Machination in *Stratagems of the Warring States*," in *After Confucius: Studies in Early Chinese Philosophy* (Honolulu: University of Hawai'i Press, 2005), 76.

40. See the outline of this text by Tsuen-hsuin Tsien in Michael Loewe, ed., *Early Chinese Texts: A Bibliographical Guide* (Berkeley, CA: Society for the Study of Early China, 1993). See also the introductions in James Crump, Jr., trans., *Chan-kuo ts'e* (Oxford: Clarendon Press, 1970) and *Legends of the Warring States: Persuasions, Romances, and Stories from Chan-Kuo Tse* (Ann Arbor: Center for Chinese Studies, The University of Michigan, 1998).

41. Goldin, "Rhetoric and Machination," 89.

42. See Major et al., *The Huainanzi*, 470.

43. *Huainanzi jishi* 淮南子集釋, ed. He Ning 何寧, Xinbian zhuzi jicheng 新編諸子集成 edition (Beijing: Zhonghua shuju, 2003), chap. 12, 880–81.

44. For more on this, see Paul van Els, "Tilting Vessels," 161–62.

45. One example of a highly elaborate narrative tapestry is *Huainanzi* chapter 18, "Renjian xun" 人閒訓 (Among Others). See Andrew Seth Meyer's elucidating analysis of the complex framing structure of this chapter in Major et al., *The Huainanzi*, 714–15.

46. Gossman, "Anecdote and History," 147.

47. Gossman, "Anecdote and History," 143.

48. Schaberg, "Chinese History and Philosophy," 395, also makes this point.

49. Schaberg, "Chinese History and Philosophy," 394.

50. Edward L. Shaughnessy, "*I Chou shu* 逸周書 (*Chou shu*)," in Loewe, *Early Chinese Texts*, 229–33.

51. Sarah Allan points out that eight out of nine manuscripts contained in the first volume of the Qinghua collection are designated *shu*. See Sarah Allan, "On *Shu* 書 (Documents) and the Origin of the *Shangshu* 尚書 (Ancient Documents) in Light of Recently Discovered Bamboo Slip Manuscripts," *Bulletin of the School of Oriental and African Studies* 75, no. 3 (2012): 547–57 (particularly note 3 on page 548).

52. Allan, "On *Shu*," 557.

53. Allan, "On *Shu*," 556.

54. As Newell Ann Van Auken has demonstrated, records were written according to regular rules that governed which types of events could be recorded and in what form. Newell Ann Van Auken, "A Formal Analysis of the *Chuenchiou* (Spring and Autumn Classic)" (PhD Diss., University of Washington, 2006), 1–2.

55. *Shisan jing zhushu fu jiaokanji* 十三經注疏附校勘記, comp. Ruan Yuan 阮元 (1764–1849) (Beijing: Zhonghua shuju, 1982), Zhuang 26, 2238–39.

56. See *Mengzi yizhu* 孟子譯注, ed. Yang Bojun 楊伯峻 (Beijing: Zhonghua shuju, [1960] 1988), "Li lou, xia" 8.21: 192.

57. For more on the *Biannianji* manuscript and annals as a distinct genre, see Edward L. Shaughnessy, "The Qin *Biannian ji* 編年記 and the Beginnings of Historical Writing in China," in *Beyond the First Emperor's Mausoleum: New Perspectives on Qin Art*, ed. Liu Yang (Seattle: University of Washington Press, 2015): 114–36. For more on the *Xinian*, see Yuri Pines "Zhou History and Historiography: Introducing the Bamboo manuscript *Xinian*," *T'oung Pao* 100, no. 4–5 (2014): 287–324, as well as his chapter in the present volume.

58. See the chapters by Andrew Seth Meyer and Sarah A. Queen in this volume.

59. Schaberg, "Chinese History and Philosophy," 403, also makes this point.

60. For a more extensive discussion of this graph, see the chapter by Christian Schwermann in this volume.

61. The various readings and meanings of 說 became clearly distinguished only from the sixth century CE onwards, as Martin Kern demonstrates in his "'Persuasion' or 'Treatise'? The Prose Genres *Shui* 說 and *Shuo* 說 in the Light of the *Guwenci leizuan* of 1779," in *Ad Seres et Tungusos: Festschrift für Martin Gimm zu seinem 65. Geburtstag am 25. Mai 1995*, eds. Lutz Bieg, Erling von Mende, and Martina Siebert (Wiesbaden: Harrassowitz, 2000), 221–43.

62. The OC (Old Chinese) reconstructions here and in the following are according to Axel Schuessler, *Minimal Old Chinese and Later Han Chinese: A Companion to Grammata Serica Recensa* (Honolulu: University of Hawai'i Press, 2009).

63. Major et al., *The Huainanzi*, 618.

64. Major et al., *The Huainanzi*, 619. For a detailed study of this *Han Feizi* chapter, see Michael Hunter, "The Difficulty with 'The Difficulties of Persuasion' ('Shuinan' 說難)," in *Dao Companion to the Philosophy of Han Fei*, ed. Paul R. Goldin (Dordrecht: Springer, 2013), 169–95.

65. *Han Feizi jijie*, 86.

66. *Han Feizi jijie*, 189–90. The main text in this edition (unlike other editions) leaves out the phrase "it thereby killed itself as well" 因自殺, which is essential to the argument.

67. See Sarah A. Queen's translation of these chapters in Major et al., *The Huainanzi*, 617–711.

68. For more on this title, see the chapter by Christian Schwermann in this volume.

69. For example: Queen (in Major et al., *The Huainanzi*, 617–711) renders the *Huainanzi* chapter titles 說山 and 說林 as "A Mountain of Persuasions" (*Shuishan*) and "A Forest of Persuasions" (*Shuilin*); Schaberg ("Chinese History and Philosophy," 400) renders the 儲說 chapters in the *Han Feizi* as "Stockpiled Persuasions" (*Chushui*); and Hunter ("Difficulty," 198) reads 說苑 as "Garden of Persuasions" (*Shuiyuan*).

70. Some philosophers (such as Cicero) do intersperse their writings with anecdotes, whereas the philosophical stunts of others (such as Diogenes) gave rise to numerous anecdotes.

Part I

Anecdotes, Argumentation, and Debate

1

Non-deductive Argumentation in Early Chinese Philosophy

PAUL R. GOLDIN[1]

The strong interest in anecdotes as a mode of philosophical discourse from the Warring States Period 戰國 (453–221 BCE) onwards can be understood as a by-product of the non-deductive nature of most early Chinese philosophical reasoning. One longstanding criticism of Chinese thought is that it is not truly "philosophical" because it lacks viable protocols of argumentation.[2] Thus it qualifies at best as "wisdom." Confucius, for example, might provide valuable guidance, or thoughtful epigrams to savor, but nothing in the way of formal reasoning that would permit his audience to reconstruct and reconsider his arguments in any conceivable context.[3] As Hu Shih 胡適 (1891–1962) put it, "China has greatly suffered for lack of an adequate logical method."[4]

Such hand-wringing bespeaks the prejudgment that satisfactory argumentation must be deductive. I have no special definition of "deduction" in mind; it suffices to use that of Aristotle: "a discourse in which, certain things being stated, something other than what is stated follows of necessity from their being so."[5] This is often called "syllogism" in older translations, because Aristotle thought that all deductive inference must be syllogistic[6]—a notion rejected by modern logicians.[7] Aristotle went on to give some examples of syllogisms, which the medieval tradition organized into types according to their "mood," that is, the nature of their premises and conclusion.[8] The mood *AAA* (sometimes called "Barbara syllogism"), for instance, holds that if all A are B, and all B are C, then all A must be C:[9]

> All elephants are mammals.
> All mammals are animals.
> ∴ All elephants are animals.

Such reasoning allows inferences that must be valid for every conceivable elephant, regardless of how many discrete elephants one happens to have seen in one's lifetime. Aristotle seems to have believed that such powers of inference were unique to human beings.[10]

As Andrew Seth Meyer notes in his contribution to this volume, China took a different tack.[11] Many of the most famous Chinese philosophical statements are patently non-syllogistic. For example:

> Ji Wenzi acted only after thinking three times. The Master heard of it, and said, "Twice would have been acceptable."

> 季文子三思而後行. 子聞之, 曰:「再, 斯可矣.」[12]

This could be construed as useful practical advice. The dangers of acting too rashly and too slowly are the subjects of contradictory aphorisms (for example, in our culture, "Look before you leap" and "He who hesitates is lost"). Here, the Master, i.e., Confucius 孔子 (551–479 BCE), recommends a prudent middle course. Think twice before acting: not once, but not three times, either. Clearly this is not a matter of deductive inference—nor is the statement applicable in every conceivable situation. One should not think twice about whether to avoid an oncoming car. It is left to us to explore the range of plausible applications, but presumably Confucius is talking about weighty moral decisions: these deserve careful consideration and reconsideration, but as soon as one has made up one's mind, further deliberation only leads to inaction. Here is another example from the *Lunyu* 論語 (Analects):

> The Master said, "Only after the year has grown cold does one know that the pine and cypress are the last to wither."

> 子曰:「歲寒, 然後知松柏之後彫也.」[13]

I have discussed this passage elsewhere,[14] and the details need not be rehearsed here, but one observation is crucial: the statement begs to be taken metaphorically, because no one would have bothered to record and preserve this line if it were really just a remark about pines and cypresses.

(The *Lunyu* is not a manual of forestry.) And metaphors have no place in deductive reasoning. When we say that all elephants are mammals, we are not speaking metaphorically; we *cannot* be speaking metaphorically, or else the very inference would be called into question. (Speakers of English sometimes refer to an obvious problem that no one wishes to address as "the elephant in the room," but that kind of elephant is not a mammal.) Thus Confucius's utterance, however we choose to interpret it (usually it is understood as a comment on the value of friends who remain true in all seasons), cannot be deductive.

Three general types of non-deductive argumentation in early Chinese philosophy merit extended discussion: paradox, analogy, and appeal to example (this last type includes anecdotes).[15]

Paradox[16]

Many of the paradoxes of the so-called "disputers" (*bianzhe* 辯者)[17] can be made to seem veridical,[18] or at least veridical in spirit, if interpreted sympathetically. For example, among the ten paradoxes ascribed to Hui Shi 惠施 (4th c. BCE), one finds: "the South has no limit but has a limit" 南方無窮而有窮.[19] We do not know how Hui Shi himself defended this paradox, but there are interpretations that would render this paradox veridical: the quadrant called "South" contains an infinite number of points, but it does not include the entire world; it is distinct, naturally, from the quadrants called "North," "East," and "West." Thus it is both limitless and limited at the same time.[20] Another (possible) example of veridical paradox is "eggs have hair" 卵有毛:[21] if this is taken to mean "Inside an egg, there is hair"—that is, the down of the unborn chick inside—then it is an unexpectedly true statement. (The Chinese word *mao* 毛 denotes body hair, such as the pelt of an animal, and could have been stretched to refer to the down of a chick.) One paradox that should have attracted more attention from modern linguists is "dogs can be sheep" 犬可以為羊,[22] which is veridical if it means "dogs may be called 'sheep' ": the word "dog" is arbitrary and has nothing to do with the nature of the dog itself.

Many of the disputers' paradoxes rely on the technique of exploiting a vulnerable keyword, either by using it in a sense different from what the audience expects, or by using it in one sense in one part of the paradox, and in a different sense in another.[23] (This is similar to the fallacy of equivocation in Western philosophy.)[24] Thus "tortoises are longer than snakes" 龜長

於蛇 if one takes "long" in the sense of "long-lived."[25] Unexpected, but not untrue. The most famous paradox of all, "a white horse is not a horse" 白馬非馬,[26] can be identified as another example of this technique if "white horse" and "horse" are taken to refer not to horses, but to sets of horses: the set of objects fulfilling the requirements "white and horse" and the set of objects fulfilling the requirement "horse" are not identical.[27]

Later Mohist exercises in semiotics attest to an interest in analyzing how such paradoxes could be constructed. A typical example: "the fruit of the peach is the peach, but the fruit of the *ji* is not the *ji*" 桃之實, 桃也; 棘之實, 非棘也,[28] which seems to be predicated on the oddity that the word *tao* 桃 (peach) refers to both the tree and the fruit that it bears (as in English), whereas the word *ji* 棘 refers only to the tree, because its fruit is called *zao* 棗 (jujube or Chinese date in English).[29] From here it would not be far to a hypothetical paradox like "peaches are not fruit" (because they are trees).

Not everyone was convinced of the value of such adventures in language—the noted philosopher Xunzi 荀子 (Master Xun, 3rd c. BCE) rejected them as useless for the enterprise of moral self-cultivation[30]—but some of the most important statements in the *Laozi* 老子 rely on the same technique of using a keyword in two different senses (and therefore probably stem from the same intellectual environment). "The highest virtue is not virtuous; therefore, it has virtue" 上德不德, 是以有德 (*Laozi* 38) is usually not treated as sophistry like "tortoises are longer than snakes," but it relies on the same rhetorical device. For "the highest virtue is not virtuous" to have any intelligible meaning, the keyword *de* 德 (virtue, inner power) must be taken in two different ways.[31] The first *de*, called *shangde* 上德, or the highest virtue, refers to *de* that is real and potent because it derives from the *dao* 道 (the Way) itself, whereas the second *de*, merely *de*, refers to the great sham that human society, in its self-induced ignorance, wrongly identifies as *de*. Thus the highest virtue has real virtue precisely because it is not the false virtue that everyone has been trained to venerate.[32] Usually such paradoxes are explained as part of a sustained rhetoric in *Laozi* whose purpose is to shake complacent readers and make them question their unnatural assumptions about the world.[33]

Analogy

Reasoning by analogy was a crucial mode of deliberation in traditional China.[34] It was one of the hallmarks of Chinese jurisprudence,[35] and also figures prominently in early Chinese poetics, where it was identified by the critical terms *bi* 比 (comparison or juxtaposition) or *xing* 興 (arousal).³⁶ In philosophy, one of the best-known examples appears in *Mengzi* 孟子 (Mencius):

> Mencius said, "I like fish; I also like bear's paw. If I cannot have both, I shall forgo fish and choose bear's paw. I like life; I also like righteousness. If I cannot have both, I shall forgo life and choose righteousness. Although I like life, there are things that I like more than life, and thus I should not keep [my life] indecorously. Although I dislike death, there are things that I dislike more than death, and thus there are some perils that I should not avoid."³⁷

> 孟子曰:「魚, 我所欲也; 熊掌, 亦我所欲也. 二者不可得兼, 舍魚而取熊掌者也. 生, 亦我所欲也; 義, 亦我所欲也. 二者不可得兼, 舍生而取義者也. 生亦我所欲, 所欲有甚於生者, 故不為苟得也; 死亦我所惡, 所惡有甚於死者, 故患有所不辟也.」³⁸

As moral philosophy, this passage conveys a certain mindset rather than formulating a definite argument (and as an argument it is obviously not deductive). Just as a gourmet is prepared to sacrifice fish for the sake of a delicacy like bear's paw, a moral connoisseur³⁹ is prepared to sacrifice his or her life for the sake of righteousness. Naturally, the analogy does not *prove* that righteousness is worth dying for; it merely illustrates Mencius's zeal.

Many such analogies refer to natural phenomena with the unstated supposition that patterns observable in nature cannot be wrong.⁴⁰ This conviction underlies arguments that are not always well-received today. For example, early in the famed debate between Mencius and Gaozi 告子 (Master Gao), the latter presents the view that human nature (*xing* 性) lacks any inherent moral orientation; like a torrent of water, it will rush in whichever direction is laid open for it. Mencius responds by assailing the analogy: water does have an inherent orientation after all, because it always flows downwards. Thus human nature is inherently good in the same way that water naturally flows downwards.⁴¹ This argument has been harshly criticized in modern times;⁴² its power must have been greater in a culture like that of ancient China, where reasoning by analogy was deeply respected.⁴³

It must also be acknowledged that appeals to natural phenomena were often used to keep women in their place. In a canonical text called "Mushi"

牧誓 (The Oath at Mu), King Wu of Zhou 周武王 (r. 1049/45–1043 BCE),[44] who went down in history as a sage king, justifies his decision to attack the last king of the Shang Dynasty 商 (ca. 1500–1045 BCE) on the grounds that the latter listens to his wife:

> The King said, "The ancients had a saying: 'The hen shall not announce the morning; when the hen announces the morning, it means that the family will wane.' Now King Shou of Shang implements only the words of his wife."[45]

> 王曰:「古人有言曰:『牝雞無晨; 牝雞之晨, 惟家之索.』今商王受惟婦言是用.」[46]

Hens should just keep quiet in the morning, because they threaten the survival of the family when they try to do the rooster's job.[47]

Not infrequently, Chinese authors saw meaningful patterns in nature that we would not recognize today. For example, the text *Baihutong* 白虎通 (Comprehensive Discussions in the White Tiger Hall) explains that women should follow their husbands because *yang chang yin he* 陽倡陰和, which is to say that *yang* 陽 (the male aspect) sings the lead and *yin* 陰 (the female aspect) harmonizes.[48] This is the problem with analogizing from nature: all observation of the natural world necessarily passes through one's peculiar interpretive filter, and therefore different people do not always apperceive the same pattern when they perceive the same set of objects.[49]

Appeal to Example

Appeals to example are nearly ubiquitous in ancient Chinese philosophy (the most prominent text not to resort to them is *Laozi*), and it seems fruitful to divide the technique into a number of subtypes. Appeal to history has been regarded as so typical of Chinese philosophy that Jeremy Bentham (1748–1832) derided it as the "Chinese argument."[50] Rarely did Chinese persuaders fail to refer to examples from the past that supposedly bolstered their case—nor did they always feel obliged to recount details accurately.[51]

A more specific category is appeal to the sages of yore and the canonical texts attributed to them. Though it is usually taken to be typical of Confucian argumentation, Mohists, i.e., followers of the philosophy of Mozi 墨子 (Master Mo, fl. late 5th c. BCE), pioneered the use of this device, because appealing to the sages was the first of the "Three Gnomons" (*san biao* 三表), also called "Three Standards" (*san fa* 三法), that they held to be indicative of valid propositions:

> This being the case, how does one judge their propositions? Master Mozi said: One must set up a gauge. Speaking without such a gauge would be like determining sunrise and sunset on the basis of a spinning potter's wheel. One could never come to know clearly the difference between right and wrong, benefit and harm. Thus one must speak in accordance with the Three Gnomons. What is meant by the "Three Gnomons"? Master Mozi said: There is "verifying the root," "verifying the origin," and "verifying the utility."[52] How does one "verify the root"? One "verifies the root" in the affairs of the sage kings of old. How does one "verify the origin"? One "verifies the origin" by investigating the things that the Hundred Surnames hear and see. How does one "verify the utility"? Observe the benefit that [the proposition] would bring to the state, its people, the Hundred Surnames, and the populace if it were disseminated by being made into law. This is what is meant by speaking in accordance with the Three Gnomons.[53]

> 然則明辨此之說將奈何哉? 子墨子言曰: 必立儀. 言而毋儀, 譬猶運鈞之上而立朝夕者也; 是非利害之辨, 不可得而明知也. 故言必有三表. 何謂三表? 子墨子言曰: 有本之者, 有原之者, 有用之者. 於何本之? 上本之於古者聖王之事. 於何原之? 下原察百姓耳目之實. 於何用之? 廢 [=發][54] 以為刑政, 觀其中國家百姓人民之利. 此所謂言有三表也.[55]

For example, the Mohists' argument against fatalism (*ming* 命), which they attributed to Confucius and his followers, runs essentially like this: the sage kings did not believe that all things were foreordained; ordinary people do not normally act on such a belief either; and fatalism is dangerous because it would lead to moral apathy if people were to put their faith in it. Thus fatalism is false.[56] The *Mozi* also dilates tirelessly on the sage kings Yao 堯, Shun 舜, Yu 禹, Tang 湯, and Kings Wen 文 and Wu 武, whom Heaven established as Sons of Heaven, in contrast to the deposed tyrants Jie 桀, Zhòu 紂, You 幽, and Li 厲, whose downfall Heaven likewise superintended.[57]

The commonplace of appealing to the example of the sages prompted a backlash in texts such as *Han Feizi* 韓非子 (Master Han Fei).[58] Teaching people how to build nests in trees or drill flint in order to make fire were crucial advances in prehistoric times, but in later eras they would have been laughable:

> If there were someone who built nests or drilled flint in the Xia dynasty, he would surely be ridiculed by Gun and Yu [i.e., the legendary father and son who tried to tame catastrophic floods and went on to found the Xia dynasty]. If there were someone who cleared water channels in the age of Yin and Zhou dynasties, he would surely by ridiculed by Tang and Wu [i.e., the sage founders of those dynasties]. Yet today there are those who praise the ways of Yao, Tang, Wu, and Yu as though they were appropriate for today's age; surely they are to be ridiculed by new sages.
>
> 今有構木鑽燧於夏后氏之世者，必為鯀, 禹笑矣. 有決瀆於殷, 周之世者，必為湯, 武笑矣. 然則今有美堯, 舜, 湯, 武, 禹之道於當今之世者，必為新聖笑矣.[59]

What may have been laudable actions by sages of the past are not necessarily appropriate to the very different society of today.

Another productive subtype is appeal to proverbs, such as the one about hens announcing the morning, mentioned above. In a later example, Jia Yi 賈誼 (201–169 BCE) wrote: "A rustic proverb says: 'Those who do not forget affairs of the past are teachers of the future'" 野諺曰：「前事之不忘, 後之師也」.[60] This is both an appeal to a proverb and an appeal to history at the same time, though Jia Yi goes on to emphasize that methods of the past might have to be adjusted to suit present circumstances. He probably did not make up this proverb, because it appears *verbatim* in an unrelated item in *Zhanguoce* 戰國策 (Stratagems of the Warring States),[61] a text that has preserved many other maxims as well (such as "three people make a tiger" 三人成虎: everyone will believe that there is a tiger if three people independently claim to have seen it).[62]

Modern readers are seldom impressed by these subtypes of appeal to example. Appeals to history are sometimes deemed persuasive, but not if the circumstances are incommensurate (and certainly not if the examples are distorted), while appeals to canonical texts and proverbs fare even worse, usually being dismissed as *argumentum ad verecundiam*, an argument from authority. But one subtype of appeal to example is not necessarily fallacious: appeal to exemplary conduct, both good and bad. This discourse is characteristic of the *Lunyu*:

> The Master said, "When I am walking [with others] in a threesome, there must be a teacher to me among them. I select what is good in them and follow it; what is not good in them, I correct."
>
> 子曰:「三人行, 必有我師焉. 擇其善者而從之, 其不善者而改之.」[63]

Like Mencius's comment about fish and bear's paw, this is more of a declaration of a certain attitude than a formal argument; it merely asserts the principle that there is always something to learn, whether positive or negative, from the example of others. The idea that we can learn by emulating other people's strengths and reforming their weaknesses has been central to Chinese philosophy for centuries,[64] and has fostered the associated conviction that we must judge people's actions fairly—including our own.[65]

Appeal to example, finally, brings us to anecdotes, the subject of the present volume. Since other chapters focus on specific cases, I shall restrict myself here to some basic observations. The appeal to an anecdote is a subtype of appeal to example because the argumentative mode and purpose are the same: the anecdote is intended to furnish an instructive example highlighting the particular philosophical issue under debate. The inferences gleaned from it are never deductive.

Take the example in *Han Feizi* of a lucky farmer who caught a rabbit that happened to kill itself by careering into a stump:

> Among the men of Song there was one who tilled his fields; in his fields there was a stump. A rabbit ran by, crashed headfirst against the stump, broke its neck, and died. Thereupon [the man] set aside his plow and kept watch by the stump, hoping to get another rabbit, but no other rabbit was to be gotten, and he became the laughingstock of Song. Now those who wish to use the governance of the Former Kings to bring order to the people of our time are all of the same type as the stump-watcher.[66]
>
> 宋人有耕田者, 田中有株, 兔走, 觸株折頸而死, 因釋其耒而守株, 冀復得兔, 兔不可復得, 而身為宋國笑. 今欲以先王之政, 治當世之民, 皆守株之類也.[67]

The argument is explicit: using "the governance of the Former Kings to bring order to the people of our time" is as foolish as waiting for a *second* rabbit (because it is equally unlikely that virtuous individuals will present themselves in government pro bono).

Such anecdotes are fungible in the sense that they can be adapted to serve different arguments, and thus their ability to convey a priori truths is limited, if not nil. The example of the stump-watcher is effectively applied in *Han Feizi* to political philosophy, but it could also be used, say, to argue against wagering one's life savings at the roulette table after winning one spin. (Essentially, its purpose is to emphasize the folly of basing one's plans for the future on the hope that a welcome but extremely rare event might happen again.) In *Han Feizi*, anecdotes are so fungible that one can occasionally find the same one marshaled in support of diametrically opposed positions. In "Shiguo" 十過 (Ten Missteps), Duke Huan of Qi 齊桓公 (r. 685–643 BCE) is criticized for ignoring Guan Zhong's 管仲 (d. 645 BCE) deathbed advice to purge three self-interested ministers,[68] while in "Nan, yi" 難一 (Critiques, No. 1), Guan Zhong's deathbed advice is itself criticized, because a lord needs to know how to extract service from self-interested ministers.[69] For if *Han Feizi* teaches us anything, it is that ministers are self-interested yet indispensable.[70]

Han Feizi does not worry about whether Guan Zhong *really* said what was attributed to him (what stenographer would have been present at his bedside, after all?); the point is that arguments about how to deal with self-interested ministers could be persuasively praised or criticized, depending on one's perspective. This is why so many appeals to historical events, as noted above, contain unconcealed factual errors. Their veracity was less of a concern than their illustrative power.

It would be unproductive, therefore, to distinguish rigidly between "anecdotes" like that of Guan Zhong's deathbed advice in *Han Feizi* and the unmistakably fictitious stories of *Zhuangzi* 莊子 (Master Zhuang), which are more commonly characterized as "parables."[71] (None of these English terms, as mentioned in the Introduction to this volume, can be mapped neatly onto Chinese vocabulary.)[72] Consider the famous parable that draws the "Inner Chapters" (*neipian* 內篇) of *Zhuangzi* to a close:

> The Emperor of the Southern Sea was named Zig; the Emperor of the Northern Sea was named Zag; the Emperor of the Center was named Dumpling.[73] Zig and Zag often met each other in Dumpling's territory, and Dumpling received them very well.

Zig and Zag planned to repay Dumpling for his kindness, saying, "All men have seven holes for seeing, hearing, eating, and breathing. [Dumpling] is the only one who does not have them. Let us try drilling them for him!" Each day they drilled another hole, and on the seventh day Dumpling died.[74]

南海之帝為儵，北海之帝為忽，中央之帝為渾沌. 儵與忽時相與遇於渾沌之地，渾沌待之甚善. 儵與忽謀報渾沌之德，曰：「人皆有七竅，以視聽食息，此獨無有，嘗試鑿之.」日鑿一竅，七日而渾沌死.[75]

No rational reader would object to this anecdote/parable on the grounds that Zig, Zag, and Dumpling are not real people.[76] We are invited to ruminate on the story, knowing full well that it must be fictitious, for the philosophical insights that it obliquely conveys—an exercise that remains fruitful to this day, with our urgent new concern for maintaining the integrity of the environment.[77] Thus appeals to history, anecdotes, and parables lie on a continuum of historicity ranging from the generally unexceptionable historical examples offered by nearly every ancient persuader at court; to more questionable historical examples, such as Guan Zhong's deathbed advice in *Han Feizi*; to parables with no pretense of factuality, such as the tale of Zig, Zag, and Dumpling in *Zhuangzi*. But fundamentally they are of the same species: devices that aim to clarify a philosophical problem by focusing on a cogent example.

Deductive Reasoning

The foregoing should not be misread as a denial that Chinese philosophers ever engaged in deductive reasoning. There are several important early Chinese arguments that can be restated in terms of propositional logic[78]—for instance, the Mohist defense of impartial care (*jian'ai* 兼愛):

> If one were to investigate where these various harms arise from, where do these things arise from?[79] Do these things arise from caring for others and benefiting others? One would have to say that this is not the case; one would have to say that they arise from despising and despoiling others. If one were to categorize things in the world by means of names, would those who hate

others and despoil others [be considered] impartial or partial? One would have to say partial. Thus is it not the case that engaging [others] with partiality gives rise to the great harms in the world? For this reason, partiality is wrong.[80]

姑嘗本原若眾害之所自生，此胡自生? 此自愛人利人生與? 即必曰非然也; 必曰從惡人賊人生. 分名乎天下, 惡人而賊人者, 兼與? 別與? 即必曰別也. 然即之交別者, 果生天下之大害者與? 是故別非也.[81]

I take this as an early attempt at a deductive argument (essentially a composite Barbara syllogism):

$p \to q$
(If one is partial, one hates and despoils others.)
$q \to r$
(If one hates and despoils others, one causes harm.)
$r \to s$
(If one causes harm, one is wrong.)
∴ $p \to s$
(If one is partial, one is wrong.)

More complex deductive arguments can be found in later texts. Xunzi's elaborate argument against abdication, which he tries to rule out as a method of transferring sovereignty in all possible situations,[82] contains an example of disjunctive elimination.

It is said, "When [the King] is dying, he should cede to someone else." This is also not so. . . . If the sage kings have already fallen, and there is no sage in the world, then there is certainly no one adequate to cede the world to. If there is a sage king in the world, and he is among [the current King's] sons or descendants, the dynasty does not change; the state does not alter its regulations. The world will be satisfied with this; there will be no respect in which this differs from [the situation] prior. If a Yao succeeds a Yao, what change would there be? If the sage is not among his sons or descendants, but among the Three Chief Ministers, then the world will come home to him as though he were restoring and sustaining it. The world will be satisfied with this; there will be no respect in which this differs from [the situation] prior. If a Yao succeeds a Yao, again, what change would there be?[83]

曰:「死而擅之.」是又不然. . . . 聖王已沒, 天下無聖, 則固莫足以擅天下矣. 天下有聖, 而在後子者, 則天下不離, 朝不易位, 國不更制. 天下厭然, 與鄉無以異也; 以堯繼堯, 夫又何變之有矣! 聖不在後子而在三公, 則天下如歸, 猶復而振之矣. 天下厭然, 與鄉無以異也; 以堯繼堯, 夫又何變之有矣![84]

This too is deductive in structure:

$\sim p \vee (q \vee r)$
(Either there is no sage or there is a sage among the King's descendants or the Three Chief Ministers.)
$\sim p \rightarrow \sim s$
(If there is no sage, there is no reason for abdication.)
$q \rightarrow \sim s$
(If there is a sage among the King's descendants, there is no reason for abdication.)
$r \rightarrow \sim s$
(If there is a sage among the Three Chief Ministers, there is no reason for abdication.)
$\therefore \quad \sim s$
(There is no reason for abdication.)

The opening premise is questionable, however: Xunzi does not seem to have envisioned a situation in which there is a sage in the world who is *neither* one of the King's descendants *nor* one of the Three Chief Ministers; nor is it entirely clear why succession by one of the Three Chief Ministers did not, in his mind, constitute the establishment of a new dynasty. (Consider the example of Yu, the sage who succeeded Shun, thereby initiating the dynasty known as Xia.) But otherwise, the reasoning is sound.

In early China audiences were so familiar with disjunctive elimination that even jokers could use it in texts intended more for entertainment than edification:

Queen Dowager Xuan of Qin [d. 265 BCE] loved Wei Choufu.[85] When the Queen Dowager fell ill and was about to die, she issued an order, saying, "When I am buried, Master Wei must accompany me in death."

Master Wei was horrified by this. Yong Rui persuaded the Queen Dowager in Master Wei's behalf, saying, "Do you consider the dead to have consciousness?"

The Queen Dowager said, "They have no consciousness."

[Yong Rui] said, "If your Majesty's godlike numen is clearly aware that the dead have no consciousness, why would you vainly take the person you loved in life, and bury him with the dead, who lack consciousness? And if the dead do have consciousness, the former king has been accumulating his wrath for many days. Your Majesty, you will scarcely have the means to make amends for your transgressions—how would you have leisure for assignations with Wei Choufu?"[86]

秦宣太后愛魏醜夫. 太后病將死, 出令曰:「為我葬, 必以魏子為殉.」魏子患之. 庸芮為魏子說太后曰:「以死者為有知乎?」太后曰:「無知也.」曰:「若太后之神靈, 明知死者之無知矣, 何為空以生所愛, 葬於無知之死人哉! 若死者有知, 先王積怒之日久矣, 太后救過不贍, 何暇乃私魏醜夫乎?」[87]

Restated in propositional form, this yields:

$p \vee \neg p$
(Either the dead have consciousness or the dead do not have consciousness.)
$p \rightarrow r$
(If the dead have consciousness, having your lover buried with you is a waste.)
$\neg p \rightarrow r$
(If the dead do not have consciousness, having your lover buried with you is a waste.)
$\therefore r$
(Having your lover buried with you is a waste.)

And that is a valid inference.

These few but memorable examples leave no doubt that audiences were aware of principles of deduction, and thus suggest that Chinese philosophers crafted non-deductive arguments as a deliberate choice. Arguments that rely wholly on deductive inference, like Xunzi's case against abdication, are not easy to find; one can only surmise that they were not preferred.

One consequence is that Chinese philosophy tends to demand a high level of interpretive participation from its audience. Perhaps this is what Confucius meant when he said, "I begin with one corner, and if [a student] cannot return with the other three corners, I do not repeat myself" 舉一隅不以三隅反, 則不復也.[88] If the strength of deductive argumentation is supposed to be that it yields correct inferences regardless of circumstance—*modus tollens* is as valid in Dallas as in Krasnoyarsk—then it follows that deductive argumentation yields the same results regardless of the audience's mood, receptiveness, perspective, and so on. By contrast, an audience presented with a statement like "only after the year has grown cold does one know that the pine and cypress are the last to wither" must ponder it sympathetically—or else derive little, if any, benefit from it. Nor is the meaning that one discovers necessarily identical at every juncture of one's life. In one's youth, the statement about the pine and cypress could mean one thing; as one matures, gains experience, and compares it to other opinions one has encountered, it could take on previously unimagined dimensions. Chinese philosophy, like literature, painting, or music, requires connoisseurship.[89] If we lack the taste—even more so if we exempt ourselves from the task of developing it—we will miss most of what Chinese philosophy has to offer.

Notes

1. I am grateful for helpful comments by participants and audience members at the venues where I delivered earlier versions of this piece.

2. The academic debate over the legitimacy of Chinese philosophy has occasioned numerous recent publications. For representative overviews, see the Introduction to this volume.

3. For an example of this sort of complaint, see Donald J. Munro, *The Concept of Man in Early China* (Stanford, CA: Stanford University Press, 1969), ix; see also the response in Bryan W. Van Norden, "What Should Western Philosophy Learn from Chinese Philosophy?" in *Chinese Language, Thought, and Culture: Nivison and His Critics*, ed. Philip J. Ivanhoe (Chicago and La Salle, IL: Open Court, 1996), 230. Also Robert M. Hartwell, "Historical Analogism, Public Policy, and Social Science in Eleventh- and Twelfth-Century China," *American Historical Review* 76, no. 3 (1971): 722ff. In earlier generations, the typical complaint was that "the Chinese mind" was incapable of higher logic; e.g., Alfred Forke (1867–1944), "The Chinese Sophists," *Journal of the North China Branch of the Royal Asiatic Society* 34

(1901–02): 5. One can only suppose that such opinions were directly or indirectly influenced by the ignorant and chauvinistic representation of China by G. W. F. Hegel (1770–1831), for which see, e.g., Sander Griffioen, "Hegel on Chinese Religion," in *Hegel's Philosophy of the Historical Religions*, ed. Bart Labuschagne and Timo Slootweg (Leiden: Brill, 2012), 21–30.

4. *The Development of the Logical Method in Ancient China* (Shanghai: Oriental Book Company, 1922), 6. For a survey of Chinese ideas about the presence or absence of logic in classical sources, see Joachim Kurtz, *The Discovery of Chinese Logic* (Leiden: Brill, 2011), esp. 277–337.

5. *Prior Analytics* 24b18–20; tr. A. J. Jenkinson in *The Complete Works of Aristotle: The Revised Oxford Translation*, ed. Jonathan Barnes (Princeton, NJ: Princeton University Press, 1984), I, 40. Richard E. Nisbett's declaration in *The Geography of Thought: How Asians and Westerners Think Differently* (New York: Free Press, 2003), 134, that "Aristotle had testable propositions about the world while the Chinese did not" is a flagrant overstatement. Consider that scientists have criticized Aristotle precisely for advancing hypotheses that are not testable; e.g., John A. Moore, *Science as a Way of Knowing: The Foundations of Modern Biology* (Cambridge, MA: Harvard University Press, 1993), 41.

6. Thus *Prior Analytics* 41b1–3. For a more precise assessment, see William Kneale and Martha Kneale, *The Development of Logic* (Oxford: Clarendon, 1962), 99: "Although Aristotle was aware that there are several kinds of valid argument which cannot be reduced to syllogistic form, he did not, so far as we know, succeed in giving a formal analysis of any of them." I am indebted to Bryan W. Van Norden for this reference.

7. Cf. Jonathan Barnes, "Aristotle," in R. M. Hare et al., *Founders of Thought* (Oxford: Oxford University Press, 1991), 120f.

8. See, e.g., W. V. Quine, *Methods of Logic*, fourth edition (Cambridge, MA: Harvard University Press, 1982), 102–08.

9. *Prior Analytics* 26a1.

10. E.g., Deborah K.W. Modrak, *Aristotle: The Power of Perception* (Chicago and London: University of Chicago Press, 1987), 128f.

11. See also Michael Nylan, "Lots of Pleasure but Little Happiness," *Philosophy East and West* 65, no. 1 (2015): 212; more generally, Zhang Wenxiu 張文修, "Zhongguo zhexue zhong de zhengming wenti" 中國哲學中的證明問題, *Wen shi zhe* 文史哲 no. 4 (2015): 136–50.

12. *Lunyu* 5.20. All translations in this chapter are my own.

13. *Lunyu* 9.28.

14. *Confucianism* (Berkeley and Los Angeles: University of California Press, 2011), 10f.

15. This is by no means an exhaustive list of types of non-deductive argumentation; for example, for my thoughts on paronomasia, see *After Confucius: Studies in Early Chinese Philosophy* (Honolulu: University of Hawai'i Press, 2005), 14ff.

16. I do not mean the same thing as riddles, which are explored as a technique of remonstrance in Wai-yee Li, "Riddles, Concealment, and Rhetoric in Early China," in *Facing the Monarch: Modes of Advice in the Early Chinese Court*, ed. Garrett P. S. Olberding (Cambridge, MA, and London: Harvard University Press, 2013), 100–132. See also Galia Patt-Shamir, "To Live a Riddle: The Transformative Aspect of the *Laozi*《老子》," *Journal of Chinese Philosophy* 36, no. 3 (2009): 408–23.

17. In previous work, e.g., Paul R. Goldin, *Rituals of the Way: The Philosophy of Xunzi* (Chicago and La Salle, IL: Open Court, 1999), 83ff., I translated *bianzhe* as "dialecticians," but I now think this is misleading.

18. I borrow this terminology from W. V. Quine, *The Ways of Paradox and Other Essays*, revised edition (Cambridge, MA, and London: Harvard University Press, 1976), 1–18.

19. Guo Qingfan 郭慶藩 (1844–1896), *Zhuangzi jishi* 莊子集釋, ed. Wang Xiaoyu 王孝魚, Xinbian zhuzi jicheng (Beijing: Zhonghua shuju, 1961), 10B.33.1103 ("Tianxia" 天下).

20. For a different interpretation, see A. C. Graham, *Disputers of the Tao: Philosophical Argument in Ancient China* (La Salle, IL: Open Court, 1989), 79f.

21. Wang Tianhai 王天海, *Xunzi jiaoshi* 荀子校釋 (Shanghai: Guji chubanshe, 2005), 2.3.81 ("Bugou" 不苟); also *Zhuangzi jishi* 10B.33.1105 ("Tianxia").

22. *Zhuangzi jishi* 10B.33.1106 ("Tianxia").

23. Cf. Goldin, *Rituals of the Way*, 91. I believe the point was first made by Mou Zongsan 牟宗三, *Mingjia yu Xunzi* 名家與荀子 (Taipei: Xuesheng shuju, 1979), 3ff.

24. E.g., Lawrence H. Powers, "Equivocation," in *Fallacies: Classical and Contemporary Readings*, ed. Hans V. Hansen and Robert C. Pinto (University Park, PA: Pennsylvania State University Press, 1995), 287–301.

25. *Zhuangzi jishi* 10B.33.1106 ("Tianxia").

26. Tan Jiefu 譚戒甫, *Gongsun Longzi xingming fawei* 公孫龍子形名發微, Xinbian zhuzi jicheng (Beijing: Zhonghua shuju, 1963), 2.24 ("Baima lun" 白馬論). Note that the *Han Feizi* 韓非子 attributes the paradox to one Ni Yue 兒說: see Chen Qiyou 陳奇猷, *Han Feizi xin jiaozhu* 韓非子新校注 (Shanghai: Guji chubanshe, 2000), 11.32.674 ("Wai chushuo, zuo, shang" 外儲說左上). For a discussion of the implications, see Goldin, *Rituals of the Way*, 138n.3.

27. The scholarship on this one line is too massive to cite in a single footnote, but the most plausible treatment, to my mind, is Christoph Harbsmeier, "The Mass Noun Hypothesis and the Part-Whole Analysis of the White Horse Dialogue," in *Chinese Texts and Philosophical Contexts: Essays Dedicated to Angus C. Graham*, ed. Henry Rosemont, Jr. (La Salle, IL: Open Court, 1991), 49–66.

28. Wu Yujiang 吳毓江, *Mozi jiaozhu* 墨子校注, ed. 孫啟治, *Xinbian zhuzi jicheng* (Beijing: Zhonghua shuju, 1993), 11.45.630 ("Xiaoqu" 小取); also A. C. Graham, *Later Mohist Logic, Ethics and Science*, reprint edition (Hong Kong: Chinese

University Press, 2003), 492 (NO 18), though his translation of *ji* as "bramble" reflects a different understanding of the statement.

29. Thus Sun Yirang 孫詒讓 (1848–1908) in *Mozi jiaozhu* 11.45.639n.64. Yiu-ming Feng, "A Logical Perspective on the Parallelism in Later Moism," *Journal of Chinese Philosophy* 39, no. 3 (2012): 348, dismisses it simply as an "invalid argument."

30. See Goldin, *Confucianism*, 92f.

31. Cf. Wim de Reu, "Right Words Seem Wrong: Neglected Paradoxes in Early Chinese Texts," *Philosophy East and West* 56, no. 2 (2006): 287. I am indebted to Paul van Els for this reference.

32. Cf. Bryan W. Van Norden, "Method in the Madness of the *Laozi*," in *Religious and Philosophical Aspects of the* Laozi, ed. Mark Csikszentmihalyi and Philip J. Ivanhoe (Albany, NY: State University of New York Press, 1999), 197.

33. Cf. Graham, *Disputers of the Tao*, 231–34.

34. For recent surveys, see Alexeï Volkov, "Analogical Reasoning in Ancient China: Some Examples," *Extrême-Orient, Extrême-Occident* 14 (1992): 15–48; and Jean-Paul Reding, "Analogical Reasoning in Early Chinese Philosophy," *Asiatische Studien* 40, no. 1 (1986): 40–56. For reasoning by analogy in mathematics, see Christopher Cullen, *Astronomy and Mathematics in Ancient China: The* Zhou bi suan jing (Cambridge: Cambridge University Press, 1996), 74–75.

35. Cf. Geoffrey MacCormack, *The Spirit of Traditional Chinese Law* (Athens, GA, and London: University of Georgia Press, 1996), 166–74; and Derk Bodde and Clarence Morris, *Law in Imperial China: Exemplified by 190 Ch'ing Dynasty Cases* (Philadelphia: University of Pennsylvania Press, 1967), 517–30.

36. The precise meanings of *bi* and *xing* are notoriously difficult to unravel, and indeed vary from one authority to another. See, e.g., Pauline Yu, *The Reading of Imagery in the Chinese Poetic Tradition* (Princeton, NJ: Princeton University Press, 1987), 57–67; also Karl S. Y. Kao, "Comparative Literature and the Ideology of Metaphor, East and West," in *Comparative Literature and Comparative Cultural Studies*, ed. Steven Tötösy de Zepetnek (West Lafayette, IN: Purdue University Press, 2003), 102ff.; Ming Dong Gu, "*Fu-bi-xing*: A Metatheory of Poetry-Making," *Chinese Literature: Essays, Articles, Reviews* 19 (1997): 1–22; and François Cheng, "*Bi* 比 et *xing* 興," *Cahiers de linguistique: Asie orientale* 6 (1979): 63–74.

37. Compare the translation in D. C. Lau, *Mencius: A Bilingual Edition*, revised edition (Hong Kong: Chinese University Press, 2003), 253.

38. *Mengzi* 6A.10.

39. On this concept, see Philip J. Ivanhoe, "McDowell, Wang Yangming, and Mengzi's Contributions to Understanding Moral Perception," *Dao* 10, no. 3 (2011): 285ff.; and Eric L. Hutton, "Moral Connoisseurship in Mengzi," in *Essays on the Moral Philosophy of Mengzi*, ed. Xiusheng Liu and Philip J. Ivanhoe (Indianapolis, IN, and Cambridge, MA: Hackett, 2002), 163–86.

40. "Zheng min" 烝民 (The Many People; *Mao* 260), a poem in the *Odes*, states this principle as clearly as any philosophical text: "Heaven engendered the many people; there are creatures; there are patterns" 天生烝民, 有物有則. Natural patterns are normative because they derive from Heaven.

41. *Mengzi* 6A.2.

42. Perhaps the sternest voice has been that of Arthur Waley (1889–1966), *Three Ways of Thought in Ancient China* (London: George Allen & Unwin, 1939), 194.

43. Cf. David B. Wong, "Reasons and Analogical Reasoning in Mengzi," in Liu and Ivanhoe, *Essays on the Moral Philosophy of Mengzi*, 187–220; and Lau, *Mencius*, 362–90.

44. Dates for the Western Zhou are necessarily tentative; I follow Edward Shaughnessy, *Sources of Western Zhou History: Inscribed Bronze Vessels* (Berkeley and Los Angeles: University of California Press, 1991), xix.

45. Compare the translation in James Legge (1815–1897), *The Chinese Classics*, 2nd edition (Oxford: Clarendon, 1893–95; rpt., Taipei: SMC, 1991), III, 302f.

46. Gu Jiegang 顧頡剛 (1893–1980) and Liu Qiyu 劉起釪, *Shangshu jiaoshi yilun* 尚書校釋譯論 (Beijing: Zhonghua shuju, 2005), III, 1098.

47. See, more generally, Paul R. Goldin, *The Culture of Sex in Ancient China* (Honolulu: University of Hawai'i Press, 2002), 48ff.

48. Chen Li 陳立 (1809–1869), *Baihutong shuzheng* 白虎通疏證, ed. Wu Zeyu 吳則虞, Xinbian zhuzi jicheng (Beijing: Zhonghua shuju, 1994), 10.452 ("Jiaqu" 嫁娶).

49. For some other thoughts on the weaknesses of analogical reasoning in Chinese thought, see Yuet Keung Lo, "From Analogy to Proof: An Inquiry into the Chinese Mode of Knowledge," *Monumenta Serica* 43 (1995): 141–58.

50. *Bentham's Handbook of Political Fallacies*, ed. Harold A. Larrabee (Baltimore, MD: Johns Hopkins University Press, 1952), 43–53.

51. See my "Appeals to History in Early Chinese Philosophy and Rhetoric," *Journal of Chinese Philosophy* 35, no. 1 (2008): 79–96.

52. The wordy phrases "verifying the root," "verifying the origin," and "verifying the utility" are necessary in English to reflect the fact that *ben* 本, *yuan* 原, and *yong* 用 are verbs.

53. Compare the translations in Burton Watson, *Mozi: Basic Writings* (New York: Columbia University Press, 2003), 120f.; and Yi-pao Mei, *The Ethical and Political Works of Motse* (London: Arthur Probsthain, 1929), 182f.

54. Following the commentary of Wang Niansun 王念孫 (1744–1832), *Mozi jiaozhu* 9.35.405n.10.

55. *Mozi jiaozhu* 9.35.400f. ("Feiming, shang" 非命上).

56. Cf. Paul R. Goldin, "Why *Mozi* Is Not Included in the *Daoist Canon*: Or, Why There Is More to Mohism Than Utilitarian Ethics," in *How Should One Live?:*

Comparing Ethics in Ancient China and Greco-Roman Antiquity, ed. R. A. H. King and Dennis Schilling (Berlin: De Gruyter, 2011), 79. The last contention is being independently confirmed, incidentally, by modern neuroscience; see, e.g., Azim F. Shariff and Kathleen D. Vohs, "The World without Free Will: What Happens to a Society That Believes People Have No Conscious Control over Their Actions?" *Scientific American* 310, no. 6 (2014): 77–79.

57. E.g., *Mozi jiaozhu* 2.9.78 ("Shangxian, zhong" 尚賢中); *Mozi jiaozhu* 7.26.295 ("Tianzhi, shang" 天志上); *Mozi jiaozhu* 7.27.306 ("Tianzhi, zhong" 天志中); *Mozi jiaozhu* 7.28.320 ("Tianzhi, xia" 天志下).

58. The best discussion is now Yuri Pines, "From Historical Evolution to the End of History: Past, Present and Future from Shang Yang to the First Emperor," in *Dao Companion to the Philosophy of Han Fei*, ed. Paul R. Goldin (Dordrecht: Springer, 2013), 25–45; see also Graham, *Disputers of the Tao*, 270–73.

59. *Han Feizi xin jiaozhu* 19.49.1085 ("Wudu" 五蠹).

60. Yan Zhenyi 閻振益 and Zhong Xia 鍾夏, *Xinshu jiaozhu* 新書校注, Xinbian zhuzi jicheng (Beijing: Zhonghua shuju, 2000), 1.17 ("Guo Qin, xia" 過秦下).

61. He Jianzhang 何建章, *Zhanguoce zhushi* 戰國策注釋 (Beijing: Zhonghua shuju, 1990), 18.613 ("Zhang Mengtan ji gu Zhao zong" 張孟談既固趙宗).

62. For this and other appeals to history, literature, and apophthegms in *Zhanguoce*, see Goldin, *After Confucius*, 82–83.

63. *Lunyu* 7.22.

64. On the *Lunyu*, see Amy Olberding, *Moral Exemplars in the* Analects*: The Good Person Is* That (New York and London: Routledge, 2012).

65. Matthias Richter, *Guan ren: Texte der altchinesischen Literatur zur Charakterkunde und Beamtenrekrutierung* (Bern: Peter Lang, 2005), argues that such moral judgments derive from the bureaucratic practice of succinctly noting an official's strengths and weaknesses. Even if this argument is correct, learning from the example of other people can still be a valid mode of moral self-cultivation.

66. Compare the translation in Burton Watson, tr., *Han Feizi: Basic Writings* (New York: Columbia University Press, 2003), 97.

67. *Han Feizi xin jiaozhu* 19.49.1085 ("Wudu").

68. *Han Feizi xin jiaozhu* 3.10.228–29. The three ministers are Shudiao 豎刁, Prince Kaifang of Wei 衛公子開方, and Yiya 易牙—who go on, in this account, to imprison Duke Huan until he starves to death. Cf. Li Xiangfeng 黎翔鳳, *Guanzi jiaozhu* 管子校注, ed. Liang Yunhua 梁運華, Xinbian zhuzi jicheng (Beijing: Zhonghua shuju, 2004), 11.32.608–09 ("Xiaocheng" 小稱); and Chen Qiyou, *Lüshi chunqiu xin jiaoshi* 呂氏春秋新校釋 (Shanghai: Guji chubanshe, 2002), 16.978–80 ("Zhijie" 知接).

69. Ibid., 15.36.849–52. Prince Kaifang of Wei does not appear in this passage.

70. Cf. Paul R. Goldin, "Introduction," in *Dao Companion to the Philosophy of Han Fei*, 2ff.

71. E.g., the subtitle of Victor H. Mair's translation, *Wandering on the Way: Early Taoist Tales and Parables of Chuang Tzu* (New York: Bantam, 1994; rpt., Honolulu: University of Hawai'i Press, 1998).

72. For more on Chinese words that overlap in some respect with the English term "anecdote," see the Introduction to this volume.

73. The name Hundun 渾沌, literally "muddy, clouded," is manifestly related to "dumpling" (*huntun* 餛飩, more familiar in the Cantonese form, "wonton," on Chinese menus in the West), so called because dumplings, like the primordial *dao* itself, lack any fixed shape.

74. Compare the translation in Mair, *Wandering on the Way*, 71.

75. *Zhuangzi jishi* 3C.7.309 ("Ying diwang" 應帝王).

76. Tamara Chin, *Savage Exchange: Han Imperialism, Chinese Literary Style, and the Imperial Imagination* (Cambridge, MA and London, UK: Harvard University Asia Center, 2014), 40–48, discusses the similar use of fictitious personages in early Chinese economic treatises.

77. Cf. Paul R. Goldin, "Why Daoism Is Not Environmentalism," *Journal of Chinese Philosophy* 32, no. 1 (2005): 80. For earlier interpretations, see for example N. J. Girardot, *Myth and Meaning in Early Taoism: The Theme of Chaos (hun-tun)* (Berkeley: University of California Press, 1983), 81–98; Max Kaltenmark, *Lao Tzu and Taoism*, tr. Roger Greaves (Stanford: Stanford University Press, 1969), 101; Joseph Needham, *Science and Civilisation in China* (Cambridge: Cambridge University Press, 1954–), II, 112ff.; Arthur Waley, *Three Ways of Thought in Ancient China* (London: George Allen & Unwin, 1939), 66ff.; Marcel Granet, *La pensée chinoise* (Paris: La Renaissance du Livre, 1934; rpt. Paris: Albin Michel, 1999), 320f.; and idem, *Danses et légendes de la Chine ancienne*, 3rd edition, ed. Rémi Mathieu (Paris: Presses Universitaires de France, 1994), 544.

78. John S. Cikoski, "On Standards of Analogic Reasoning in the Late Chou," *Journal of Chinese Philosophy* 2, no. 3 (1975): 325, proposes a passage from *Lüshi chunqiu* 呂氏春秋 as an example of "the syllogism form," but I fail to see how it qualifies as a syllogism; cf. Janusz Chmielewski, "Concerning the Problem of Analogic Reasoning in Ancient China," *Rocznik orientalistyczny* 40, no. 2 (1979): 67n.4. There are also some examples of syllogisms in the Mohist Canons in Zhan Jianfeng 詹劍峰, *Mojia de xingshi luoji* 墨家的形式邏輯, 2nd edition (Wuhan: Hubei renmin chubanshe, 1979), 110–18.

79. This sentence is no less repetitive in the original Chinese.

80. Compare the translations in Watson, *Mozi*, 41; and Mei, 87.

81. *Mozi jiaozhu* 4.16.175 ("Jian'ai, xia" 兼愛下).

82. Cf. Goldin, "Appeals to History in Chinese Philosophy and Rhetoric," 88f. My understanding of this passage differs slightly from that of Yuri Pines, "Disputers of Abdication: Zhanguo Egalitarianism and the Sovereign's Power," *T'oung Pao* 91, no. 4–5 (2005), 289ff. Cf. also Luo Genze 羅根澤, *Zhuzi kaosuo* 諸子考索 (Beijing: Renmin chubanshe, 1958), 72ff.

83. Compare the translation in John Knoblock, *Xunzi: A Translation and Study of the Complete Works* (Stanford, CA: Stanford University Press, 1988–94), III, 40.

84. *Xunzi jiaoshi* 12.18.722f. ("Zhenglun" 正論).

85. This name appears to mean "The Grotesque Man from Wei."

86. Compare the translation in J. I. Crump, *Chan-kuo Ts'e*, rev. edition (Ann Arbor, MI: Center for Chinese Studies, University of Michigan, 1996), §98.

87. *Zhanguoce zhushi* 4.148 ("Qin Xuan taihou ai Wei Choufu" 秦宣太后愛魏醜夫).

88. *Lunyu* 7.8.

89. Cf. Sarah Mattice, "Artistry as Methodology: Aesthetic Experience and Chinese Philosophy," *Philosophy Compass* 8, no. 3 (2013): 199–209.

2

The Frontier between Chen and Cai

Anecdote, Narrative, and Philosophical Argumentation in Early China

Andrew Seth Meyer[1]

In his groundbreaking study of early Chinese historiography, David Schaberg described the centrality of the anecdote to the historiographic enterprise. Anecdotes did not function simply as vectors for the transmission of facts about the past; their formal structure provided the intrinsic mechanism by which the past became meaningful. The medium was the message: "the morphology and thematics of the anecdote" were "specially adapted to substantiate certain kinds of judgments," making "the world and its history a laboratory." Schaberg acknowledges that this blurs the line between historiography and philosophy, noting the frequent similarity between anecdotal material anthologized in "historical" works such as the *Zuozhuan* 左傳 (Zuo Commentary) and "philosophical" works such as the *Xunzi* 荀子 (Master Xun) or *Han Feizi* 韓非子 (Master Han Fei).[2]

This raises a question that (understandably, given the scope of his project) Schaberg initially left unexplored: were anecdotes in early China as instrumental to philosophy as they were to historiography?[3] There are two ways to conceptualize this question that respect the integrity of early Chinese texts and the categories native to early Chinese discourse. The first is in terms of genre. Did or could anecdotes perform the same determinatively instrumental role in the writings directly conveying the teachings of the "Masters," the early Chinese analogues of the ancient Mediterranean's "philosophers," as Schaberg has shown for "annals" or "records" such as

63

the *Zuozhuan* or *Guoyu* 國語 (Discourses of the States)? The second is in terms of basic cognitive tasks. Schaberg has shown that when early Chinese elites set out to explore the question "What does event X mean?," that the anecdote provided a principal mechanism by which this problem could be addressed and resolved. Could the same be true when early thinkers began with a more abstract question of truth or value such as "What is humaneness?" Were the formal properties and applied uses of the anecdote as critical within this domain of inquiry?

In this chapter I would like to explore this latter "philosophical" use of the anecdote as a literary form in early China through the examination of a large group of related stories: those depicting the sojourn of Kongzi 孔子 (551–479 BCE), better known to Western readers as Confucius, on the frontier between the southern states of Chen 陳 and Cai 蔡. The basic framework of these sojourn anecdotes is fairly stable and consistent. The scene always opens upon Confucius and his disciples, surrounded by hostile forces on the frontier between Chen and Cai during the Master's wanderings in search of a sage ruler. The exact reasons for Confucius's detention are most often left vague. All accounts agree that conditions were desperate; Confucius and his followers were without food and held to the brink of starvation. Here accounts diverge. Different texts populate the scene with different characters, and portray varying events. Some accounts reflect favorably on the demeanor and behavior of Confucius and his students, others depict them in a much more negative light. The sheer number of such anecdotes and the variety of different texts in which they appear marks this as a significant case-in-point for any investigation of the use of anecdotes more generally. The repeated recasting of this scene tells us a great deal about the discursive norms and practices being negotiated by the participants in early Chinese intellectual culture.

The origins of the sojourn narrative are difficult to determine with any certainty. If the various articulations of this anecdote do in fact stem from some actual event, it may have begun as an element of oral lore surrounding the life of Confucius, transmitted within the community of his latter-day followers.[4] Whatever the case, it is clear that by the late fourth century BCE the sojourn story had become an established and relatively stable point of reference within the larger discourse of early Chinese thinkers, recounted as "fact" with the same frequency and consistency as, for example, the story of Yao's 堯 abdication to Shun 舜 or the early wanderings of Duke Wen of Jin 晉文公 (r. 636–628 BCE).[5] However, the copious anecdotal depictions of the sojourn are not chiefly intriguing as empirical reports of historical events. Rather, the permutations and distortions to which the scene is subjected from text to text can be seen to encode rhetorical assertions about and logical formulations of issues and values that transcend the particular circumstances of Confucius's life.

Taken together, the various versions of the narrative allow us to reconstruct a kind of philosophical conversation. Ancient Chinese literati used the sojourn anecdote to formulate logical arguments concerning ethics, politics, and cosmology. Looked at comparatively, we find that though these arguments do not employ the type of logic privileged in the post-Socratic Greco-Roman tradition, they are nonetheless substantively "philosophical," utilizing the logical potential of narrative in a manner comparable to the "thought experiments" identified and employed by philosophers in the modern academy. In fact, this use of anecdotes exemplifies a general methodological orientation among the "Masters and disciples" that, though not entirely incommensurate with the logical methods and worldview of Greco-Roman philosophy, nonetheless distinguishes early Chinese and Greco-Roman discourses from one another in certain respects.

Beyond Exempla: The Sojourn Narrative as Philosophical Reasoning

Any brief perusal of the writings of the early Chinese Masters discloses the ubiquity of the anecdote within that discourse. Both transmitted "Masters texts" and archaeologically recovered manuscripts are replete with anecdotes. As we might expect, the most characteristic use to which anecdotes are put in Masters writings are as exempla deployed to support discrete propositions. This usage is epitomized by the *Lüshi chunqiu* 呂氏春秋 (Spring and Autumn Annals of Mr. Lü), most of which consists of chapters comprising a propositional statement followed by anecdotes presented in evidence.[6] It is likewise in evidence in the *Shuoyuan* 說苑 (Garden of Illustrative Examples), a composition of the Han scholar Liu Xiang 劉向 (79–8 BCE), as Christian Schwermann makes clear in his contribution to this volume. In other texts, such as the "Shuolin" 說林 (Forest of Illustrative Examples) chapters of the *Han Feizi* and *Huainanzi*, "loose" anecdotes (that is to say, anecdotes unattached to particular logical propositions) are collected, presumably for use as exempla in oral argumentation.[7] As David Schaberg noted in a recent study, while such uses of anecdotal evidence may often be rhetorically and polemically very powerful, they ultimately lack philosophical sophistication: "a philosophy that merely carried on its reliance upon anecdotal demonstration . . . could never rise above the prejudices of its favourite stories."[8]

If anecdotes were only ever used as exempla within early Masters discourse, they would have little to teach about Chinese philosophical method. In the various instances of the sojourn narrative, however, we see the formulation of anecdotes that are not reducible to historical exempla. For example, the simplest version of the tale, found in *Lunyu* 論語 (Analects) 15.2, reads:

> In Chen, provisions were cut off and the followers were so ill that they could not rise. Zilu, expressing resentment, said, "Does even a gentleman reach dire straits?" The Master said, "The gentleman is invariably in dire straits.[9] A petty person, in such circumstances, loses self-control."

> 在陳絕糧，從者病，莫能興．子路慍見曰：「君子亦有窮乎？」子曰：「君子固窮，小人窮斯濫矣．」[10]

The basic kernel of the sojourn narrative is found here, though certain key details are absent: nowhere does the text mention either the setting of the frontier (only Chen is mentioned, not Cai) or the presence of an armed threat, as other versions do. Nonetheless, as brief as this passage is, it manifests all of the formal characteristics of an anecdote identified by Schaberg and is indeed structurally indistinguishable from the stories in the *Zuozhuan*: it is a tale "constructed around opportunities for judgment" and "favoring themes of vision."[11]

Generic as it is as an anecdote, *Lunyu* 15.2 is not reducible to a typical "exemplum." It is not deployed in support of a proposition, but rather poses a proposition internally in the form of Confucius's judgment. Indeed, this instance of the sojourn narrative (like many others) works as proposition and exemplum simultaneously. Confucius models the principle articulated in his judgment even as he declares it to his disciple Zilu 子路. In this sense, if *Lunyu* 15.2 is an exemplum, it is one constructed to resist its use in support of any proposition that contradicts the one to which it gives voice.

Fundamentally, *Lunyu* 15.2 uses the anecdote as a form to take up a "philosophical" question lying latent in Zilu's query: what is a "gentleman" (*junzi* 君子)? The situation that the passage depicts, especially their experience of hunger, would conventionally have called the status of Confucius and his disciples as "gentlemen" into doubt. Confucius and his followers were not high-born aristocrats possessed of their own ancestral temples; they were "knights" (*shi* 士) inhabiting the fringe of the aristocratic social order. For such men to go publicly hungry was a clear sign of status degradation,[12] marking them as having fallen from the circle of "gentlemen" entitled to a share of meat from the ancestral altars.[13] *Lunyu* 15.2 challenges this conventional understanding of gentlemanly status.

This challenge may at first seem entirely rhetorical: the story could be construed as a simple appeal to authority. If the question at hand is "what disqualifies an individual as a gentleman," then, in the eyes of Confucius's latter-day followers, anything that happened to Confucius must be discarded. If we examine more deeply, however, the logical assertions formulated by the anecdote are more sophisticated. To a readership that is expected to already hold that hunger and gentlemanly status were mutually incommensurate, *Lunyu* 15.2 presents a "what if?" What if *even* Confucius experienced hunger, would *he* then no longer be a gentleman? The plot of the narrative further complicates the hypothetical. Setting aside Confucius's particular persona and cachet, his behavior as depicted in the anecdote problematizes the conventional construction of "gentleman" as a category. What if we had an individual (*any* individual) who was suddenly threatened with starvation, but who remained steadfast and calm in the face of death; if that man is not a "gentleman," then is the category of "gentleman" still useful in describing personal excellence? Anyone who answered "no" to either of these questions would be forced to assent to the principle implicit in Confucius's judgment: a gentleman can not be defined by his objective circumstances, but only by the quality of his subjective responses to those circumstances.

That the producers and transmitters of early texts were critically aware of the logical implications of the sojourn narrative is evinced by their repeated recasting of this scene. More elaborate, perhaps later sojourn anecdotes further explore the logical implications of the situation. In *Xunzi* 28, we read:

> When Confucius was going south to Chu, he was trapped on the border between Chen and Cai. For seven days they lit no fire, they ate only a soup of wild greens without rice. The disciples all looked hungry. Zilu asked, "I have heard, 'Heaven will repay those who do good with good fortune, and will repay those who transgress with calamity.' Now you, Master, have stored virtue, accumulated righteousness and perfected your conduct for so

long. Why have you been eclipsed?" Confucius replied, "You do not understand, so I will tell you. Do you suppose the wise will necessarily be employed? Did not Prince Bigan have his heart cut out?[14] Do you suppose that the loyal will necessarily be employed? Did not Guan Longfeng meet with punishment?[15] Do you suppose that one who admonishes will necessarily be employed? Was not Zixu of Wu dismembered outside the east gate of Gusu?[16] Success or failure depends on the age. Worthiness or unworthiness is a question of character. Many gentlemen who learn broadly and plan profoundly do not meet with the [right] age. If looked at from this perspective, those who did not meet with their age were legion, how am I unique? Moreover, if the orchid and angelica grow in a deep forest, though there are no people about they are no less fragrant. The learning of the gentleman is not undertaken in order to succeed. It is done so that when he is in dire straits anxiety will not hinder him nor will his will flag. He understands calamity and fortune, the ends and beginnings of things, thus his mind is unconfused. Worthiness or unworthiness depends on character. Doing it or not depends on the person. Success or failure depends on the age. Death or life depends on fate. If now there is a person who does not meet his age, though he is worthy, can he act? If he meets his age, what difficulty will he have? Thus the gentleman learns broadly and plans deeply, cultivating his person and correcting his conduct in anticipation of his age."

孔子南適楚, 厄於陳蔡之間, 七日不火食, 藜羹不糝, 弟子皆有飢色. 子路進而問之曰:「由聞之: 為善者天報之以福, 為不善者天報之以禍. 今夫子累德積義懷 美, 行之日久矣, 奚居之隱也?」孔子曰:「由不識, 吾語女. 女以知者為必用邪? 王子比干不見剖心乎! 女以忠者為必用邪? 關龍逢不見刑乎! 女以諫者為必用 邪? 吳子胥不磔姑蘇東門外乎! 夫遇不遇者, 時也; 賢不肖者, 材也; 君子博學深謀, 不遇時者多矣! 由是觀之, 不遇世者眾矣, 何獨丘也哉! 且夫芷蘭生於深林, 非以無人而不芳. 君子之學, 非為通也, 為窮而不困, 憂而意不衰也, 知禍福終始而心不惑也. 夫賢不肖者, 材也; 為不為者, 人也; 遇不遇者, 時也; 死生者, 命 也. 今有其人, 不遇其時, 雖賢, 其能行乎? 苟遇其時, 何難之有! 故君子博學深謀, 修身端行, 以俟其時.」[17]

Here the anecdote shifts focus from the social dimensions of gentlemanly status to the metaphysical parameters of moral identity. Zilu's query opens up a basic philosophical problem: how do the empirical conditions faced by Confucius and his disciples impact their understanding of the moral universe? If one accepts, as Zilu suggests (and as Confucius and his disciples implicitly held), that Heaven in some sense favors the good and opposes the wicked, the situation on the frontier between Chen and Cai posed a paradox. A starving worthy and a moral universe, proposes Zilu, are mutually irreconcilable. Either Confucius was somehow blameworthy, or the conventional understanding of Heaven as a moral agent must be abandoned.

Confucius's lengthy answer to Zilu works through some of the basic doctrinal debates between the latter-day disciples of Confucius (or Ru 儒, as they are identified in early texts) and their philosophical opponents, particularly the Mohists.[18] In the *Mozi* 墨子 (Master Mo) we find a close echo of the adage Zilu claims to have heard: "Heaven will give good fortune to those who love and benefit others, Heaven will bring calamity to those who hate and steal from others" 愛人利人者, 天必福之, 惡人賊人者, 天必禍之.[19] In suggesting on this basis that there is something wrong with Confucius's situation, Zilu has failed (from the perspective of the anecdote) to understand the evidence with which he has been confronted. On the most basic level, Zilu has misunderstood the manner in which Heaven's preferences are revealed in the phenomenal world. His expectation that virtue will be materially rewarded is refuted by history, which is replete with exempla of virtuous actors that met bad ends.

Here Zilu effectively serves as a kind of Mohist "straw man."[20] The *Mozi* explicitly asserts that the worthy will be materially rewarded and the wicked materially punished, such outcomes are a function of the operation of "Heaven's Will" (*tianzhi* 天志).[21] But this, according to Confucius, is to misunderstand the basic nature of "worthiness," which is an intrinsic state of excellence complete unto itself: "if the orchid and angelica grow in a deep forest, though there are no people about they are no less fragrant." The worthy are worthy irrespective of any reward or punishment.

The confict between *Xunzi* 28 and the *Mozi* on some level turns upon an article of faith. The latter text asserts that Heaven consistently intervenes in worldly affairs in a way that the former text denies, and each cites its own precedents in favor of its position.[22] The sojourn narrative does not merely serve as a vector for the "prejudices" of the *Xunzi* (to borrow Schaberg's phrase), however. The text utilizes the story as an opportunity to formulate logical objections to its opponents' arguments. In the conclusion of the sojourn tale in *Xunzi* 28 we read:

> Confucius said, "You (i.e., Zilu) stay, I will tell you. Of old Prince Chong'er of Jin's (Duke Wen 文公, r. 636–628 BCE) will to become hegemon was born at Cao. King Goujian of Yue's (r. 496–465 BCE) will to become hegemon was born at Kuaiji. The will of Xiaobai, Duke Huan of Qi (r. 685–643 BCE) to become hegemon was born at Ju.[23] Thus one who does not live in obscurity can not have far-reaching thoughts, one whose person is not eclipsed can not have expansive aspirations. How can you know I have not gotten it beneath the falling leaves of this mulberry?"
>
> 孔子曰:「由! 居! 吾語女. 昔晉公子重耳霸心生於曹, 越王句踐霸心生於會稽, 齊桓公小白霸心生於莒. 故居不隱者思不遠, 身不佚者志不廣; 女庸安知吾不得之桑落之下?」[24]

Here the *Xunzi* makes the hypothetical extension of the sojourn narrative and its logical implications explicit. In the same way that *Lunyu* 15.2 presents readers with a "what if?" that forces them to reassess conventionally held concepts of gentlemanly status, *Xunzi* 28 constructs a scenario that tests the existential viability of a concept like *Mozi*'s "Heaven's Will." In asking "How can you know?" Confucius probes the utility of Zilu's adage (and by extension, the *Mozi*'s doctrine) as a gauge to moral action. Even if one accepts hypothetically that any material event could be an instance of Heavenly reward or punishment, drawing ethical guidance from such signs would be impossible. As Confucius notes, history is not only full of people who met with final calamity though they enjoyed a reputation for virtue, but of those who, like Duke Huan, Duke Wen, and King Goujian, won through to triumph after a period of adversity. As with *Lunyu* 15.2, *Xunzi* 28 confronts the reader with a logical question: could anyone caught in the situation portrayed in the anecdote know whether they were being punished for past crimes or prepared for future greatness? If the answer is "no," then the value of "Heaven" as an external gnomon by which to objectively measure conduct *right now* is negated. Where the *Mozi* argues that Heaven's will provides an organizing principle by which the moral society may be realized, *Xunzi* 28 demonstrates that once that model is applied within "real time" its efficacy crumbles.

Further inferences are drawn from the sojourn narrative in other versions of the story that reflect a "Ru" or "Confucian" perspective. In *Lüshi chunqiu* 14.6[25] we read:

> Confucius was brought to extreme straits between Chen and Cai. For seven days they did not eat, they had only a soup of wild greens without grain. Zai Yu was exhausted, Confucius was playing and singing within the house. Yan Hui was gathering vegetables outside. Zilu spoke with Zigong, saying, "The Master was driven out of Lu twice, had to erase his tracks in Wei, had a tree felled upon him in Song, and now has come to extremity between Chen and Cai. One who kills the Master will not be punished, one who extorts the Master will not be restrained. [Yet] the Master has played, sung, and danced without ceasing. Can it be that the gentleman so lacks shame?" Yan Hui had no reply, he entered and told Confucius. Confucius pushed his zither away impatiently, sighing he said, "You and Si are petty men. Summon them, I will speak with them." Zilu and Zigong entered. Zigong said, "Our condition now may be called extreme." Confucius said, "What kind of talk is this? The gentleman calls attaining the Way attainment, being bereft of the Way extremity. Now I grasp the Way of humaneness and righteousness in meeting the vagaries of a chaotic age. How can this position be called extremity? Thus if within one reflects and is blameless in the Way, one will not lose one's virtue in the face of adversity. When the great cold comes and the frost and snow fall, then I see the splendor of the pines and poplars. Of old Duke Huan attained it at Ju, Duke Wen attained it at Cao, the King of Yue attained it at Kuaiji. On the frontier between Chen and Cai lies my good fortune!" Confucius ardently returned to his zither and played, Zilu fervently took up the baton and danced. Zigong said, "I did not understand the loftiness of Heaven, I did not understand the profundity of the Earth." Of old those who attained the Way were happy in extremity or success. What made them happy was not extremity or success; if the Way had been attained extremity and success were the same, like the alternation of cold and heat, wind and rain. Thus Xu You was content on the north bank of the Ying, the Earl of Gong settled for Mount Gongshou.

孔子窮於陳, 蔡之間, 七日不嘗食, 藜羹不糝. 宰予備矣, 孔子弦歌於室, 顏回擇菜於外. 子路與子貢相與而言曰:「夫子逐於魯, 削跡於衛, 伐樹於宋, 窮於陳, 蔡, 殺夫子者無罪, 藉夫子者不禁, 夫子弦歌鼓舞, 未嘗絕音, 蓋君子之無所醜也若此乎?」顏回無以對, 入以告孔子. 孔子憱然推琴, 喟然而歎曰:「由與賜, 小人也. 召, 吾語之.」子路與子貢入. 子貢曰:「如此者可謂窮矣.」孔子曰:「是何言也? 君子達於道之謂達, 窮於道之謂窮. 今丘也拘仁義之道, 以遭亂世之 患, 其所也, 何窮之謂? 故內省而不疚於道, 臨難而不失其德. 大寒既至, 霜雪既降, 吾是以知松柏之茂也. 昔桓公得之莒, 文公得之曹, 越王得之會稽. 陳, 蔡之 阨, 於丘其幸乎!」孔子烈然返瑟而弦, 子路抗然執干而舞. 子貢曰:「吾不知天之高也, 不知地之下也.」古之得道者, 窮亦樂, 達亦樂. 所樂非窮達也, 道得於此, 則窮達一也, 為寒暑風雨之序矣. 故許由虞乎穎陽, 而共伯得乎共首.²⁶

Here the focus has shifted again, into the political realm.²⁷ Within the context of the narrative, Confucius and his disciples form a state in microcosm, with Confucius as its ruler. This is accentuated by the crux of Zilu's description of the Master's "extremity": "One who kills the Master will not be punished, one who extorts the Master will not be restrained." The two forces to which Zilu alludes, coercive force and material suasion, are the two basic powers that undergird the sovereignty of the state in much Warring States Masters discourse.²⁸ In Zilu's assessment Confucius has become a kind of "anti-ruler": not only is he incapable of rewarding or punishing his disciples, he is himself on the brink of starvation and vulnerable to whomever would seek to do him physical harm. It is on this basis that Zilu implies Confucius should feel ashamed; he falls short by every material measure of leadership.

Confucius's rebuttal to Zilu applies the same logic to political leadership as *Lunyu* 15.2 does to social status. When Confucius declares that he need only be ashamed of lacking the "Way" (*dao* 道, a general signifier in early Masters discourse denoting ultimate truth or the normatively correct path), he implicitly excludes wealth and weapons from this domain. In this respect *Lüshi chunqiu* 14.6 parallels the logic of *Lunyu* 12.7, where Confucius instructs Zigong that the state should give up weapons and food before it gives up the trust of the people.²⁹ Confucius's self-defense in *Lüshi chunqiu* 14.6 is easy to follow. Wealth and weapons are naturally alienable assets; a person can not necessarily be blamed for lacking them. Humaneness and righteousness, by contrast, are within the scope of a person to develop or not, thus Confucius could only be held accountable if he were without these virtues.

Again the reader is confronted with hypothetical questions. It is easy to envision rulers that lead through threats and bribes, but is another kind of leadership imaginable, one that operates solely through the personal qualities of the leader? If so, would not that type of leadership be more admirable than the kinds that do so through the mundane mechanisms of coercion and bribery? A reader who answered "yes" to these questions would take the first step to assenting to an array of Ru propositions concerning the nature of kingship and the moral mission of the state.

As in *Lunyu* 15.2, in *Lüshi chunqiu* 14.6 Confucius models the principle articulated in his judgment, giving form to ideas concerning political morality. Confucius's singing and dancing provides the matrix of his leadership as the narrative unfolds. It is the proximal stimulus that sets off Zilu's "mutiny," and it is the sign that harmony has been restored when Zilu takes up the baton and dances to the Master's tune at the story's conclusion. Readers would have of course been aware of the *Mozi*'s proposition that, because it wasted material resources, "making music is wrong."[30] *Lüshi chunqiu* 14.6 confronts the reader with a countervailing hypothetical on this score: if all other material resources (the "benefit" that the *Mozi* declares to be wasted by the pursuit of music) were lacking and the threat of death imminent, would music be consoling? A "yes" in answer to this question again opens the door to a series of propositions that contradict the doctrine of the *Mozi*. If music would retain its value and motive power on the dire frontier between Chen and Cai, then the *Mozi*'s strictly materialist concepts of the human condition and the social good are revealed to be flawed.

Understood in the contexts that would have informed early readers, these versions of the sojourn narrative are not reducible to historical exempla. They compel the reader to confront logical problems, and lay down the conceptual pathways by which those problems are most cogently (from the perspective of the anecdotes' proponents) resolved. These anecdotes are thus not fodder for reasoning, but rather instances of philosophical reasoning in and of themselves. In their architecture and function, they are most closely analogous to what have been termed "thought experiments" in present-day scientific and philosophical literature.[31]

An example of an early philosophical thought experiment can be found in Book I of Plato's *Republic*:

> [If] one took over weapons from a friend who was in his right mind and then the lender should go mad and demand them back . . . we ought not to return them in that case and . . . he who did so would not be acting justly.
>
> εἴ τις λάβοι παρὰ φίλου ἀνδρὸς σωφρονοῦντος ὅπλα, εἰ μανεὶς ἀπαιτοῖ, ὅτι οὔτε χρὴ τὰ τοιαῦτα ἀποδιδόναι, οὔτε δίκαιος ἂν εἴη ὁ ἀποδιδούς.[32]

This experiment was reformulated in the twentieth century by Dale Jamieson and Tom Regan, as a dilemma in which one is asked to fulfill the promise of returning a chainsaw to a neighbor who is drunk and accompanied by a bound and beaten companion.[33] We can see the parallels between the kinds of reasoning these hypothetical scenarios embody and the logical formulations expressed in various instances of the sojourn narrative. Each engages an abstract question ("must one always fulfill a promise," "does well-fed leisure define the gentleman," "is kingliness a function of material power," "is music wrong"), reasoning toward a conclusion by placing figures within a conceptual terrain and observing the logical trajectory of their evolution.

Inversions between Chen and Cai

Though they serve the same function as instruments of reasoning, anecdotes like the sojourn narratives were not strictly equivalent to thought experiments, in that they were not presented as purely hypothetical. Another distinction to be drawn between thought experiments as they are used in modern philosophy and anecdotes in early Masters' writings is the latters' discursive malleability across texts and traditions.[34] However concretely the sojourn between Chen and Cai may have been established as "fact," its meaning quickly became an open and contested issue. In the "Fei Ru" 非儒 (Against the Ru) chapter of the *Mozi*, for example, we read:

> When Confucius was brought to extreme straights between Cai and Chen, the stew was only of wild greens without grain. On the tenth day Zilu produced a boiled pig. Confucius did not ask where the meat had come from and ate it. [Zilu] also stole someone's robe and exchanged it for wine. Confucius did not ask where the wine came from and drank it. When Duke Ai

[of Lu] (r. 494–477 BCE) welcomed Confucius, if his mat were not straight he would not sit, if the food were not cut properly he would not eat. Zilu came forward and asked, "Why do you [now] do the opposite [of what you did between] Chen and Cai?" Confucius said, "Come here, I will tell you. Formerly, we expediently survived; now we are expediently righteous." Thus when he was starving and penurious he did not refuse to grasp licentiously to preserve his person. Secure and replete he falsified his conduct to adorn himself. What greater corruption and hypocrisy is there?

孔丘窮於蔡陳之閒, 藜羹不糝, 十日, 子路為享豚, 孔丘不問肉之所由來而食; 號人衣以酤酒, 孔丘不問酒之所由來而飲. 哀公迎孔子, 席不端弗坐, 割不正弗食, 子路進, 請曰:「何其與陳, 蔡反也?」孔丘曰:「來! 吾語女, 曩與女為苟生, 今與女為苟義.」夫飢約則不辭妄取, 以活身, 贏飽則偽行以自飾, 汙邪詐偽, 孰大於此!³⁵

This version of the sojourn narrative is obviously closely related to those contained in the *Xunzi* and the *Lüshi chunqiu*. The language that establishes the setting closely mirrors that used in these latter texts. Once again Zilu appears as interlocutor, and Confucius's injunction "Come here, I will tell you" is a deeply ironic echo of Ru accounts.

In this sense it would be tempting to read this passage as mere satire or slander. Where *Xunzi* 28 and *Lüshi chunqiu* 14.6 present "proof" contradicting the notion of Heavenly material reward and punishment; *Mozi* 39 recasts the scene to demonstrate that Confucius was, in fact, guilty of hypocrisy, thus his experience of calamity was entirely deserved. This is, of course, one unmistakable message of the recast narrative, and cannot be discounted as one of its rhetorical uses.

If we look more closely at *Mozi* 39, however, we can see that the particular way it reconstructs the sojourn narrative confronts and refutes many of the specific arguments made in Ru accounts of the scene. This is underscored by Confucius's final response to Zilu: "Formerly, we expediently survived; now we are expediently righteous." Righteousness (*yi* 義) was a label used by both Ru and Mohists to denote a moral value of ultimate importance. The *Mozi* uses the sojourn narrative to demonstrate that Confucius's construction of this category precludes consistent assessment of morality in conduct. Confucius's shifting of righteousness into the subjective realm has divorced righteousness from the material realities that control our lives from moment to moment; if "survival" and "righteousness" can be analytically distinguished then one is operating with a standard of morality that is prone to shift and change in response to exigency. By contrast, the *Mozi*'s equation of righteousness and benefit acknowledges (from its own perspective) the real conditions within which a moral agent must live and act, thus it is an unerring and unchanging standard in all times and all places.

The elegance of this argument is that one does not have to believe the particulars of the *Mozi*'s account to appreciate the way in which it critiques Ru values. In structural terms, *Mozi* 39 presents the same form of hypothetical expressed in *Lunyu* 15.2, *Xunzi* 28, and *Lüshi chunqiu* 14.6. Like these latter texts the *Mozi* presents the frontier between Chen and Cai as a state in microcosm, but asks: What if Confucius and his disciples had reached the actual point of starvation in that domain? Would there still be moral constraints on their acquisition of food?

Lunyu 15.2, *Xunzi* 28, and *Lüshi chunqiu* 14.6 define the righteous community as one whose members conduct themselves with courage and decorum, but courage and decorum are not sustainable indefinitely without food. We might concede that even brave people might steal food in order to survive, but if they did so, would their personal qualities make that action "right"? Anyone who answered "no" to this question moves toward conceding the *Mozi*'s position that "righteousness" is an objectively definable condition, and that to speak, as the opening passage of the *Mengzi* 孟子 (Mencius) enjoins, of "righteousness" wholly apart from "benefit"[36] is to open a chasm between moral ideals and lived reality. This reworking of the "thought experiment" embodied in the sojourn narrative thus expresses subtle understanding of the logical differences between Mohist and Ru doctrine and contributes a sophisticated critique to the philosophical exchange.

Other texts in the classical corpus induce similar logical inversions on the frontier between Chen and Cai, reconfiguring the hypothetical questions posed by the sojourn narrative to produce conclusions opposed to those implied by Ru texts. The extant *Zhuangzi* contains three full accounts of the sojourn narrative, one of which is shared with the *Lüshi chunqiu*.[37] The two unique accounts are anthologized in chapter 20 of the extant text, "Shanmu" 山木 (Mountain Tree). Though both accounts introduce similar distortions to the narrative, the second account depends less on emplotment, using the frontier between Chen and Cai chiefly as a backdrop for a prototypically "skewed" dialogue between Confucius and his disciple Yan

Hui. The first account is more plot-driven, and thus more analogously comparable to instances of the sojourn narrative found in the *Lunyu*, *Xunzi*, and *Mozi*. It reads:

> Confucius was besieged between Chen and Cai, and for seven days he ate no cooked food. Taigong Ren[38] went to offer his sympathy. "It looks as if you are going to die," he said.
> "It does indeed."
> "Do you hate the thought of dying?"
> "I certainly do!"
> Ren said, "Then let me try telling you about a way to keep from dying. In the eastern sea there is a bird and its name is Listless. It flutters and flounces, but seems to be quite helpless. It must be boosted and pulled before it can get into the air, pushed and shoved before it can get back to the nest. It never dares to be the first to advance, never dares to be the last to retreat. At feeding time, it never ventures to take the first bite, but picks only at the leftovers. So, when it flies in file, it never gets pushed aside, nor do other creatures such as men ever do it any harm. In this way it escapes disaster. The straight-trunked tree is the first to be felled; the well of sweet water is the first to run dry. And you, now—you show off your wisdom in order to astound the ignorant, work at your good conduct in order to distinguish yourself from the disreputable, going around bright and shining as though you were carrying the sun and moon in your hand! That's why you can't escape! . . . The Perfect man wants no repute. Why then do you delight in it so?"
> "Excellent!" exclaimed Confucius. Then he said good-bye to his friends and associates, dismissed his disciples, and retired to the great swamp, wearing furs and coarse cloth and living on acorns and chestnuts. He could walk among the birds without alarming their flocks. If even the birds and beasts did not resent him, how much less would men!

孔子圍於陳, 蔡之間, 七日不火食. 大公任往弔之, 曰:「子幾死乎?」曰:「然.」「子惡死乎?」曰:「然.」任曰:「予嘗言不死之道. 東海有鳥焉, 其名曰意怠. 其為鳥也, 翂翂翐翐, 而似無能; 引援而飛, 迫脅而棲; 進不敢為前, 退不敢為後; 食不敢先嘗, 必取其緒. 是故其行列不斥, 而外人卒不得害, 是以免於患. 直木先伐, 甘井先竭. 子其意者飾知以驚愚, 修身以明汙, 昭昭乎若揭日月而行, 故不免也. . . . 至人不聞, 子何喜哉?」孔子曰:「善哉!」辭其交遊, 去其弟子, 逃於大澤; 衣裘褐, 食杼栗; 入獸不亂群, 入鳥不亂行. 鳥獸不惡, 而況人乎!³⁹

As in the *Mozi*, though even more prominently, this narrative has the elements of satire and even farce, as one would expect from the *Zhuangzi*. The account begins by establishing that Confucius is besieged; then moves directly to the odd hermit Taigong Ren dropping in to pay his condolences. At the end the fact of the siege does not hinder Confucius from simply wishing everyone farewell and heading off into the swamp. All of these absurdities are deployed to comic effect.

All this casts doubt on whether such a farcical account can serve other than rhetorical purposes. But again, as in the *Mozi*, the *Zhuangzi* colonizes the narrative of Ru texts by way of expressing a logical critique of Ru doctrine. If one of the central messages of the sojourn narrative running through the *Lunyu*, *Xunzi*, and *Lüshi chunqiu* 14.6 versions is that moral individuals are defined by their subjective responses to exigent circumstances, *Zhuangzi* 20 explores the subjectivity of the individual and exposes its weakness as a beacon of moral value.

It would be tempting to see the text as ridiculing the values by which Confucius has lived, but if we read closely we see that this is not so. Taigong Ren does not say that Confucius was a fool to live as he had, he only points out that Confucius's chosen path has led him to the frontier between Chen and Cai, and the question he must ask himself at that juncture is, is he prepared to die? Though this version of the sojourn narrative contains many elements that are obviously ironic and constructed for humorous effect, it simultaneously lays out a serious argument by inviting readers to project themselves into the narrative, raising hypothetical questions structurally identical to those posed by the *Lunyu* and *Xunzi* versions of the story. We are enjoined to ask ourselves: do we fear death? Have we control of our desires? If not, we must seriously reconsider the wisdom that would lead us to the impasse between Chen and Cai. In the *Zhuangzi* that frontier has lost its status as a particular moment in time and space, it has become the threshold at which we all land if we insist on living our lives in accordance with values such as humaneness and righteousness and the imperatives to social engagement these entail.

A final articulation of the sojourn narrative I will examine is also contained in the *Lüshi chunqiu*, in Book 17, "Shenfen lan" 審分覽 (Exposition on Examining Divisions). In the third essay of that chapter, titled "Renshu" 任數 (Relying on Technique), we read:

> When Confucius was in extremity between Chen and Cai, there was not even a soup of wild greens to be had, for seven days they did not taste grain and slept during the day. Yan Hui went in search of grain. Finding some, he cooked it. When it was almost done, Confucius saw him put his hand into the pot and eat from it. After a little while, when the food was done, [Yan Hui] summoned Confucius and offered the food. Confucius pretended he had not seen [what Yan Hui had done].
>
> Rising, Confucius said, "Just now I dreamed of my father. If the food is pure I will make an offering of it."[40]
>
> Yan Hui said, "This is not possible. Just before an ash got into the pot. It was inauspicious to discard the food, thus I scooped it out and ate it."
>
> Confucius sighed and said, "What I trusted was my eyes, and my eyes cannot be trusted, what I relied on was my mind, and my mind cannot be relied upon. Remember this, my disciples. Knowing others is never easy."
>
> In fact, knowing is not difficult. That by which Confucius sought to know [made it] difficult.

孔子窮乎陳, 蔡之間, 藜羹不斟, 七日不嘗粒, 晝寢. 顏回索米, 得而爨之, 幾熟. 孔子望見顏回攫其甑中而食之. 選間, 食熟, 謁孔子而進食. 孔子佯為不見之. 孔子起曰:「今者夢見先君, 食潔而後饋.」顏回對曰:「不可. 嚮者煤室入甑中, 棄食不祥, 回攫而飯之.」孔子歎曰:「所信者目也, 而目猶不可信; 所恃者心也, 而心猶不足恃. 弟子記之, 知人固不易矣.」故知非難也, 孔子之所以知人難也.[41]

This account of the sojourn narrative is antagonistic to its Ru versions in ways similar to that of *Zhuangzi* 20. Once again the text picks up the theme of the subjective responses of the individual being the true measure of the gentleman. In this version Confucius's response to Yan Hui's actions would have been completely gentlemanly *had Yan Hui actually done what*

Confucius thought he did. If the whole ideal normative order described by *Lüshi chunqiu* 14.6 is based on the trust that Confucius as "ruler" inspires in his disciples, then *Lüshi chunqiu* 17.3 declares that that trust hangs, even among the morally elevated, by a very slender thread.

Lüshi chunqiu 17.3 makes a similar argument to *Zhuangzi* 20, though it focuses on the cognitive rather than the emotional faculties. The weakness of the Ru perspective, these texts argue, is that it emphasizes the subjectivity of the individual without looking closely or deeply enough into the workings of consciousness and the mind. Beginning, as Ru texts do, from the premise that the mind's responses must be made moral, bypasses a genuine understanding of how the emotional and cognitive functions of the mind operate. If the hypothetical question posed by *Lunyu* 15.2 is whether we must look at an individual's character to determine if he is a "gentleman," the sojourn narratives in *Lüshi chunqiu* and *Zhuangzi* 20 asks whether even a gentleman so conceived is truly suited to the challenges of the age. Can any individual, given the limitations of human perception and intellect, build and sustain the kind of trust that Ru texts deem essential for virtuous leadership?

More counter-articulations of the sojourn narrative could be examined, but these three examples provide ample evidence of the way in which Warring States authors appropriated this same anecdote as a logical instrument in formulating arguments diametrically opposed to one another. In a sense, through the writings of these authors the frontier between Chen and Cai took on a new significance. It became a meeting point at which opposing intellectuals of the Warring States could encounter and engage one another in philosophical debate.

Implications: Comparing the Philosophical Uses of Narrative in Early China and Ancient Greece

David Schaberg noted that, in the techniques that they developed for the crafting of events into anecdotes, the authors of the *Zuozhuan* had turned "the world and its history into a laboratory." A study of the various permutations of the sojourn anecdote demonstrates that this phenomenon was wide-ranging. Anecdotes were not only instrumental for ancient authors engaged in the task of historiography (viz. the recording and interpretation of the past), but were a versatile and important component of the "philosophical" toolkit employed by the producers of Masters' writings.

In this capacity, though anecdotes were most frequently employed as exempla, they at times served as the medium in which philosophical propositions were formulated and through which they were resolved. In other words, anecdotes like the sojourn narrative are not merely emblematic expressions of prior logically derived ideas, but concrete instances of their authors' "thinking through" the philosophical implications of particular problems. Schaberg's evocation of the "laboratory" was thus particularly apt in this regard, as textual expressions like the sojourn narrative use the structural properties of the anecdote to produce the same kind of logical effects achieved by "thought experiments" in modern philosophical reasoning.

What, then, can we learn about the distinct nature of early Chinese philosophical discourse from a study of anecdotes like the sojourn narrative? Most prominently, we are alerted to a distinctive mode of philosophical exchange. Ideas formulated and expressed in anecdotal form gave rise to a unique form of discourse that exploited all of the potential for plasticity and multivalence inherent in narrative. Thus a single "thought" (in the form of a single anecdote) could represent a working-through of multiple problems on multiple levels. This we have seen in the case of the sojourn narrative, which in any instance may simultaneously reflect on the relationship of the gentleman to society, humanity to Heaven, the sage to history, the state to morality, and etcetera. Authors that appropriated and transformed one another's anecdotes could thus conduct a kind of "conversation" that played out in many dimensions at once.

This is not to suggest that this type of manipulation of narrative was unique to early China. If we examine the literary culture of other areas in the ancient world, we may perceive similar discursive dynamics at work. In the late antique Mediterranean world, for example, early Christian authors engaged in reformulations of the Passion narrative by way of debating questions of theology and orthopraxy.[42] However, the logical uses of narrative exemplified by the sojourn anecdotes reveal marked differences between the conventions of early Chinese Masters' discourse and that of classical Greco-Roman philosophy.

In the Platonic dialog *Euthyphro*, for example, the eponymous priest of that text defines "piety" for Socrates as "what the gods all love," implicitly claiming that this can be known from stories of the gods recorded on the sacred robe of Athena. This elicits a Socratic critique, prompting Socrates to pose the famous query: "Is what is pious pious because the gods approve it, or do they approve it because it is pious?"[43] The logical appeal of the latter answer undermines the value of Euthyphro's stories of the gods: no universal truth can be deemed grasped if it must be defined in terms particular to a specific narrative. This imperative exerted a powerful influence on the subsequent development of "philosophy" as an enterprise in the greater Mediterranean world; so much so that within the modern discipline of philosophy "thought experiments," as logical implements employing narrative reasoning, remain controversial.[44]

By contrast, the sojourn narrative and other anecdotes similarly employed evince a "philosophical culture" much more at ease with narrative as an instrument of logic. Indeed, the early Chinese Masters' discourse may fairly be characterized as generally (with some significant exceptions) preferring narrative reasoning to the syntactic logic more esteemed by Greco-Roman philosophy. This orientation was not unreflective or uncritically arrived at, moreover, but may be linked to a general statement of method that is articulated in various forms in many disparate Masters' writings of the Warring States. A pristine exemplar of this methodological dictum is found in *Lunyu* 9.28: "The Master said: 'Only after the year has grown cold does one know that the pine and the poplar are the last to wither.'" 子曰：「歲寒，然後知松柏之後彫也。」[45] Though this passage reads as a somewhat innocuous adage, as Paul R. Goldin notes in his contribution to this volume, it is in fact an example of "non-deductive reasoning." In contrast to Socrates's insistence that the "one form" of a quality like "piety" must be abstracted from any and all particular contexts, *Lunyu* 9.28 asserts that certain qualities can only be known (indeed, can only be said to exist at all) through the unique context that reveals them. This is a baseline observation that is reaffirmed persistently throughout the transmitted texts of the Warring States. The *Xunzi* states this concept in spatial rather than temporal terms, declaring that, "If one does not climb high mountains, one does not know the loftiness of Heaven, if one does not descend into deep gorges, one does not know the profundity of earth." 不登高山，不知天之高也；不臨深谿，不知地之厚也。[46] The *Mozi* voices the idea negatively, warning against "trying to determine the location of sunrise and sunset from atop a spinning potter's wheel" 運鈞之上而立朝夕。[47] The *Zhuangzi* repeatedly notes the impossibility of recognizing dreams except after waking,[48] and of comprehending death from the vantage of life.[49] Perhaps the most vivid and oft-cited articulation of this principle is the image of the "Jade Disk of Mr. He" 和氏之璧, a seemingly ordinary stone that, when cut and polished, becomes a priceless gem. The fullest account of this anecdote is in the eponymous "Mr. He" chapter of the *Han Feizi*.[50] The *Han Feizi* works this story into a kind of thought experiment[51] analogous in certain structural respects to that of "Pascal's wager,"[52] it is thus another example of a "philosophical" use of an anecdote like that embodied by the various instances of the sojourn narrative.

Taken together, these expressions outline a point of general consensus among the authors of Warring States texts, and a point of general contrast with the emerging conventions of philosophical discourse in the Greco-Roman world: a broad emphasis on the idea that abstract, universal truths were often contingent upon and could only be known through particular actualizing contexts.[53] This orientation facilitated the development of the unique form of discourse embodied by the sojourn narratives and other anecdotes like them. Assessing the nature or value of a phenomenon such as "righteousness" or "music" was understood to be accomplishable by finding the conditions in which the truth about it is rooted and would be discernible. As with modern philosophical "thought experiments,"[54] this revelatory context was often to be found at extreme boundaries or marginal states (winter, high mountains, deep gorges) of the phenomenal world, thus it is no wonder that "the frontier between Chen and Cai" would provide so much grist for the philosophical mill.

This is not to suggest that early Chinese and Greco-Roman authors were engaging in modes of thought beyond one another's comprehension. For example, in the *Lüshi chunqiu* we find this observation:

> All the methods of the former kings were essential to their age, and the age has not persisted with the methods. Even though some methods may have been transmitted to today, they still may not be followed. Thus we must relinquish the particular methods of the former kings and [model] our methods on that by which they fashioned methods. What was that by which the former kings fashioned methods? That by which the former kings fashioned methods was humans. And we are humans as well.

> 凡先王之法, 有要於時也, 時不與法俱至. 法雖今而至, 猶若不可法. 故擇先王之成法, 而法其所以為法. 先王之所以為法者何也? 先王之所以為法者人也. 而己亦人也.[55]

Here we see an application of the same reasoning to be found in the *Euthyphro*. In the same way that Socrates prods Euthyphro to abandon contemplation of what the gods love and instead focus on why they love it, the author(s) of *Lüshi chunqiu* 15.8 advocate rejection of the specific methods of the former kings in favor of the underlying realities upon (and for) which those methods were instituted. In similar fashion, we might compare the parable of the "Jade of Mr. He" to Plato's allegory of the cave: both posit a more fundamental reality underlying the world of appearances that is hidden from those without the wisdom to grasp it.[56]

Though neither Greco-Roman nor Chinese authors were engaging in forms of reasoning that were completely exotic from the perspective of one another, they were yet affirming radically different priorities in negotiating the respective discursive conventions within which each group operated. Thus in the same *Lüshi chunqiu* in which we see an echo of the "Euthyphro dilemma," we see this argument made against verbal argumentation abstracted from practical concerns: "On the Zhou tripods there is pictured the ancient artisan Chui chewing on his own fingers. By this means did the former kings illustrate the uselessness of excessive skill" 周鼎著倕而齕其指，先王有以見大巧之不可為也.[57] Contrast this with Plato's implicit denigration of Euthypho's faith in the scenes pictured on the sacred cloak of Athena. In the same *Republic* in which we find the allegory of the cave, moreover, we find Socrates making this answer to the claim that astronomy leads to the study of "higher things":

> You seem to me in your thoughts to put a most liberal interpretation on the "study of higher things," . . . for apparently if anyone with back-thrown head should learn something by staring at decorations on a ceiling, you would regard him as contemplating them with the higher reason and not with the eyes. Perhaps you are right, and I am a simpleton. For I, for my part, am unable to suppose that any other study turns the soul's gaze upward than that which deals with being and the invisible. But if anyone tries to learn about the things of sense, whether gaping up or blinking down, I would never say that he really learns—for nothing of the kind admits of true knowledge. . . .
>
> οὐκ ἀγεννῶς μοι δοκεῖς, ἦν δ' ἐγώ, τὴν περὶ τὰ ἄνω μάθησιν λαμβάνειν παρὰ σαυτῷ ἥ ἐστι: κινδυνεύεις γάρ. καὶ εἴ τις ἐν ὀροφῇ ποικίλματα θεώμενος ἀνακύπτων καταμανθάνοι τι, ἡγεῖσθαι ἂν αὐτὸν νοήσει ἀλλ' οὐκ ὄμμασι θεωρεῖν. ἴσως οὖν καλῶς ἡγῇ, ἐγὼ δ' εὐηθικῶς. ἐγὼ γὰρ αὖ οὐ δύναμαι ἄλλο τι νομίσαι ἄνω

ποιοῦν ψυχὴν βλέπειν μάθημα ἢ ἐκεῖνο ὃ ἂν περὶ τὸ ὄν τε ᾖ καὶ τὸ ἀόρατον, ἐάν τέ τις ἄνω κεχηνὼς ἢ κάτω συμμεμυκὼς τῶν αἰσθητῶν τι ἐπιχειρῇ μανθάνειν. οὔτε μαθεῖν ἄν ποτέ φημι αὐτόν—ἐπιστήμην γὰρ οὐδὲν ἔχειν τῶν τοιούτων.[58]

Expressions like this one are as common in early Greco-Roman letters as those akin to the adage about the pine and the poplar in the early Chinese corpus. Post-Socratic Greco-Roman philosophy privileged knowledge arrived at through "pure reasoning," abstracted from any and all empirical particularities. Such a discourse might be amenable to purely allegorical narratives such as Plato's cave, but it was not strongly disposed to grant ultimate cogency to anecdotes, like the sojourn narratives, that used the phenomenal world as a laboratory for the exploration of abstract truths.

This, again, was a matter of preference, frequency, and emphasis, and not an untraversable chasm of mutual incommensurability. The difference between these two emergent discourses is more persuasively explained by the divergent social conditions in which they evolved than by differences in "deep structures" of language or thought. Greek philosophers like Socrates were making assertions about ultimate value and reality in competition with priests like Euthyphro, who claimed secret knowledge of the words and deeds of the gods, thus there was a strong incentive to devalue empirical knowledge in favor of "pure reason." By contrast, as evinced by *Lunyu* 15.2, the authors of early Chinese Masters' writings were handicapped by their low (by the standards of Zhou society) birth-status. They thus had every incentive to maximally value the empirical knowledge gained from personal experience, as this distinction was one of the only ways to overcome the perceived deficits disqualifying them as "gentlemen" within a society that invested absolute importance in uniqueness of birth.

Conclusion

The divergences between Chinese and Greco-Roman authors thus do not reflect the unconscious assumptions of writers in the grips of forces of which they were unaware. As Michael Puett writes in his own study of Chinese notions of divinity: "The interesting issues for comparative studies are how and why the claims were made in each culture, and how and why various solutions came to be institutionalized."[59] Preferences for particular patterns of reasoning were arrived at in each context (Chinese and Greco-Roman) through a complex negotiation between individuals impacted by diverse social, economic, political, and cultural forces.

An appreciation of how anecdotes like the sojourn narratives were employed as a form of reasoning and argumentation in early China compels us to realign the reading strategies with which we approach Warring States texts. We must remain vigilant for the vast array of aesthetic, rhetorical, historiographical, and philosophical meanings that can be carried by an anecdote. Moreover, we must be aware that such a narrative can operate on many different levels simultaneously, formulating profound ethical or cosmological concepts at the same time that it indulges in base satire or brute polemics. Are there hermeneutical guidelines that we might develop to aid in cultivating such vigilance? One good one might be: to read one Warring States text, one must read all (available) Warring States texts. As the many permutations of the sojourn anecdote demonstrate, and as Ting-mien Lee notes in her contribution to this volume, within any given text the meaning of any narrative, symbol, or utterance may be amplified by resonance with some other text in which it is echoed, reconfigured, or transformed. It is thus incumbent upon us as informed readers to read as broadly and discursively as possible. While this of course cannot guarantee invariably "correct" readings, it should produce consistently rich and intriguing ones.

Notes

1. This essay has benefitted from the input of the scholars gathered at the Anecdotes Workshop in Leiden (2013), and especially from the editorial work of Paul van Els and Sarah A. Queen. Thanks also to the anonymous reviewers for their feedback.

2. David Schaberg, *A Patterned Past: Form and Thought in Early Chinese Historiography* (Cambridge, MA: Harvard University Press, 2001), 190.

3. Here I do not mean to impose upon early Chinese discourse an alien or anachronistic categorical distinction. We do not have to suppose that the producers of early Chinese texts conceived of "history" and "philosophy" in the terms of today's academy for this question to be meaningful and its exploration illuminating.

4. Sima Qian 司馬遷 (ca. 145–90 BCE), in his reconstruction of Confucius's biography in the *Shiji* 史記 (Records of the Historian), fixes the sojourn into the timeline of Confucius's life, placing it in 489 BCE In that year, the *Shiji* reports, during his travels through the south and while residing in Cai, Confucius responded to a summons from King Zhao of Chu 楚昭王 (r. 515–489 BCE).

Fearing the consequences if a worthy of Confucius's eminence was employed in Chu, the aristocracy of Chen and Cai sent armed forces to surround Confucius and block his progress. Confucius remained trapped until his disciple Zigong was able to reach Chu with a message for King Zhao, who sent troops to lift Confucius's imprisonment (*Shiji* [Beijing: Zhonghua shuju, 1959], 47.1930–32). It is impossible to know whether Sima Qian's account is entirely credible. He was working with centuries of accrued lore concerning Confucius life, much or most of which may have been fabricated in the wake of Confucius's death. If indeed the event or something like it took place, it may have been perceived by contemporary observers as a sign that Confucius possessed a significant destiny, enhancing his charisma. As I will argue below, however, the historicity of the event has little bearing on its use as anecdote. If the sojourn were not detachable from the broad sweep of Confucius's life and examinable from various angles, it would not have been amenable to "anecdotalization."

5. The currency of this story as "fact" is evinced by the sheer volume of references to it in the textual record. A *terminus ante quem* for the story's institutionalization as "Confucius lore" is provided by the excavated text *Zi dao e* 子道餓 (The Master Was Hungry on the Road). See: Ma Chengyuan 馬承源, *Shanghai bowuguan cang Zhanguo Chu zhushu* 上海博物館藏戰國楚竹書, Vol. 8 (Shanghai: Shanghai guji chubanshe, 2011), 13–20, 117–136.

6. A good example would be *Lüshi chunqiu* 2.2, "Guisheng" 貴生 (Valuing Life), which begins with the proposition, "In profoundly contemplating the world the sage values nothing more than life." This is followed by several anecdotes depicting sages who declined or resisted being given the throne or high office out of concern for their own lives (*Lüshi chunqiu zhuzi suoyin* 呂氏春秋逐字索引, eds. D. C. Lau 劉殿爵 and Chen Fong Ching 陳方正 [Hong Kong: Commercial Press, 1994], 2.2/7/6–8/1).

7. *Han Feizi* 22/46/9–23/55/23; *Huainanzi* 16/154/1–17.243/185/16. See the Introduction to this volume, and see also the discussion of this genre in John Major and Sarah A. Queen, "A Mountain of Persuasions and A Forest of Persuasions," in John S. Major, Sarah A. Queen, Andrew Seth Meyer, and Harold D. Roth, translators, *The Huainanzi: A Guide to the Theory and Practice of Government in Early Han China* (New York: Columbia University Press, 2010), 617–24.

8. David Schaberg, "Chinese History and Philosophy," in *The Oxford History of Historical Writing: Beginnings to AD 600*, eds. Andrew Feldherr and Grant Hardy (Oxford: Oxford University Press, 2011), 404.

9. As one reviewer noted, the translation could also read here "the gentleman responds to adversity with firmness."

10. *Lunyu zhuzi suoyin* 論語逐字索引, eds. D. C. Lau and Chen Fongjing (Hong Kong: Commercial Press, 2006), 15.2/42/1–2. All citations of primary sources, unless otherwise noted, are to ICS concordance editions: D. C. Lau 劉殿爵 and Chen Fong Ching 陳方正, eds. *Xian Qin Liang Han guji zhuzi suoyin congkan*

先秦兩漢古籍逐字索引叢刊 (Hong Kong: Commercial Press, 1992–2002). Citations are in the form of chapter/page/line. Where the ICS edition is divided into *juan* rather than *pian*, the *pian* number will be provided in parentheses after the chapter. All translations are my own unless otherwise noted.

11. Schaberg, *Patterned Past*, 190.

12. The evidence for this is laid out more fully in: Andrew Meyer, "The Baseness of Knights Truly Runs Deep 士之賤也, 亦甚矣: The Crisis and Negotiation of Aristocratic Status in the Warring States," New York: Presented at the Early China Seminar of Columbia University, October 1, 2011. See, for example, the case of Yue Shifu 越石父 in the *Yanzi chunqiu* 宴子春秋. Yue was a knight driven into indentured servitude by hunger and poverty. Yan Ying redeems him from bondage, but then treats him with what Yue perceives to be insufficient courtesy, prompting Yue to request that he be sold again (*Yanzi chunqiu* 5.24/47/20–48/5).

13. One phrase denoting the aristocracy was "those who eat meat (*rou shi zhe* 肉食者);" i.e., those entitled to a share of meat from the ancestral altars. See *Chunqiu Zuozhuan* 春秋左傳 B3.10.1/46/17,18; B12.13.4/454/27; *Shuoyuan* 說苑 11.7/87/12.

14. Prince Bigan was a loyal and worthy minister of the tyrannical Zhòu 紂, last monarch of the Shang Dynasty 商 (ca. 1500–1045 BCE). To punish his remonstrance, the king had Bigan's heart cut out.

15. Guan Longfeng was a worthy minister of the tyrannical Jie 桀, last monarch of the legendary Xia Dynasty 夏. He was executed for remonstrating against Jie's construction of a "Pond of Wine."

16. Wu Zixu 伍子胥 was a loyal minister of the King Fuchai 夫差 (r. 495–473 BCE), last monarch of the southern state of Wu 吳. Because he repeatedly warned the king of the danger of his vassal, Goujian 勾踐 of Yue 越 (who would ultimately rebel, killing Fuchai and destroying Yue), Wu Zixu fell out of favor and met with death.

17. *Xunzi* 28/140/17–18–141/1–8.

18. The Mohists were the latter-day disciples of Mo Di 墨翟 (fl. late 5th c. BCE), or Master Mo 墨子, whose putative teachings have been preserved in an eponymous text. The Mohists propounded a doctrine which contradicted that of Confucius on several key points.

19. *Mozi* 1.4 (4)/4/26–27.

20. Note that this is not an assertion about "authorial intent." Even the fact that the anecdote in question contains language that closely mirrors phrases found in the *Mozi* does not definitively prove that this story was constructed in *deliberate* response to the Mohists. Whether or not that was the case, however, in the discursive context of the Warring States the anecdote as it reads is anti-Mohist *in effect*. Though many people could (and most likely did) give voice to the idea that Heaven materially rewards the good and punishes the bad, the Mohists were exceptional in grounding their entire discursive position in this proposition. If this

thesis is negated, the *Mozi*'s entire system of ethics, politics, and social engineering collapses. Given the prominent position of the Mohists in the discourse of the Warring States, the sojourn anecdote in *Xunzi* 28 is made implicitly anti-Mohist by the context in which it was produced, irrespective of any authorial "intent." It is analogous to a text written in Moscow circa 1917 that declared the sanctity of private property. Whether its author had ever read *Das Kapital* or heard of Vladimir Lenin, such a statement would have been implicitly anti-Marxist in that context.

21. *Mozi* 7.1 (26)/43/7–16.

22. Again, this is not to suggest that we can definitively read these texts as intentionally composed in response to one another. Nevertheless, even absent such intent the *Mozi* and *Xunzi* do conflict with one another and encode countervailing proofs and propositions. This is clearly manifest by the *Mozi*'s own account of the sojourn between Chen and Cai (*Mozi* 9.7 [39]/66/18–22), which (as will be discussed later in this essay) configures it as "proof" that Heaven materially punishes the wicked. Whether or not the composers of the *Mozi*'s account knew that the composers of *Xunzi* 28 had adduced this incident to argue that Heaven does not materially punish the wicked, the Mohists' own ideological commitments compelled them to construct this event as proving the opposite.

23. Prince Chong'er (b. 677 BCE), a younger son of Duke Xian of Jin (r. 676–651 BCE), was disinherited and exiled in his youth, but returned to reign as Duke Wen of Jin (r. 636–628 BCE), during which time he raised Jin to the position of hegemon (*ba* 霸), or leader of the vassal states. During his exile he met with many hardships. In Cao he was insulted by that state's ruler, who looked in as the Prince was bathing so that he could catch sight of the Prince's "linked ribs," a congenital deformity. King Goujian of Yue was surrounded on Mount Kuaiji and forced to surrender by his enemy, King Fuchai of Wu. He later defeated Fuchai and also claimed the title of hegemon. Prince Xiaobo, like Chong'er, was a younger scion of the ruling house of Qi. He was initially forced into exile in the small state of Ju, but was able to return to Qi as Duke Huan, where he became the first regional lord to claim the title of hegemon.

24. *Xunzi* 28/141/8–10.

25. Though the *Lüshi chunqiu* is an eclectic text, I include the following anecdote among "Ru" articulations of the sojourn narrative. Structurally and thematically it clearly originated in the same discourse that produced *Lunyu* 15.2 and *Xunzi* 28. The book in which it is contained, "Xiaoxing lan" 孝行覽 (Exposition on Filial Conduct) is largely Ru in perspective.

26. *Lüshi chunqiu* 14.6/76/14–28.

27. This is not to imply that versions of the anecdote found in the *Lunyu* and *Xunzi* are wholly apolitical. John Makeham sees large disparities in the depiction of Confucius and his political ambitions (or lack thereof) in comparing between the sojourn anecdotes in the *Lunyu*, *Xunzi*, and *Lüshi chunqiu* 14.6, but I would contend that these texts express closely related perspectives, their differences being

principally a matter of emphasis. See John Makeham, "Between Chen and Cai: *Zhuangzi* and the *Analects*," in *Wandering at Ease in the Zhuangzi*, ed. Roger T. Ames (Albany, NY: State University of New York Press, 1998), 75–100.

28. For example, as the titular "Erbing" 二柄 (Two Handles) of *Han Feizi* 7/9/15–10/16.

29. *Lunyu* 12.7/31/12–17.

30. *Mozi* 8.4 (32)/55/17–57/25.

31. I am indebted to Paul R. Goldin for pointing me toward thought experiments as an analogue for the kind of anecdote exemplified by the sojourn narratives. For theoretical discussions of thought experiments in European and American philosophy, see Ray A. Sorenson, *Thought Experiments* (New York: Oxford University Press, 1992); Tamar Szabó Gendler, *Intuition, Imagination, and Philosophical Methodology* (Oxford: Oxford University Press, 2010).

32. Plato, "Republic," trans. Paul Shorey, in *Plato: The Collected Diaolgues*, eds. Edith Hamilton and Huntington Cairns (Princeton, NJ: Princeton University Press, 1961), 580.

33. Peg Tittle, *What If? Collected Thought Experiments in Philosophy* (New York: Pearson, 2005), 164.

34. This is not to assert that thought experiments lack all malleability. Philosophers often alter the terms of one another's thought experiments by way of logical argumentation. But because early Chinese anecdotes purport to narrate "actual" events, by changing the terms of an anecdote an author could shift or expand its significance into new realms of meaning, engaging different logical questions. In this sense anecdotes always retained a robust rhetorical dimension, even when deployed in logical argumentation.

35. *Mozi* 9.7/66/18–22.

36. *Mengzi* 1.1/1/5.

37. *Zhuangzi* 28/84/13–85/5 corresponds largely to *Lüshi chunqiu* 14.6. The two unique accounts are at *Zhuangzi* 20/54/13–22 and 20/55/12–28.

38. Taigong Ren is unattested in other early sources. The commentator Cheng Xuanying 成玄英 (fl. 7th c. CE) takes *taigong* to be "an expression for an old person," thus following him we might translate the name as "Grandfather Ren." I have followed Yu Yue 俞樾 (1821–1907), however, in rendering it as a double surname (See Guo Qingfan 郭慶藩, *Zhuangzi jishi* 莊子集釋, Vol. 3 [Beijing: Zhonghua shuju, 1961], 680). The character appears to be a hermit figure, and stands proxy for the composer of the anecdote.

39. *Zhuangzi* 20/54/13–22. The translation is from Burton Watson, *The Complete Works of Chuang Tzu* (New York: Columbia, 1968), 213–14.

40. Confucius is gently rebuking Yan Hui here. He knows that the food is not fit for offering because Yan Hui put his hand into it, and is offering Yan Hui an opportunity to confess.

41. *Lüshi chunqiu* 17.3/102/14–19.

42. Elaine Pagels, *The Gnostic Gospels* (New York: Random House, 1979), 70–101.

43. Plato, "Euthyphro," trans. Lane Cooper, in *Plato: The Collected Diaolgues*, eds. Edith Hamilton and Huntington Cairns (Princeton, NJ: Princeton University Press, 1961), 178. I have changed the translation of "holy" to "pious."

44. See Sorenson, *Thought Experiments*, 21–50.

45. *Lunyu* 9.28/22/14.

46. *Xunzi* 1/1/7. Note that both this adage and the *Lunyu* 9.28 passage about poplars and pines are invoked in the lengthy version of the sojourn narrative recorded in *Lüshi chunqiu* 14.6.

47. *Mozi* 9.3 (35)/58/19.

48. For example, *Zhuangzi* 2/7/1–4; 2/21–24; 6/19/1–6.

49. For example, *Zhuangzi* 2/6/25–30; 18/48/19–26.

50. *Han Feizi* 13/23/4–27. It is unclear whether *Han Feizi* is the *locus classicus* of this image, but the "Jade of Mr. He" became a stock symbol invoked in many early texts (see, for example, *Lüshi chunqiu* 10.4/51/15–17; *Xunzi* 27/134/6–8).

51. Paul R. Goldin, email to author, May 23, 2014.

52. Pascal's wager and *Han Feizi*'s "Jade of Mr. He" are both concerned with the logical economy of belief. Pascal demonstrated that to err on the side of belief in God is more logical, as wrongly believing in a nonexistent God is harmless, while the inverse is not. In like manner the *Han Feizi* demonstrates that to err on the side of accepting what people offer the throne "no questions asked" makes more sense than not, as there is no harm in accepting something worthless, while there is great harm in losing out on what is valuable.

53. See Sarah A. Queen's chapter in this volume that makes a similar point with respect to the anecdotes in the *Gongyangzhuan*.

54. Modern thought experiments are more often than not set on desert islands, lifeboats at sea, in outer space, or in purely ideal realms such as a rural district filled with perfect paper-mâché facsimiles of barns (Tittle, *What If?*, 126–27, 182–85, 194–95, 210–15, 216–17).

55. *Lüshi chunqiu* 15.8/88/28–30.

56. Plato, "Republic," 747–750.

57. *Lüshi chunqiu* 18.4/113/13. The excessive skill in question is specifically that of the sophist Chunyu Kun, who undermined himself by giving equally strong arguments both for and against the same policy.

58. Plato, "Republic," 761.

59. Michael Puett. *To Become a God: Cosmology, Sacrifice, and Self-Divinization in Early China* (Cambridge, MA: Harvard-Yenching Institute, 2002), 322.

3

Mozi as a Daoist Sage?
An Intertextual Analysis of the "Gongshu" Anecdote in the *Mozi*

TING-MIEN LEE[1]

Anecdotal narrative as a rhetorical, hermeneutical, literary, or argumentative device, is ubiquitous in early Chinese texts. Throughout these texts, we encounter and re-encounter many anecdotes through re-narration and allusion. Many chapters in the present volume contain examples of these recurrent or stock anecdotes.[2] As these chapters demonstrate, stock anecdotes often served as analogies, precedents, or historical allusions that were employed to illustrate ruling principles, elaborate moral norms, amplify arguments, or explicate canonical citations. Being evoked to support a wide range of positions, rather than as subjects of primary interest, the details (of plots, scenes, or wordings) of stock anecdotes could be adapted, abridged, or even omitted for each incarnation.

Some modified details in a version of a stock anecdote could appear quite trivial, yet upon close examination, these details reveal what might be otherwise overlooked about the history and thought of the text in which they occur. The case study examined in the current chapter is a version of a stock anecdote—Mozi's rescue of the state of Song—as it appears in *Mozi* 墨子 (Master Mo) chapter 50, titled "Gongshu" 公輸 after the surname of one of the main protagonists in the chapter. (Hereafter I will refer to the chapter as *Mozi* 50.) As this "Gongshu" version is included in the book *Mozi*, scholars generally think, implicitly or not, that it was composed or edited by a Mohist author with the intent of illustrating or reiterating the standpoints of the *Mozi*. Yet, by paying close attention to the details of its ending, we discover that they contain conceptual and perspectival elements that depart from the rest of the *Mozi*. More specifically, we will see that the anecdote employs the concepts *shen* 神 (invisible) and *ming* 明 (visible) differently from other *Mozi* chapters, and it praises Mozi for his lack of recognition. This praise spells out a view in conflict with the typical Mohist view of the positive correlation between one's merit and one's esteem. Such a conceptual pairing of *shen* and *ming* and the celebration of an unrecognized Mozi do not cohere with the rest of *Mozi*, but they do resonate with other discourses in the received *Shizi* 尸子 (Master Shi), *Lüshi chunqiu* 呂氏春秋 (Spring and Autumn Annals of Mr. Lü), and *Huainanzi* 淮南子 (The Master of Huainan). These discourses all refer to Mozi (and Confucius 孔子 in conjunction), and they advocate ideas that are more generally associated with Daoism than with Mohism.

These particulars carry implications for the research on the *Mozi* as an evolving text[3] and on the history of Mohist thought.[4] They suggest that the ending of the "Gongshu" anecdote might have been added to *Mozi* 50 after the completion and circulation of the main body of the anecdote, or that the ending might have been adapted by subsequent editors whose thought was somehow affiliated with a type of Daoism,[5] or that *Mozi* 50 was composed by a Mohist author whose discursive habit or standpoint departed from the majority of Mohist authors. Thus, this case study of *Mozi* 50 might either show a glimpse of how an early (perhaps pre-Han) *Mozi* may have differed from the received version as we know it,[6] or reveal the diversity (e.g., the Daoist influence) of early Mohist thought.[7]

In this chapter, I first describe the discontinuity between the body and the ending of the "Gongshu" anecdote, and highlight the "un-Mohist" concepts and perspectives in the anecdotal ending. In a second step, I trace the "un-Mohist" elements in the *Shizi*, *Lüshi chunqiu*, and *Huainanzi* discourses, in an attempt to (1) explain the rupture between the body and the ending of the "Gongshu" anecdote, (2) interpret the "un-Mohist" message conveyed by the "Gongshu" ending, and (3) indicate the Daoist tinges surrounding these discourses.

Inherent Tensions in the "Gongshu" Anecdote

Mozi 50, the "Gongshu" chapter, is an extended anecdote about Mozi, who, with persuasive and strategic skills, convinces the king of Chu 楚 to suspend his military campaign against the state of Song 宋.[8] Compared to other chapters, *Mozi* 50 has been relatively little studied.[9] As a result, the incongruity between the body of this anecdote and its ending has been overlooked. I shall first outline the body of the anecdote, before presenting its remarkable ending, and conclude with an analysis of the tensions between them.

The Body of the "Gongshu" Anecdote

The body of the "Gongshu" anecdote contains four consecutive scenes: (1) a conversation between Mozi and Gongshu Ban, (2) a conversation between Mozi and the king of Chu, (3) a simulated war game between Mozi and Gongshu Ban, and (4) Mozi's proclamation of his defensive preparations in Song. The narratives are relatively homogeneous in content and in style: they admiringly present Mozi's enthusiasm and talents in saving the state of Song from invasion by the state of Chu.

The story begins with Mozi learning that Gongshu Ban, a military engineer of Chu, has just built some "cloud ladders" (an apparatus in siege warfare that allows the assailant to gain access to defensive walls) and the king of Chu is about to use them to attack the state of Song.[10] Alarmed by the news, Mozi travels for ten days and nights to visit this military engineer. He begins the conversation by soliciting Gongshu Ban for a contract killing. Perhaps feeling insulted, Gongshu Ban is displeased and clarifies that he regards killing as unrighteousness. Mozi then reproaches him for being either self-contradictory or ignorant about what is really righteous: "If righteousness prevents you from killing a few and yet you kill many [with cloud ladders], you cannot be said to understand proportions"[11] 義不殺少而殺眾, 不可謂知類.[12] He also condemns Gongshu Ban for failing to conform to the principle of humaneness: "to attack Song while it is innocent, cannot be called humane" 宋無罪而攻之, 不可謂仁.[13] Gongshu Ban is persuaded by Mozi and presents him to the king of Chu, to whom Mozi poses the following hypothetical trick question:

> Suppose there is a man who, dismissing his elegant carriage, intends to steal his neighbor's shattered sedan; dismissing his embroidery and finery, intends to steal his neighbor's short garment; and dismissing his refined grains and meat, intends to steal his neighbor's husks and chaff. What kind of a man would this be?

今有人於此, 舍其文軒, 鄰有敝轝, 而欲竊之; 舍其錦繡, 鄰有短褐, 而欲竊之; 舍其梁肉, 鄰有糠糟, 而欲竊之. 此為何若人?[14]

The king offhandedly answers that this kind of person must be suffering kleptomania. Following the king's answer, Mozi starts to enumerate the ample natural resources of Chu in comparison to the deficient resources of Song; he then states that the king's attempt to invade Song in fact resembles the behavior of a kleptomaniac. This analogical argument, however, does not convince the king to give up his plan to invade Song.

The subsequent scene implies that Mozi had foreseen this and came prepared. He invites Gongshu to simulate the siege, intending to show the king of Chu that Gongshu's military technique has been overestimated. Mozi unties his belt, places it in a circle to represent a city, and adds small sticks as defensive implements. Gongshu tries nine times to break through Mozi's defense, but fails each time. While Gongshu has exhausted his weapons, Mozi still has much to spare in defense. Embarrassed, Gongshu says to Mozi: "I know how to defeat you" 吾知所以距子矣.[15] The king of Chu is curious to hear his plan. Mozi then explains to the king that Gongshu thinks of having him killed: with Mozi out of the way, the state of Song would become defenseless, or so Gongshu Ban seems to think. The "Gongshu" chapter then portrays a fearless Mozi who declares that even in the event of him being killed, hundreds of his disciples, armed with his defensive implements, have already been garrisoned in Song waiting for the Chu troops. With this threat, Mozi finally convinces the king to call off the attack on Song.

As I will show below, most other accounts of Mozi's rescue of Song end at this point in the story, with the king calling off the attack. In the *Mozi*, by contrast, the "Gongshu" anecdote ends in the following manner.

The Ending of the "Gongshu" Anecdote

Despite Mozi's success with the king of Chu, his reputation is unknown to the lowly gatekeepers of Song who deny him shelter upon his return. *Mozi* 50 recounts: "On his way back, Master Mozi passed Song. Since it was raining, he sought shelter within the gate, but the gatekeepers did not let him in" 子墨子歸, 過宋. 天雨, 庇其閭中, 守閭者不內也.[16] This rain scene in some way affects our impression of the entire story. Providing a stark contrast with the preceding array of descriptions about Mozi's respectable compassion, persuasive skill, strategic prowess, keen foresight, and intrepidness, this scene introduces a sense of disappointment and bitterness into the narrative. This shade of gloom, however, is immediately spun by the closing remark:

> Thus it is said, "If you operate at [the level of] the invisible (*shen*), the multitudes will not be aware of your merits; if you struggle at [the level of] the visible (*ming*), the multitudes will be aware of them."[17]

> 故曰:「治於神者, 眾人不知其功; 爭於明者, 眾人知之.」[18]

This closing remark again reverses the tone by citing an adage to celebrate the unrecognized Mozi: one's merits are not recognized by the public if one operates at the level of the "invisible" (*shen* 神); and one's achievement are easily recognized if one struggles at the level of the "visible" (*ming* 明). The closing remark suggests that Mozi's great merit went unnoticed because he did not manage affairs in the open but in subtle and unnoticeable ways. This suggests that the rain scene may not be intended to dishearten the reader but to indicate something else. This something else, according to Sun Yirang 孫詒讓 (1848–1908), is that Song was still unaware at that time that the crisis had been lifted by Mozi. That is to say, Song was still in a state of high alert and might have prohibited access from outsiders to prevent espionage.[19] While Sun Yirang's interpretation is plausible, it does not account for the tension between the ending of the anecdote and its main body as well as the other *Mozi* chapters.

Tensions Introduced by the "Gongshu" Ending

The ending to *Mozi* 50 conflicts with the main body of the "Gongshu" anecdote and with the rest of the *Mozi* in three important regards:

First, the rain scene alters the tone of the story: it shares neither a focus nor a sentiment congruent with the preceding narratives. Following the litany of narratives about Mozi's deep compassion, strong will, outstanding oratory, and military talent, the rain scene transforms the glorious hero Mozi into an unwelcome intruder. *Mozi* scholars rarely consider this tension. Liang Qichao 梁啟超 (1873–1929) and Fang Shouchu 方授楚 (1898–

1956), for example, read the "Gongshu" as intending to exalt Mozi's compassion in saving the people of Song and to reiterate Mozi's pacifist ideal.[20] Their interpretation does not take into account the rain scene. The novelist Lu Xun 魯迅 (1881–1936), however, did explore the satirical potential of the story in a short fiction titled "Feigong" 非攻 (Against Military Aggression), which is adapted from the "Gongshu" anecdote.[21] In Lu Xun's fiction, Mozi as the real savior of Song was rudely rummaged at the Song border control and his belongings were forcedly "recruited" by Song's Fundraising National Salvation Squad (*mukuan jiuguo dui* 募款救國隊). Following these humiliations, a cloudburst appeared. Mozi returned to Song for shelter but was chased away by the armed guards and he unluckily caught a cold. By turning the hero Mozi into a "drowned rat," Lu Xun indeed magnifies the tension created by the rain scene and brings its oddity to our attention.

Second, while the rain scene takes place in a cloudy atmosphere, the final ending spins the discouraging feeling with the *shen-ming* (visible-invisible) adage. While this adage celebrates Mozi, its key concepts—*shen* and *ming*—do not seem in tune with the rest of the book. In the *Mozi*, *shen* mainly refers to spirits and is habitually juxtaposed with *gui* 鬼 (ghosts).[22] Moreover, in the *Mozi*, the spirits (*shen*) are usually not contrasted with *ming*, but described as being *ming* (perspicacious) or being *ming*-ed (clarified) by the author. The "Gongshu" adage, however, invokes the conceptual pair in a divergent way: it contrasts *ming* to *shen* implying that struggling at the visible (*ming*) level is less creditable than operating at the level of the invisible (*shen*). All this suggests that the ending of *Mozi* 50 deploys the terms *shen* and *ming* in a different way from other *Mozi* chapters.

Finally, the combination of the rain scene and the *shen-ming* adage in *Mozi* 50 yields a view that potentially challenges the typical Mohist opinion regarding the relationship between one's merit and one's reputation. It suggests that the Song gatekeepers do not recognize Mozi's merit because it belongs to a higher, less visible level. This view, albeit favoring Mozi, does not fit the book well. The whole *Mozi*, and especially its "core chapters" (8–39) express an optimistic opinion that if one's virtues and merits are both magnificent and comply with the will of Heaven or the spirits, and if they also benefit the people in significant ways, then one's name will be known broadly and it will endure.[23] The "dialogue chapters" (46–51) contain some awareness that invisible intentions are to be valued and that good deeds might go unnoticed.[24] But they never portray lack of recognition as a sign of excellence. According to the optimistic opinion permeating most of the book, a person with superior virtues and merits should be recognized by the multitudes.²⁵ The "Gongshu" ending's perspective that unnoticed merits is a sign of exceptional powers does not seem to cohere with the rest of the book.

The tensions outlined above suggest that the "Gongshu" ending is incongruous with the main body of the anecdote and that it even challenges the general outlook of the *Mozi*. In particular, its use of the term *shen* differs remarkably from the typical Mohist terminology and its portrayal of an unrecognized hero contrasts sharply with the typical Mohist tendency to positively correlate moral achievement with reputation. The task facing modern interpreters, then, is to explain the textual rupture within *Mozi* 50 and to interpret the apparently un-Mohist elements in the ending of the "Gongshu" anecdote.

Identifying the Discourse Circles of the "Gongshu" Anecdote

The "Gongshu" anecdote in *Mozi* 50, as we have seen, appears to consist of two different and somewhat incongruent parts. This dichotomy is confirmed by the textual parallels or echoes that it shares with other texts, or what I will tentatively call "discourse circles." The first part, or the body of the story, shows affinity with the Song rescue stories in *Shizi*, *Lüshi chunqiu*, and *Huainanzi*, which I collectively call "Discourse Circle A." The un-Mohist ending of the *Mozi* anecdote does not occur in any of these parallel stories, but it echoes tenuously with other chapters of the same texts, which I tentatively gather under the label "Discourse Circle B," which either praise an unrecognized Mozi concluding with an un-Mohist adage or consider war-prevention a *shen* achievement that contrasts with a *ming* achievement.

Discourse Circle A

Parallels to the body of the "Gongshu" anecdote appear in *Shizi* 14 "Zhi Chu shi" 止楚師 (Stopping the Chu Army), *Lüshi chunqiu* 21.5 "Ailei" 愛類 (Caring for One's Own Kind), and *Huainanzi* 19 "Xiuwu" 脩務 (Cultivating Effort).²⁶ Like the main body of the "Gongshu" version, they all begin with Mozi learning of Chu's plan to attack Song, and they end with Mozi's success in persuading the king of Chu to alter his course of action. Below I quote the beginning and ending of the anecdote in these texts.

Mozi 50 (main body)

Gongshu Ban made a cloud ladder mechanism for Chu and, having completed it, was about to use it to attack Song. When Master Mozi heard of this, he set out from Qi and traveled for ten days and ten nights to reach Ying [the capital of Chu] and see Gongshu Ban. [. . .] The King of Chu said, "Good! I no longer wish to attack Song!"

公輸盤為楚造雲梯之械，成，將以攻宋. 子墨子聞之，起於齊，行十日十夜而至於郢，見公輸般. [. . .] 楚王曰：「善哉，吾請無攻宋矣.」

Shizi 2.129

Gongshu Ban made a ladder that reached the sky. Upon completion, he was about to use it to attack Song. When Mozi heard of this, he left for Chu. He traveled for ten days and ten nights to reach Ying and see Ban. [. . .] The king said, "Good! I no longer wish to attack Song."

公輸般為蒙天之階，階成將以攻宋. 墨子聞之，赴於楚. 行十日十夜而至於郢，見般 [. . .] 王曰：「善哉，請無攻宋.」[27]

Lüshi chunqiu 21.5

Gongshu Ban made tall cloud ladders, and wished to attack Song with them. When Mozi heard of this, he left Lu to go there. He ripped pieces from his garments to wrap his feet; he did not rest day or night; and after going for ten days and ten nights, he reached Ying and saw the king of [Chu] [. . .] [Chu] therefore called off the attack on Song.

公輸般為高雲梯，欲以攻宋. 墨子聞之，自魯往. 裂裳裹足，日夜不休，十日十夜而至於郢，見荊王 [. . .] 故荊輟不攻宋.[28]

Huainanzi 19

Long ago, Chu wanted to attack Song. When Mozi heard about it, he was deeply grieved over it. From Lu he hurried off, traveling for ten days and ten nights. Though his feet were swollen and blistered, he did not pause. He ripped pieces from his garments to wrap his feet. Having reached Ying, he went to see the king of Chu [. . .] Thereupon [Chu] put down the weapons and called off the attack on Song.

昔者楚欲攻宋，墨子聞而悼之，自魯趨而十日十夜．足重繭而不休息，裂衣裳裹足，至於郢，見楚王 [. . .] 於是乃偃兵，輟不攻宋．[29]

A detailed comparison of all these parallels would be tantalizing but lies beyond the limits of the present essay.[30] It is interesting to note, however, that both *Lüshi chunqiu* and *Huainanzi* further down add a didactic message that identifies Mozi as a sage concerned with the people's benefit: "There are no sage-kings and erudite scholars who do not act from the desire to benefit the people" 聖王通士不出於利民者無有 (*Lüshi chunqiu* 21.5) and "Thus the hearts of sages never deviate, day or night, from the desire to benefit others" 夫聖人之心，日夜不忘於欲利人 (*Huainanzi* 19).[31] This didactic message is very much in line with the Mohist ideal of a sage who cares for the people. But surprisingly, unlike the *Lüshi chuqiu* and *Huainanzi*, the "Gongshu" anecdote does not end the story with "Mohist" views.

Discourse Circle B

As I mentioned previously, the "Gongshu" version of the Song rescue story has a peculiar ending that contains two un-Mohist elements: it praises Mozi for a lack of recognition and it cites an adage that uses *shen* and *ming* with the connotations of "invisible" and "visible." The former has no close parallels in the early corpus, but it echoes the discourses about Mozi (and Confucius) in *Lüshi chunqiu* 15.1 "Shenda" 慎大 (Being Cautious When [the State is] Large) and *Huainanzi* 12 "Daoying" 道應 (Responses of the Way). The *shen-ming* adage finds a parallel in *Shizi* 2 "Guiyan" 貴言 (Valuing Good Advice).

Though generally not associated with Mohist views, these discourses resonate with the "Gongshu" ending as they either praise Mozi for trying to remain unrecognized or cite a *shen-ming* adage to celebrate unrecognized merits. Thus, I suggest they belong to what I would call "Discourse Circle B." I will first describe the links between the "Gongshu" ending and

Discourse Circle B, and then indicate that while Discourse Circle A portrays Mozi as a Mohist sage (that is, a sage who cares for the well-being of the people), Discourse Circle B portrays a sage with Daoist characteristics.

Let us first examine the links (marked in italics) between the "Gongshu" ending and the descriptions of Mozi in *Lüshi chunqiu* 15.1 and *Huainanzi* 12.

> *Mozi* 50 (ending)
>
> On his way back, Master Mozi passed Song. Since it was raining, he sought shelter within the gate. But the gatekeepers did not let him in. Thus it is said, "*If you operate at [the level of] the invisible, the multitudes will not know your merits*; if you struggle [at the level of] the visible, the multitudes know them."
>
> 子墨子歸, 過宋, 天雨, 庇其閭中, 守閭者不內也. 故曰:「治於神者, 眾人不知其功, 爭於明者, 眾人知之.」³²
>
> *Lüshi chunqiu* 15.1
>
> Confucius's strength could lift the bolt on the gate of the capital, yet he refused to be known for his force. Mozi made defenses against attacks, forcing Gongshu Ban to surrender, yet *he did not want to be renowned for his military prowess*. Those who are skilled at preserving victory use methods of weakness (*ruo*) to be strong (*qiang*).
>
> 孔子之勁, 舉國門之關, 而不肯以力聞; 墨子為守攻, 公輸般服, 而不肯以兵知.³³ 善持勝者, 以弱術彊.³⁴
>
> *Huainanzi* 12
>
> Confucius's strength could lift the bolt on the gate of the capital, yet he refused to be known for his force. Mozi made defenses against attacks, forcing Gongshu Ban to surrender, yet *he did not want to be renowned for his military prowess*. Those who are skilled at preserving victory consider strength (*qiang*) as weakness (*ruo*).
>
> 孔子之勁, 舉國門之關, 而不肯以力聞; 墨子為守攻, 公輸般服, 而不肯以兵知. 善持勝者, 以強為弱.³⁵

Lüshi chunqiu 15.1 and *Huainanzi* 12 discourses differ from the "Gongshu" ending about whether Mozi deliberately keeps himself unknown—they state that Mozi does not wish to establish a reputation for his strategic talent, whereas the "Gongshu" ending simply states that Mozi is not recognized by the Song gatekeepers. However, similar to the "Gongshu" ending, they undermine or moderate the Mohist optimistic opinion that achievements necessarily lead to reputation or that reputation is an indication of one's great achievement. *Lüshi chunqiu* 15.1 and *Huainanzi* 12 praise Mozi for making his achievements unrecognized, and the "Gongshu" ending praises Mozi for his unrecognized achievement. Despite the difference, they are closer to the ending of *Mozi* 50 than to the typical Mohist view that upholds the close connection between merit and reputation.

Challenging the perspective that reputation manifests one's excellence reminds us of some views in the *Laozi* and *Zhuangzi*. After stating that Mozi does not want to be known, *Lüshi chunqiu* 15.1 and *Huainanzi* 12 cite an adage in terms of strength 強 (*qiang*) and weakness 弱 (*ruo*). They suggest that keeping a low profile conforms to the principle of weakness and therefore Mozi is praiseworthy. The view that weakness is superior to strength is elaborated in several places of the *Laozi*.[36] The connection between the praise of Mozi's "weakness" and the *Laozi*'s view of the superiority of "weakness" is reinforced by the *Huainanzi* 12 fragment, which immediately adds a reference to the *Laozi*: "the Way is empty, yet when you use it, you need not refill it" 道沖, 而用之又弗盈也.[37] This suggests that the portrayal of an unrecognized Mozi might have been utilized to illustrate the *Laozi*'s views instead of typical Mohist perspectives. It is also noteworthy that the "Gongshu" ending, which celebrates the unrecognized Mozi, is reminiscent of the *Zhuangzi*'s view that a sage is without fame (*wuming* 無名) or accomplishment (*wugong* 無功).[38]

The second "un-Mohist" element in the "Gongshu" anecdote—the *shen-ming* adage and the view that *shen* merit is inevitably unnoticeable—bears strong resemblance to the reconstructed *Shizi* 2 (marked in italics).[39]

> *Mozi* 50 (ending)
>
> On his way back, Master Mozi passed Song. Since it was raining, he sought shelter within the gate. But the gatekeepers did not let him in. Thus it is said, "*If you operate at [the level of] the invisible, the multitudes will not know your merits; if you struggle at [the level of] the visible, the multitudes will know them.*"

子墨子歸，過宋．天雨，庇其閭中，守閭者不内也．
故曰：「治於神者，眾人不知其功，爭於明者，眾人知之．」⁴⁰

Shizi 1.2

The beginnings of fortune are like flames and tree sprouts: easy to stop. But when they are neglected and become great matters, even worthies such as Confucius and Mo Di cannot save people from them. When a house burns and someone saves people, they will know their debt to him. But when an old person puts earth on chimney cracks to make them safe, so that during their whole life people are free from disasters caused by stray flames, they do not know their debt to him. [. . .] Misfortune also has "chimneys." If a worthy travels around the world working at stuffing them, the world would suffer no military disasters, but nobody would know their debt to him. Thus it is said, *"A sage operates in the invisible; a fool struggles in the visible."*

夫禍之始也，猶熛火蘗足也，易止也．及其措於大事，雖孔子，墨翟之賢，弗能救也．屋焚而人救之，則知德之；年老者使塗隙戒突，終身無失火之患，而不知德也．[. . .] 夫禍亦有突，賢者行天下而務塞之，則天下無兵患矣，而莫之知德也．故曰「聖人治于神，愚人爭於明」也．⁴¹

This *Shizi* passage not only cites a *shen-ming* adage akin to that in the "Gongshu" ending, but it could even be used to interpret the "Gongshu" ending.⁴² It explains that *shen* refers to the accomplishment of eliminating disasters such as warfare just as they begin to germinate; and *ming* to the stopping of disasters that have already taken a discernable shape.⁴³ Visibly striving to save people from disasters, one will obviously win their esteem. In contrast, eliminating the germination of a disaster belongs to the realm of *shen*: it is highly meritorious but unnoticeable because people have not yet become aware of the calamity-to-come.

This *Shizi* 2 passage shares with the "Gongshu" ending the conceptual pair *shen-ming* and the view about the invisibility of the merit of efficient war-prevention. It does not recommend that one should practice virtues in an inconspicuous manner (the didactic message of *Lüshi chunqiu* 15.1 and *Huainanzi* 12); rather, it suggests that real achievements at the level of *shen* (including war-prevention) are invisible in nature, whether they have been done publicly or not. However, like the aforementioned fragments from Discourse Circle B, *Shizi* 2 reminds us of Daoist concepts and perspectives. As using the concept *shen* opposed to *ming* is relatively uncommon in early texts, the connection between *Shizi* 2 and *Zhuangzi* 32 is noteworthy.[44] *Zhuangzi* 32 elaborates on the contrast between *shen* and *ming*:

> Those who cultivate the visible are only being utilized by others, while those who cultivate the invisible know how to employ others.[45] That the visible does not surpass the invisible has long been so, but the foolish relies on what one sees and forces it upon others. Their merits are outward; is it not pathetic!

> 明者唯為之使, 神者徵之. 夫明之不勝神也久矣, 而愚者恃其所見入於人. 其功外也, 不亦悲乎![46]

Similar to the "Gongshu" ending and *Shizi* 2, *Zhuangzi* 32 regards what is visible as less meritorious and hence inferior to what is invisible. In addition, *Shizi* 2 also shares with the *Zhuangzi* the term *shenren* 神人 (numinous man, with "numinous" bearing the connotation of "invisible").[47]

> The way of Heaven and Earth is to let things grow while nobody sees how they make them grow, and to let things perish while nobody sees how they make them perish. The way of the sages is also like that: when they bring about good fortune, good fortunes is brought about while nobody sees it; when they take away ill fortune, ill fortune is taken away while nobody knows it. Thus they are called *shenren*.

> 天地之道, 莫見其所以長物而物長, 莫見其所以亡物而物亡. 聖人之道亦然, 其興福也, 人莫之見而福興矣; 其除禍也, 人莫之知而禍除矣, 故曰「神人」.[48]

In *Shizi* 2, a sage helps people avoid disasters and ill fortunes that they did not foresee, so his merit is invisible and complies with the way of Heaven and Earth. Such a sage is therefore comparable to the model of *shenren*, which is described in the *Zhuangzi* as having no conspicuous merit and not caring about fame. By reading the "Gongshu" ending in light of *Shizi*'s explanation of *shen*, *ming*, and *shenren*, we can apprehend why Mozi's merit can be considered *shen*. This is because he stopped a war before any possible causality had become visible (to the others). Since a *shen* merit is easily overlooked, the gatekeepers did not recognize Mozi as the real hero of Song.

This "un-Mohist" message departs from the traditional interpretation, which tends to understand the "Gongshu" anecdote as a plain reiteration of the Mohist theses of caring for the people and opposing military aggression. The traditional interpretation might appear obvious when the main body of the "Gongshu" anecdote is exclusively considered and read solely against Discourse Circle A. Yet, an analysis of the anecdote's ending and the resonance between its details and Discourse Circle B, suggests that the "Gongshu" anecdote attempts to portray Mozi as a sage who does not only comply with Mohist but Daoist ideals as well.

Conclusion

The foregoing analysis has shown that there is an implicit rupture between the main body and the ending of the "Gongshu" anecdote. Moreover tensions between the "Gongshu" ending and other *Mozi* chapters abound. This is confirmed by their connections with two different discourse circles. In Discourse Circle A, parallel sources such as the *Lüshi chunqiu* and *Huainanzi* use the anecdotal body to illustrate that a sage endeavors to benefit the people, an ideal in line with the *Mozi*. Yet, the narratives in Discourse Circle B use the image of the unrecognized Mozi (along with Confucius) to illustrate the principle of keeping a low profile, a perspective explicitly associated with the *Laozi*, or they employ the *shen-ming* distinction to describe the *shenren*, a model advocated by the *Zhuangzi*. These narratives that refer to Mozi touch upon the merit-reputation issue, praise unrecognized worthies or sages, and they contain adages with Daoist tinges to conclude their arguments. Additionally, in preferring the invisible (*shen*) over the visible (*ming*), or the weak (*ruo*) over the strong (*qiang*), they come closer to the ideas in the *Zhuangzi* and *Laozi*, most explicitly in the *Huainanzi* passage that ends by quoting the *Laozi*.

These two discourse circles can potentially shed some light on why the "Gongshu" version of the Song rescue anecdote looks incoherent: it contains narratives that otherwise occur separately and that refer to different ideals. While the received *Lüshi chunqiu*, *Huainanzi*, and *Shizi* do not conflate the two separate clusters of narratives, the "Gongshu" anecdote does. It is unsurprising that the "Gongshu" anecdote contains narratives commensurate with Discourse Circle A, for these narratives illustrate the Mohist ideal of a sage caring for the people's well-being. Yet, the "Gongshu" anecdote also incorporates aspects of Discourse Circle B, which clearly undermines the typical Mohist view which positively correlates merit and reputation.

Considering the incongruity between the body and the ending of the Gongshu anecdote as well as the tensions between the "Gongshu" ending and the rest of the *Mozi*, the question arises whether the author(s) of the main body of the "Gongshu" anecdote devised this peculiar ending or subsequent authors or editor(s) of the *Mozi* incorporated it. One can develop many scenarios to explain this peculiar ending. For example, it is possible that the anecdote was influenced by and adopted from other sources, which postdate the earliest part of *Mozi* 50. As all the narratives from Discourse Circle B refer to Mozi and Confucius as a pair and tackle the issue of the relationship between achievement and reputation, it is also possible that the "Gongshu" ending was added in a time when Confucius and Mozi were praised together, and when concern for reputation had become a major but uncertain issue.[49] Such conjectures are inevitably tentative since little is known about Mohist authors and the composition and the editorial history of the *Mozi*. Although we may never determine precisely the historical context and intellectual motivation, which generated the received *Mozi* 50, an analysis of its curious content provides a better idea of how Mohist thought and the book *Mozi* may have developed and evolved.

Notes

1. This chapter was presented at the Anecdotes Workshop in Leiden (2013). I thank my discussant Paul R. Goldin and other workshop participants for their encouragement and insightful remarks. I am grateful to Carine Defoort, Nicolas Standaert, Eric Schmitt, and Wai-chun Leong for their incisive comments on an earlier draft. I am especially indebted to the editors of the present volume, Paul van Els and Sarah A. Queen, for their substantive suggestions regarding various aspects of my chapter, and I am also grateful to the anonymous reviewers for their feedback.

2. See also David Schaberg, "Chinese History and Philosophy," in *The Oxford History of Historical Writing Volume 1: Beginnings to AD 600*, ed. Andrew Feldherr and Grant Hardy (Oxford: Oxford University Press, 2011), 394–414; Sarah A. Queen, "The Creation and Domestication of the Techniques of Lao-Zhuang: Anecdotal Narrative and Philosophical Argumentation in *Huainanzi* 12," *Asia Major* 21, no. 1 (2008): 201–47; Paul van Els, "Tilting Vessels and Collapsing Walls— on the Rhetorical Function of Anecdotes in Early Chinese Texts," *Extrême-Orient Extrême-Occident* 34 (2012): 141–66.

3. On the idea of *Mozi* being an evolving text, see Carine Defoort and Nicolas Standaert, "Introduction: Different Voices in the *Mozi*: Studies of an Evolving Text," in *The Mozi as an Evolving Text: Different Voices in Early Chinese Thought*, ed. Carine Defoort and Nicolas Standaert (Leiden: Brill, 2013), 1–34.

4. One of the most specific and concrete accounts on this exclusion is given by Chris Fraser in footnote 1 in the following article: Chris Fraser, "The Ethics of the Mohist Dialogues," in *The Mozi as an Evolving Text*, 175–204.

5. It might also be possible that some later Mohist or non-Mohist author(s) had composed or recrafted this fragment, which was added by the *Daozang* 道藏 (Daoist Canon) editor(s) to the "Gongshu" chapter. Such conjectures are inevitably tentative since little is known about the history of the composition of the *Mozi*, or about what the *Daozang* editor(s) might have done to the *Mozi*. Relevant observations are provided in Stephen W. Durrant, "The Taoist Apotheosis of Mo Ti," *Journal of the American Oriental Society* 97, no. 4 (1977): 545; Paul R. Goldin, "Why *Mozi* Is Included in the *Daoist Canon*—Or, Why There Is More to Mohism Than Utilitarian Ethics," in *How Should One Live? Comparing Ethics in Ancient China and Greco-Roman Antiquity*, ed. R. A. H. King and Dennis Schilling (Berlin: Walter de Gruyter, 2011), 61–91.

6. As it has been argued, pre-Han texts (including the book *Mozi*) may have been relatively unstructured growing anthologies of fragments and textual building blocks. See e.g., Eric Maeder, "Some Observations on the Composition of the 'Core Chapters' of the *Mozi*," *Early China* 17 (1992): 27–82; William G. Boltz, "The Composite Nature of Early Chinese Texts," in *Text and Ritual in Early China*, ed. Martin Kern (Seattle: University of Washington Press, 2005), 50–78.

7. For an analysis of the relationship between Mohism and Daoism in the Warring States Period, see Franklin Perkins, "The *Mozi* and the *Daodejing*," *Journal of Chinese Philosophy* 41, no. 1–2 (2014): 18–32.

8. This might refer to King Hui of Chu 楚惠王 (r. 489–432 BCE). See Sun Yirang 孫詒讓, *Mozi jiangu* 墨子閒詁 (Beijing: Zhonghua shuju, [1894] 2007), 483; Qian Mu 錢穆, *Xian-Qin zhuzi xinian* 先秦諸子繫年 (Shijiazhuang: Hebei jiaoyu chubanshe, [1935] 2000), 170.

9. Scholars typically mention the "Gongshu" chapter to illustrate Mozi's deep concern for the world, to speculate about the life of the historical figure Mozi, or to interpret the religious Daoist portrayal of Mozi. E.g., Liang Qichao 梁啟超, *Mozi xue'an* 墨子學案 (Shanghai: Shanghai shangwu yinshuguan, [1921] 1926), 71–73; Stephen W. Durrant, "Taoist Apotheosis," 545; Angus C. Graham, *Later Mohist Logic, Ethics and Science* (Hong Kong: The Chinese University of Hong Kong, [1978] 2003), 6–7; Ren Jiyu 任繼愈, *Mozi yu Mojia* 墨子與墨家 (Beijing: Shangwu yinshuguan, 1998), 26–29; Robert F. Campany, *To Live as Long as Heaven and Earth: A Translation and Study of Ge Hong's Traditions of Divine Transcendents* (Berkeley: University of California Press, 2002), 508–09; John Knoblock and Jeffrey

Riegel, *Mozi: A Study and Translation of the Ethical and Political Writings* (Berkeley: University of California Press, 2013), 5–6.

10. For the features and functions of cloud ladders, see Joseph Needham and Robin Yates, *Science and Civilisation in China. Vol. 5: Chemistry and Chemical Technology; Part 6: Military Technology: Missiles and Sieges* (Cambridge: Cambridge University Press, 1994), 446–55.

11. The expression *zhi lei* 知類 could also simply mean "have common sense" or "be intelligent." See also Johnston, *The Mozi*, 725, and Knoblock and Riegel, *Mozi*, 388.

12. *Mozi* 50: 116/5–6. All my references to primary sources are to D. C. Lau, *ICS Ancient Chinese Texts Concordance Series* (Hong Kong: Commercial Press, 1995–present). The chapter number is given first, followed by a colon and then the page number and line number separated by a slash. I often refer to an existing translation ("see also") without strictly following it.

13. *Mozi* 50: 116/4–5. See also Knoblock and Riegel, *Mozi*, 387–88.

14. *Mozi* 50: 116/7–9. See also Knoblock and Riegel, *Mozi*, 388.

15. *Mozi* 50: 116/15. See also Knoblock and Riegel, *Mozi*, 389.

16. *Mozi* 50: 116/19. See also Knoblock and Riegel, *Mozi*, 390.

17. Johnston, *The Mozi*, 729 attributes this *shen-ming* adage to master Mozi and renders *shen* as "the spirit." Durrant ("Taoist Apotheosis," 545) also puts this adage in Mozi's mouth. Knoblock and Riegel (*Mozi*, 390) consider it an anonymous saying.

18. *Mozi* 50: 116/19–20. See also Knoblock and Riegel, *Mozi*, 3

19. See Sun, *Mozi jiangu*, 489.

20. See Liang, *Mozi Xue'an*, 71–73; Fang Shoucu 方授楚, *Moxue yuanliu* 墨學源流 (Shanghai: Zhonghua & Shanghai shudian, 1989), 22.

21. Lu Xun 魯迅, *Lu Xun quanji* 魯迅全集, vol. 2 (Beijing: Renmin wenxue chubanshe, [1934] 2005), 468–84.

22. This usage of *shen* is found in many paragraphs of the core chapters of the *Mozi*; for example, *Mozi* 35: 59/6–6: "Having the righteous above, those under heaven will certainly be set in order. The supreme Lord, and the ghosts and spirits of mountains and rivers will certainly have chief sacrificers, and the people will receive the great benefits" 義人在上，天下必治. 上帝山川鬼神必有幹主，萬民被其大利 (see also Knoblock and Riegel, *Mozi*, 292–93). An uncommon usage of *shen* and *ming* occurs in *Mozi* 48: 109/4–5 (titled "Gongmeng" 公孟 after the surname of one of Mozi's interlocutors), which applies *shen* to the percipient capacity of Heaven and *ming* to the divine capacity of ghosts. Both refer to the superb capacities of sacred forces, not human operations. Furthermore, *shen* here parallels *ming*, whereas the "Gongshu" adage employs *shen* to denote something surpassing *ming* (see also Knoblock and Riegel, *Mozi*, 361).

23. For example, *Mozi* 9: 12/20–13/19 and 27: 46/6–15.

24. For example, *Mozi* 48: 107/4–6 exhibits some embarrassment in admitting that Mozi was not noticed and admired by others. Gongmeng insinuates that Mozi must not be a good man; otherwise he would have been recognized by the public and would not need to travel around and promote himself. In his defense, Mozi does not express a preference for operating in an invisible level, in line with the "Gongshu" ending. He admits with slight regret that what is good is not always recognized by the multitudes, and reiterate with firmness that even if it is so, one should still maintain good faith and promote what one considers good.

25. This optimistic opinion concerning the merit-repute relation may be an application of the Mohist belief or teaching that good deed must be rewarded. This is termed by Goldin "intransigent optimism." As Goldin indicates, with this "intransigent optimism" Mohist authors reveal "unwillingness to admit that bad things sometimes happen to good people." See Goldin, "Why Mozi Is Included in the Daoist Canon," 70–71.

26. The *Shizi* is a Qing dynasty reconstruction on the basis of quotes attributed to Master Shi in secondary sources, most importantly the *Qunshu zhiyao* 群書治要 (Essentials of Government Extracted from Documents), of 631 CE. The reconstructed "Zhi Chu shi" chapter is even more questionable since it does not belong to that core and is not included in every current *Shizi* edition. See Wang Jipei 汪繼培, *Shizi* 尸子 (Shanghai: Shanghai guji chubanshe, 1986), 379; and Paul Fischer, *Shizi: China's First Syncretist* (New York: Columbia University Press, 2012), 42–53.

27. *Shizi* 2.129: 24/22–30. See also Fischer, *Shizi*, 111–112.

28. *Lüshi chunqiu* 21.5: 142/11–7. See also John Knoblock and Jeffrey Riegel, *The Annals of Lü Buwei: A Complete Translation and Study* (Stanford, CA: Stanford University Press, 2000), 560–61.

29. *Huainanzi* 19: 203/21–28. See also John S. Major et al., *The Huainanzi: A Guide to the Theory and Practice of Government in Early Han China* (New York: Columbia University Press, 2010), 771–73.

30. Since I believe that each of these chapters uses the anecdote in an interestingly different way, a fuller analysis of their differences would lead us astray from the peculiar ending of the "Gongshu" anecdote which this chapter focuses upon. For comparative studies of these stories and their relation to the "Gongshu" version, see e.g., Fang, *Moxue yuanliu*, 52; Zhou Diande 周典德, "'Gongshu' Kaobian" 《公輸》考辨, *Liaoning shifandaxue xuebao (shehui kexue ban)* 遼寧師範大學學報(社會科學版), no. 3 (1982); Hirabayashi Moegi 平林綠萌, "Bokushi kyu Sou setsuwa kou" 墨子救宋說話考, *Chūgoku kodaishi ronsō* 中國古代史論叢, no. 3 (2006): 75–95.

31. *Lüshi chunqiu* 21.5: 142/19 (see also Knoblock and Riegel, *The Annals of Lü Buwei*, 561); *Huainanzi* 19: 204/10–11 (see also Major et al., *The Huainanzi*, 773).

32. *Mozi* 50: 116/19–20.

33. Following Knoblock and Riegel, *The Annals of Lü Buwei*, 341 in reading 加 as 知.

34. *Lüshi chunqiu* 15.1: 81/5–6. Following Knoblock and Riegel, *The Annals of Lü Buwei*, 341 in emending 以術彊弱 into 以弱術彊.

35. *Huainanzi* 12: 107/12–3. Major et al., *The Huainanzi*, 445.

36. See e.g., *Laozi* 36: 13/4, 40: 14/12, 76: 25/22–3, 78: 26/12–3.

37. *Huainanzi* 12: 107/13–4; see also Major et al., *The Huainanzi*, 445. A further comparison between them would be interesting but lead away from the focus of this chapter. For a detailed analysis of the anecdotal argumentation of *Huainanzi* 12, see Queen, "Creation and Domestication." The reverence for Laozi does not necessarily imply a "Daoist" identity of the *Huainanzi*. On the issue of the intellectual affiliation of the *Huainanzi*, see Sarah A. Queen, "Inventories of the Past: Rethinking the 'School' Affiliation of the 'Huainanzi,'" *Asia Major* 14, no. 1 (2001): 51–72; Paul R. Goldin, "Insidious Syncretism in the Political Philosophy of Huai-Nan-Tzu 1," *Asian Philosophy* 9, no. 3 (1999): 90–111.

38. *Zhuangzi* 1: 2/2–3. The view that one should avoid fame is expressed in many places of the *Zhuangzi*; see, for example, *Zhuangzi* 4: 9/3–4, 4: 9/11, and 24: 71/2–4.

39. The parallel between the "Gongshu" ending and *Shizi* 2 is indicated by Sun, *Mozi jiangu*, 489. A brief discussion is provided by Paul A. Fischer, "The Formation of the *Shi Zi*" (PhD Diss., University of Chicago, 2007), 18.

40. *Mozi* 50: 116/19–20.

41. *Shizi* 1.2: 3/13–7. See also Fischer, *Shizi*, 67. It should be noted that the *ming* 明 in the retrieved *Shizi* quote was originally written as *shen* 神 too: it was changed into *ming* according to the "Gongshu" chapter; see Wang, *Shizi* 尸子, 368.

42. The problems surrounding the authenticity and periodization of the *Shizi* do not prevent us from appreciating its interaction with the texts discussed in this chapter. Moreover, following Defoort's argument, I read the *Shizi* 2 chapter as containing sources, or reflecting views, able to be situated in a context with the *Lüshi chunqiu*. For the dating issue of the *Shizi* and its implications for our understanding of early Chinese thought, see Carine Defoort, "Ruling the World with Words: The Idea of *Zhengming* in the *Shizi*," *Bulletin of the Museum of Far Eastern Antiquities* 7, no. 3 (2001): 217–42; Paul A. Fischer, "The Formation of the *Shi Zi*" (PhD Diss., University of Chicago, 2007); and Paul R. Goldin's review of Fishers' translation in *Dao* 12, no. 1 (2013): 117–19.

43. Other early texts make similar points such that a sage or the wise is able to discern the root of disasters or stop them in advance. See Paul van Els, "Persuasion through Definition: Argumentative Features of the Ancient *Wenzi*," *Oriens Extremus* 45 (2006): 211–34.

44. We read numerous occurrences of *shen*, *ming*, and *shenming* in purportedly early Chinese texts, but in most cases, *shen* and *ming* do not appear in the same context as a contrasting pair. The *Xunzi* 荀子 (Master Xun), *Guanzi* 管子

(Master Guan), *Heguanzi* 鶡冠子 (Pheasant Cap Master), *Lüshi chunqiu*, *Huangdi sijing* 黃帝四經 (Four Canons of the Yellow Emperor), *Huainanzi* 淮南子 (The Master of Huainan), and *Wenzi* 文子 (Master Wen), to name but a few, employ the two concepts side by side in a positive light. As an example, see Guanzi 10.5: 80/32–81/1 and Xunzi 3: 11/5.

45. I translate the *zheng* 徵 as "employ" because in the same chapter, the term *zheng* is used to refer to methods of testing and evaluating others so as to determine whether they are the inferior or not. See *Zhuangzi* 32: 96/12–6.

46. *Zhuangzi* 32: 97/8–9.

47. Yet, *Shizi*'s standpoint differs considerably from *Zhuangzi*. Whereas *Zhuangzi* 32 implicitly suggests that the *imposition* of popular values is a visible (*ming*) struggle, *Shizi* 2 states that the *inculcation* of the values is an invisible merit and ascribes this merit to the ideal of *shenren*.

48. *Shizi* 1.2: 3/19–20; see also Fischer, *Shizi*, 68.

49. Nylan casts lights on the reputational anxiety behind the Confucius-Mozi narratives and the combination of *Ru* and *Mo*. See Michael Nylan, "Kongzi and Mozi, the Classicists (Ru 儒) and the Mohists (Mo 墨) in Classical Era Thinking," *Oriens Extremus* 48 (2009): 1–20.

4

Anecdotal Barbarians in Early China

Wai-yee Li[1]

To use categories like "barbarians" or "Chinese" for early Chinese texts is to beg the question of definitions. "China" is *zhongguo* 中國 in Chinese, but in Warring States texts the term *zhongguo* refers to the "central domains" ruled by the lords who claimed theoretical allegiance to the Zhou Dynasty 周 (ca. 1045–256 BCE).[2] Geographically, the area covered the lower reaches of the Yellow River 黃河 and the east-central regions of modern day China. In later periods the geographic reach expands and shifts, and *zhongguo* is sometimes translated as "middle kingdom." The term *zhongguo*, like its synonyms *hua* 華, *xia* 夏, *zhuhua* 諸華 (the various *hua*), and *zhuxia* 諸夏 (the various *xia*),[3] often implies a sense of filiation with a shared cultural and textual tradition. After the Zhou Dynasty, these terms continued to be used to refer to the territories ruled by the Qin 秦 (221–206 BCE), Han 漢 (202 BCE–220 CE), and later dynasties. Do terms like "Chinese" or "Sino" introduce anachronistic associations of ethnicity or the nation-state to the awareness of belonging to a cultural tradition, a group of related political entities, or (under Qin and Han) a unified empire? Does the absence of a precise equivalent for the term "barbarians"—there are specific groups identified as "aliens" or "cultural others" (such as Man 蠻, Yi 夷, Rong 戎, Di 狄, Miao 苗, Qiang 羌, Xianyun 獫狁, and Xiongnu 匈奴), but no category that encompasses all these groups—problematize its usage?[4] Despite possible elisions, I would like, for want of better alternatives, to use these terms to participate in the ongoing scholarly discussion of cultural identity and cultural difference in early China. By "Chinese" I refer to the sense of belonging to the central domains during the centuries of disunity (ca. 8th to 3rd c. BCE), to the jurisdiction of the reigning dynasty after Qin unification, or to a common cultural tradition based on shared texts, both oral and written. The term "barbarian" here encompasses all the groups described as foreign or culturally different. Ultimately I am less concerned with definitions than with the rhetorical and heuristic functions of these terms.

Discussions of "Chinese" and "barbarians" in early China typically focus on these questions: How do we define these groups? How do definitions change or evolve? How and why do boundaries between Chinese and barbarians shift? How do ethnic or cultural perspectives converge or diverge? Are views of barbarians uniformly negative, or is there room for more flexible or positive appraisals? Are representations of cultural others necessarily tied to cultural self-definition?[5] These are indeed important and interesting questions, and I hope in the course of the following discussion to weigh in on some of them. With these questions, the dominant underlying issue remains historical inquiry into cultural attitudes: How did the Chinese define cultural others? How did they regard barbarians? What accounts for those views? Consideration of different historical and geographical contexts introduces nuances, gradations, and variations into these arguments. In what follows I will discuss anecdotes in early Chinese texts that feature barbarians. Circumstantial details in these anecdotes draw attention to contextual differences and to rhetorical functions more generally. The beauty of thinking through anecdotes is to be guided by their details to consider possible agendas underlying ostensible concerns (i.e., who counts as barbarians or how did the Chinese regard them). Anecdotes about barbarians, in addition to revealing possible historical attitudes toward these groups, also address major concerns in early Chinese thought. My discussion will focus on three issues debated through "anecdotal barbarians": (1) perspectives on cultural refinement (*wen* 文) and substance (*zhi* 質); (2) tradition and transformation, and (3) the rhetorical contexts of policy arguments and diplomatic confrontations. One may even go further and think of some anecdotes about barbarians as being imagined and transmitted as one way to engage in these cultural and political debates.

Cultural Refinement and Substance: How Much Culture Is Too Much Culture?

Among the diverse positions taken up in early Chinese thought, the writings associated with Mozi 墨子 (Master Mo; fl. late 5th c. BCE) are well known for their emphasis on frugality and disparagement of ritual as excessive and wasteful. The implied skepticism toward the ornaments of culture leads, not surprisingly, to the praise of "barbarian simplicity." As Pines points out, "most challenges to the Chinese superiority paradigm came from those thinkers who disputed the pivotal role of ritual in social life."⁶ The chapter entitled "Jiezang" 節葬 (Restraining Funerals) in the *Mozi* describes the simple burial of the legendary sage kings Yao 堯, Shun 舜, and Yu 禹, all said to have "died on the road" (*daosi* 道死) as they were "teaching" (*jiao* 教) barbarians—Yao in the north among the eight Di tribes, Shun in the west among the seven Rong tribes, Yu in the east among the nine Yi tribes. Three articles of clothing, a thin coffin bound by hemp, and graves either unmarked or marked only by a clump of earth characterize these funerals.⁷ The implication seems to be that these sage rulers can moderate the excesses of funerals precisely because they are among barbarians. One may argue that abstemious funerals mark the sage kings' virtues irrespective of their movements or location. Nevertheless, being among barbarians may also lead one to question the necessity of elaborate rituals. The word *jiao* (to teach) here suggest prolonged interaction, as compared to other early texts that presents the sage kings' journeys to the margins of civilization as merely incidental.⁸

Barbarians in *Mozi* serve to illustrate the relativity of standards. Values appear sacrosanct because "one gets used to the practice and honors the custom as proper" 便其習而義其俗. In order to question the propriety of "lavish funeral and prolonged mourning" 厚葬久喪, the text enumerates three barbarian customs. In the Kingdom of Kaimu 輆沐之國 in the far southeast, the firstborn is cut up and eaten to bring younger brothers into being, and after the grandfather's death, the grandmother is called the "ghost wife" (*guiqi* 鬼妻) and abandoned. In the Kingdom of Cannibals 啖人國 in the deep south, only those who leave their dead kin to rot and then bury the bare bones are called filial sons. In the Kingdom of Yiqu 義渠之國, only those who gather firewood to burn up the corpses of their dead kin and let the smoke rise are deemed filial.⁹ Customs justify what must seem barbaric to those from the central domains. Likewise, from the perspective of these barbarian kingdoms, lavish funerals sanctioned by tradition are anathema. Cultural difference functions to relativize value judgments and put into question the claim of ritual prescriptions to be self-evident and absolute.

In the above examples, the goal is to manipulate perspectives and question assumptions rather than to praise barbarian mores per se. The move to criticize the excesses of elaborate ritual and music by extolling the simplicity and frugality of cultural others is taken up in other texts; it is epitomized by the "wise barbarian" You Yu 由余, the Rong envoy who ends up becoming a Qin minister. His story appears in various Warring States and Han texts, including *Han Feizi* 韓非子 (Master Han Fei), *Lüshi chunqiu* 呂氏春秋 (Spring and Autumn Annals of Mr. Lü), *Shiji* 史記 (Records of the Historian), *Hanshi waizhuan* 韓詩外傳 (Han's Supplementary Commentary to the Odes),[10] and *Shuoyuan* 說苑 (Garden of Illustrative Examples). In the *Han Feizi* chapter "Shiguo" 十過 (Ten Missteps), the anecdote featuring You Yu is told as a cautionary tale about the baleful consequences of indulging in music.

> Formerly, the Rong king sent You Yu on a diplomatic mission to Qin. Duke Mu [of Qin, r. 659–621 BCE] asked him, "I have heard of the Way, but have not seen it with my own eyes. I would like to hear about the enlightened rulers of the past: as a rule, on what basis did they gain their domains or lose them?" You Yu replied, "I have managed to learn about that: as a rule they gained them by frugality and lost them by extravagance." Duke Mu said, "I have not been ashamed to ask you, sir, about the Way, why do you just respond by speaking of frugality?" You Yu replied, "I have heard: formerly when Yao ruled the world, he ate from earthen ware and drank from earthen cups. His land reached southwards to Jiaozhi [Cross Toes], northwards to the Youdu [Dark City], eastwards and westwards to where the sun and the moon rise and set: there was none who did not submit tribute. Yao gave up rule over the world and Shun, receiving it, had utensils for meals fashioned from wood, polished off traces of the saw, painted them with lacquer and ink, and transported them to the palace to be used as vessels for food. The regional lords considered this extravagant, and insubordinate domains numbered thirteen. Shun gave up rule over the world and passed it to Yu, who made sacrificial vessels coated with black lacquer outside and painted red inside. Beddings were made of cloth and mats were elaborately edged. Wine cups had patterns, and wine vessels had decorations. This was even more extravagant, and insubordinate domains numbered thirty-three. After the Xia lineage came to an end, the men of Shang received the mandate to rule. They created the great royal carriage and banners with nine streams, their food vessels were carved, their wine cups were engraved, their four walls were plastered white, their beddings and mats were elaborate and patterned. This was even more extravagant, and insubordinate domains numbered

fifty-three. The gentlemen all knew about culture and refinement, but those willing to submit dwindled. That is why I said that frugality is the Way." You Yu came out, and the lord then summoned the court scribe Liao and told him about this, "I have heard that when a neighboring domain has a sage, it is the bane of its rival. Now You Yu is a sage, and I am worried about it. What should I do?" Court scribe Liao said, "I have heard that the place where the Rong king lives is remote and nondescript, being a long way away. They have not heard of the music of the central domains. You, my lord, should send him female entertainers and musicians to disrupt his government, and then request on behalf of You Yu a later date of return so that the Rong king will meet but scant remonstrance. Only when a rift develops between them, lord and subject, can we further our plans." The lord said, "I agree." He then had court scribe Liao send sixteen female entertainers and musicians to the Rong king, and followed through by requesting on behalf of You Yu a later date of return. The Rong king assented, saw these female entertainers and musicians and delighted in them. He set forth wine and tents for drinking. Day after day he listened to music, not desisting through the year, and half of the cattle and horses died. You Yu returned and on this account remonstrated with the Rong king, who did not heed him. You Yu thus left and went to Qin. Duke Mu of Qin went to meet him, bowed to honor him as high minister, and asked him about the military situation and topography of the Rong. Having obtained the information, he raised an army to attack it, annexing twelve domains and opened up a thousand *li* of territories. That is why it is said: to indulge in the pleasures of female entertainers and musicians and to neglect affairs of state means the calamity of a domain's downfall.

昔者戎王使由余聘於秦，穆公問之曰：「寡人嘗聞道而未得目見之也，願聞古之明主得國失國何常以？」由余對曰：「臣嘗得聞之矣，常以儉得之，以奢失之.」穆公曰：「寡人不辱而問道于子，子以儉對寡人何也？」由余對曰：「臣聞昔者堯有天下，飯於土簋，飲於土鉶，其地南至交趾，北至幽都，東西至日月之所出入者，莫不賓服. 堯禪天下，虞舜受之，作為食器，斬山木而財之，削鋸修之迹，流漆墨其上，輸之於宮, 以為食器, 諸侯以為益侈, 國之不服者十三. 舜禪天下而傳之於禹, 禹作為祭器, 墨染其外, 而朱畫其內, 縵帛為茵, 蔣席額緣, 觴酌有采, 而樽俎有飾, 此彌侈矣, 而國之不服者三十三. 夏后氏沒, 殷人受之, 作為大路, 而建九旒, 食器雕琢, 觴酌鏤刻, 四壁堊墀, 茵席雕文, 此彌侈矣, 而國之不服者五十三. 君子皆知文章矣, 而欲服者彌少, 臣故曰儉其道也.」由余出, 公乃召內史廖而告之, 曰:「寡人聞鄰國有聖人, 敵國之憂也. 今由余, 聖人也, 寡人患之, 吾將奈何?」內史廖曰:「臣聞戎王之居, 僻陋而道遠, 未聞中國之聲, 君其遺之女樂, 以亂其政, 而後為由余請期, 以疏其諫, 彼君臣有間, 而後可圖也.」君曰:「諾.」乃使史廖以女樂二八遺戎王, 因為由余請期, 戎王許諾. 見其女樂而說之, 設酒張飲, 日以聽樂, 終歲不遷, 牛馬半死. 由余歸, 因諫戎王, 戎王弗聽, 由余遂去之秦. 秦穆公迎而拜之上卿, 問其兵勢與其地形. 既以得之, 舉兵而伐之, 兼國十二, 開地千里. 故曰:「耽於女樂, 不顧國政, 則亡國之禍也.」[11]

There are many stories about the dangers of indulging in music in early Chinese texts. In one case, Confucius plays a role analogous to that of You Yu: both are forced to leave when the ruler or powerful minister become entranced by music and neglect their duties:

> The men of Qi sent female entertainers and musicians [to Lu]. Ji Huanzi accepted them and did not attend court for three days.[12] Confucius left.
>
> 齊人歸女樂. 季桓子受之, 三日不朝. 孔子行.[13]

The *Han Feizi* account is notable for resolutely linking abstinence from musical pleasures to political unity and control over subordinate domains. Music facilitates aggression: it is here turned into a strategy for sowing discord and instigating corruption and decline.

You Yu's speech implies that the frugality of the sage kings is comparable to the simple ways of the Rong. For a domain boasting of supposed cultural superiority to take its cue from a "barbarian" (though highly cultured and knowledgeable) envoy and use the power of culture to corrupt the barbarians and thus achieve victory is a plot fraught with irony, which becomes even more evident in "Qin benji" 秦本紀 (Basic Annals of Qin) in the *Shiji*:[14]

The Rong king sent You Yu as envoy to Qin. You Yu's ancestors were men of Jin who fled to the Rong. He could speak the Jin language. The Rong heard that Duke Mu was worthy, that was why You Yu was sent to observe Qin. Duke Mu of Qin showed him the palaces and the storage, and You Yu said, "If ghosts were to accomplish this, their numinous power would have been worn out. If humans were to accomplish this, the people would indeed suffer!" Surprised, Duke Mu asked, "The central domains govern by the *Odes*, the *Documents*, ritual, music, rules and laws, and even then there is periodic disorder. Now the Rong and Yi have none of these, on what basis do they govern? Is that not difficult?" You Yu smiled, "This is precisely why the central domains suffer disorder. For when the sages of high antiquity and the Yellow Emperor created ritual, music, rules and laws, they first embodied them in their lives, and on that basis they attained governance on a small scale. By the time we got to their descendants in later eras, they became ever more arrogant and excessive, relying on the authority of rules and laws to discipline and make demands on those below. As for those below, worn out in the extreme, they use the criteria of humaneness and righteousness to justify their rancor and resentment against those above. Those above and those below vie to blame each other, a mutual rancor that results in usurpation and assassination, so much so that whole lineages are exterminated—such are all examples of this kind. The Rong and the Yi are different. Those above encompass a pure and simple virtue whereby they interact with those below them. Those below hold loyalty and good faith wherewith they serve those above them. The government of a domain is like the regulation of a body—one does not know how the regulation is achieved. This is truly the regulation of a sage."

戎王使由余於秦. 由余, 其先晉人也, 亡入戎, 能晉言. 聞繆公賢, 故使由余觀秦. 秦繆公示以宮室, 積聚. 由余曰:「使鬼為之, 則勞神矣. 使人為之, 亦苦民矣.」繆公怪之, 問曰:「中國以詩書禮樂法度為政, 然尚時亂, 今戎夷無此, 何以為治, 不亦難乎?」由余笑曰:「此乃中國所以亂也. 夫自上聖黃帝作為禮樂法度, 身以先之, 僅以小治. 及其後世, 日以驕淫. 阻法度之威, 以責督於下, 下罷極則以仁義怨望於上, 上下交爭怨而相篡弒, 至於滅宗, 皆以此類也. 夫戎夷不然. 上含淳德以遇其下，下懷忠信以事其上，一國之政猶一身之治，不知所以治，此真聖人之治也。」[15]

The remainder of the story in the *Shiji* differs only in details and wording from other Warring States accounts. Female entertainers and musicians are sent to "rob [the Rong king] of his will" 以奪其志. You Yu is detained so that he would "miss the appointed date [of return]" 以失其期. Right after Scribe Liao propounds his scheme, the Qin ruler and You Yu are already closely conferring on the military situation and topography of the Rong. The main difference then is how You Yu couches his argument not as a warning against extravagance and sensual indulgence but as a contrast between civilization as burden and strife and barbarity as ease and harmony. Music is no longer just a marker of excess but a cypher for all other constituents of culture—ritual, classical texts, rules and laws. There are distinct Daoist echoes in You Yu's argument, as noted in the comments of the Song historian-statesman Sima Guang 司馬光 (1019–1086) and the Ming scholar and poet Wang Wei 王韋 (fl. late 15th–early 16th c.).[16] But this is Daoism with a twist: instead of simply glorifying simplicity, this account tells of the triumph of a civilized domain over the barbarians by strategically corrupting them with culture. The Rong sends You Yu to the Qin court in order to learn from its superior culture but ends up being undermined by its excesses. We are not told whether Qin adopts Rong ways as propounded by You Yu. The barbarians fall because they learn "Chinese" ways, but Qin seems to have achieved victory through an amalgamation of Chinese and barbarian perspectives, relying on a barbarian advisor with a Jin ancestor.

What might have been the historical context for the production of the story in the *Shiji*? Why turn Qin appropriation of Rong perspectives into the explanation of how Qin "thus became the hegemon among the Western Rong" 遂霸西戎? Warring States and Han critiques of Qin sometimes characterize Qin as "a domain of tigers and jackals" 虎狼之國 steeped in barbarian ways and far removed from the culture of the central domains. The "Qin benji" chapter contains numerous references to Qin conflicts and interactions with the Rong. However, the introduction of Rong elements in this anecdote obviously does not imply critical intent. On the contrary, it glorifies Qin for differentiating itself from and raising itself above *both* the central domains and the Rong. As the civilized domain triumphing over the barbarian one by "civilizing" the latter and by recruiting a barbarian advisor, Qin is shown to be deciding and manipulating the very boundary between Chinese and barbarians. The story might have its provenance in

Qin records: as the great Han historian Sima Qian 司馬遷 (ca. 145–90 BCE) reminds us, Qin records were available while the historical records of the other domains had been mostly burnt. The Qin court might have used this story to foreground its distinctiveness or superiority precisely on account of its barbarian connection even as it emphasizes its ties with the central domains. In that sense, this anecdote could function as an implicit rebuttal of the accusation that Qin is "less civilized" than the central domains: It does so both by asserting Qin cultural superiority and by dramatizing the fluidity of cultural distinctions. Alternatively, if Sima Qian were responsible for drawing attention to the idea of barbarian simplicity, the issue could have contemporary resonance: both as implicit critique of Emperor Wu's 漢武帝 (r. 141–87 BCE) extravagance and interventionist policies and as recognition that "barbarian ways" can be vindicated, as Zhonghang Yue 中行說, the Han envoy who defected to remain among the Xiongnu, argues.[17] Zhonghang Yue's defense of Xiongnu customs could in turn make expensive campaigns against the Xiongnu seem less justified.[18]

Tradition and Transformation

In the stories about You Yu cited above, we are not told whether Qin ends up adopting Rong ways. They emphasize criticism of excessive cultural refinement and ritual prescriptions and draw attention to the advantages of manipulating the boundaries between "Chinese" and "barbarians." In this section we will focus on anecdotes urging adoption of barbarian ways. Concomitant debates on the claims of tradition mean that perspectives on "Sino-barbarian" polarity overlap with judgments on the necessity of change and on the respective merits of the old and the new. The point is driven home by the accounts of King Wuling of Zhao's 趙武靈王 (r. 326–298 BCE) reforms instituting Hu clothing (*hufu* 胡服) and mounted archery (*qishe* 騎射) in *Zhanguoce* 戰國策 (Stratagems of the Warring States) and closely parallel passages in *Shangjunshu* 商君書 (Book of Lord Shang), chapter 1, "Gengfa" 更法 (Altering Laws).

"Hu clothing," so named after the "Hu" northern nomadic peoples, probably involved sartorial changes that would facilitate riding—some version of breeches and a shirt or jacket with tighter sleeves.[19] The choice to adopt cavalry, a radical departure from the dominance of chariot warfare from about eighth to fifth century BCE,[20] showed the influence of the Xiongnu, Zhao's northern neighbor.[21] Historians dispute the reality or the extent of

King Wuling's reforms. According to an entry from *Zhushu jinian* 竹書紀年 (Bamboo Annals), an annalistic history of Wei 魏 unearthed from the tomb of a Wei king in 279 BCE that now exists only in fragments, the Zhao court ordered commanders, officers, and their families, as well as garrison guards to adopt He clothing (*hefu* 貉服) in 302 BCE.[22] (*He* is a fox-like animal; here it is synonymous with "Hu" and refers to northern nomadic peoples.) In *Shiji* 43, "Zhao shijia" 趙世家 (Hereditary Family of Zhao), King Wuling is said to undertake these reforms in the nineteenth year of his reign (307 BCE), and the debates about them become one episode in a colorful account of the king's ambitions, resoluteness, and errors of judgments.

The most detailed account of the debates about adopting barbarian ways is found in *Zhanguoce*.[23] A series of entries pit the king against various interlocutors, whose endorsement and—more typically—opposition allow conflicting perspectives to unfold. The story-interest is minimal; the momentum of these passages is rhetorical. The arguments partially overlap, but closer inspection reveals subtle shifts and reversals. The first exchange, between the king and the minister Fei Yi 肥義, harps on the strategic advantage of adopting "Hu clothing and mounted archery" 胡服騎射, the importance of following heroic precedents set by earlier Zhao rulers, and normative duties for rulers and ministers.[24] The king's only concern is opposition:

> Now I want to continue the enterprise of Duke Xiang, and open up territories that belong to the Hu and the Di, but the whole world fails to see it. [. . .] Those who have accomplishments that rise above the world must bear the burden of leaving customs behind; those who have the deliberations of singular insights must abide the resentments of commoners. I am about to teach the people about Hu clothing and mounted archery, and the world will surely criticize me.
>
> 今吾欲繼襄主之業, 啟胡, 翟之鄉, 而卒世不見也. [. . .] 夫有高世之功者, 必負遺俗之累, 有獨知之慮者, 必被庶人之怨. 今吾將胡服騎射以教百姓, 而世必議寡人矣.

Fei Yi tries to dispel the king's doubts:

> Your servant has heard, "A deed beset by doubts will not accomplish anything, an action beset by doubts will garner no fame." [. . .] Those who discourse on supreme virtue are not

in harmony with customs, those who achieve great merit do not confer with the multitude. Formerly, the sage king Shun danced among the Miao, and the sage king Yu bared his flesh in the Naked Domain: they were not nourishing desires and taking pleasure in their will, they wanted thereby to discourse on virtue and achieve merit.

臣聞之: 疑事無功, 疑行無名. [. . .] 夫論至德者, 不和于俗; 成大功者, 不謀于眾. 昔舜舞有苗, 而禹袒入裸國, 非以養欲而樂志也, 欲以論德而要功也.

The king is ultimately swayed by the expectation of territorial gain:

> If the world complies with me, the beneficial effects of Hu clothing is beyond estimation. Even if the whole world derides me, I will certainly gain the territories of Hu and Zhongshan.

世有順我者, 胡服之功未可知也. 雖驅世以笑我, 胡地中山吾必有之.

The king has his second round of negotiations with his uncle Prince Cheng 公子成. Through his proxy Wangsun Xie 王孫緤, the king declares his plan to preside at court dressed in Hu clothes, and enjoins Prince Cheng to do the same, citing the minister's imperative to obey so that royal decrees can be properly implemented. Prince Cheng pleads sickness and indicates his opposition by reiterating the moral, intellectual, and material superiority of the central domains, which should serve as the exemplar for barbarians, not the other way around. The king personally visits Prince Cheng to press his case, which revolves around ideas of facilitation or expediency (*bian* 便) and efficacy or benefit (*li* 利):

> For clothing is what facilitates use, and ritual propriety is what facilitates action. That is why sages observe regional origins and go along with what's fitting, follow the course of events and institute ritual propriety. The purpose is to benefit the people and enrich the domain. The people from Ouyue[25] let loose their hair and tattoo their bodies, they cross their arms and have their lapels fold left. The people from the great Wu blacken their teeth and brand their foreheads, they wear sharkskin hats and roughly

sewn clothes. Rituals and clothing may differ, but they are the same in being expedient.

> 夫服者, 所以便用; 禮者, 所以便事也. 是以聖人觀其鄉而順宜, 因其事而制禮, 所以利其民而厚其國也. 被髮文身, 錯臂左衽, 甌越之民也, 黑齒雕題, 鯷冠秫縫, 大吳之國也. 禮服不同, 其便一也.²⁶

If regional variations apply even among central domains, how much more so then should they obtain in distant lands? The primacy of efficacy or profit dictates a functional understanding of ritual propriety that allows the king to rise above mere customs and to claim to abide by "the factor that defines customs" 所以制俗.²⁷

In the next round of debates, the ministers Zhao Wen 趙文 and Zhao Zao 趙造 uphold the sanctity of tradition, and in arguing against them, the king moves inexorably toward a more general justification of changing rules and laws:

> In the three eras, the kings wore different clothes yet became kings, the five hegemons did not have the same teachings yet achieved governance. The wise ones create the teachings, and the foolish ones are constrained by them. The worthy ones challenge customs, and the unworthy ones are bound by them. [. . .] That is why those who plan for themselves do not wait for others, and those who establish rules for the present do not imitate the ancients.

> 且夫三代不同服而王, 五伯不同教而政. 知者作教, 而愚者制焉. 賢者議俗, 不肖者拘焉. [. . .] 故為己者不待人, 制今者不法古.²⁸

When Zhao Zao reiterates the need to follow tradition and rejects Hu clothing as a marker of disorder and "licentious thoughts" (*zhiyin* 志淫), the king offers a vision of history as relentless changes:

> Past and present do not share the same customs. What past can one emulate? Rulers and kings do not borrow from each other, what rituals can one follow? Fuxi and Shennong taught but did not use capital punishment. The Yellow Emperor, Yao and Shun

used capital punishment but did not let rage take over.²⁹ [. . .] Moreover, if strange clothes mean licentious thoughts, then the people of Zou and Lu are guilty of no deviant acts. If outlandish customs mean that the people are loose, then Wu and Yue boast of no good people. [. . .] As the saying goes, "Riding a horse by the rules of the book, one cannot fully be in tune with the nature of the horse; using the past to control the present, one cannot understand the changing situation of things." That is why the merit of following rules does not suffice to raise the era above earlier ones, using past learning as model does not suffice to control the present.

古今不同俗, 何古之法? 帝王不相襲, 何禮之循? 慮羲神農教而不誅, 黃帝堯舜誅而不怒. [. . .] 且服奇而志淫, 是鄒魯無奇行也; 俗僻而民易, 是吳越無俊民也. [. . .] 諺曰: 以書為御者, 不盡於馬之情, 以古制今者, 不達于事之變. 故循法之功, 不足以高世, 法古之學, 不足以制今.³⁰

From an initial emphasis on precedents and the ruler's authority, the argument shifts to justifying functional ritual and context-determined mores, and concludes with the inevitability and rationality of fundamental changes. Three more entries present the king convincing the imperial tutor Zhou Shao 周紹 and the noble Zhao Yan 趙燕 to adopt Hu costume and winning over the commander Niu Zan 牛贊 on the issue of cavalry. No new arguments are advanced, however, except a more explicit attack on "moral diplomacy": "Humaneness, righteousness, the Way, and virtue will not bring [foreign envoys] to our court" 仁義道德, 不可以來朝.³¹

Various scholars, including Sun Yirang 孫詒讓 (1848–1908) and Takigawa Kametarō 瀧川龜太郎 (1865–1946), have noted the close parallels—with many identical passages—between the debates about King Wuling's reforms in *Zhanguoce* and "Gengfa" in *Shangjunshu*.³² In the latter, Gongsun Yang 公孫鞅 (i.e., Shang Yang 商鞅) propounds his views by refuting Gan Long 甘龍 and Du Zhi 杜摯 as Duke Xiao of Qin 秦孝公 (r. 361–338 BCE) presides. Miao Wenyuan 繆文遠 argues that the anecdotes about King Wuling are based on "Gengfa," and since the latter involve policy changes on a grand scale, King Wuling's reforms are retrospectively recast as having broad ramifications when they might have been just targeted toward the elite and were more local in application.³³ The chapter "Gengfa" in the *Shangjunshu*, much shorter than the *Zhanguoce* account, emphasizes the need to enforce the ruler's authority and to override opposition. It also uses the focus on function to justify challenging tradition. Both versions preserve the structure of the anecdote about advice or remonstrance—different perspectives are presented, but the position of choice is vindicated by a brief mention of success at the end, as evinced by the expansion of territories for Zhao in the *Zhanguoce* and the "Kencaoling" 墾草令 (Decree of Opening Up Untilled Land) that concludes the chapter in the *Shangjunshu*. Irrespective of the direction of borrowing, the parallels between these two texts show the affinities between the arguments justifying radical policy changes and "beneficial barbarization," respectively. The ways of barbarians, both as challenge and as a model to emulate, justify reforms and radical changes; even as the argument for radical changes provides the paradigm for adopting barbarian ways.

In this sense the accounts of Shang Yang's reforms and King Wuling's adoption of barbarian ways can be juxtaposed as mutually illuminating contexts, irrespective of the direction of derivation. In both cases, a fuller contextualization also unravels the "message" of change. In *Shiji* 68, "Shangjun liezhuan" 商君列傳 (Biography of Lord Shang), after Shang Yang prevails in the debates with Gan Long and Du Zhi, his policies augmenting severe laws and challenging the authority of nobles and princes are fully implemented. Qin is said to enjoy good governance as a result. When questioned about his policies, Shang Yang maintains in self-defense that he has transformed the barbarian customs of Qin:

> Formerly Qin was defined by the ways of the Rong and the Di. There were no distinctions between fathers and sons; they inhabited the same rooms. Now I have remade its rules and created the separation of the sexes. Palaces and towers were widely built, so that Qin's situation is comparable to Lu and Wei.
>
> 始秦戎翟之教, 父子無別, 同室而居. 今我更制其教, 而為男女之別, 大築冀闕, 營如魯衛矣.[34]

The same reasoning about radical changes can thus support both "barbarization" and the adoption of Chinese ways. Beyond this ironic twist, the story of Shang Yang is ultimately one of failure and self-destruction as he falls victim to the relentless web of punishment he created. The same is true of King Wuling's story in the "Zhao shijia" chapter of the *Shiji*. After victory over Zhongshan[35] and Dai, King Wuling puts his oldest son in power in

Dai while he abdicates his position, chooses a younger son by a favored concubine as successor, and styles himself "the royal father" (*zhufu* 主父). The consequent power struggle pits the king and Fei Yi against the erstwhile opponents of reform, notably Prince Cheng. In the end the king dies of starvation during the prolonged siege of his Shaqiu Palace. The inexorable logic of the reasoning justifying changes and emphasizing adaptability in the more discrete anecdotes is in some ways undermined by the larger contexts of the ignominious deaths of Shang Yang and King Wuling.

Rhetorical Contexts of Sino-Barbarian Boundaries

In the *Zhanguoce* passage quoted above, Fei Yi argues that even sage kings adopt barbarian customs (Shun dances, Yu goes naked) when they go to barbarian domains.[36] This plea for instigating changes in the name of adaptability (*yin* 因) and flexibility can also be turned into a statement on how barbarians are not teachable (even sage kings fail to "civilize" them). Thus the Han thinker Wang Chong 王充 (27–100 CE) uses these examples to question Confucius's reported wish to go and live among the Nine Yi tribes.[37] In the *Lunyu*, the sage's transformative power is such that he would have no fear of the backwardness (*lou* 陋) of the barbarian domains. But Wang Chong quibbles, citing Yu's nakedness among the barbarians: "Yu could not teach the Naked Domain to wear clothes, how could Confucius turn the Nine Yi tribes into gentlemen?" 禹不能教躶國衣服, 孔子何能使九夷為君子?[38] The same detail supports opposite arguments—both approbation for accepting barbarian ways and denigration of their recalcitrance, both permeable and insuperable boundaries between Chinese and barbarians.

"Yu's nakedness" reminds us how contexts determine meanings. Among the numerous references to barbarians in early texts, one can find many statements declaring their inferiority and difference. One can also garner counter-arguments describing their superior knowledge and customs. On the whole the "culturalist" position, whereby culture determines "Chineseness," prevails over narrowly "ethnic" or biological distinctions. As Pines points out, one consistent strand is the belief in the "changeability of the other."[39] One can indeed tabulate these views and construct a spectrum of cultural attitudes, possibly tracing changes over time. It is important, however, to note that these positions are often embedded in historical contexts. Circumstantial details often take us to power politics as we consider the motivations and functions of avowed views on barbarians.

As an example we may consider this brief entry dated to 638 BCE from the *Zuozhuan* 左傳 (Zuo Commentary), compiled in the fourth century BCE, a vast repertory of narratives and speeches related to events spanning two hundred and fifty-five years (722 BCE–468 BCE) and traditionally understood as an exegetical tradition of *Chunqiu* 春秋 (Spring and Autumn Annals):

> Sometime earlier, when King Ping had moved the capital to the east, Xin You had gone to Yichuan and, upon seeing someone with unbound hair offering a sacrifice in the countryside, had said, "Within a hundred years, this will likely be the Rong's! Ritual propriety has been lost already!" In autumn, Qin and Jin moved the Rong tribes of Luhun to Yichuan.
>
> 初，平王之東遷也，辛有適伊川，見被髮而祭于野者，曰：「不及百年，此其戎乎! 其禮先亡矣.」秋，秦晉遷陸渾之戎于伊川.[40]

The fall of the Zhou capital Haojing 鎬京 (modern day Xi'an 西安) and the relocation of the Zhou capital to Luoyi 雒邑 (modern-day Luoyang 洛陽), traditionally accepted as the end of Western Zhou 西周 (ca. 1045–771 BCE) and the beginning of Eastern Zhou 東周 (770–256 BCE), took place in 770 BCE. The Zhou minister Xin You's prediction of Yichuan taken over by barbarians is recalled (or invented) as explanation of the relocation of the Rong tribes of Luhun to Yichuan in the autumn of 638 BCE. The prediction seems to tally with a cultural definition of "Sino-barbarian" boundaries. The figure with unbound hair offering sacrifice in the wilds symbolizes the demise of proper rituals and heralds the infiltration of barbarians. Closer inspection, however, reveals other possible readings. Yichuan refers to areas in the royal Zhou domain along the banks of the Yi River within the region still known as Yichuan County in Henan. The Rong tribes of Luhun were originally in Guazhou in Gansu.[41] Why would Qin and Jin move the Rong in the northwestern parts of their territories to an area close to the Zhou capital? Presumably their goal is to take over the land formerly inhabited by the Rong. The hegemons of the Spring and Autumn Period 春秋 (770–453 BCE) all claim to "honor the king and expel the Yi tribes" (*zun wang rang yi* 尊王攘夷).[42] We have here a flagrant violation of that principle; as a result barbarians on the outer margins are brought close to the center of Zhou power.[43] The new proximity of Rong to Zhou is to give King Zhuang of

Chu 楚莊王 (r. 613–591 BCE) the excuse to threaten Zhou in the name of fending off the Rong thirty-two years later (606 BCE).[44] Jin also later arrests a Zhou envoy to curry favor with the Rong (568 BCE).[45] In other words, apparently "cultural" explanation of how a region is "barbarized" may mask the actual maneuvers of domains (in this case Qin and Jin) seeking territorial expansion and political advantage.

The obverse side of the "acculturation paradigm," featuring "civilized barbarians," also yields new ambiguities when we consider how articulating cultural mastery is one way to defend political self-interest. Views of Sino-barbarian boundaries are often implicated in rhetorical contexts, of which policy debates and diplomatic negotiations feature most prominently. A good example is the diplomatic confrontation between the Jin minister Fan Xuanzi 范宣子 (d. 548 BCE) and the Rong chief Juzhi 駒支 during a meeting summoned by the Jin to mobilize support for an attack against the southern state Chu. Fan Xuanzi, who presides over the meeting, accuses Juzhi of leaking Jin's secrets and passing on rumors that undermine the regional lords' allegiance to Jin.

> Jin was about to arrest Juzhi, leader of the Rong. Fan Xuanzi personally reprimanded him at court, saying, "Come! You chief of the Jiang Rong lineage! Formerly, the men of Qin pressed your ancestor Wuli hard and drove him from Guazhou. Your ancestor Wuli, draped in a white rush cape and wearing a headdress made from brambles, came to our former lord for protection. Though our former lord, Duke Hui, had but meager lands, he divided them with you to provide you with sustenance. Now the reason why the regional lords no longer serve our lord in the same way as before is because words leaked out, and this could have happened only on account of you. You are not to take part in the event of the next morning. If you do, we shall have your arrested."
>
> Juzhi replied, "Formerly, the men of Qin, relying on their numbers and covetous of territory, expelled us, the various Rong tribes. Duke Hui, making manifest his great virtue, said that we were the descendants of the lords of the Four Peaks, and that we were not to be pruned off or abandoned. He bestowed on us the lands of Jin's southern march, where foxes and wild cats dwelled, and where jackals and wolves howled. We, the various Rong, removed and cut down their brambles and drove away

their foxes and wild cats, jackals and wolves, and became subjects of the former lord. Neither aggressive nor rebellious, we have been unwavering in our allegiance until now. Formerly, Duke Wen, together with Qin, attacked Zheng. Qin secretly swore a covenant with Zheng and set up garrisons there. That was why armies were mobilized at Yao. Jin resisted Qin from above, and the Rong withstood it from below. That the Qin army did not come back is due to none other than us. Just as in the pursuit of a deer, the men of Jin seized its antlers, and the various Rong tribes caught its legs, and with Jin brought it to the ground. How have the Rong failed to absolve themselves from charges against them? From that time until the present, in the hundred campaigns of Jin, we, the various Rong tribes, have taken part unremittingly. Following those in charge of Jin government, our intent has ever been the same as at Yao. How would we dare to distance ourselves or go against you? Now is it not your officials of various ranks who themselves are remiss, and who have in this way alienated the regional lords, while you lay the blame on us, the various Rong tribes? Our drink, our food, our clothing and our regalia are all different from the central domains. We do not exchange gifts with them, and our language and theirs do not allow communication. What harm can we possibly do? Not to participate in the meeting will be no cause for grief." He chanted "Blue Flies" and withdrew. Fan Xuanzi acknowledged his error and made Juzhi take part in affairs at the meeting, thus realizing the attributes of being "joyous and civil."

將執戎子駒支, 范宣子親數諸朝, 曰:「來! 姜戎氏! 昔秦人迫逐乃祖吾離于瓜州, 乃祖吾離被苫蓋, 蒙荊棘來歸我先君, 我先君惠公有不腆之田, 與女剖分而食之. 今諸侯之事我寡君不如昔者, 蓋言語漏洩, 則職女之由. 詰朝之事, 爾無與焉. 與, 將執女.」對曰:「昔秦人負恃其眾, 貪于土地, 逐我諸戎. 惠公蠲其大德, 謂我諸戎, 是四嶽之裔冑也, 毋是翦棄. 賜我南鄙之田, 狐狸所居, 豺狼所嗥. 我諸戎除翦其荊棘, 驅其狐狸豺狼, 以為先君不侵不叛之臣, 至于今不貳. 昔文公與秦伐鄭, 秦人竊與鄭盟而舍戍焉, 於是乎有殽之師. 晉禦其上, 戎亢其下, 秦師不復, 我諸戎實然. 譬如捕鹿, 晉人角之, 諸戎掎之, 與晉踣之. 戎何以不免? 自是以來, 晉之百役, 與我諸戎相繼于時, 以從執政, 猶殽志也, 豈敢離逷? 今官之師旅無乃實有所闕, 以攜諸侯, 而罪我諸戎! 我諸戎飲食衣服不與華同, 贄幣不通, 言語不達, 何惡之能為? 不與於會, 亦無眚焉.」賦〈青蠅〉而退. 宣子辭焉, 使即事於會, 成愷悌也.[46]

Both Rong and Jin appeal to history to justify their respective stance. According to Fan Xuanzi, Duke Hui of Jin 晉惠公 (r. 651–637 BCE) gave land to the Rong, thereby protecting it from Qin aggression.[47] Juzhi in response gives another historical retrospection. He proclaims Rong allegiance to Jin but also stakes out its independence from Jin. Juzhi also qualifies Rong indebtedness to Jin, claiming that the land Jin ceded to Rong was inhospitable wilderness tamed only through Rong efforts. This is one of the rare occasions when the barbarian is given a voice. Far from being the "wild people," Rong is presented as the agent of civilization. In return, Rong's ties with Jin are to be defined through negation, as the absence of aggression and rebellion (*bu qin bu pan* 不侵不叛). Instead of acknowledging Jin protection of Rong against Qin, Juzhi emphasizes the contributions of Rong as Jin's ally in Qin-Jin conflicts, which are chronicled elsewhere in *Zuozhuan*.[48]

Beyond past grudges or obligations, Juzhi probes the factors determining amity or confrontation between the central domains and barbarian realms. His approach is two-pronged. On the one hand, he emphasizes radical difference. Rong culture (food, clothing, language) is so different that it is not capable of meddling in affairs of the central domains. Also, Rong distinctiveness is such that isolation is no punishment, and it would not be troubled by Jin's threat of removing it from the covenant meeting. On the other hand, Juzhi avers common roots with the central domains. Juzhi claims that, by helping the Rong, Duke Hui of Jin implicitly recognized them as "descendants of the lords of the Four Peaks," identified in various early texts as ancient rulers in four corners of the land. This means that the Rong deserves to be treated as Jin's equal. Most ironic of all, having emphasized cultural difference and obstacles to communication, Juzhi shows his mastery of a shared cultural heritage by chanting "Blue Flies," an ode that laments the perniciousness of slander:

營營青蠅	Buzzing blue flies
止于樊	Gather on the fence.
豈弟君子	Joyous and civil is the gentleman:
無信讒言	He does not believe in words of slander.
營營青蠅	Buzzing blue flies
止于棘	Gather at the brambles.

讒人罔極	The slander-mongers know no limit,
交亂四國	And wreak havoc in domains on four sides.
營營青蠅	Buzzing blue flies
止于榛	Gather at the thickets.
讒人罔極	The slander-mongers know no limit,
構我二人	And sow discord between you and me.[49]

Confucius connects knowledge of the odes to verbal skill and diplomatic competence.[50] In *Zuozhuan*, there are many examples of Eastern Zhou aristocrats who quote or recite the odes (most of them found in the received text *Shijing* 詩經 [Book of Odes]) to convey their political vision, policy recommendation, or diplomatic finesse. The ability to *fushi* 賦詩 (variously translated as reciting, chanting, or singing the odes), to use apposite odes to define one's position and to negotiate for advantages, mark participation in a shared cultural and textual tradition.[51] Commentators such as Zheng Xuan 鄭玄 (127–200), Kong Yingda 孔穎達 (574–648), and Zhu Xi 朱熹 (1130–1200) characterize "blue flies" (*qingying* 青蠅) as an "affective, arousing image" (*xing* 興) that prompts the poet to versify about the scourge of slander. Loathed for their propensity to "invert black and white," blue flies may also bear a more direct metaphorical connection with "slander-mongers." By chanting the ode "Blue Flies," Juzhi displaces the burden of "cultural otherness" to the instigators of discord. One may say that he erases Rong's status as "cultural other" by reciting an ode and by redefining amity in terms of shared values.[52] Juzhi's recitation apparently clinches the case for Fan Xuanzi, who in acknowledging his error proves himself to be the "joyous and civil noble man" praised in "Blue Flies." The *Zuozhuan* passage ends thus:

> On this occasion Zishu Qizi served as Ji Wuzi's assistant to attend the meeting. From then on the leaders of Jin reduced the obligatory contributions of Lu and treated its envoys with even greater respect.

> 於是子叔齊子爲季武子介以會. 自是晉人輕魯幣而益敬其使.[53]

It is customary to send one high officer to assist a minister on a diplomatic mission. Here Lu is sending two ministers to show its respect, and Jin reciprocates by lightening the burden of contributions from Lu. Fan Xuanzi might have been prompted to scale back demands on lesser domains because of Juzhi's speech. In this sense Juzhi's chanting of "Blue Flies" is also effective remonstrance.

Juzhi recites "Blue Flies" to imply cultural common ground and also to assert the rights of the "cultural other." There is behind the recitation a complex negotiation of demands and rebuttals, of self-definition and attempts to define the other, between the speaker and the addressee. What obtains is not a simple picture of barbarian otherness or acculturation but a heightened sense of how such assertions function in a diplomatic confrontation. The articulation of cultural difference can also motivate rhetorical competition, as in this example from *Hanshi waizhuan*, a collection of anecdotes supposed to illustrate the meanings of examples from the *Book of Poetry* and linked to sayings attributed to Confucius:[54]

> Goujian, the King of Yue, sent Lian Ji to offer captives to the king of Chu.[55] The Chu king's messenger said, "Yue is a domain of the Yi and Di barbarians. Your subject begs to get the better of its envoy." The Chu king said, "The Yue king is a worthy man. His envoy is also worthy. You should be careful!" The envoy came out, received Lian Ji and said, "You have to put a cap on for a customary audience;[56] no cap, no audience." Lian Ji said, "Yue was also among those who received office and land from the Zhou house. It does not get to be situated among the great domains, but is instead located by rivers and seas, having fish, turtles, and other marine creatures for companions. Only when we tattooed our bodies and cut our hair did we find a place for ourselves. Now we have come to your exalted domain, and you found it necessary to say, 'Put a cap on for a customary audience; no cap, no audience.' In that case, when the envoy from your exalted domain comes to Yue, he will have to cut his nose, brand his forehead, tattoo his body, cut his hair—and only then will he get a customary audience. Is that acceptable?" When the Chu king heard of this, he put on his robe, came out, and apologized.
>
> Confucius said, "One who is sent as envoy to the four directions without bringing shame to the lord's command can be called a proper man."[57]

越王勾踐使廉稽獻民於荊王, 荊王使者曰:「越, 夷狄之國也, 臣請欺其使者.」荊王曰:「越王, 賢人也, 其使者亦賢, 子其慎之!」使者出, 見廉稽曰:「冠, 則得以俗見, 不冠, 不得見.」廉稽曰:「夫越, 亦周室之列封也, 不得處於大國, 而處江海之陂, 與魭鱣魚鱉為伍, 文身翦髮, 而後處焉. 今來至上國, 必曰:『冠, 得俗見, 不冠, 不得見.』如此, 則上國使適越, 亦將劓墨文身翦髮, 而後得以俗見, 可乎?」荊王聞之, 披衣出謝. 孔子曰:「使於四方, 不辱君命, 可謂士矣.」[58]

One may read this as a straightforward statement of cultural relativism: a cap, which may be regarded as a marker of superior ritual propriety, is shown to be the cultural equivalent of tattoos and short hair. All are products of specific traditions and geographic location—there is no intrinsic hierarchy to their cultural meanings. The keyword is *chu* 處 (located, situated, find a place for): historical and geographic contexts determine customs. It is a matter of necessity and survival.[59] It is also ironic that Chu, cast as a barbarian domain in some accounts, should be presented as being arrogantly assured of its cultural superiority as one of the "central domains." By quoting the line from the *Lunyu* (13.20), however, the teller of the anecdote makes clear that the point is rhetorical prowess in defending the honor of one's domain, especially in a diplomatic context. Like the Rong chief Juzhi, the Yue envoy Lian Ji claims common origins with the central domains and earns the right to redefine the meanings of "barbarian"—Lian Ji's proper fulfillment of the ruler's command is the structural counterpart of Juzhi's mastery of Chinese cultural traditions.

Conclusion

The anecdotes discussed above imply fluid boundaries between "Chinese" and "barbarians." The actual issues debated may be the dangers of excessive refinement, the importance of frugality, the need to challenge tradition, or the grounds for diplomatic negotiations. Yet the collateral effect, or the lynchpin that delivers the message for these anecdotes, is the notion that cultural difference is not immutable. For thinkers like Xunzi 荀子 (Master Xun, 3rd c. BCE), this just goes to prove the transformative power of learning and teaching (*jiao* 教).[60] We also find frequent assertions about shared humanity and comparable goals, as in this passage from *Huainanzi*:

> The three Miao [tribes] bind their heads with hemp; the Qiang people bind their necks; the [people of] the Middle Kingdom

use hat and hairpin; the Yue people shear their hair. In regard to getting dressed, they are as one. [. . .] Thus the rites of the four Yi ["barbarians"] are not the same, [yet] they all revere their ruler, love their kin, and respect their elder brothers.

三苗髽首, 羌人括領, 中國冠笄, 越人劗鬋, 其於服, 一也. [. . .] 故四夷之禮不同, 皆尊其主而愛其親, 敬其兄.[61]

If in some anecdotes the barbarian does not learn Chinese ways properly, the issue is ultimately less about unchangeable nature than about the desirable method of learning, as in this anecdote from *Shuoyuan*:

> Zilu asked Confucius, "I beg leave to put aside ancient learning and follow my own mind. Is that acceptable?" Confucius said, "That will not do. In the old days, the eastern Yi admired the righteousness of the central states. Among them was a woman whose husband died. They let her have clandestine relations with her son-in-law, and to the end of her days she never married again. True enough, she did not remarry, but this cannot be the righteousness of chaste integrity. [. . .] Now you want to leave aside ancient learning and follow your mind. How do we know that you do not turn what is wrong into what is right and turn what is right into what is wrong? If you fail to follow the right course from the beginning, even if you want to get it right, it will be difficult indeed!

子路問於孔子曰: 「請釋古之學而行由之意, 可乎? 」孔子曰: 「不可, 昔者東夷慕諸夏之義, 有女, 其夫死, 為之內私婿, 終身不嫁, 不嫁則不嫁矣, 然非貞節之義也. [. . .] 今子欲釋古之學而行子之意, 庸知子用非為是, 用是為非乎! 不順其初, 雖欲悔之, 難哉! 」[62]

The person who trusts his own imperfect understanding (in this case Confucius's rash disciple Zilu 子路) is likely to err, mistaking appearance for reality. The point is not the stupidity of barbarians who fail to grasp the true meaning of ritual propriety but the dangers of not adhering to "ancient learning."

At the same time, it is not hard to find categorical statements about the immutable nature of barbarians placed in a spatial order, as in this passage from "Wangzhi" 王制 (The Institutions of Kings) in *Liji* 禮記 (Records of Ritual), a third to second century BCE compilation of Confucian precepts and ritual prescriptions:

> Those who live in the central domains, the Rong, the Yi, [and other barbarians, in other words] the people in the five directions: they all have their nature that cannot be changed. In the east they are called the Yi. Their hair unbound and their bodies tattooed, they are those who do not eat cooked food. In the south they are called the Man. Their forehead branded and their toes crossed, they are those who do not eat cooked food. In the west they are called the Rong. With unbound hair and dressed in leather, they are those who do not eat grains. In the north they are called the Di. Dressed in feather coats and dwelling in caves, they are those who do not eat grains. [. . .] For people in the five directions, their languages do not let them communicate, and their desires and inclinations are not the same.
>
> 中國戎夷, 五方之民, 皆有其性也, 不可推移. 東方曰夷, 被髮文身, 有不火食者矣. 南方曰蠻, 雕題交趾, 有不火食者矣. 西方曰戎, 被髮衣皮, 有不粒食者矣. 北方曰狄, 衣羽毛穴居, 有不粒食者矣. [. . .] 五方之民, 言語不通, 嗜欲不同.[63]

Such formulations find analogues in other markers of difference, from musical styles to positioning in imaginary early Zhou court audience. In view of the examples we have seen, such accounts seem to be abstract visions of order imposed on materials of great flux and variations.

Anecdotes about barbarians and barbarian ways demonstrate how their multifarious representations are tied to debates about cultural values and policies and are often determined by rhetorical contexts. Our examples span Warring States to Han, which begs the question of whether the emergence of a drastically different geopolitical situation—Qin-Han unification and the dominance of Xiongnu over other nomadic groups in the north—yields different perspectives on barbarians. Warring States writings depict the admixture and frequent intermarriage between different groups identified as Chinese and barbarians. The building of the Great Wall confirmed the polarity of Chinese and barbarians and upheld their separation as normative.[64] The Xiongnu problem emerged as one of the central issues in early Han policy debates.

We expect a formidable enemy up north to reshape the discourse on barbarians. The retelling of Warring States anecdotes in Han histories and anecdotal collections, however, display no significant rupture: we see comparable arguments as fluid boundaries are replayed. This may be in part because the domains formerly identified as "semi-barbarian" on occasions (e.g., Chu, Wu, Yue) are now brought within the compass of the unified empire. Even when it comes to the Xiongnu, comparable arguments on sameness or difference and the contextual determination of culture are invoked in the justification of war or appeasement.

In the anecdotes discussed above, the barbarian (You Yu, Juzhi, Lian Ji) often claims common origins with the central domains for himself or for his domain. In *Shiji*, we are told that the ancestor of the Xiongnu "was a descendant of the Xia ruling lineage by the name of Chunwei" 其先祖夏后氏之苗裔也, 曰淳維.[65] The first ruler of the Xia dynasty, the sage king Yu, was the great-great grandson of the Yellow Emperor.[66] As told in the *Shiji*, rulers of almost all the domains from the Spring and Autumn era and the Warring States era could trace their genealogies to the Yellow Emperor. Sima Qian is also interested in using genealogical stories to think about the common traits of and differences among peoples. The myth of common origins forestalls arguments of the Xiongnu's dehumanizing otherness, such as what obtains in Ban Gu's concluding comments on their feature of "human on the outside, beast on the inside" (*renmian shouxin* 人面獸心) in his chapters on the Xiongnu in *Hanshu*.[67] At the same time, the absence of stories about joining lineages, interdependence, or crossing boundaries that underpin many other genealogical accounts of rulers of various domains or tribal groups in *Shiji* points to the fundamental, unassimilable difference of the Xiongnu.

Such difference is evident in the detailed description of Xiongnu mores and customs at the beginning of "Xiongnu liezhuan" 匈奴列傳 (Account of the Xiongnu), which has no real counterpart in the other chapters on border peoples (*Shiji* 113, 114, 115, 116, 123). Their lack of writing and clan names, discrimination against the old, marriages that violate the boundaries of kinship—all these seem to amount to a complete reversal of the values of Han society. The judgment of their warlike nature or their "ignorance of ritual propriety and righteousness" (*bu zhi liyi* 不知禮義) apparently follows from such radical differences.[68] Halfway through the chapter, however, after the shared history of the Chinese and their barbarian (usually northern) neighbors has unfolded, Zhonghang Yue, the aforementioned Chinese "turncoat" who defects to the Xiongnu side, offers an eloquent justification of Xiongnu ways, thereby enacting a dialogue with the perspective implied in the initial description. Emperor Wen had sent the eunuch Zhonghang Yue to accompany a Han princess for the latter's marriage to the Xiongnu ruler. Disgruntled with the mission, Zhonghang Yue stays in the land of the Xiongnu and strategizes for them. He urges Xiongnu leaders to disdain Chinese luxuries that can potentially "soften" or corrupt the Xiongnu and foster dependence on China. He defends Xiongnu customs to a Han envoy, arguing that the exigencies of war necessitate preferential treatment of the young and healthy—when Han soldiers are sent off to war, their family would also offer them their best food and clothing. When a father or a brother dies, the Xiongnu takes the stepmother or sister-in-law as wives only "for fear of losing the seeds of the lineage" 惡種姓之失也.

Zhonghang Yue's story echoes earlier anecdotes justifying barbarian ways. Like You Yu, Fei Yi, King Wuling, Juzhi, or Lian Ji, Zhonghang Yue commands both Chinese and barbarian perspectives. This is a kind of vigilant self-justification that anticipates the detraction or opposition of the other side. This implicitly dialogic perspective often looks for Sino-barbarian common grounds even as it extols functional reasoning as well as barbarian simplicity and efficacy. Zhonghang Yue's speech carries verbal echoes of You Yu's (e.g., both compare the government of a domain to the care of the body), although the contexts are symmetrically opposite (You Yu defects to Qin, Zhonghang Yue to the Xiongnu). The policy implications of justifying barbarian ways are also divergent. Juzhi wants Jin to treat Rong as more of an equal partner in peaceful coexistence. King Wuling instigates the adoption of Hu clothing and mounted archery to pursue expansionist ambitions. Zhonghang Yue uses the rhetoric of Xiongnu superiority to force Han to continue appeasement by sending tribute. While Zhonghang is obviously justifying his own political decision, Sima Qian's motives for including his speech are somewhat more ambiguous. Tamara Chin argues persuasively that Zhonghang Yue's speech represents a self-reflexive gesture that sets out to "transform anthropological discourse into the object of scrutiny or doubt."[69] One may also say that the self-reflexive mode is a logical consequence of Sima Qian's historical goal of "comprehending changes from past to present." Reading the Zhonghang Yue episode in the light of earlier anecdotes justifying barbarian ways, some of which are included as pre-history of the Xiongnu in *Shiji* 110, evaluating the center from the margins seems an inevitable trajectory. In this sense, anecdotes about barbarians and barbarian ways, besides playing a tangible role in shaping attitudes toward non-Sinitic groups, also define the premise of historical understanding.

Early Chinese anecdotes about barbarians, just like categorical assertions on the subject, are shaped by various issues in cultural and intellectual debates dominant in the period of their formation. The difference between an anecdote and a plain statement is that narrative momentum and a plethora of descriptive details heighten our awareness that much more is at stake than the definition of "cultural others" or the proper relationship between "Chinese" and "barbarians." The issue is not so much distilling the "message" of these anecdotes—that is, asking what people were "really" talking about when they tell stories about barbarians—rather, we should see how these anecdotes function to shape ideas and arguments. In many cases, the barbarian functions to question or reverse established perspectives. With the story about Zhonghang Yue in *Shiji*, the shift of perspectives becomes something central to the whole enterprise of writing an impartial and comprehensive history.

Notes

1. This chapter was presented at the Anecdotes Workshop in Leiden (2013). I am grateful to the scholars gathered at the workshop, and to the volume's editors and anonymous reviewers for their comments and suggestions.

2. On the term *zhongguo*, see Hu Axiang 胡阿祥, *Wei zai si ming: Zhongguo gujin chengwei yanjiu* 偉哉斯名: 中國古今稱謂研究 (Wuhan: Hubei jiaoyu chubanshe, 2000); Peter K. Bol, "Geography and Culture: The Middle-Period Discourse on the *Zhong guo*—the Central Country," in *Kongjian yu wenhua changyu: Kongjian zhi yixiang, shijian yu shehui de shengchan* 空間與文化場域: 空間的意象, 實踐與社會的生產, ed. Huang Yinggui 黃應貴 (Taipei: Hanxue yanjiu zhongxin, 2009), 61–106.

3. The related terms *huaxia* 華夏 and *zhongxia* 中夏 are used much more rarely.

4. See Nicola di Cosmo, *Ancient China and Its Enemies: The Rise of Nomadic Power in East Asian History* (Cambridge: Cambridge University Press, 2002), 95n.7; Yuri Pines, "Beasts or Humans," in *Mongols, Turks, and Others: Eurasian Nomads and the Sedentary World*, eds. Reuven Amitai and Michal Biran (Leiden: Brill, 2005), 61n.8.

5. See Pines, "Beasts or Humans"; Mu-chou Poo, *Enemies of Civilization: Attitudes toward Foreigners in Ancient Mesopotamia, Egypt, and China* (Albany, NY: State University of New York Press, 2005); di Cosmo, *Ancient China and Its Enemies*; Wai-yee Li, "Hua Yi zhi bian yu yizu tonghun" 華夷之辨與異族通婚, in *Tanqing shuoyi* 談情説異 (Taipei: Center for the Study of Foreign Cultures, Shih-hsin University, 2012), 45–63.

6. Pines, "Beasts or Humans," 75.

7. Sun Yirang 孫詒讓, *Mozi jiangu* 墨子閒詁 (Taipei: Huazheng shuju, 1987), 25.165–67.

8. In *Huainanzi* 淮南子, Shun is said to die at Cangwu during his southern military expedition against the three Miao tribes 三苗, see Liu Wendian 劉文典 comp., *Huainan honglie jijie* 淮南鴻烈集解 (Beijing: Zhonghua shuju, 1989), 19.631. In *Lunheng* 論衡 (Balanced Discourses), Wang Chong 王充 cites (and refutes) Confucian texts that claim that Shun and Yu die on the road in frontier regions during tours of ritual inspection (*xunshou* 巡狩).

9. *Mozi jiangu*, 25.170–73. In another chapter, "Luwen" 魯問 (Lu's Questions), eating one's sons is said to be the custom in the Kingdom of Cannibals, and the character Mozi uses this barbaric custom to question the practice of putting the father to death while rewarding the son (e.g., the flood-controller Yu and his father Gun) (*Mozi jiangu* 49.432). Unlike Kaimu and the Kingdom of Cannibals, Yiqu is the actual domain of western Rong tribes mentioned in historical texts.

10. See James Hightower, *Han shih wai chuan: Han Ying's Illustrations of the Didactic Application of the Classic of Songs* (Cambridge, MA: Harvard University Press, 1952).

11. *Han Feizi jishi* 韓非子集釋, comp. Chen Qiyou 陳奇猷 (Beijing: Zhonghua shuju, 1958), 10.186–87. All translations in this essay are my own, unless otherwise indicated.

12. Ji Huanzi was the head of the powerful Jisun lineage and the de facto chief minister of Lu.

13. *Lunyu* 18.4.

14. *Hanshi waizhuan* and *Shuoyuan* retell the story with the same emphasis on frugality. The *Shuoyuan* account, almost identical with that in *Han Feizi*, in a chapter entitled "Fanzhi" 反質 (Returning to Essentials), concludes with a warning against "departing from substance" (*li zhipu* 離質樸). See Liu Xiang, *Shuoyuan jinzhu jinyi* 說苑今註今譯, comp. Lu Yuanjun 盧元駿 (Taipei: Shangwu yinshuguan, 1995[1988]), 20.713. In *Lüshi chunqiu*, this story appears in the "Bugou" 不苟 (Not Compromising) chapter. You Yu's speech is omitted and the issue is the Qin minister Jianshu's scruples: he refuses to participate in the scheme to detain You Yu and Scribe Liao comes up with the plan to corrupt the Rong king with music. See: *Lüshi chunqiu xin jiaoshi* 呂氏春秋新校釋, comp. Chen Qiyou 陳奇猷 (Shanghai: Shanghai guji chubanshe, 2002), 24.1584.

15. Sima Qian 司馬遷, *Shiji*, with annotations by Pei Yin 裴駰, Sima Zhen 司馬貞, Zhang Shoujie 張守節 (Taipei: Dingwen shuju, 1981), 5.192–93.

16. Takigawa Kametaro 瀧川龜太郎, *Shiji huizhu kaozheng* 史記會注考證 (Taipei: Hongye shuju, 1990), 5.33b; Ling Zhilong 凌稚隆 comp., *Shiji pinglin* 史記評林 (Taipei: Diqiu shuju, 1993), 1:158.

17. *Shiji* 110.2898–2900.

18. Zhonghang Yue's speech is discussed in Nicola di Cosmo, *Ancient China and Its Enemies*, 276–80. It is central to Tamara Chin's argument that Sima Qian critiques "ethnographic knowledge and practice" in *Shiji* 110, see her article "Defamiliarizing the Foreigner: Sima Qian's Ethnography and Han-Xiongnu Marriage Diplomacy," in *Harvard Journal of Asiatic Studies* 70, no. 2 (2010): 311–54. See also Wai-yee Li, "Historical Understanding in 'The Account of the Xiongnu' in the *Shiji*," in *Views from Within, Views from Beyond: Approaches to the Shiji as an Early Work of Historiography*, eds. Hans van Ess, Olga Lomová, and Dorothee Schaab-Hanke (Wiesbaden: Harrassowitz Verlag, 2015), 79–102.

19. See Wang Guowei 王國維 (1877–1927), "Hufu kao" 胡服考, in *Guantang jilin wai fu bieji* 觀堂集林附別集 (Beijing: Zhonghua shuju, [1959] 1991), 4:1069–1113.

20. On the evidence of chariot technology during the Shang and its possible role in the Zhou conquest of Shang, see Edward Shaughnessy, "Historical Perspectives on the Introduction of the Chariot to China," *Harvard Journal of Asiatic Studies* 48, no. 1 (1988): 189–237. *Zuozhuan* gives ample evidence for the importance of chariot warfare from the eighth to the fifth century BCE.

21. On the evidence of riding in ancient China, see Chauncey S. Goodrich, "Riding Astride and the Saddle in Ancient China," *Harvard Journal of Asiatic Studies* 44, no. 2 (1984): 279–306; on how mounted warriors redefined warfare during the Warring States Period, see Yang Kuan 楊寬, *Zhanguo shi* 戰國史 (Shanghai: Shanghai renmin chubanshe, 1998), 311–17.

22. Li Daoyuan 酈道元 (d. 527) cites this information from *Zhushu jinian*. See his *Shuijingzhu jiaoshi* 水經注校釋, ed. Chen Qiao 陳橋 (Hangzhou: Hangzhou daxue chubanshe, 1999), 3.42. See also Fang Shiming 方詩銘 and Wang Xiuling 王修齡, *Guben zhushu jinian jizheng* 古本竹書紀年輯證 (Shanghai: Shanghai guji chubanshe), 154, 290.

23. See Liu Xiang 劉向 comp., *Zhanguoce* 戰國策 (Shanghai: Shanghai guji chubanshe, 1978), "Zhao ce" 趙冊, 2.653–75.

24. *Zhanguoce*, "Zhao ce," 2.653–55.

25. Ouyue was an ancient kingdom, which was also known as Dong'ou 東甌.

26. *Zhanguoce*, "Zhao ce," 2.657.

27. *Zhanguoce*, "Zhao ce," 2.657.

28. *Zhanguoce*, "Zhao ce," 2.661.

29. Some commentators read *nu* 怒 as variant for *nu* 孥, "family and dependents": "Yao and Shun used capital punishment but did not extend it to the family and dependents of the accused."

30. *Zhanguoce*, "Zhao ce," 2.663.

31. *Zhanguoce*, "Zhao ce," 2.674.

32. Sun Yirang, cited by Zhu Shiche 朱師轍 in *Shangjunshu jiegu* 商君書解詁 (Taipei: Shijie shuju, 1990), 1; Takigawa Kametaro, *Shiji huizhu kaozheng*, 43.59.

33. Miao Wenyuan, "Hufu qishe kao" 胡服騎射考, *Lishi luncong* 歷史論叢 no. 2 (1981): 215–27.

34. *Shiji* 68.2234.

35. Two overlapping Warring States anecdotes, in *Zhanguoce* and *Han Feizi* respectively, tells why Zhongshan is vulnerable—it constitutes a kind of mirror image reversal of Zhao reforms. Zhongshan is a barbarian domain undermined by the adoption of Chinese cultural values. (The logic here is reminiscent of the anecdotes about You Yu.) King Wuling, after his abdication, asks Li Ci whether Zhao should attack Zhongshan. Li Ci replies in the affirmative, citing the Zhongshan ruler's respect for recluses and poor scholars. He then explains why these apparent markers of a worthy ruler would promote the wrong values and weaken the kingdom. See *Han Feizi jishi*, 32.654; *Zhanguoce*, "Zhongshan," 1181–82.

36. This detail also appears in *Huainan zi*, "Yuandao xun" 原道訓, in *Huainan honglie jijie*, 1:20; *Lüshi chunqiu*, "Guiyin" 貴因 (*Lüshi chunqiu jiaoshi*, 15.927).

37. *Lunyu* 9.14. The stated desire to leave the central domains implies Confucius's discontent. See also *Lunyu* 5.7: "When the Way does not prevail, I would board a raft and drift away on the seas."

38. Wang Chong, *Lunheng*, "Wen Kong" 問孔, see *Lunheng jiaoshi* 論衡校釋, ed. Huang Hui 黃暉 (Beijing: Zhonghua shuju, 1990), 28.417.

39. Pines, "Beasts or Humans," 69–75.

40. Yang Bojun 楊伯峻, *Chunqiu Zuozhuan zhu* 春秋左傳註 (Beijing: Zhonghua shuju, 1990), Xi 22.4 (i.e., fourth entry in the twenty-second year of Duke Xi of Lu), 1:394.

41. Guazhou is traditionally identified as a place in Gansu, but Gu Jiegang claims that it refers to the northern and southern slopes of the Qin Mountains. See Yang Bojun, *Chunqiu Zuozhuan zhu*, 3:1005.

42. The word "Yi" here does not refer to Yi tribes per se but encompasses various groups classified as unconnected to the "central domains."

43. Many years later (Zhao 9 [533 BCE]), in a territorial dispute between Zhou and Jin, a Zhou minister is to blame Jin for subverting the ideal political order based on banishing barbarians to the margins by citing this incident, see Yang Bojun, *Chunqiu Zuozhuan zhu*, 4:1309.

44. See Ibid., 2:669–72 (Xuan 3.2).

45. See Ibid., 3:942 (Xiang 5.2).

46. See Ibid., 3:1005–07 (Xiang 14.1).

47. As noted above, Qin and Jin might have been both responsible for relocating the Rong.

48. See Yang, *Chunqiu Zuozhuan zhu*, 1:479–482, 1:494–501. These events are dated to 630 BCE (Xi 30.3) and 627 BCE (Xi 33.1, 33.3).

49. *Maoshi zhushu* 毛詩註疏, 14C.489–90, in Ruan Yuan et al., *Chongkan Song ben Shisan jing zhushu fu jiaokan ji* 重刊宋本十三經注疏附校勘記 (Taipei: Yiwen yinshu guan, 1965).

50. *Lunyu* 13.5, 16.13.

51. Studies of the *fushi* phenomenon include Van Zoeren, *Poetry and Personality: Reading, Exegesis, and Hermeneutics in Traditional China* (Stanford, CA: Stanford University Press, 1991); Schaberg, *A Patterned Past: Form and Thought in Early Chinese Historiography* (Cambridge, MA: Harvard University Asia Center, 2001); Zhang Suqing 張素卿, *Zuozhuan chengshi yanjiu* 左傳稱詩研究 (Taipei: Taiwan daxue chubanshe, 1991); Mao Zhenhua 毛振華, *Zuozhuan fushi yanjiu* 左傳賦詩研究 (Shanghai: Shanghai guji chubanshe, 2001); Fu Daobin 傅道斌, *Shi keyi guan: liyue wenhua yu Zhou dai shixue jingshen* 詩可以觀: 禮樂文化與周代詩學精神 (Beijing: Zhonghua shuju, 2010); Wai-yee Li, "Aesthetics and Politics: Poetry and Diplomacy in *Zuozhuan*," *Journal of Chinese Literature and Culture* (2014): 242–262. For the list of *fushi* instances in *Zuozhuan*, see Gu Donggao 顧棟高 (1679–1759), *Chunqiu dashi biao* 春秋大事表, 3 vols. (Beijing: Zhonghua shuju, 1993), 3:2555–61.

52. For other examples of the barbarian's mastery of ritual tradition and esoteric knowledge, see *Zuozhuan*, Xi 29.4, Zhao 17.3 (Yang, *Chunqiu Zuozhuan zhu* 1:477, 4:1386–89).

53. Ji Wuzi (d. 535 BCE) was the chief minister in Lu. Zishu Qizi (d. 551 BCE) was also a Lu minister. These lines conclude the passage on the exchange between Fan Xuanzi and Juzhi (Yang Bojun, *Chunqiu Zuozhuan zhu*, 3:1007).

54. The text is linked to the Han scholar Han Ying (200 BCE?–120? BCE). On the structure and meaning of this text, see Paul van Els, "Tilting Vessels and Collapsing Walls—On the Rhetorical Function of Anecdotes in Early Chinese Texts," *Extrême-Orient, Extrême-Occident*, 34 (2012), 141–66.

55. Lian Ji may be a Yue minister. He is not mentioned in any other extant early Chinese texts. The "captives" refer to those captured upon a Yue victory in a battle. The Yue king is offering the Chu king a share of his spoils of war, a ritual known as *xianjie* 獻捷 in early texts.

56. Some versions of the text have *li* 禮 for *su* 俗: "Put a cap on and you will be received with proper rituals."

57. A modified quotation from *Analects* 13.20.

58. *Hanshi waizhuan jinzhu jinyi* 韓詩外傳今註今譯, comp. Lai Yanyuan 賴炎元 (Taipei: Shangwu yinshu guan, 1986), 8.317.

59. In *Huainanzi*, people in the watery wilds in the south are said to "let loose their hair and tattoo their bodies in order to resemble scaly creatures" 披髮文身, 以像鱗蟲 (*Huainan honglie jijie*, 1.19). Liu Wendian suggests that when humans look like scaly creatures, they can enter water without harm.

60. "Men of Gan, Yue, Yi, and He, they sound the same when they are born but grow up to have different customs. It is learning that makes this happen" 干, 越, 夷, 貉之子, 生而同聲, 長而異俗, 教使之然也. See *Xunzi jianshi* 荀子柬釋, compiled by Liang Qixiong 梁啟雄 (Taipei: Shangwu yinshu guan, 1993), 2.

61. *Huainan honglie jijie*, 11.355. Sarah A. Queen's translation, in *The Huainanzi*, translated and edited by John S. Major, Sarah A. Queen, Andrew Seth Meyer, and Harold D. Roth (New York: Columbia University Press, 2010), 406–07. The last line about the "four barbarians" (or "barbarians in the four directions") conclude earlier arguments about how different cultures can share moral principles despite varying customs. Despite this apparent relativism, the moral and social tenets of the "Middle Kingdom" are not really challenged.

62. *Shuoyuan*, ed. Lu Yuanjun 盧元駿 (Taipei: Shangwu yinshu guan, 1988), *juan* 3, 94.

63. *Liji zhushu* 禮記注疏, with commentaries by Zheng Xuan and Kong Yingda, *juan* 12, 247–48, in *Chongkan Song ben shisan jing zhushu fu jiaokan ji*.

64. In one of Emperor Wen's letters to the Xiongnu, he articulates the vision of peaceful co-prosperity and non-competitive expansion: "Following what was instituted by the former emperor, north of the Great Wall is the domain of those who draw the bow, and they receive their command from the Chanyu; within the Great Wall are the abodes of those who wear cap and gown, and we will likewise be obeyed." 先帝制, 長城以北, 引弓之國, 受命單于; 長城以內, 冠帶之室, 朕亦如之 (*Shiji* 110.2903).

65. *Shiji* 110.2879.

66. *Shiji* 2.49.

67. *Hanshu* 94B.3834.

68. *Shiji* 110.2879.

69. Tamara Chin, "Defamiliarizing the Foreigner," 319.

Part II

Anecdotes and Textual Formation

5

Anecdote Collections as Argumentative Texts
The Composition of the *Shuoyuan*

Christian Schwermann[1]

> It is a trite but true observation, that examples work more forcibly on the mind than precepts: and if this be just in what is odious and blameable, it is more strongly so in what is amiable and praise-worthy. Here emulation most effectually operates upon us, and inspires our imitation in an irresistible manner. A good man therefore is a standing lesson to all his acquaintance, and of far greater use in that narrow circle than a good book.
>
> But as it often happens that the best men are but little known, and consequently cannot extend the usefulness of their examples a great way: the writer may be called in aid to spread their history farther, and to present the amiable pictures to those who have not the happiness of knowing the originals; and so, by communicating such valuable patterns to the world, he may perhaps do a more extensive service to mankind than the person whose life originally afforded the pattern.
>
> —Henry Fielding[2]

Anecdotes or anecdote collections are not normally considered to be argumentative texts. In literary studies, anecdotes are defined as entertaining and/or didactic short narratives, which due to their being steeped in historical detail may succeed in enticing their readers to believe in their being factual accounts and at the same time express timeless truths by describing exemplary characters or events in a pointed way.[3] Although early Chinese literature did not have this generic concept of anecdotes, it abounds with anecdotal narratives. Instead of conceiving of these as tales, early Chinese scholars subsumed them under the genre of "explanations" (*shuo* 說), which can be traced back to an argumentative mode of writing, i.e., *shuo*, OC (Old Chinese) *lhot, "to explain," as distinguished from its exoactive form, *shui*, OC *lhots, "to persuade."⁴ That is, they defined short narratives with regard to their use in an argumentative frame and treated them as exempla, which in classical European literature can be traced back to the *paradeigmata* of Aristotle's *Rhetoric*, i.e., rhetorical forms of induction.⁵ In regard to their argumentative context, these "explanations" or "illustrative examples" (*shuo*) were used to exemplify "guidelines" or "propositions" (*jing* 經), which normally preceded them.⁶

Taking chapter 9, "Zhengjian" 正諫 (Rectifying Remonstrance), of the *Shuoyuan* 說苑 (Garden [i.e., Collection] of Illustrative Examples) as an example,⁷ I will analyze how in a so-called "anecdote collection" different types of arguments, including exempla, are combined to form an elaborate tapestry of argumentation in support of a proposition, and how received anecdotes are adapted to a new argumentative context to make for a more persuasive text. As this implies that the *Shuoyuan* is not a mere collection of received anecdotal narratives and that Liu Xiang 劉向 (79–8 BCE) should be considered its *author* rather than its compiler,⁸ I will begin with a short discussion of his role in the composition of the text, starting with his extant memorial on the occasion of submitting the text to the throne in 17 BCE.⁹

The Textual Fabric of the *Shuoyuan* and the Question of Liu Xiang's Authorship

The *Shuoyuan*, also referred to as *Shuiyuan* (Garden [i.e., Collection] of Persuasions) by some scholars,¹⁰ is traditionally ascribed to the Han bibliographer and scholar Liu Xiang.¹¹ Ever since Luo Genze 羅根澤 (1900–1960) contended that Liu Xiang did not compose the *Shuoyuan* but rather collected and edited the material in the received text from older sources, his authorship and the homogeneity of the text have been widely called into question.¹² Although Xu Fuguan 徐復觀 (1903–1982) in 1977 marshalled a whole array of arguments to reestablish Liu Xiang's claim to authorship and, more recently, Xie Mingren 謝明仁 as well as Du Jiaqi 杜家祁 tried to show in two book-length studies that Liu Xiang both edited the *Shuoyuan* and composed parts of it,¹³ there is, especially among non-Chinese sinologists, still a strong scholarly consensus that the work—similar to the *Xinxu* 新

序 (Newly Arranged [Anecdotes]) or the *Lienüzhuan* 列女傳 (Biographies of Exemplary Women)[14]—merely constitutes a relatively haphazard compilation of older documents and that Liu Xiang's sole contribution to the formation of it was the thematical arrangement of its segments.[15]

However, this view neither accounts for the sophisticated structure of the text and the homogeneity of both its style and its contents, nor does it consider that "literary or essay-like texts, authored by a single writer, in the way we typically think of a text in the modern world, do not reflect the norm for early China but were, at best, the exception."[16] Authoring a scholarly text in early imperial China normally meant to build arguments on the basis of earlier texts, which were alluded to or quoted to illustrate, enforce, expand, or even form an argument and, finally but not most importantly, to endow it with the prestige of the quoted text.[17] In quite a few works, including the *Shuoyuan*, this was taken to an extreme insofar as the thesis was first presented in discursive introductions to individual chapters and developed in a progression of allusions and quotations, and then illustrated by strings of received textual units, most of them anecdotes and exempla, but also parables, didactic speeches, sayings, memorials to the throne, pseudepigraphy,[18] and other types of short prose items, all of which, if required, were modified and adapted to the context.[19] In his *Danses et légendes de la Chine ancienne*, Marcel Granet (1884–1940) compared both these compositions and more recent literary texts to richly decorated cloths, albeit with the felicitous qualification that the collage of allusions and quotations in the former forms the weft and not the décor of the textual fabric:

> Acceptons le fait. La littérature chinoise est une littérature de centons: vérité fort simple, que bien peu, sans doute, refuseraient d'admettre parmi ceux qui ont une connaissance directe des textes, mais vérité qui, prise à la rigueur et dans toutes ses conséquences, fait éviter de fausses démarches et peut engager sur une bonne route. On connaît l'importance des *allusions littéraires* dans les ouvrages récents. Ces ouvrages sont des compositions qui visent à l'Art et que l'on pare d'élégances empruntées: étoffes de luxe décorées au poncif de motifs éternellement plagiés. – Les œuvres anciennes sont tournées vers la pratique; leur objet est l'éducation du Prince et des Sages qui pourront l'aider. De ces œuvres faites pour l'usage, les centons forment la trame et non le décor: sentences oratoires, symboles philosophiques, thèmes d'action, destinés à persuader et à guider, ayant valeur de proverbes, non

pas copiés de texte à texte mais passant d'âme à âme, imposés
à l'auteur, s'imposant au lecteur par l'empire des traditions.[20]

This collage-style way of writing was probably influenced by philosophical works of the early and middle Warring States Period (5th to 3rd c. BCE), which seem to have been assembled, transmitted, and perhaps also revised by scholarly lineages over several generations.[21] However, late Warring States and early imperial texts (3rd to 1st c. BCE) differ from these predecessors in that they place authority both in statements of individual masters and in arguments, and accordingly replace the teaching scene with an attachment to textual traditions.[22] Moreover, early Han texts not only show the first signs of individual authorship but also develop elaborate notions of it.[23] Their writers no longer cast themselves in the role of secretaries "transcribing the speech of another."[24] This is also true for the *Shuoyuan*. By analyzing Liu Xiang's memorial on the text and collating his illustrative examples therein with certain aspects of the composition of its chapter on "Rectifying Remonstrance" (Zhengjian), it can be demonstrated that he created a self-conscious literary as well as argumentative artifice, which explores important political topics of the last century BCE. As it does so by adapting received anecdotes to new contexts, some attention has also to be paid to the problem of intertextuality, i.e., to the question of to what extent the "deeper meaning" of the *Shuoyuan* is shaped by the interplay of references to other works and to what extent allusions and quotations form argumentative elements or even help to structure the text.[25]

Liu Xiang's Memorial on the Occasion of Submitting the *Shuoyuan* to the Throne

To determine to what extent Liu Xiang *authored* the *Shuoyuan* we turn to the text itself and to Liu Xiang's memorial, which contains valuable information on the formation of the *Shuoyuan*. Contrary to what many interpreters claim,[26] the text preserved in Yan Kejun's 嚴可均 (1762–1843) anthology *Quan shanggu Sandai Qin Han Sanguo Liuchao wen* 全上古三代秦漢三國六朝文 (Complete Collection of Prose Works from Remote Antiquity, the Three Dynasties, Qin and Han Dynasties, Three Kingdoms, and Six Dynasties) is not corrupt, but is entirely reliable, as my following reading demonstrates:

The Commissioner of the Eastern Metropolitan Area River Conservancy and Imperial Household Grandee, Your servant [Liu] Xiang speaks [to the Throne]: I completely[27] collated the various historical accounts of an Imperial Library collection of illustrative examples, which I had put together, with my own documents and those from private libraries.[28] Their categories of accounts were varied, the order of sections and sentences was jumbled. In some places, the sequence was illogical, and it was difficult to divide [into sections] and to arrange in order. I removed the duplicates of [accounts in] the *Xinxu*. As for what remained, I compiled [accounts] that were shallow and not commensurate with the pattern of righteousness separately as the *Baijia* 百家 ([Accounts of] the Hundred Thinkers). Thereafter I had [the accounts] follow each other according to their categories, allocated a chapter heading to every division [of the text], modified[29] [the text] and thus created[30] new accounts [numbering] more than one hundred thousand words.[31] The total of twenty chapters with 784 sections I have called "New Collection" (*Xinyuan* 新苑). All of it is ready for your inspection. Your servant [Liu] Xiang, at the risk of [committing a crime that merits the] death [penalty].[32]

護左都水使者光祿大夫臣向言. 所校中書說苑雜事及臣向書民間書誣校讎. 其事類眾多. 章句相溷. 或上下謬亂. 難分別次序. 除去與新序復重者. 其餘者淺薄不中義理別集以為百家. 後令以類相從. 一一條別篇目. 更以造新事十萬言以上. 凡二十篇七百八十四章號曰新苑. 皆可觀. 臣向昧死.[33]

According to this memorial, Liu Xiang proceeded in several steps and, amongst other things, was responsible for collation, emendation, elimination, abridgement, and thematical arrangement of parts of a received anecdotal repertoire, and for the division of the resulting work into chapters, to which he added titles. He first collated a collection of historical accounts (*shi* 事)[34] stored in the Imperial Library (*zhongshu* 中書) with materials of his own and those from other private libraries. The term *shuoyuan* 說苑 in the expression *zhongshu shuoyuan zashi* 中書說苑雜事 ("various historical accounts of an Imperial Library collection of illustrative examples"), may refer either to an official title of a work in the imperial collection or to an untitled and unpolished "collection of illustrative examples," i.e., a mere random assemblage of unrelated narratives, which Liu Xiang himself in his function as imperial bibliographer and librarian might have put together in view of providing raw material for possible later editorial projects.³⁵ Zuo Songchao 左松超 believes the latter to be the case, since the memorial on the *Shuoyuan* differs from other extant memorials, for example those on the *Guanzi* 管子 (Master Guan), *Xunzi* 荀子 (Master Xun), *Yanzi chunqiu* 晏子春秋 (Spring and Autumn Annals of Master Yan), or *Liezi* 列子 (Master Lie), insofar as it does not mention the number of chapters (*pian* 篇) that constituted the source text (i.e., the *Shuoyuan zashi*).³⁶ Quite to the contrary, says Zuo, Liu Xiang's account indicates that (1) this and the other manuscripts from private collections were in poor condition and had to be emended and arranged in sections, and that (2) there was no previously established text.³⁷

In what constituted the next step in this process of text production, he eliminated duplicates of accounts in the collection *Xinxu*, which therefore must have been submitted to the throne before the *Shuoyuan*,³⁸ and selected objectionable textual units for separate compilation in the *Baijia*. His explanation indicates that the latter abridgement amounted to an act of censorship: because they were deemed shallow (probably in the sense of being morally deficient) and not in accord with proper ritual conduct, i.e., *bu zhong yi li* 不中義理 (not commensurate with the pattern of righteousness),³⁹ a disproportionately large number of items (the *Hanshu* 漢書 [History of the (Former) Han Dynasty] lists the *Baijia* as a work of 139 *pian*)⁴⁰ was sorted out and put together in a collection that soon ceased to be handed down.⁴¹

Having thus "cleansed" the text and given it a thorough Classicist (Confucian) orientation, Liu Xiang arranged the remaining constituents thematically in chapters, which were then given titles. His conclusion that he created a new collection of accounts through modification is perfectly in line with the preceding report. He did not re-edit a preexisting work but composed a new text on the basis of older materials. He adapted these received textual units, mostly items of short anecdotal prose, and modified them according to his intentions. On the most obvious plane, these are expressed by the chapter titles, which he inserted and which, together with the references to other texts in his discursive introductions, can be interpreted as indicators of the meaning of the text as a whole.⁴² Judging from the fact that he referred to his redactions of *Xunzi* and *Liezi* as *Sun Qing xinshu* 孫卿新書 (New Documents by Sun Qing) and *Liezi xinshu* 列子新書 (New Documents by Master Lie), respectively, it does not come as a surprise that he submitted the *Shuoyuan* under the title *Xinyuan* (New Collection). In contrast to the former two redactions, however, he did not ascribe it to an author figure, presumably because he conceived of himself as being the author of it. This is also warranted by the fact that he claimed authorship for himself by asserting that he created (*zao* 造) not only individual accounts within that collection but the entire work, i.e., "new accounts [numbering] more than one hundred thousand words."

Explanation and/or Persuasion?
The *Shuoyuan* as a Discursive Text

In the following, I will present more textual evidence that Liu Xiang's "modification" of a received repertoire entailed both the adaptation of these transmitted materials and their supplementation with argumentative and narrative items that he had composed himself. Before comparing the information given in the memorial with the composition of the *Shuoyuan*, however, it seems advisable to first analyze the meaning of the term *shuo* 說, which may provide us with clues to the nature of the whole text. Since the verbs *shuo*, OC *lhot, "to speak, discuss, explain," and *shui*, OC *lhots, "to exhort, persuade," both of them written 說, are closely related (the second being an exoactive derivation of the first), the deverbal nouns *shuo*, explanation, and *shui*, persuasion, are complementary insofar as the first refers to the contents of an argument, and the second to its application and intention.[43] As an exoactive verb, *shui* governs personal nouns that refer to a "specific audience."[44] Setting aside this difference for a while, we can safely assume that the shared semantic component of *shuo* and *shui* is "argument," and that both refer to discursive speech.[45]

In spite of the close etymological relationship and semantic complementarity of the two nouns, it should not prove impossible to decide whether the received title of Liu Xiang's work refers to arguments as explanations or as persuasions, and thus to finally settle the problem as to how its title should be read at least with regard to its first part—the crucial question being whether it refers to arguments primarily in view of their contents or of their application.[46] To come straight to the point, I propose to settle for the pronounciation *Shuoyuan*, for the following reasons.

Although some of the anecdotal prose in the *Shuoyuan*, especially in chapter 9, "Zhengjian" (Rectifying Remonstrance), and chapter 11, "Shanshui" 善說 (Skilled at Persuasion) resembles the persuasions contained in the *Zhanguoce* 戰國策 (Stratagems of the Warring States), which occasionally use exempla as arguments, most of the narratives in the *Shuoyuan* do not have an obvious persuasive context, i.e., a frame text relating to a discussion between a persuader and his audience, normally a ruler.[47] In the abovementioned two chapters, persuasion is of topical interest only within the majority of anecdotes themselves and in the introduction to chapter 11.

Of course, one might argue that the short narratives, which constitute the lion's share of the work, have to be regarded as the argumentative "flesh" on its conceptual "backbone," which is formed by introductions to individual chapters and acquaints the readers with the topics of the work,[48] and may be interpreted as constituents of an extended persuasion directed at the ruler as reader. Following this line of thought, Du Jiaqi comes to the conclusion that both *Xinxu* and *Shuoyuan* are remonstrances on a grand scale addressed to the emperor.[49] What can be cited in support of this proposition, which strikes one as rather bold in its generalization, and what can be said against it? Du's view would imply that the work was addressed to a Han ruler, presumably Emperor Cheng of the Han Dynasty 漢成帝 (i.e., Liu Ao 劉鷔, r. 33–7 BCE), since it can be demonstrated that—even if the date of submission to the throne as given in the fragment transmitted in Chao Gongwu's *Junzhai dushu zhi* is not accepted—the *terminus ante quem non* for the text is 33 BCE.[50] At first sight, the hypothesis that the whole text is a persuasion on a grand scale, a sort of "grand remonstrance" directed at the emperor, appears to dovetail nicely with the fact that Liu Ao was notorious for his licentiousness, irresponsibility, and imperviousness to criticism.[51] His alleged shortcomings can be argued to be reflected in the *Shuoyuan*, which, from a Classicist point of view, deals with central aspects of rulership and governance such as the optimum performance of rulers and officials, guidelines for political action and personal conduct of decision-makers, basic political principles (especially the priority of rule by virtue over rule by law), recruitment of administrative personnel, the art of remonstrance, political circumspection, the art of persuasion (and the complementary virtue of heeding advice), diplomacy, tactics, and stratagems (only to be employed for the purpose of advancing the commonweal), the priority of the public good over private interest, military readiness and provision of defensive armament, observance of omens and portents, ritual and music as means of ordering and harmonizing society, and, finally, the maintenance of simplicity and frugality as a precondition for political ascendancy. Moreover, Liu Xiang's *Hanshu* biography tells us that he composed both *Xinxu* and *Shuoyuan* in order to "lay out standards and warnings" (*chen fa jie* 陳法戒) to the emperor.[52]

However, the abovementioned aspects of rulership and governance would have been of vital importance to any Chinese ruler, not just Emperor Cheng of the Han Dynasty. Caution is recommended when dealing with the biographical chapters of dynastic histories and their rhetorical commonplaces like the topos of the uncompromising critic of monarchic misrule, which clearly informs Liu Xiang's biography.[53] In fact, the *Shuoyuan* is not a remonstrance but, at most, a very opaque attempt at an "indirectly allusive remonstrance" (*fengjian* 諷諫), disguised under a welter of delightful stories.[54] And what is decisive is that these anecdotal narratives do not serve as persuasions but as illustrative "explanations" to the chapter introductions. Even in the case of chapters 9, "Zhengjian" (Rectifying Remonstrance), and 11, "Shanshui" (Skilled at Persuasion), the tales primarily serve to exemplify the propositions made in the introductory paragraphs.[55] With regard to the reference of the term *shuo* in the title *Shuoyuan*, it is important to note that Han Classicists developed the genre of "explanatory commentaries" (*shuo*), which are listed in the bibliographical treatise of the *Hanshu*.[56] Unfortunately, none of these works has survived. Although most of these commentaries such as the *Lu Wang Jun shuo* 魯王駿說 (Explanations [to the *Lunyu*] by Wang Jun of Lu) in 21 *pian* 篇[57] or the *Zhongyong shuo* 中庸說 (Explanations to the *Doctrine of the Mean*) in 2 *pian*,[58] were probably purely exegetical in nature, some of them, similar to the extant *Hanshi waizhuan* 韓詩外傳 (Han's Supplementary Commentary to the Odes), which in terms of narrative materials is closely related to the *Shuoyuan*,[59] may have contained anecdotal illustrations of passages in the Classics.[60] This is definitely true for those works that are listed in the section on *xiaoshuo* 小說, "inferior explanations," of the bibliographical treatise.[61]

Moreover, received *shuo*-chapters in other texts indicate that *shuo* were conceived of as illustrative explanations of discursive guidelines (*jing* 經).[62] The *shuo*-chapters in the *Han Feizi* 韓非子 (Master Han Fei) establish this subgenre of illustrative explanations by serializing anecdotes and usually introducing them with discursive guidelines. Whereas chapters 22 and 23, "Shuolin, shang, xia" 說林上下 (Forest [i.e., Collection] of Illustrative Examples, Part One and Part Two) are purely narrative and consist of strings of anecdotes,[63] which serially illustrate certain aspects of political thought, the six chapters "Nei chushuo" 內儲說 (Inner Collection of Illustrative Examples) and "Wai chushuo" 外儲說 (Outer Collection of Illustrative Examples) are structured differently insofar as they commence with lists of discursive guidelines, which are then illustrated by explanations, most of these being anecdotal in nature.[64] To give an example, chapter 30, "Nei chushuo, shang, qi shu" 內儲說上七術 (Inner Collection of Illustrative

Examples, Part One, Seven Methods) introduces seven political guidelines for the ruler, which are then illustrated by short narrative items serving as exempla. Some of these guidelines even refer to the following illustrations by the formula *qi shuo zai* 其說在, "for illustrative examples, see [. . .]."⁶⁵ We also find this formula in chapter 32, "Wai chushuo, zuo, shang" 外儲說左上 (Outer Collection of Illustrative Examples, Part One of the Left).⁶⁶ Moreover, this as well as the following three chapters 33 through 35 insert the editorial remark *you jing* 右經, "guidelines on the right [i.e., above]," to detach the sections containing the guidelines from the anecdotes explaining or illustrating these guidelines.⁶⁷ The structure of these chapters thus closely resembles that of most chapters of the *Shuoyuan*. As mentioned above, these normally commence with discursive introductions, the main arguments of which are then illustrated by strings of short narrative textual units.

Judging from this evidence, we may conclude that the *Shuoyuan* consists of explanations, mostly in the form of anecdotes, which address certain political issues of the late Western Han and illustrate "guidelines" or propositions formulated in the introductions to the chapters, and that the basic-level category *shuo*, "explanations," can be traced back to an argumentative and/or explanatory "mode of writing."⁶⁸ As for the title of the work, it does not seem advisable to read 說 as *shui* (persuasions). As I have argued above, the *Shuoyuan* is not a "grand remonstrance," and persuasion, if mentioned at all, is only of topical interest within a mere fraction of its textual units. Structurally, these serve as constituents of a discursive text that relies on illustrative arguments to advertise certain Classicist positions in central political issues such as administrative performance and personal conduct of decision-makers, personnel recruitment, political criticism, and/or the advancement of the public good or military policy.

The Composition of Chapter 9, "Zhengjian" (Rectifying Remonstrance) in the *Shuoyuan*

To understand the composition of the *Shuoyuan*, it is particularly important to investigate how these received textual units, which correspond to the sections (*zhang* 章) of the text and which can be interpreted as explanations of or arguments for Liu Xiang's political claims, are tied together and adapted to their context. In early Chinese prose, textual units can be interlaced by means of at least four types of transphrastic text-structuring devices, i.e., structural expedients that pass across groups of words, clauses, or even sentences, namely (1) formal, argumentative, and thematic bracketing, (2) associative coupling, (3) non-associative coupling, and (4) associative sampling.[69] The first and last of these four are the most important means of text composition in the *Shuoyuan*. As shown above, most chapters have introductions, which serve as discursive guidelines (*jing*) for the subsequent anecdotal explanations (*shuo*), but they typically lack short associative or thematic connective links, by which individual anecdotes can be tied together. In the following I will also take into account a more sophisticated type of bracketing technique, namely the use of intertextual references as text-structuring devices. To narrow down the task, I will focus on the composition of chapter 9, "Zhengjian" (Rectifying Remonstrance), of the *Shuoyuan*.

As this chapter is a deliberative text and deals with an important aspect of the art of persuasion, namely the question of how to remonstrate with one's ruler most effectively, it seems to be particularly suited for a rhetorical analysis. Like most chapters of the *Shuoyuan*, it commences with a discursive introduction into its subject. This introduction presents a string of arguments in favor of a particular strategy of remonstrance:

> The *Changes* say, "A royal minister is outspoken, but not for his own sake."[70] The reason for his being outspoken, causing trouble and remonstrating with his lord is not that he [seeks advantage] for himself but that he wants thereby to correct the mistakes of his lord and make amends for his failures. If a lord has mistakes and failures, then this is the sprout of danger and destruction. To see the mistakes and failures of one's lord and yet not to remonstrate with him, this is to take lightly his danger and destruction. Now, as for taking lightly one's lord's danger and destruction, it is what a loyal minister does not bear to do.
>
> If he has remonstrated three times [with his lord], and [his advice] has not been heeded, he [ought to] leave. If he does not leave, he will bring destruction upon himself.[71] To bring destruction upon himself is what a humane man does not do.
>
> For this reason there are five [types] of remonstrance. The first is called straightforward remonstrance. The second is called submissive remonstrance. The third is called faithful remonstrance. The fourth is called stupid remonstrance. The fifth is called indirectly allusive remonstrance.[72] Confucius said, "As far as I am concerned, I am for the indirectly allusive remonstrance!"

Now, if you do not remonstrate with your lord, you will put him in danger. If you remonstrate stubbornly, you will put yourself in danger. If you put yourself in danger and in the end [your advice] is not heeded, the remonstrance will surely be fruitless. The wise man assesses the lord and weighs the proper time. By adjusting his relaxing and urging, he does what is appropriate in his situation. Above he does not dare to put [his] lord in danger, below he thereby does not put himself in danger. Therefore he is concerned with [his own] state so that [his] state is not in danger, and he is concerned with [his own] person so that [his] person is not in danger.

Once Lord Ling of Chen [r. 613–599 BCE] did not heed Xie Ye's remonstrance and had him killed. Cao Ji remonstrated three times with the lord of Cao and left when he was not heeded. Although the *Chunqiu* 春秋 (Spring and Autumn Annals) rates[73] both of them as worthies, it was Cao Ji who accorded with the rites.[74]

《易》曰：「王臣蹇蹇，匪躬之故。」人臣之所以蹇蹇為難而諫其君者，非為身也，將欲以匡君之過，矯君之失也. 君有過失者，危亡之萌也；見君之過失而不諫，是輕君之危亡也. 夫輕君之危亡者，忠臣不忍為也. 三諫而不用則去，不去則亡身，亡身者，仁人所不為也. 是故諫有五：一曰正諫，二曰降諫，三曰忠諫，四曰戇諫，五曰諷諫. 孔子曰：「吾其從諷諫矣乎！」夫不諫則危君，固諫則危身，與其危君寧危身. 危身而終不用，則諫亦無功矣. 智者度君權時，調其緩急，而處其宜，上不敢危君，下不以危身. 故在國而國不危，在身而身不殆. 昔陳靈公不聽泄冶之諫而殺之，曹羈三諫曹君不聽而去，《春秋》序義雖俱賢，而曹羈合禮.[75]

This introduction contains three appeals to authority, which are crucial for the progress of Liu Xiang's argumentation. The first is a quotation from the *Book of Changes*, better known in the West as the *I Ching*, which in some modern editions and translations of the Classic is still interpreted as it was by Liu Xiang more than two thousand years ago,[76] namely as a reference to straightforward remonstrance. Placed right at the beginning of the text, the quotation not only serves as an introduction into the subject of the chapter, i.e., the minister's strategy of communicating with his lord when exercising criticism, but also as an *argumentum ad verecundiam* in favor of outspokenness.

In what follows, however, this apparent call for candidness is qualified. Whereas the first section emphasizes that ministerial criticism of wrong views or decisions or misdemeanour on the ruler's part is not only useful but indispensable for the future well-being of lord, land, and people, the second section, introducing a new point of view by referring to the oft-quoted rule that a minister ought to resign after having remonstrated thrice in vain,[77] goes on to argue that it is just as important that the remonstrant does not sacrifice his own life for the sake of outspokenness. The following list of five types of remonstrance ranges from the straightforward to the indirectly allusive remonstrance. It is concluded by a quotation attributed to Confucius, which gives precedence to the latter, i.e., indirectly allusive remonstrance. This reference constitutes the second appeal to authority and serves as a "pivot" that marks a break between sections insofar as it brings the discussion of the various types of remonstrance to a close and at the same time segues into the topic of the following section—the art of expediency. Slightly different versions of Confucius's endorsement of indirect remonstrance can also be found in *Kongzi jiayu* 孔子家語 (School Sayings of Confucius) and *Baihutong* 白虎通 (Comprehensive Discussions in the White Tiger Hall).[78]

Thus, at first sight it would seem that Liu Xiang prefers indirect remonstrance,[79] but in fact the following section once again points in a different direction. Quite obviously, the line of argumentation is not that one particular type of remonstrance is superior to all others. Rather, it is proposed that it is important for the remonstrant to be flexible and adapt to the respective circumstances and power constellations at court to be successful, i.e., to both convince his lord of his point of view *and* stay alive. By alluding to the cases of Xie Ye and Cao Ji and their rating in the *Chunqiu*—the third appeal to authority—in the final part of his introduction, Liu Xiang seems to indicate that it is better to be adaptable to unpredictable changes and hazards and to "accord with the rites" (here meaning to abide by the rule not to submit more than three futile remonstrances) than to insist stubbornly on one's own point of view, even though one is in the right. However, this does not mean that indirectness is a panacea for effective communication with the ruler. It all depends on the situation. Under certain circumstances it is necessary to be outspoken, sometimes it is better not to speak at all—or even to feign incompetence or madness.[80]

Thus, in order to both get one's message across and to survive, it is essential to base one's actions on political expediency and to be able to cover the full range of remonstrance.

This is exactly what the following series of anecdotes illustrates. All of them document cases of successful remonstrances.[81] The ratio between indirect and direct remonstrances does not seem to be in perfect balance but slightly in favor of direct remonstrance.[82] This finding is further corroborated by the fact that the penultimate and final sections of the chapter, i.e., *Shuoyuan* 9.25 and 9.26, do not deal with remonstrances but contain two speeches, in which Confucius and Yan Ying 晏嬰, the prime minister of Qi 齊 who is supposed to have lived from 589 to 500 BCE, argue in favor of "outspokenness" (*ee* 諤諤) and a climate of open-mindedness and openness to criticism at court as preconditions for good government.[83] Whereas the first speech, which is put into the mouth of Confucius, compares "loyal words" (*zhong yan* 忠言) to a "good medicine" (*liang yao* 良藥), which may have a bitter taste but is of benefit for curing a disease,[84] Yan Ying argues that if severity (*yan* 嚴) holds sway at court, there will be a silence that is "detrimental to ordering the country and the ruling house" (*hai yu zhi guo jia* 害於治國家).[85] As both speeches readdress the topic of outspokenness introduced at the beginning of the chapter, they help to establish an argumentative frame bracketing the illustrative anecdotes.[86] Moreover, some indirect remonstrances begin with theatrical performances, which are not decoded by the ruler but explained by the remonstrant himself and thus prepare the ground for ensuing straightforward censure.[87] In these cases, the performances merely serve as delightful preludes, intended to distract the addressee and make him feel receptive and well-disposed toward the speaker or curious about his intention. Therefore, they can also be seen as direct remonstrances supplemented and thus made palatable by preceding acts of entertainment.

For example, an anecdote in *Shuoyuan* 9.4 tells us about a man called Jiu Fan 咎犯, who criticizes Duke Ping of Jin 晉平公 (r. 557–532 BCE) for his extravagance, which, among other things, manifests itself in his excessive indulgence in music.[88] Jiu Fan introduces himself as a music master, is invited to give a performance at court but then informs the ruler that he is not able to play his instruments and suggests to pose a riddle instead.[89] He stretches out his left arm, makes a fist and asks his audience to guess what it signifies. As no one is able to solve the riddle, he explains it himself, stretching out one finger of his left hand after the other and enumerating the mistakes of Duke Ping, in this manner bluntly criticizing him for wasting resources and causing his people to starve. Instead of putting the remonstrant to death, the accused decides to henceforth rule his country together with Jiu Fan.

What should not be overlooked is that Jiu Fan is a telling name meaning "to blame (someone) for an offence"—clearly a reference to direct remonstrance—and that the anecdote is anachronistic: the historical *jiu* Fan 舅犯, on whom the protagonist seems to be modeled, was active in the second half of the seventh century BCE, but Liu Xiang turns him into a remonstrant of the second half of the sixth century BCE.[90] Both details possibly suggest that Liu Xiang adapted this narrative to make it better suit its context. As both *Lienüzhuan* and *Hou Hanshu* 後漢書 (History of the [Later] Han Dynasty) only have fragmentary parallels to Jiu Fan's remonstrance itself but different protagonists and different or no frame narratives,[91] it is even conceivable that Liu Xiang in this case might have composed large parts of the story, i.e., its framework, himself, in other words: might have "modified [the text] and thus created a new account" (*geng yi zao xin shi* 更以造新事), as he terms it in his memorial.[92]

In tales of direct remonstrance, censors explicitly raise the issue of outspokenness and thus readdress a central topic of the argumentative frame. In *Shuoyuan* 9.10 Duke Huan of Qi 齊桓公 (r. 685–643 BCE) wants to have cast a bell with an inscription commemorating his achievements and vaingloriously compares his own deeds to those of the mythical rulers Yao 堯 and Shun 舜. Bao Shu 鮑叔[93] counters him by referring to his own (as well as his lord's) straightforwardness: "As you have been straightforward, my lord, my reply will also be straightforward."[94] He then proceeds to enumerate his lord's wrongdoings, starting with his having usurped the throne of Qi by eliminating the legitimate heir to it.[95]

In all of these narratives, the remonstrant's audacity is rewarded, and he finally succeeds in persuading his lord to mend his ways.[96] In *Shuoyuan* 9.2, for example, Yan Zhuqu 顏燭趨 censures Duke Jing of Qi 齊景公 (r. 547–490 BCE) for traveling to the seaside and enjoying himself there for six months on end without fulfilling his official duties. When the duke, boiling with rage, picks up a battle axe to chop off his head, Yan Zhuqu even musters the courage to provoke him. Comparing Lord Jing to the two infamous tyrants Jie 桀 and Zhòu 紂,[97] he exclaims:

> Why does my lord not chop off my head? In the past King Jie killed Guan Longfeng, King Zhòu killed Prince Bigan. The worthiness of my lord does not match that of these two rulers, the competence of your subject does not match that of these two masters. Why does my lord not chop off my head? Is it

not acceptable to put me on a par with these two persons [i.e,. Guan Longfeng and Prince Bigan who fell victim to the wrath of Jie and Zhòu]?

君奚不斫也？昔者桀殺關龍逄，紂殺王子比干；君之賢，非此二主也，臣之材，非此二子也，君奚不斫？以臣參此二人者，不亦可乎？[98]

Adopting the strategy that attack is the best defense, Yan Zhuqu in the end induces his lord to drop his battle axe by putting him under pressure with being compared with two tyrants and thus acquiring a bad name.[99] In a similar fashion, Protector Shen 保申, who in *Shuoyuan* 9.12 criticizes King Wen of Jing (also known as Chu 楚) 荊文王 (r. 689–677 BCE) for indulging in his passion for hunting and women instead of attending to his duties, finally even succeeds in inducing his lord to accept corporal punishment.[100] A close parallel to this anecdote is classified as a direct remonstrance (*zhijian* 直諫) in the *Lüshi chunqiu* 呂氏春秋 (Spring and Autumn Annals of Mr. Lü).[101]

Quite obviously, these anecdotes not only serve as illustrative exempla related to the line of reasoning in the introduction but also add new aspects to Liu Xiang's argumentation, thus in fact giving another "turn of the screw" to it and transcending the argumentative frame of the chapter. For example, in section 9.9 we are given the formula for successful remonstrating, which is all the more convincing as it is put into the mouth of someone who is at the receiving end of a direct remonstrance.[102] King Zhuang of Chu 楚莊王 (r. 613–591 BCE), who has been criticized by a reclusive farmer called Zhuyu Ji 諸御己 for sacrificing his people to build a stepped terrace of enormous proportions, not only heeds the recluse's advice but also explains his reasons for doing so:

The people who tried to persuade me before—their persuasions did not serve to move my heart, and they imposed them on me haughtily. That's why all of them had to die. Now your persuasion does serve to move my heart, and you don't impose it on me haughtily, so I will heed your remonstrance.[103]

先日說寡人者，其說也不足以動寡人之心，又危加諸寡人，故皆至而死；今子之說，足以動寡人之心，又不危加諸寡人，故吾將用子之諫。[104]

Those who had tried before—and according to King Zhuang had remonstrated haughtily with him—were great ministers (*da chen* 大臣), 72 in number, all of them dead by the time when Zhuyu Ji, who had previously fled Chu because of the building of the terrace, decides to lay down his plough, return to Chu, and take up speaking.[105] At first glance, his remonstrance is as plain and simple as one would expect from a peasant, but in fact it is a rhetorical masterpiece. As such, I would suggest, it is much more than (in fact something quite different from) "the bold rejection of any tropic language and the staging of archaic directness."[106] Certainly, part of the fascination of this tale, as well as part of its protagonist's success lie in the yawning social gap between the remonstrating rustic and his royal audience. However, this is a narrative device that only affects the surface of the plot. The real spell of this story lies in the stark contrast between appearance as well as expectation of simplicity on the one hand and rhetorical craft on the other hand—and in the fact that the speaker succeeds in persuading his addressee and affecting him emotionally with his contrived artlessness, which in fact is an artifice.[107] Zhuyu Ji criticizes that the excessive royal demands are wearing down the people (note the hyperbole employed in the quotation below) but at the same time politely insinuates that this is commonly seen as a punishment for their previous crimes in order to allow the addressee of his remonstrance to save his face. Moreover, he implies that the commoners, including himself, are not only too scared but also too humble (and maybe too good-natured) to complain, and thus manages to remonstrate with his king by seemingly denying himself the right to remonstrate:

> My Lord is building a stepped terrace that extends to a thousand courses of stone and across a hundred *li* of land. The blood [paid] for the criminal offenses of the people is filling the streets but they have not yet dared to remonstrate. How should I dare to remonstrate?[108]
>
> 君築層臺, 延石千重, 延壤百里, 民之釁咎, 血成於通塗, 然且未敢諫也, 己何敢諫乎?[109]

He then adds a list of nine rulers who perished because they did not heed the remonstrances of their ministers.[110] In spite of the Zhuyu Ji's pretended self-restraint, which culminates in the rhetorical question "How should I dare to remonstrate?," this address is not exactly indirect, as it explicitly mentions the enormous death toll of the king's building project on his populace.¹¹¹ At the same time, however, the remonstrant follows the advice given in the chapter introduction. By using figures of speech such as rhetorical questions and hyperboles, he "adjusts his relaxing and urging" (*tiao qi huan ji* 調其緩急) flexibly. By feigning simplicity and pretending self-restraint, he "does what is appropriate in his situation" (*chu qi yi* 處其宜), i.e., behaves according to his humble station in front of his monarch and fulfills the expectations of his addressee. Thus, the anecdote is an illustration of persuasion as the art of expediency.

However, as argued above, the narrative also expands on the arguments of the introduction by having the royal addressee reveal the secret of conversational success in remonstrance, which according to King of Zhuang of Chu consists in (1) the ability to affect the recipient emotionally and (2) modesty. In another instance of argumentative amplification of what has been said in the introduction, the abovementioned anecdote about Bao Shu's censure in section 9.10 exemplifies—and thus *argues* according to the early Chinese understanding of anecdotes as rhetorical forms of induction—that the successful remonstrant, apart from being modest and applying fundamental communication tactics (3) uses certain shared cultural and political concepts to apply moral pressure on his opponent. In the remonstrance under review, Bao Shu uses Heaven's disapproval as a powerful lever for reform. He alludes to the theory of Heaven's Mandate (*tian ming* 天命) and threatens his lord indirectly with its withdrawal:

> [Although] Heaven is situated way up above, its hearing reaches way down below. Since I correct your mistaken words, Heaven will accordingly hear them.
>
> 天處甚高, 其聽甚下. 除君過言, 天且聞之.¹¹²

Finally, I would like to offer a few additional remarks and summarizing observations on Liu Xiang's techniques of adapting received narratives to the argumentative frame of *Shuoyuan* 9.

As regards the modification of "wandering anecdotes" (German: *Wanderanekdoten*), Du Jiaqi, whose study of the composition of both *Xinxu* and *Shuoyuan* is based on a thorough analysis of their numerous textual parallels in other sources, distinguishes four major types of intervention into a received text. These are (1) textual addition (*zengtian* 增添) at the beginning or end of a story, (2) abridgement (*shanjian* 刪減) of received narratives, (3) rewriting (*gaixie* 改寫) aiming at adapting wandering anecdotes to their new argumentative context or at making them accord with Classicist views, (4) reorganization (*chongzu* 重組) of fragments from different variants of a wandering anecdote into yet another version of it, and (5) synthesis (*zonghe* 綜合) of several or all of the abovementioned strategies of textual intervention.¹¹³

Many of these strategies seem to have been applied in chapter 9 of the *Shuoyuan*. As I have argued above, a close look at the narrative structure of section 9.4 reveals that Liu Xiang seems to have made textual additions by devising a frame narrative about a fake music master posing a riddle. Moreover, he might have given his protagonist a telling name and transposed him into an anachronistic setting in order to better adapt the story to its argumentative context. Apparently, he also made substantial abridgements, most of them aiming at radically reducing the plot structures to those elements that are indispensable in the context of "Rectifying Remonstrance."¹¹⁴ As a corollary, the narrative structure is simplified and reduced to its bare essentials. By cutting tales short in this way, Liu Xiang has often succeeded in producing versions that from the point of view of argument and contents seem to be more focused, from the narratological point of view more satisfying than their parallels in other early Chinese texts. The most intriguing example of an adaptation of a wandering anecdote is section 9.6, which contains a variant of the famous mantis parable illustrating the calamitous chain of predation. To match its argumentative context in the *Shuoyuan*, it is integrated into an anecdote that tells the story of a remonstrant named Shao Ruzi 少孺子, literally "Young Weakling":¹¹⁵

> The king of Wu wanted to attack Chu and told his [ministers on the] left and right, "Whosoever dares to remonstrate will die." Among the retainers there was a certain Shao Ruzi. He wanted to remonstrate with the king but did not dare to and therefore wandered about in the back garden, carrying pellets in his breast pocket and holding a pellet bow in his hands, soaking his clothes with dew. This happened on three mornings in a row. The king of Wu said, "Come, sir, why do you soak your clothes with dew like this?" He replied: "In the garden there is a tree. / In it there was a cicada. / He was sitting high up [there], chirping mournfully and drinking dew. / He did not know that there was a mantis behind him. / The mantis, curving his body and bending his forelegs,¹¹⁶ wanted to catch the cicada, / But he did not know that there was a siskin¹¹⁷ beside him. /

The siskin, stretching the neck, wanted to peck at the mantis, / But he did not know that there were pellet bow and pellet beneath him.[118] These three were all occupied with wanting to gain the advantage before them, but they did not notice that there was serious trouble [waiting] behind them." The king said, "Excellent!" Then he withdrew his army.

吳王欲伐荊，告其左右曰：「敢有諫者死．」舍人有少孺子者，欲諫不敢，則懷丸操彈，遊於後園，露沾其衣，如是者三旦．吳王曰：「子來，何苦沾衣如此．」對曰：「園中有樹，其上有蟬，蟬高居悲鳴飲露，不知螳螂在其後也；螳螂委身曲附欲取蟬，而不知黃雀在其傍也；黃雀延頸欲啄螳螂，而不知彈丸在其下也；此三者，皆務欲得其前利，而不顧其後之有患也．」吳王曰：「善哉．」乃罷其兵．[119]

As Maggie Bickford has pointed out, the point here is not the preying on others in itself, i.e., the implication of all living beings in the calamity of "serial predation," as in the variant transmitted in chapter 20 of the *Zhuangzi* 莊子 (Master Zhuang), "but rather the consequences of the ruler's fixation on near-term advantage blinding him to greater threats beyond."[120] In this case, the differences between the textual variants are particularly revealing, especially if we compare the version in *Shuoyuan* 9.6 to its closest parallel in the *Hanshi waizhuan*.[121] First of all, Liu Xiang added a highly attractive frame narrative to the parable in order to adapt it to the context of remonstrance, in particular to illustrate the technique of indirect remonstrance.[122] When doing this, he ingeniously turned a protagonist of the parable, namely the boy shooting the siskin with his pellet bow, into a remonstrant, who criticizes his ruler's military policy by staging a dumb show and feigning to shoot the siskin in the back garden of the royal palace with his pellet bow. Quite consequentially, this character is given the telling name Shao Ruzi, "Young Weakling," and is addressed as *zi* 子 (sir) by the king. The little rascal of the parable, who is referred to as an unnamed *tongzi* 童子 (boy or brat) in the *Hanshi waizhuan* version of this tale,[123] has been transformed into a remonstrating scholar-official, who even gives his central piece of advice in rhymed prose to highlight the negative consequences of focusing merely on short-term benefit. Only his telling name provides a clue pointing to the origin of this character, whom the text ranks among the king's *sheren* 舍人 (officials, retainers, servants).

Conclusion

It is inconceivable that the composition of *Shuoyuan* 9 and the employment of the abovementioned literary and rhetorical devices are the result of mere chance, i.e., that Liu Xiang by accident stumbled across textual units that perfectly suited his design. It is likewise inconceivable that prefabricated argumentative modules were at his disposal, which he only had to allocate to chapters and place at the beginning and end of them. As Xu Fuguan, Zuo Songchao, Du Jiaqi, and Xie Mingren have convincingly shown, not only the chapter "Rectifying Remonstrance" but the entire *Shuoyuan* was composed in the fashion analyzed above. Moreover, it could be demonstrated that Liu Xiang's memorial on the occasion of submitting the text to the throne is not only not corrupt but contains an implicit claim to individual authorship. All of which leads to the following conclusions:

The *Shuoyuan* was not only "arranged" or "compiled" but *composed* by Liu Xiang, who may even have conceived of himself as the author of the text.

In all probability, he himself was responsible for writing the argumentative introductions to the chapters as well as other ratiocinative textual units, which are spread across the whole of the *Shuoyuan* and sometimes even conclude individual chapters, thus contributing to an argumentative frame bracketing the narratives in between, as is the case in "Rectifying Remonstrance."

These anecdotes were conceived of as illustrative arguments. They served as exempla, which substantiated and verified the "propositions" (*jing*) that preceded them. Therefore they were subsumed under the generic term of "explanations" (*shuo*).

Hence follows that the transliteration of the title should be *Shuoyuan*, "Garden of Illustrative Examples" rather than *Shuiyuan*, "Garden of Persuasions." As the author conceived of arguments in view of their contents and not of their application, the transliteration *Shuiyuan* appears to be misleading. Persuasions (*shui*) are only of topical interest within a small fraction of textual units, most of them part of chapters 9 and 11 of the text.

As for chapter 9, its sophisticated design primarily rests on an argumentative frame, which serves to bracket 23 anecdotes. Moreover, the author has employed transphrastic text-structuring devices like thematic or associative links to organize his text, for example the recurrent topic of outspokenness or the repeated intertextual reference to Cao Ji as the incarnation of the proprietous remonstrant.

Most of the 23 anecdotes have parallels in other early Chinese texts. Sample analyses indicate that Liu Xiang modified wandering anecdotes in order to adapt them to his argumentative frame. This finding is perfectly in line with his memorial, which mentions that he "modified [the text] and thus created new accounts [numbering] more than one hundred thousand words."

When revising received anecdotes, he abridged and rewrote them and made textual additions, i.e., furnished them with new frame narratives. Moreover, he invented telling names for his protagonists, transposed them into new, sometimes anachronistic settings, and emphasized their central pieces of advice by employing rhyme. All of these revisions serve the purpose of bringing plot structures and contents in line with his argument concerning the "Rectification of Remonstrance."

On closer examination, Liu Xiang does not argue in favor of indirect remonstrance. Instead he proposes that it is important to be flexible and adapt to the respective circumstances and power constellations to be both successful *and* survive. Thus he recommends to base one's actions on political expediency and to be able to cover the full range of remonstrance, including direct remonstrance, which he actually seems to favor.

To conclude, I would like to add a final remark on the argumentative functions of anecdotes and their implications for Liu Xiang's "author functions."[124] The above findings corroborate Rolf Trauzettel's observation that exempla form the core of many early Chinese philosophical texts and to a large extent replace abstract analysis.[125] In the *Shuoyuan*, however, they are more than mere décor that is experimentally assembled to visualize matters of certainty.[126] Apart from illustrating the propositions put forward at the beginning and end of the chapter, the anecdotes in *Shuoyuan* 9 also amplify and enhance the argumentation of the introduction by addressing important aspects of communicative strategy and tactics, namely modesty, the ability to affect the recipient emotionally, and the use of shared cultural and political concepts to apply moral pressure on the addressee of the remonstrance, for example by threatening him with conferring a bad posthumous name to him. As his biography in the *Hanshu* attests, Liu Xiang was not only fully aware of the importance of these strategies but also applied them in his own remonstrances.[127] Once again, we have to conclude that he was responsible for composing the *Shuoyuan* in its entirety, including the received narratives, which he adapted not only to illustrate his propositions but also to develop these into more complex and far-reaching insights into fundamental aspects of human nature and their implications for political culture. He did so with a creative passion that still resonates to this day. Writing at a time when the notion of individual authorship was first conceived and developed by scholars like Sima Qian 司馬遷 (145–86 BCE), Yang Xiong 揚雄 (53 BCE–18 CE), and Wang Chong 王充 (27–100 CE),[128] Liu Xiang ought to be acknowledged not only as compiler but as the creator of the *Shuoyuan*, i.e., as its author in Bonaventura's above-given sense of the term *auctor*.

Notes

1. It is my great pleasure to dedicate the present paper to Christoph Harbsmeier, fellow "connoisseur of accounts" and pioneer of the study of authorial presence in pre-Buddhist Chinese texts, on the occasion of his seventieth birthday. I would like to thank Newell Ann Van Auken, Paul van Els, Sarah A. Queen, and the anonymous reviewers for their helpful comments to earlier versions of the paper.

2. Henry Fielding, *Joseph Andrews*, ed. R. F. Brissenden (Harmondsworth, UK: Penguin, [1742] 1977), 39.

3. For example, see Hans Peter Neureuter, "Zur Theorie der Anekdote," *Jahrbuch des Freien Deutschen Hochstifts* (1973): 458–480, and Jürgen Hein, "Die Anekdote," in *Formen der Literatur: in Einzeldarstellungen*, ed. Otto Knörrich (Stuttgart: Kröner, [1981] 1991), 14–20. Compare Ulrich Unger, *Abriß der Literatur des chinesischen Altertums: Prodesse aut delectare?* (Münster: Hao-ku, 2005), 109–133, 138, for early Chinese anecdotal literature.

4. See section three below and Christian Schwermann, "Gattungsdynamik in der traditionellen chinesischen Literatur: Von der 'Erläuterung' (*shuō*) zur 'Erzählung' (*xiǎoshuō*)," in *Was sind Genres? Nicht-abendländische Kategorisierungen von Gattungen*, ed. Stephan Conermann and Amr El-Hawary, Studien des Bonner Zentrums für Transkulturelle Narratologie 1 (Berlin: EB-Verlag, 2011), 67–68; compare Christoph Harbsmeier, *Language and Logic in Traditional China*, vol. 7, part 1 of *Science and Civilisation in China*, ed. Joseph Needham (Cambridge: Cambridge University Press, 1998), 267–68, and Unger, *Abriß der Literatur des chinesischen Altertums*, 115. For the early history of the genre of "inferior explanations" (*xiaoshuo* 小說), which was derived from this mode of writing, see Schwermann, "Gattungsdynamik in der traditionellen chinesischen Literatur." Old Chinese reconstructions here and in the following are according to Axel Schuessler, *Minimal Old Chinese and Later Han Chinese: A Companion to* Grammata Serica Recensa (Honolulu: University of Hawai'i Press, 2009), if not otherwise specified.

5. For exempla and their use in medieval European literature see Ernst Robert Curtius, *Europäische Literatur und lateinisches Mittelalter* (Bern and München: Francke, [1949] 1973), 67–70. Compare Rolf Trauzettel, "Stellenwert und Funktion des Beispiels in antik-chinesischen philosophischen Texten," in *Form und Gehalt in*

Texten der griechischen und chinesischen Philosophie. Akten der 11. Tagung der Karl und Gertrud Abel-Stiftung vom 18.–19. Juli 2008 an der Universität Trier, ed. Karl-Heinz Pohl and Georg Wöhrle, Philosophie der Antike 29 (Stuttgart: Franz Steiner Verlag, 2011), 77–89, for exempla in ancient Chinese literature.

6. See section three below and Schwermann, "Gattungsdynamik in der traditionellen chinesischen Literatur," 67–68; compare Unger, *Abriß der Literatur des chinesischen Altertums*, 115–16.

7. In the following, I will refer to the text as established by Xiang Zonglu 向宗魯 (1895–1941) in his *Shuoyuan jiaozheng* 說苑校證 (Beijing: Zhonghua shuju, 1987). For Xiang Zonglu and his work on the *Shuoyuan jiaozheng*, which was compiled between 1922 and 1931 but only published more than half a century later, see the introduction by Qu Shouyuan 屈守元, in *Shuoyuan jiaozheng*, 1–11. David Schaberg, "Playing at Critique: Indirect Remonstrance and the Formation of *Shi* Identity," in *Text and Ritual in Early China*, ed. Martin Kern (Seattle and London: University of Washington Press, 2005), 201, interprets the chapter title "Zhengjian" as referring to "direct remonstrance." However, this does not seem to be justified in view of the contents of the chapter; see part four below. For a discussion of the reading of the character 苑 in the title of the collection see note 35 below.

8. I.e., he did not compose the *Shuoyuan* by merely collecting and assembling older materials from various sources but also adapted and rewrote received textual units or even composed original ones himself in order to create an entirely new work that expressed his own political ideas. Thus, he embodies Bonaventura's (1221–1274) authorial mode of the "auctor," as distinguished from "scriptor," "compilator" and "commentator," i.e., of "someone who combines received textual materials and self-composed texts, while treating the received material as secondary;" see Raji C. Steineck and Christian Schwermann, "Introduction," in *That Wonderful Composite Called Author: Authorship in East Asian Literatures from the Beginnings to the Seventeenth Century*, eds. Christian Schwermann and Raji C. Steineck, East Asian Comparative Literature and Culture 4 (Leiden and Boston: Brill, 2014), 7; compare *S. Bonaventurae opera omnia*, ed. Adolphe C. Peltier, vol. 1 (Paris: Vivès, 1864), 20. In the following I refer to Liu Xiang as an author in Bonaventura's sense of the term *auctor* in order to establish that he was a "creator" and not just a "transmitter."

9. For the date see note 33 below.

10. For a discussion of how to transliterate the first character of the title see section three below. For an alternative reading of the title's second character as as a loan for *yun* 蘊, "collection," see note 35 below.

11. The bibliographical treatise of the *Suishu* 隋書, 6 vols. (Beijing: Zhonghua shuju, 1973), *juan* 卷 34, 997, records the *Shuoyuan* as a work in 20 scrolls (*juan* 卷) compiled (*zhuan* 撰) by Liu Xiang. According to Zeng Gong's 曾鞏 (1019–1083) preface to the *Shuoyuan* (*Shuoyuan jiaozheng*, 1–2), by the Northern Song period the work was lost except for five chapters (*pian* 篇) preserved in the imperial library. Chao Gongwu 晁公武 (d. 1171) reports in his *Junzhai dushu zhi* 郡齋讀

書志 that Zeng Gong restored the text by using 15 *pian* which he had obtained from other scholars. According to the same source, however, he formed *pian* no. 20 by dividing *pian* no. 19 into two parts and thus in fact only succeeded to reestablish 19 *pian*; see *Junzhai dushu zhi* 郡齋讀書志, 6 vols., Shumu xubian 書目續編 (Taipei: Guangwen shuju, 1967), *juan* 3 *shang* 上, vol. 3, 668 / *juan* 10, 15b. The last *pian* is said to have later been taken from an intact Korean text. For the textual history, see Xie Mingren 謝明仁, *Liu Xiang* Shuoyuan *yanjiu* 劉向《說苑》研究 (Lanzhou: Lanzhou daxue chubanshe, 2000), 36–75, and David R. Knechtges, "*Shuo yüan* 說苑," in *Early Chinese Texts: A Bibliographical Guide*, ed. Michael Loewe, Early China Special Monograph Series 2 (Berkeley: The Society for the Study of Early China and The Institute of East Asian Studies, University of California, 1993), 444. The *Shuoyuan* was first ascribed to Liu Xiang by Ban Gu 班固 (32–92 CE) in *Hanshu* 漢書 (History of the [Former] Han Dynasty), 12 vols. (Beijing: Zhonghua shuju, 1959), *juan* 30, 1727, and *juan* 36, 1958. Whereas Ban Gu's note in the bibliographical treatise refers to him as having arranged (*xu* 序) the text, his biography in *Hanshu*, chapter 36, says that he wrote (*zhu* 著) it.

12. See Luo Genze 羅根澤, "*Xinxu, Shuoyuan, Lienüzhuan* bu zuo shi yu Liu Xiang kao"《新序》,《說苑》,《列女傳》不作始於劉向考, *Tushuguanxue jikan* 圖書館學季刊 4, no. 1 (1930): 45–47, reprinted in *Gushibian* 古史辨, ed. Gu Jiegang 顧頡剛, 7 vols. (Hong Kong: Taiping shuju, 1962–1963), vol. 4, 227–29. Actually, the first scholar to deny Liu Xiang's authorship was Shen Qinhan 沈欽韓 (1775–1832), who, basing himself on the memorial of the text's official presentation to the throne, argued that Liu did not create the *Shuoyuan* but merely revised an older edition of it. See his *Hanshu shuzheng* 漢書疏證 as quoted by Wang Xianqian 王先謙 (1842–1918) in his *Hanshu buzhu* 漢書補注, 2 vols. (Beijing: Zhonghua shuju, 1983), *juan* 36, 24a / vol. 2, 963. For the first expression of the idea that Liu Xiang merely collected older materials see *Lunheng jiaoshi* 論衡校釋, ed. Huang Hui 黃暉, 4 vols. (Beijing: Zhonghua shuju, 1990), vol. 2, 607–08.

13. See Xu Fuguan 徐復觀, "Liu Xiang *Xinxu, Shuoyuan* de yanjiu" 劉向《新序》,《說苑》的研究, *Dalu zazhi* 大陸雜誌 55.2 (1977), 51–74, Xie, *Liu Xiang* Shuoyuan *yanjiu*, and Du Jiaqi 杜家祁, *Liu Xiang bianxie* Xinxu, Shuoyuan *yanjiu* 劉向編寫《新序》,《說苑》研究 (PhD Diss., Chinese University of Hong Kong, 1999). The latter two studies seem to have gone largely unnoticed by academia, perhaps due to its current preoccupation with excavated manuscripts. Whereas the value of Xie Mingren's book primarily rests with its substantial account of the formation of the *Shuoyuan*, its textual history and relationship with the *Xinxu* 新序, Du Jiaqi's study stands out due to its detailed analysis of the structure of both *Shuoyuan* and *Xinxu* and of their textual parallels in other early Chinese texts, including the bamboo manuscript "Rujiazhe yan" 儒家者言 (Words of the Ru Lineage) unearthed 1973 in Dingzhou 定州, Hebei 河北 province, in a Han dynasty tomb, which is dated to the mid-first century BCE. (For an account of the discovery see Paul van Els, "Dingzhou: The Story of an Unfortunate Tomb,"

Asiatische Studien/Études asiatiques 63 (2009): 909–41.) Du's study is influenced by Zuo Songchao's 左松超 articles on the composition of the *Shuoyuan* and its relation to the "Rujiazhe yan;" see Zuo Songchao 左松超, "Lun Liu Xiang bianzhuan *Shuoyuan*" 論劉向編撰《說苑》, *Xianggang Jinhui Xueyuan xuebao* 香港浸會學院學報 13 (1986): 51–56; and Zuo Songchao 左松超, "Lun 'Rujiazhe yan' ji qi yu *Shuoyuan* de guanxi" 論《儒家者言》及其與《說苑》的關係, *Xianggang Jinhui Xueyuan Zhongwen xi jikan* 香港浸會學院中文系集刊 1992, 1–33. The contents of the *Shuoyuan*, especially its Classicist background and political intentions, are analyzed by Ikeda Shūzō 池田秀三, "Ryū Kō no gakumon to shisō" 劉向の學問と思想, *Tōhōgaku hō* 東方學報 50 (1978): 109–90; and Xu Sufei 許素菲, Shuoyuan *tanwei* 《說苑》探微 (Taipei: Taibai shushi, 1989).

14. For a different view on the *Lienüzhuan* see Bret Hinsch, "The Composition of *Lienüzhuan*: Was Liu Xiang the Author or Editor?," *Asia Major*, Third Series 20 no. 1 (2007): 21, who finds evidence "that Liu Xiang combined editorial work with original writing when he put together *Lienüzhuan*. [. . .] By writing or heavily rewriting most of the stories in *Lienüzhuan*, he was able to turn out a series of pointed ideological essays in narrative form."

15. See Yan Lingfeng 嚴靈峯, "Liu Xiang '*Shuoyuan* xu lu' yanjiu" 劉向《說苑敍錄》研究, *Dalu zazhi* 大陸雜誌 56 no. 6 (1978): 287–92. According to David R. Knechtges, "*Shuo yüan*," 444, "[. . .], the *Shuo yüan* is basically a collection which was edited rather than composed by Liu Hsiang, [. . .]." Compare Martin Kern, "Die Anfänge der chinesischen Literatur," in *Chinesische Literaturgeschichte*, ed. Reinhard Emmerich (Stuttgart and Weimar: J. B. Metzler 2004), 77: "Hinter keiner dieser Sammlungen [i.e., the *Zhanguoce, Xinxu, Shuoyuan*, and *Lienüzhuan*] steht Liu Xiang als Autor; seine Rolle als Kompilator ergibt sich aus seiner offiziellen Bestallung als kaiserlicher Bibliothekar und Kollationator der alten Texte, d.h. als Leiter einer Kommission, der die Sammlung und Ordnung der bis dahin chaotischen schriftlichen Tradition historischer, philosophischer, literarischer und technischer Literatur oblag." In his analysis of *Shuoyuan*, chapter 11: "Shanshui" 善說 (Skilled at Persuasion), Ulrich Unger, "Der gute Redner: *Shuoh-yüan* 11," in *Han-Zeit: Festschrift für Hans Stumpfeldt aus Anlaß seines 65. Geburtstages*, eds. Michael Friedrich et al., Lun Wen: Studien zur Geistesgeschichte und Literatur in China 8 (Wiesbaden: Harrassowitz, 2006), 229, comes to the following conclusion concerning the structure of the whole text: "Eine gezielte Strukturierung der Beispielsammlung ist hier—und auch sonst—kaum anzunehmen. Vielmehr folgt die Anordnung der Stücke eher dem Assoziationsprinzip, welches auch bei manch anderen älteren Texten zu beobachten ist, wie etwa beim *Lun-yü*."

16. See William G. Boltz, "The Composite Nature of Early Chinese Texts," in *Text and Ritual in Early China*, ed. Martin Kern (Seattle and London: University of Washington Press, 2005), 59. Compare Du, *Liu Xiang bianxie* Xinxu, Shuoyuan *yanjiu*, 327–28. See also Matthias L. Richter, *The Embodied Text: Establishing Textual Identity in Early Chinese Manuscripts*, Studies in the History of Chinese Texts

3 (Leiden: Brill, 2013), who argues that even excavated texts were intentionally modified to suit new ideas and meanings and that not all changes in manuscripts are unintentional or due to corruption.

17. As I see it, the argumentative functions of quotations in early Chinese texts are at least as important as their authority function; see Christian Schwermann, "Rhetorical Functions of Quotations in Late Pre-Imperial and Early Imperial Memorials on Questions of Civilian-Military Leadership," *Asiatische Studien / Études asiatiques* 68 no. 4 (2014): 1069–1114. And as quotations are inevitably torn out of their original contexts and as the original meaning of the quoted passages is usually contaminated by the new context (i.e., as citations in general have to span the gap between quoting and quoted text), it does not seem helpful to set up a strict dichotomy between quotations of authority and "subversive" quotations, as Jean Levi, "Quelques exemples de détournement subversif de la citation dans la littérature classique chinoise," *Extrême-Orient, Extrême-Occident* 17 (1995): 41–65, has done. The borrowing text may quote a prestigious text to provide authority to its argument and at the same time subvert the original meaning of the quoted passage; see below. Moreover, early imperial texts often contain alleged quotations, which in fact are not part of the quoted text as received. Some of these may well be genuine quotations taken from lost repertoires, others seem to be "pseudo-quotations" invented for the sake of lending force to an argument and thus can possibly be interpreted as specimens of so-called imputed words (*yuyan* 寓言), a rhetorical device described in the *Zhuangzi* 莊子 chapter of the same title. Mark Edward Lewis, *Writing and Authority in Early China* (Albany, NY: State University of New York Press, 1999), 90, argues that "the enunciatory strategy of imputing words to multiple authorities avoids the weakness of a single author. By placing itself in multiple standpoints and proving the case from each of them, the argument acquires persuasive force and, in theory, escapes from the limits of an individual viewpoint."

18. For possible examples in received literature, amongst them an inscription-style text in chapter 10 of the *Shuoyuan*, see Mark Csikszentmihalyi, "Reimagining the Yellow Emperor's Four Faces," in *Text and Ritual in Early China*, ed. Martin Kern (Seattle and London: University of Washington Press, 2005), 226–48.

19. Therefore, Ban Gu's characterization of Liu Xiang's literary activities as both *xu* and *zhu* is not inconsistent at all: the two terms were near synonyms at this time. Accordingly, Ban Gu also refers to Yang Xiong's 揚雄 (53 BCE–18 CE) composition of the *Fayan* 法言 (Exemplary Sayings) and the *Taixuan* 太玄 (Supreme Mystery) as *xu* (*Hanshu*, *juan* 30, 1727). Obviously, it is not acceptable to cite *Hanshu*, *juan* 30, 1727, as evidence that Liu Xiang merely compiled the *Shuoyuan*, as Luo, "*Xinxu*, *Shuoyuan*, *Lienüzhuan* bu zuo shi yu Liu Xiang kao," did; compare Xu Fuguan, "Liu Xiang *Xinxu*, *Shuoyuan* de yanjiu," 56.

20. See Marcel Granet, *Danses et légendes de la Chine ancienne* (Paris: Librairie Félix Alcan, 1926), 34–35.

21. See Lewis, *Writing and Authority in Early China*, 54–56. Besides, the predominance of the injunction "to transmit but not to innovate" (*shu er bu zuo* 述而不作, *Lunyu* 論語 7.1) was conducive to the development of an aesthetic ideal of indirectness. For collage-style composition in early Chinese literature see Christian Schwermann, "Collage-Technik als Kompositionsprinzip klassischer chinesischer Prosa: Der Aufbau des Kapitels 'Tāng wèn' (Die Fragen des Tāng) im *Liè zǐ*," in *Komposition und Konnotation—Figuren der Kunstprosa im Alten China*, ed. Wolfgang Behr and Joachim Gentz, *Bochumer Jahrbuch zur Ostasienforschung* 29 (2005): 125–57.

22. See Lewis, *Writing and Authority in Early China*, 62–63, for the origin of this paradigm shift in late Warring States texts.

23. Compare Lewis, *Writing and Authority in Early China*, 63: "In Chinese philosophy 'authorship' emerged in the space vacated by the shift of authority to the 'classic.'" For collective authorship in pre-imperial China and the emergence of individual authorship in early imperial China see Christian Schwermann, "Composite Authorship in Western Zhōu Bronze Inscriptions: The Case of the 'Tiānwáng guì' 天亡簋 Inscription," in *That Wonderful Composite Called Author: Authorship in East Asian Literatures from the Beginnings to the Seventeenth Century*, eds. Christian Schwermann and Raji C. Steineck, East Asian Comparative Literature and Culture 4 (Leiden: Brill, 2014), 30–57.

24. See Lewis, *Writing and Authority in Early China*, 57.

25. See Schwermann, "Rhetorical Functions of Quotations," for argumentative and structural functions of quotations in early imperial memorials. In his influential *Semiotics of Poetry*, Michael Riffaterre (1924–2006) refers to this deeper meaning as "significance," characterizes it as the formal and semantic unity of a poem, which transcends the plane of mimesis and is indicated by "indices of indirection" such as titles or references to other texts; see Michael Riffaterre, *Semiotics of Poetry* (Bloomington, IN, and London: Indiana University Press, 1978), 1–22. He comes to the conclusions that "the poem carries meaning only by referring from text to text" (*Semiotics of Poetry*, 150) and that "the reader's manufacture of meaning is thus not so much a progress through the poem and a half-random accretion of verbal associations, as it is a seesaw scanning of the text, compelled by the very duality of the signs—ungrammatical as mimesis, grammatical within the significance network" (*Semiotics of Poetry*, 166). Except for its metaphysical underpinnings, this concept of "significance" seems to be well-suited both for the analysis of the textual fabric of early Chinese prose with its "weft-threads" of intertextual references and for the description of the circular process of manufacturing meaning involved in reading nonlinear collage texts. For the nonlinearity of early Chinese texts and for text-structure related reading strategies see Schwermann, "Collage-Technik als Kompositionsprinzip klassischer chinesischer Prosa."

26. The existing translations and paraphrases of, as well as commentaries on, this text deviate in crucial points, often seem to misrepresent important details and are

marred by unnecessary emendations. For example, compare the Japanese translation by Ikeda, "Ryū Kō no gakumon to shisō," 112, and the German translation by Dagmar Zißler-Gürtler, *Nicht erzählte Welt noch Welterklärung: Der Begriff "Hsiao-shuo"* 小説 *in der Han-Zeit*, Münstersche Sinologische Mitteilungen 3 (Bad Honnef: Bock und Herchen, 1994), 130; see also the paraphrase by Knechtges, "*Shuo yüan*," 443, and the partial translations by Jens Østergård Petersen, "Which Books *Did* the First Emperor of Ch'in Burn? On the Meaning of *Pai Chia* in Early Chinese Sources," *Monumenta Serica* 43 (1995): 20, and Donald Holzman, "Liu Xiang's Attitude towards Fiction," *Recarving the Dragon: Understanding Chinese Poetics*, ed. Olga Lomová, Studia Orientalia Pragensia 23 (Prague: Karolinum, 2003), 79. The most extensive modifications of the text are proposed by Yan, "Liu Xiang '*Shuoyuan* xu lu' yanjiu," 290, who liberally revises the text and even suggests a rearrangement of sentences because he thinks it to be largely corrupt. A useful, but not exhaustive, compilation of earlier glosses on the text may be found in Du, *Liu Xiang bianxie* Xinxu, Shuoyuan *yanjiu*, 19–22.

27. One might be inclined to follow the suggestion of Ikeda, "Ryū Kō no gakumon to shisō," 181n.10, and read *wu* 誣, "to lie, to deceive, to cheat" as a misspelling of *jin* 謹, "carefully." As *wu* does not make any sense here, the text would appear at first glance to be corrupted. Moreover, this emendation seems to be corroborated by the fact that in the memorials on both *Yanzi chunqiu* 晏子春秋 and *Liezi* 列子 the verb *jiaochou* 校讎, "to collate," is also qualified by the adverb *jin*. However, in both cases *jin* is not directly collocated with *jiaochou* as 誣 is with 校讎 in the memorial on the *Shuoyuan*. Instead, we find the following formula: "Together with [Fu] Can, Commandant of Changshe, I have carefully collated [them, i.e., the chapters of the text]." 臣向謹與長社尉臣參校讎. See *Quan shanggu Sandai Qin Han Sanguo Liuchao wen* 全上古三代秦漢三國六朝文, ed. Yan Kejun 嚴可均, 9 vols., Zhongguo xueshu mingzhu 中國學術名著 edition (Taipei: Shijie shuju, 1963), vol. 1: "Quan Han wen" 全漢文, *juan* 36, 4a, 6b. For Fu Can 富參 see Piet van der Loon, "On the Transmission of the Guan-tzǔ," *T'oung Pao* 41 (1952): 361n.2, and Michael Loewe, *A Biographical Dictionary of the Qin, Former Han and Xin Periods (221 BC–AD 24)*, vol. 16 of Handbuch der Orientalistik: Section 4, China (Leiden: Brill, 2000), 105; his surname Fu 富 is mentioned in the memorial on *Guanzi* 管子, see *Quan shanggu Sandai Qin Han Sanguo Liuchao wen*, vol. 1, *juan* 36, 3a. Therefore I follow Xu Fuguan, "Liu Xiang Xinxu, Shuoyuan de yanjiu," 73n.16, who, basing himself on a gloss in Lu Wenchao's 盧文弨 (1717–1796) *Shuoyuan jiaozheng* 說苑校正, proposes to read 誣, OC *ma, as a loan for *wu* 憮, OC *maʔ, hmâ (compare Gao Heng 高亨, *Gu zi tongjia huidian* 古字通假會典 [Ji'nan: Qi-Lu shushe, 1989], 853), in the sense "completely, equally, together," i.e., to interpret the verbal phrase *wu jiaochou* 誣〔憮〕校讎 as "to completely collate"; see also Yan, "Liu Xiang '*Shuoyuan* xu lu' yanjiu," 287.

28. The terms *jiao* 校 and *jiaochou* 校讎, which both occur in this sentence, are synonyms. Accordingly, I translate them—slightly differently—as "to collate" and "to put together (for comparison)," respectively.

29. For a comparable use of *geng* 更 see *Shiji* 史記 (Records of the Historian), 10 vols. (Beijing: Zhonghua shuju, 1959), *juan* 87, 2561: 斯更以其實對, 輒使人復榜之. Compare *Ssu-ma Ch'ien: The Grand Scribe's Records*, ed. William H. Nienhauser, vol. 7: *The Memoirs of Pre-Han China*, trans. Tsai-fa Cheng, Zongli Lu, William H. Nienhauser, and Robert Reynolds (Bloomington and Indianapolis, IN: Indiana University Press, 1994), 355: "Whenever [Li] Ssu changed his confession to state the truth, the men who had been sent beat him again."

30. The use of the term *zao* 造, "to create, to compose, to draw up," in this sentence is exceptional and implies a claim to individual authorship; compare for example *Shiji*, *juan* 84, 2481, where the context clearly indicates that the composition of a law code is conceived of as an act of individual authorship and its product the intellectual property of its author: 上官大夫與之同列, 爭寵而心害其能. 懷王使屈原造為憲令, 屈平屬草稿未定. 上官大夫見而欲奪之, 屈平不與 [. . .]. Compare *Ssu-ma Ch'ien: The Grand Scribe's Records*, ed. William H. Nienhauser, vol. 7: *The Memoirs of Pre-Han China*, 295: "The Grand Master Shang-kuan held the same rank as he [i.e., Qu Yuan]. He strove for favor and was secretly envious of his abilities. King Huai had Ch'ü Yüan draw up laws; he was writing a draft, but it was not finished. The Grand Master Shang-kuan saw it and wanted to take it. Ch'ü P'ing did not give [it to him]." See also Schwermann, "Composite Authorship in Western Zhōu Bronze Inscriptions," 32.

31. According to Du Jiaqi's count (Du, *Liu Xiang bianxie* Xinxu, Shuoyuan *yanjiu*, 49), the received *Shuoyuan* has 101,984 characters. Therefore, Liu Xiang's statement that he "modified [the text] and thus created new accounts [numbering] more than one hundred thousand words" (*geng yi zao xin shi wan yan yi shang* 更以造新事十萬言以上) has to be understood as referring to the whole of the *Shuoyuan*, not only to a fraction that he composed himself to supplement received parts of the text, as Luo, "*Xinxu, Shuoyuan, Lienüzhuan* bu zuo shi yu Liu Xiang kao," 46, apparently believed.

32. Enno Giele, *Imperial Decision-Making and Communication in Early China. A Study of Cai Yong's Duduan*, Opera Sinologica 20 (Wiesbaden: Harrassowitz, 2006), 92–94, shows that *mei si* 昧死 is an abbreviation for the formula *mei fan sizui* 昧犯死罪, "to risk committing a crime that merits the death penalty."

33. See *Quan shanggu Sandai Qin Han Sanguo Liuchao wen*, vol. 1, *juan* 37, 8b–9a, punctuation is mine. Compare *Qilüe bielu yiwen. Qilüe yiwen* 七略別錄佚文 • 七略佚文, ed. Yao Zhenzong 姚振宗 (Shanghai: Shanghai guji chubanshe, 2008), 47, which adds the date of the presentation of the text to the throne as transmitted in Chao Gongwu's *Junzhai dushu zhi*: 《說苑》鴻嘉四年三月己亥上. "Submitted to the Throne on the 22nd of April 17 BCE."

34. The term *shi* 事, here translated as "historical account," refers both to historical events and to narratives about these, i.e., to *historia ipsa* and *narratio historica*, and also occurs twice in Liu Xiang's memorial on the *Zhanguoce* 戰國策, see *Quan shanggu Sandai Qin Han Sanguo Liuchao wen*, vol. 1, *juan* 37, 1a, compare

Qilüe bielu yiwen, 32. It is related to the genre designation *shiyu* 事語, "sayings about historical events," i.e., "historical narratives," which is likewise mentioned in the memorial on the *Zhanguoce* as an alternative title of this collection; see *Quan shanggu Sandai Qin Han Sanguo Liuchao wen*, vol. 1, *juan* 37, 1a, compare *Qilüe bielu yiwen*, 32. Compare Xu Jianwei 徐健委, Shuoyuan *yanjiu* 《說苑》研究 (Beijing: Beijing daxue chubanshe, 2011), 237–72, who defines *shi* as literary units, i.e., as "stories belonging to the genre of historical narratives" (*shiyu lei gushi* 事語類故事). For another early use of the generic terms *shi*, "account," and *gu shi* 故事, "old accounts," see *Shiji*, *juan* 126, 3203: "Mr Chu [i.e., Chu Shaosun, 104?–30? BCE] says: 'Due to my mastery of the Classics, I was so lucky as to be given the opportunity to become Court Gentleman and liked to recite the transmitted sayings of the outer masters. I took the liberty not to content myself [with that] and moreover composed six sections of old accounts and sayings of jesters and tied them together on the left [i.e., below]. They can thus be perused to arouse ideas and thus be presented to connoisseurs of accounts in later generations to be recited by them in order to delight their hearts and stun their ears. I appended them to the above three sections of His Honour the Grand Scribe" (褚先生曰: 臣幸得以經術為郎, 而好讀外家傳語. 竊不遜讓, 復作故事滑稽之語六章, 編之於左. 可以覽觀揚意, 以示後世好事者讀之, 以游心駭耳, 以附益上方太史公之三章). This passage not only illustrates that the metonymic semantic change from "historical event" to "account (of that event)," which led to the establishment of *shi* as a generic literary term, had taken place as early as by the first century BCE when Liu Xiang composed his reports, but is also perfectly in line with the uses of *shi* and *shiyu* in his reports on the *Zhanguoce* and the *Shuoyuan*. Moreover, it helps us to better understand the origin and semantics of the expression *hao shi zhe* 好事者, originally "connoisseur of accounts," literally "someone who likes accounts," i.e., in later usage a person who also likes to tell these to other people and thus is prone to bragging. The contents of these "histories" were conceived of as setting historical precedents and therefore conveying valuable ethical and political insights. This usage of the term *shi* marks an important point of semantic change from "affairs" to "story" (later *gushi*), a transformation that is directly related to the development of fictional texts, which at that time were still conceived of as being factual historical accounts. See Schwermann, "Gattungsdynamik in der traditionellen chinesischen Literatur." For Liu Xiang's view of fictitious composition see Holzman, "Liu Xiang's Attitude towards Fiction." For the absence of a generic differentiation of factual and fictional writing see Rainer von Franz, "Fiktionalität in der klassischen chinesischen Literatur," in *Der Abbruch des Turmbaus: Studien zum Geist in China und im Abendland. Festschrift für Rolf Trauzettel*, ed. Ingrid Krüßmann et al., Monumenta Serica Monograph Series 34 (Nettetal: Steyler Verlag, 1995), 199–209, and Rolf Trauzettel, "Die klassische Skizze (*biji*)," in *Die klassische chinesische Prosa: Essay, Reisebericht, Skizze, Brief. Vom Mittelalter bis zur Neuzeit*, ed. Marion Eggert et al., vol. 4 of *Geschichte der chinesischen Literatur*, ed. Wolfgang Kubin (München: Saur,

2004), 248–51. I am grateful to Jens Østergård Petersen, whose incisive questions at the conference helped me to improve my argument.

35. According to Xu Fuguan, "Liu Xiang *Xinxu, Shuoyuan* de yanjiu," 56, who bases his argument on a quotation of a fragment of the *Fengsu tongyi* 風俗通義 (Comprehensive Meaning of Customs) transmitted in the *Chuxueji* 初學記 (Records for Elementary Studies), the character 苑, OC *ʔonʔ, here has to be read as a loan for *yun* 蕰, OC *ʔunʔ, ʔuns, "collection;" see *Chuxueji* 初學記, ed. Xu Jian 徐堅 (Beijing: Zhongguo Shudian, 2012), *juan* 24, 29a; compare Xu Fuguan 徐復觀 *Liang Han sixiang shi* 兩漢思想史, vol. 3 (Taipei: Taiwan xuesheng shuju, 1979), 63. The evidence furnished by Gao, *Gu zi tongjia huidian*, 111, 160–61, indicates that this loan is phonologically acceptable. See also Axel Schuessler, *ABC Etymological Dictionary of Old Chinese* (Honolulu: University of Hawai'i Press, 2007), 594, 598, who gives OC *ʔonʔ and *ʔunʔ as reconstructions. Thus, it might be wrong to interpret the term *yuan* 苑, "garden," in the title *Shuoyuan* as a metaphorical expression for "collection." Rather, the title might have to be spelled "Shuo yun." In fact, there are no further instances of *yuan* being used as a metaphorical expression for "collection (of documents)" in early Chinese texts. Only the metaphorical use of the word *lin* 林, "forest," in the title "Shuolin" 說林 (Forest [i.e., Collection] of Illustrative Examples) of chapters 22 and 23 of the *Han Feizi* 韓非子 can be regarded as a distant parallel. However, since the use of 苑 as a loan for *yun* 蕰 cannot be proved with certainty in this case, I retain the traditional spelling "Shuoyuan."

36. See Zuo, "Lun Liu Xiang bianzhuan *Shuoyuan*," 54–55; compare Xu Fuguan, "Liu Xiang *Xinxu, Shuoyuan* de yanjiu," 56.

37. See Zuo, "Lun Liu Xiang bianzhuan *Shuoyuan*," 55, and Zuo, "Lun 'Rujiazhe yan' ji qi yu *Shuoyuan* de guanxi," 11. See also Du, *Liu Xiang bianxie Xinxu, Shuoyuan yanjiu*, 23, who accepts Zuo's proposition that there was no previously established text but argues, not very convincingly, that even such an accumulation of raw narrative materials as the *zhongshu Shuoyuan zashi* can still be conceived of as a "book."

38. Possibly as early as 24 BCE, see note 50 below, compare Du, *Liu Xiang bianxie* Xinxu, Shuoyuan *yanjiu*, 46–47. Du thinks that Liu's aim in producing the *Shuoyuan* was to create a collection of illustrative examples that was more refined than the *Xinxu*; compare Xu Sufei, Shuoyuan *tanwei*, ii, and Xu Fuguan, *Liang Han sixiang shi*, vol. 3, 66. Zuo, "Lun 'Rujiazhe yan' ji qi yu *Shuoyuan* de guanxi," shows that distribution of parallels to *Shuoyuan* and *Xinxu*, respectively, in the "Rujiazhe yan" gives evidence of a systematic elimination of duplicates. Zuo, ibid., 13, argues that 13 of the 15 parallels between the *Shuoyuan* and the 10 extant chapters of the *Xinxu*, which originally comprised 30 chapters (see *Suishu*, *juan* 34, 997), are not close enough to count as duplicates, i.e., that the variations of these parallel textual units are meaningful in their respective contexts. For the parallels between *Shuoyuan* and *Xinxu* see also Xie, *Liu Xiang* Shuoyuan *yanjiu*, 76–95, who comes to the conclusion that only one of 18 parallels can be considered a duplicate.

39. For a definition of *yi li* 義理 as the outward appearance of ritual conduct see *Liji* 禮記 (Records of Ritual), chap. 10: "Liqi" 禮器 (The Vessels of Rites): "When the earlier kings established the rites, they depended on roots and embellishment. Loyalty and trust are the roots of the rites. The pattern of righteousness is the embellishment of the rites. Without roots, they are not established. Without embellishment, they are not practiced." See *Liji zhushu* 禮記注疏, ed. Ruan Yuan 阮元, Sibu beiyao 四部備要 edition (Taipei: Zhonghua shuju, 1965), *juan* 23, 1b: 先王之立禮也, 有本有文. 忠信, 禮之本也. 義理, 禮之文也. 無本不立, 無文不行.

40. See *Hanshu*, *juan* 30, 1745.

41. Jens Østergård Petersen argues that the term *bai jia*, "hundred persons," refers to the "many wise men" of the past, who express their moral and political maxims in such didactic stories as are contained in the *Shuoyuan*. For the textual history of the *Baijia*, possible fragments and for the view of it as not being in accordance with orthodoxy see Petersen, "Which Books Did the First Emperor of Ch'in Burn?" 19–22; Zißler-Gürtler, *Nicht erzählte Welt noch Welterklärung*, 130–34; and Holzman, "Liu Xiang's Attitude towards Fiction."

42. Compare Riffaterre, *Semiotics of Poetry*, 99–109, for the function of titles in poems.

43. See Schwermann, "Gattungsdynamik in der traditionellen chinesischen Literatur," 67–68, compare Schuessler, *ABC Etymological Dictionary of Old Chinese*, 476–77, and Zißler-Gürtler, *Nicht erzählte Welt noch Welterklärung*, 9. For the assumed word family and apparent etymology of *shuo/shui* from the OC root *lo, "to loosen, relax," see Schuessler, *ABC Etymological Dictionary of Old Chinese*, 585–86; compare William G. Boltz, *The Origin and Early Development of the Chinese Writing System*, American Oriental Series 78 (New Haven, CT: American Oriental Society, 1994), 101.

44. I suggest that the directedness at a "specific audience," which according to Michael Hunter, "The Difficulty with 'The Difficulties of Persuasion' ('Shuinan' 說南)," in *Dao Companion to the Philosophy of Han Fei*, ed. Paul R. Goldin (Dordrecht: Springer, 2013), 173, is the "key difference" between *shuo* and *shui*, is a corollary of the difference between an endoactive and an exoactive verb or, put semantically in relation to the nouns *shuo* and *shui*, that between the contents and the application of an argument.

45. In certain contexts, the noun *shuo* takes on the meaning "argument." For example, see *Mozi* 墨子 (Master Mo), chap. 17: "Feigong, shang" 非功上 (Against Military Aggression, Part One), in *Mozi jiangu* 墨子閒詁, ed. Sun Yirang 孫詒讓, 2 vols., Xinbian zhuzi jicheng 新編諸子集成 edition (Beijing: Zhonghua shuju, 2001), vol. 1, *juan* 5, 129: 殺一人謂之不義, 必有一死罪矣. 若以此說往, 殺十人十重不義, 必有十死罪矣; 殺百人百重不義, 必有百死罪矣. "When someone has killed a single person and one calls it wrong, he must have the criminal responsibility for one death. If one goes on with this argument, then someone who has killed ten people and [thus] has done ten times as much wrong must have

the criminal responsibility for ten deaths. If someone has killed a hundred people and [thus] has done a hundred times as much wrong, he must have the criminal responsibility for a hundred deaths." (For more on this *Mozi* chapter, see Paul van Els, "How to End Wars with Words: Three Argumentative Strategies by Mozi and his Followers," in *The Mozi as an Evolving Text: Different Voices in Early Chinese Thought*, eds. Carine Defoort and Nicolas Standaert [Leiden: Brill, 2013], 69–94.)

46. For the currently unresolvable question as to whether the character 苑 in the title should be read *yuan*, "garden/collection," i.e., as a metaphorical reference to a group of documents, or as a loan for *yun* 蘊, "collection," see note 35 above. For the problem as to whether the character 說 in the title should be read *shuo* or *shui*, see section one above. Robert E. Hegel and Martin Kern, "A History of Chinese Literature?," *Chinese Literature: Essays, Articles, Reviews* 26 (2004): 173–74n.21, have chosen to transliterate *Shuiyuan*, i.e., to interpret the title as referring to a collection of "persuasions." I am grateful to Elisa Sabattini for referring me to this review of the *Columbia History of Chinese Literature*, ed. Victor H. Mair (New York: Columbia University Press, 2001). Compare Martin Kern, "Die Anfänge der chinesischen Literatur," 77, who likewise opts for transliterating the title as *Shuiyuan*. See also Martin Kern, "'Persuasion' or 'Treatise'? The Prose Genres *Shui* 說 and *Shuo* 說 in the Light of the *Guwenci leizuan* of 1779," in *Ad Seres et Tungusos. Festschrift für Martin Gimm zu seinem 65. Geburtstag am 25. Mai 1995*, ed. Lutz Bieg et al., Opera sinologica 11 (Wiesbaden: Harrassowitz, 2000), 227, who argues that only from the early seventh century CE onwards rhyme dictionaries explicitly related the phonological and semantic differences between *shuo* and *shui* to each other and that this was the precondition for making a clear distinction between persuasive and explanatory forms of argumentation and, later on, between different literary genres. However, as I have shown in Schwermann, "Gattungsdynamik in der traditionellen chinesischen Literatur," *shuo*, as distinguished from *shui*, is attested both as a mode of argumentative writing and as a generic term in the early Han at the latest. Moreover, not only Old Chinese reconstructions but also the usages of *shuo/shui* in early Chinese texts clearly indicate that the terminological differentiation between contents and application of an argument must have been in place even earlier. See for example *Zhanguoce* 戰國策, 3 vols. (Shanghai: Shanghai guji chubanshe, 1978): vol. 3, *juan* 29, 1069: 秦王之志, 苟得窮齊, 不憚以一國都為功。然而王何不使布衣之人, 以窮齊之說說秦, 謂秦王曰: 〔. . .〕. "As for the king of Qin's ambition, if he is given the opportunity to cause distress to Qi, he will not shrink from rewarding the achievement with [the command of] the capital of the whole country. This being the case, why does your majesty not send a plain-clothed commoner to *persuade* the king of Qin with an *explanation* how to cause distress to Qi, addressing the king and saying: [. . .]?" (Italics are mine.)

47. See James I. Crump's definition of persuasion as opposed to oratory in his *Intrigues: Studies of the* Chan-kuo Ts'e (Ann Arbor: The University of Michigan Press, 1964), 36: "Since we know of no early oratorical tradition in China—that is,

one which involves exhorting groups of people to certain actions or attitudes—but have almost numberless examples of the adviser exhorting a single person (a ruler) to undertake actions, to revise or adopt certain attitudes, the term persuasion is used instead of oratory." Actually, there are quite a few examples of oratory in early China, for example the orations ascribed to late Shang and Western Zhou rulers in the *Shangshu* 尚書 (Ancient Documents), which are paralleled by the public speeches of kings in Western Zhou bronze inscriptions relating court investiture ceremonies. Notwithstanding this qualification, it makes sense to distinguish between oration and persuasion along the lines of Crump's definition. For anecdotal persuasions in the *Zhanguoce* see Crump, *Intrigues: Studies of the* Chan-kuo Ts'e, 35–39, 53.

48. According to my count, 16 out of 20 chapters commence with introductions, which are unparalleled in other texts of the period and were probably written by Liu Xiang himself. Only chapters 1, "Jundao" 君道 (The Way of the Ruler), 16, "Tancong" 談叢 (Collection of Sayings), 18, "Bianwu" 辨物 (Discriminating Varieties), and 20, "Fanzhi" 反質 (Returning to Essentials) lack formal introductions. The introductory paragraphs of three of these chapters (1, 18, 20) are dialogues between historical personages, who outline the main arguments of the subsequent textual units. Since these dialogues are tailored to match the topics of the chapters and their anecdotal items and since none of them is attested elsewhere, they are likely to have been composed by Liu Xiang as well. Two of these three synopses (the introductory paragraphs of chapters 18 and 20) are put into Confucius' mouth. The introduction to chapter 12, "Fengshi" 奉使 (Diplomatic Missions) is a condensed paraphrase of a passage in the *Chunqiu fanlu* 春秋繁露 (Luxuriant Gems of the Spring and Autumn), see *Chunqiu fanlu yizheng* 春秋繁露義證, ed. Su Yu 蘇輿, Xinbian zhuzi jicheng 新編諸子集成 edition (Beijing: Zhonghua shuju, 2002), *juan* 3, chap. 5, 88–91. Compare the overview of discursive sections in Du, *Liu Xiang bianxie* Xinxu, Shuoyuan *yanjiu*, 322, who only counts 13 introductory paragraphs but finds 21 further ratiocinative components scattered across the 20 chapters of the *Shuoyuan*.

49. See Du, *Liu Xiang bianxie* Xinxu, Shuoyuan *yanjiu*, 327.

50. The latest items of the text relate events that occurred during the reign of Emperor Xuan of the Han 漢宣帝 (i.e., Liu Bingyi 劉病已, r. 74–48 BCE), the grandfather of Liu Ao; see *Shuoyuan* 5.14, 6.6, and 13.20 (*Shuoyuan jiaozheng*, 102–05, 123, 323–24). As Liu Xiang was dismissed in 47 or 46 BCE and rehabilitated at the accession of Liu Ao in 33 BCE (Loewe, *A Biographical Dictionary*, 372–73), the work cannot have been submitted before the latter date. In his discussion of the date of the *Shuoyuan*, Xie Mingren comes to the conclusion that it must have been composed later than 26 BCE when Liu Ao commissioned Chen Nong 陳農 to search for lost writings throughout the empire and ordered Liu Xiang to collate the works gathered in the Imperial Library; see Xie, *Liu Xiang* Shuoyuan *yanjiu*, 32–35, compare *Hanshu*, *juan* 10, 310, and *juan* 30, 1701; see also Loewe, *A Biographical Dictionary*, 34, 251, 374. As mentioned above, according to Chao

Gongwu's *Junzhai dushu zhi, juan* 3 *shang*, vol. 3, 667–68 / *juan* 10, 15a–b, the *Shuoyuan* was submitted in 17 BCE, the *Xinxu*, which—as shown above—must have been composed before the *Shuoyuan*, seven years earlier, in 24 BCE. These dates were later adopted by Wang Yinglin 王應麟 (1223–1296) in his *"Hanshu Yiwenzhi" kaozheng* 《漢書藝文誌》考證 (Evidential Studies on the "Treatise on the Arts" of the *History of the [Former] Han Dynasty*) and in the *Yuhai* 玉海 (Sea of Jade); see Xie, *Liu Xiang* Shuoyuan *yanjiu*, 32. As regards the date for the submission of the *Xinxu*, the statement of Chao Gongwu can be traced back to the Tang scholar Ma Zong 馬總 (d. 823); see his *Yilin* 意林 (Forest of Ideas), Sibu beiyao 四部備要 edition (Taipei: Zhonghua shuju, 1965), *juan* 3, 5a.

51. See Loewe, *A Biographical Dictionary*, 245–52, 373.

52. See *Hanshu, juan* 36, 1958.

53. I would like to thank Wai-yee Li for reminding me at the conference that it is always better to think twice before turning someone into a hero. See Hunter, "The Difficulty with 'The Difficulties of Persuasion' ('Shuinan' 說難)," 185–86, for Liu Xiang's realistic view of persuasion as the art of "expediency" (*quan* 權).

54. See David Schaberg, "Remonstrance in Eastern Zhou Historiography," *Early China* 22 (1997), 133–79, and David Schaberg, "Playing at Critique," 194–225, for remonstrance in general and indirect remonstrance in particular. As coincidence would have it, the latter is one of the subjects of chapter 9 of the *Shuoyuan*, which is under examination here. As I will show in section four, Liu Xiang, contrary to what is commonly believed, does not argue in favor of indirect remonstrance here.

55. Accordingly, Unger, "Der gute Redner," 229, characterizes the narratives of chapter 11 as "evidentiary anecdotes" (*Beleganekdoten*), i.e., as exemplifications of the propositions preceding them in the introduction to the chapter.

56. See the survey in Zißler-Gürtler, *Nicht erzählte Welt noch Welterklärung*, 51–53.

57. See *Hanshu, juan* 30, 1716.

58. See *Hanshu, juan* 30, 1709.

59. For the textual relations between *Xinxu, Shuoyuan* and *Hanshi waizhuan* see Xu Fuguan, "Liu Xiang *Xinxu, Shuoyuan* de yanjiu," 57–61, and Xu Fuguan, *Liang Han sixiang shi*, vol. 3, 68–77.

60. For example, this may have been the case with the *Han shuo* 韓說 (Explanations of the Han [School of the *Shijing* 詩經]) in 41 *juan*, which is listed directly after the *Han neizhuan* 韓內傳 (Inner Commentary of the Han School) and *Han waizhuan* 韓外傳 (Outer Commentary of the Han School) in the bibliographical treatise of the *Hanshu*; see *Hanshu, juan* 30, 1708. Zißler-Gürtler, *Nicht erzählte Welt noch Welterklärung*, 52–53, argues that the *Shishuo* 世說 (Explanations of the World), which in *Hanshu, juan* 30, 1727, is listed as a Classicist text arranged by Liu Xiang, was a collection of anecdotes and sayings. For anecdotal commentaries see Hans Stumpfeldt, "Ein verschollener Konfuzius-Kommentar? Notizen zu elf

Anekdoten in der spätklassischen chinesischen Literatur," in *Über Himmel und Erde. Festschrift für Erling von Mende*, ed. Raimund Theodor Kolb and Martina Siebert, Abhandlungen für die Kunde des Morgenlandes LVII, 3 (Wiesbaden: Harrassowitz, 2006), 419–30.

61. See *Hanshu*, *juan* 30, 1744–1745. Five out of 15 titles contain the element *shuo*. Liu Xiang's account of the formation of the *Baijia*, which is also listed in this section, in his memorial on the *Shuoyuan* and his son Liu Xin's 劉歆 (46 BCE–23 CE) pejorative description of the *xiaoshuo*, which is preserved in the bibliographical treatise of the *Hanshu*, *juan* 30, 1745, both imply that these works consisted of anecdotal materials which were considered non-factual and/or morally subversive. For the *xiaoshuo* see the valuable collection of fragments of the 15 titles in Zißler-Gürtler, *Nicht erzählte Welt noch Welterklärung*, 54–134; see also Holzman, "Liu Xiang's Attitude towards Fiction," and Schwermann, "Gattungsdynamik in der traditionellen chinesischen Literatur."

62. For the following, see Schwermann, "Gattungsdynamik in der traditionellen chinesischen Literatur," 67–68. Compare Zißler-Gürtler, *Nicht erzählte Welt noch Welterklärung*, 19–22, and Lewis, *Writing and Authority in Early China*, 300.

63. I therefore suggest that it is not advisable and also slightly self-contradictory to refer to the "Shuolin" chapters of the *Han Feizi* as a "'Forest of Persuasions,' a collection of anecdotes." See Hunter, "The Difficulty with 'The Difficulties of Persuasion' ('Shuinan' 說難)," 176.

64. For a discussion of these chapters see Heng Du's chapter in this volume. See also Zißler-Gürtler, *Nicht erzählte Welt noch Welterklärung*, 20–21.

65. See *Han Feizi jijie* 韓非子集解, ed. Wang Xianshen 王先慎, Xinbian zhuzi jicheng 新編諸子集成 edition (Beijing: Zhonghua shuju, 2003), chap. 30, 212 (two instances), 213–14, 214, 216. For another five instances of *qi shuo zai* see *Han Feizi jijie*, chap. 31, 240, 241, 242, 243 (two instances). The formula can be traced back to the Mohist Canons and their explanations; see the numerous instances of the collocation *shuo zai* 說在 in *Mozi*, chaps. 41, "Jing, xia" 經下, and 43, "Jingshuo, xia" 經說下. For one typical example see *Mozi jiangu*, vol. 1, *juan* 10, 320–21: 知而不以五路, 說在久. Compare Angus C. Graham's translation in his *Later Mohist Logic, Ethics and Science* (Hong Kong: The Chinese University Press, 1978), 415, which I have slightly modified: "When one knows, it is not by the means of the 'five roads.' The explanation consists in duration." The expression *wu lu* 五路, "five roads," refers to the five senses (*wu guan* 五官), the term *jiu* 久, duration, to the duration, i.e., persistence, of knowledge; compare Graham, *Later Mohist Logic, Ethics and Science*, 416: "The crucial point about knowing for the Mohist is that it persists even when the object is no longer in front of your eyes. Seeing is by means of the eye, knowing is by means of *chih* 'intelligence' (A 3). [. . .] It is this persistence of knowing which shows that we do not know by means of the five senses."

66. See *Han Feizi jijie*, 261.

67. See *Han Feizi jijie*, 265, 293, 311, 332. For the microstructure of chapter 32, which has six subsections of guidelines and accordingly six subsections of exempla with fluctuating numbers of textual units, see Unger, *Abriß der Literatur des chinesischen Altertum*, 115–18.

68. This is my translation of the German technical term *Schreibweise*, on which see Schwermann, "Gattungsdynamik in der traditionellen chinesischen Literatur," 68.

69. For these four types of collage-like text assemblage see Schwermann, "Collage-Technik als Kompositionsprinzip klassischer chinesischer Prosa." In the first case, preexisting textual units are connected by means of transphrastic text-structuring devices such as introductions, dialogical frames, rhyme nets or intertextual references, in the second they are joined by associative connective links, in the third case they are coupled by connective links focussing on a shared theme, and in the fourth case, the theme is illustrated by a series of exempla having formal or thematic parallels. For rhyme nets as phonological text-structuring devices see Wolfgang Behr, "Three Sound-Correlated Text Structuring Devices in Pre-Qín Philosophical Prose," in *Komposition und Konnotation—Figuren der Kunstprosa im Alten China*, eds. Wolfgang Behr and Joachim Gentz, *Bochumer Jahrbuch zur Ostasienforschung* 29 (2005): 19–24.

70. See *Yijing* 易經 (Book of Changes), second line statement "Six in the Second" of hexagram *jian* 蹇, in *Zhouyi dazhuan jinzhu* 周易大傳今注, ed. Gao Heng 高亨 (Ji'nan: Qi-Lu shushe, 1979), 344. Gao Heng interprets the line statement according to Liu Xiang's reading, treats 蹇, OC *kanʔ, as a loan character for *jian* 謇, OC *kanʔ, "to be outspoken," and explains that it refers to "launching straightforward remonstrations incessantly" (*zhijian bu yi* 直諫不已).

71. Both here and in the following sentence Xiang Zonglu, *Shuoyuan jiaozheng*, 206, basing himself on a passage in the early Song encyclopaedia *Taiping yulan* 太平御覽 (Imperial Readings of the Taiping Era), ed. Li Fang 李昉, 4 vols. (Beijing: Zhonghua shuju, 1960), vol. 2, 2095 / *juan* 455, 8b, emends *shen wang* 身亡 to *wang shen* 亡身.

72. Compare the five-partite typologies in *Baihutong* 白虎通 (Comprehensive Discussions in the White Tiger Hall), in *Baihutong shuzheng* 白虎通疏證, ed. Chen Li 陳立, 2 vols., Xinbian zhuzi jicheng 新編諸子集成 edition (Beijing: Zhonghua shuju, 1997), vol. 1, *juan* 5, 235–37, in He Xiu's 何休 (129–82) commentary on *Gongyangzhuan* 公羊傳 (Gongyang Commentary), Zhuang gong 莊公 24.8–9, in *Gongyang yishu* 公羊義疏, ed. Chen Li 陳立, *Sibu beiyao* 四部備要 edition (Taipei: Zhonghua shuju, 1965), *juan* 23, 17b, and in *Kongzi jiayu* 孔子家語 (School Sayings of Confucius), Zhongguo xueshu mingzhu 中國學術名著 edition (Taipei: Shijie shuju, 1962), *juan* 3, chap. 14, 33, with different sequences and partly different terminologies. However, all of them appear to give precedence to the indirectly allusive remonstrance, which occupies either the first or the last

position in the sequence. Whereas the typologies in *Baihutong* and He Xiu's commentary on the *Gongyangzhuan* are arranged anticlimactically, the classifications in *Shuoyuan* and *Kongzi jiayu* have an onion-like structure, i.e., categories one and five as well as two and four are related to each other by contrast or similarity and thus form two layers surrounding category three.

73. Reading 義, OC *ŋaih, as a loan character for *yi* 議, OC *ŋaih, "to assess, evaluate."

74. For Xie Ye 泄冶, who openly criticized the debauchery of his lord, see *Zuozhuan* 左傳 (Zuo Commentary), Xuan gong 宣公 9.6, in *Chunqiu Zuozhuan zhu* 春秋左傳注, ed. Yang Bojun 楊伯峻, 4 vols. (Beijing: Zhonghua Shuju, 1981), vol. 2, 701–02; here, Xie is written 洩. Compare *Chunqiu*, Xuan gong 9.14 (*Chunqiu Zuozhuan zhu*, vol. 2, 700) as well as the corresponding entry in *Guliangzhuan* 穀梁傳 (Guliang Commentary [to the *Spring and Autumn Annals*]), in *Chunqiu jingzhuan yinde* 春秋經傳引得. *Combined Concordances to Ch'un-Ch'iu, Kung-yang, Ku-liang and Tso-chuan*, ed. William Hung, 4 vols., Harvard-Yenching Institute Sinological Index Series, Supplement No. 11 (Taipei: Ch'eng-wen, [1937] 1966), vol. 1, 191: 稱國以殺其大夫, 殺無罪也. 泄冶之無罪如何? 陳靈公通于夏徵舒之家. 公孫寧, 儀行父亦通其家. 或衣其衣, 或衷其襦, 以相戲於朝. 泄冶聞之, 入諫曰:「使國人聞之則猶可. 使仁人聞之則不可.」君愧於泄冶. 不能用其言而殺之. Compare the translation by Göran Malmqvist, "Studies on the Gongyang and Guuliang Commentaries I," *Bulletin of the Museum of Far Eastern Antiquities* 43 (1971): 183–84: "When the state is given as the agent of a killing of a great officer, it indicates the killing of one without guilt. Under what circumstances was Shieh-yee without guilt? Duke Ling of Chern had illicit relations with [the woman in] the family of Jeng-shu of Shiah. Gong-suen Ning and Yi Shyng-fuu also had illicit relations with [the woman of] that family. Sometimes they put on her clothes, sometimes they wore her jackets innermost [on their bodies] and made fun of this together at the court. Shieh-yee heard of this and went in to remonstrate, saying: 'It may be permissible to make the people of the state hear of this. But it is not permissible to make a benevolent man hear of this.' The duke felt ashamed before Shieh-yee. He could not follow his advice and therefore killed him." Compare also *Kongzi jiayu*, *juan* 5, chap. 19, 48–49. For Cao Ji 曹羈 see *Han Feizi*, chap. 10 (*Han Feizi jijie*, *juan* 3, 76–77), *Zuozhuan*, Xi gong 僖公 23.6 (*Chunqiu Zuozhuan zhu*, vol. 1, 407) and 28.3 (*Chunqiu Zuozhuan zhu*, vol. 1, 453–454). According to this tradition, Xi Fuji 僖負羈 (i.e., Cao Ji) unlike his lord showed the due respect to Prince Chong'er 重耳 of Jin 晉, who later ruled Jin under the posthumous name of Duke Wen of Jin 晉文公 from 636 to 628 BCE, i.e., "accorded with the rites" and thus escaped Duke Wen's revenge. For his remonstrating three times in vain with the lord of Cao 曹 see *Shuoyuan* 8.2 (*Shuoyuan jiaozheng*, 176) and the *Gongyangzhuan*'s commentary on *Chunqiu*, Zhuang gong 24.8-9: 冬, 戎侵曹. 曹羈出奔陳. (*Chunqiu Zuozhuan zhu*, vol. 1, 228) The commentary (*Chunqiu jingzhuan yinde*, vol. 1, 71) says: 曹羈者何? 曹

大夫也. 曹無大夫. 此何以書? 賢也. 何賢乎曹羈? 戎將侵曹. 曹羈諫曰:「戎眾以無義. 君請勿自敵也.」曹伯曰:「不可.」三諫不從, 遂去之. 故君子以為得君臣之義也. Compare Malmqvist, "Studies on the Gongyang and Guuliang Commentaries I," 140: "In Winter the Rong invaded Tsaur. Ji of Tsaur left [his state] and fled to Chern. Gongyang: Who was this Ji of Tsaur? A great officer of Tsaur. There were no great officers in Tsaur. Why, then was this entry made? [Ji] was worthy. In what respect was Ji of Tsaur worthy? The Rong was about to invade Tsaur. Ji of Tsaur remonstrated [with his ruler], saying: 'The Rong are many and do not act with righteousness. I beg of you, Sir, not to lead the troops in person!' The earl of Tsaur said: 'This cannot be!' Having remonstrated three times without success [Ji] left him. Therefore the superior man considered that [Ji] had fulfilled his obligations of a minister towards his ruler." Compare also the entries in *Gongyangzhuan* and *Guliangzhuan* related to *Chunqiu*, Zhuang gong 26.3 (*Chunqiu jingzhuan yinde*, vol. 1, 72; Malmqvist, "Studies on the Gongyang and Guuliang Commentaries I," 142).

75. See *Shuoyuan jiaozheng*, 206–07.

76. See, for example, Gao Heng's interpretation in his *Zhouyi dazhuan jinzhu*, 344, compare the most recent German translation by Dennis Schilling, *Yijing: Das Buch der Wandlungen* (Frankfurt am Main/Leipzig: Verlag der Weltreligionen, 2009), 131: "Die Minister des Königs bringen Ermahnung um Ermahnung vor, auch wenn es nicht ihre eigene Sache ist."

77. See *Liji*, chap. 2: "Quli, xia" 曲禮下 (Minute Rituals, Part Two): "As for the ritual propriety of a minister, he does not remonstrate in public. If he has remonstrated thrice but is still not heeded, he [may] abscond from his lord. As for a son serving his parents, if he has remonstrated thrice but is still not heeded, he [may] pursue them, wailing and weeping." (*Liji zhushu*, *juan* 5, 8b–9a): 為人臣之禮, 不顯諫. 三諫而不聽, 則逃之. 子之事親也, 三諫而不聽, 則號泣而隨之. Compare *Gongyangzhuan*, Zhuang gong 24.8–9 (*Chunqiu jingzhuan yinde*, vol. 1, 71), *Baihutong shuzheng*, vol. 1, *juan* 5, 228–29, and *Lunheng* 論衡 (Balanced Discourses), chap. 34, in *Lunheng jiaoshi* 論衡校釋, ed. Huang Hui 黃暉, 4 vols. (Beijing: Zhonghua shuju, 1990), vol. 2, 534–35. Compare also *Shiji*, *juan* 38, 1610, and *juan* 127, 3217.

78. See *Kongzi jiayu*, *juan* 3, chap. 14, 33, and *Baihutong shuzheng*, vol. 1, *juan* 5, 236: 孔子曰:「諫有五, 吾從諷之諫.」Compare the translation by Tjan Tjoe Som, *Po Hu T'ung* 白虎通. *The Comprehensive Discussions in the White Tiger Hall*, 2 vols., Sinica Leidensia 6 (Leiden: Brill, 1949–1952), vol. 2, 469: "Therefore [sic!] Confucius said: 'There are five kinds of admonitions. I follow the Allusive Admonition.'"

79. Compare Schaberg, "Playing at Critique," 202–03: "Yet the only type of remonstrance found in all of the lists, and the type given clear priority in all of them, is indirect remonstrance, an act not provided for in institutional or ritual writings.

The imperial courts took over the old practice of direct criticism, but on terms that implied its subordination to an imaginary ideal of tact and self-preservation."

80. For the strategy of feigning madness see Christian Schwermann, "Feigned Madness, Self-Preservation and Covert Censure in Early China," in *Zurück zur Freude. Studien zur chinesischen Literatur und Lebenswelt und ihrer Rezeption in Ost und West. Festschrift für Wolfgang Kubin*, ed. Marc Hermann and Christian Schwermann, Monumenta Serica Monograph Series 57 (Nettetal, Sankt Augustin: Steyler Verlag, 2007), 531–72.

81. Even the items in the two sections 9.20 (*Shuoyuan jiaozheng*, 227–32) and 9.21 (*Shuoyuan jiaozheng*, 232–33), in which the remonstrants do not survive, can be interpreted as successful examples, since their lords in the end admit their mistakes and repent that they did not heed their ministers' advice.

82. According to my count, ten anecdotes, namely the narratives in *Shuoyuan* 9.4 (*Shuoyuan jiaozheng*, 209–10), 9.5 (*Shuoyuan jiaozheng*, 210–12), 9.6 (*Shuoyuan jiaozheng*, 212–14), 9.7 (*Shuoyuan jiaozheng*, 214), 9.11 (*Shuoyuan jiaozheng*, 220–21), 9.13 (*Shuoyuan jiaozheng*, 223), 9.14 (*Shuoyuan jiaozheng*, 223–24), 9.16 (*Shuoyuan jiaozheng*, 224–25), 9.17 (*Shuoyuan jiaozheng*, 225), and 9.24 (*Shuoyuan jiaozheng*, 237–38), can be interpreted as tales of indirect remonstrance, 13 anecdotes, namely the narratives in *Shuoyuan* 9.2 (*Shuoyuan jiaozheng*, 207–08), 9.3 (*Shuoyuan jiaozheng*, 208), 9.8 (*Shuoyuan jiaozheng*, 215–17), 9.9 (*Shuoyuan jiaozheng*, 217–19), 9.10 (*Shuoyuan jiaozheng*, 219–20), 9.12 (*Shuoyuan jiaozheng*, 221–23), 9.15 (*Shuoyuan jiaozheng*, 224), 9.18 (*Shuoyuan jiaozheng*, 225–27), 9.19 (*Shuoyuan jiaozheng*, 227), 9.20 (*Shuoyuan jiaozheng*, 227–32), 9.21 (*Shuoyuan jiaozheng*, 232–33), 9.22 (*Shuoyuan jiaozheng*, 233–34), and 9.23 (*Shuoyuan jiaozheng*, 234–37), as tales of direct remonstrance.

83. See *Shuoyuan jiaozheng*, 238–39.

84. See *Shuoyuan jiaozheng*, 238. Compare the parallel in *Kongzi jiayu*, juan 4, chap. 15, 35.

85. See *Shuoyuan jiaozheng*, 239. Compare the parallel in *Yanzi chunqiu jishi* 晏子春秋集釋, ed. Wu Zeyu 吳則虞, 2 vols. (Beijing: Zhonghua shuju, 1962), vol. 1, juan 2, 140.

86. Note that they are not included in Du's list of 34 discursive sections in the *Shuoyuan*; see his *Liu Xiang bianxie* Xinxu, Shuoyuan *yanjiu*, 322.

87. See Schaberg, "Playing at Critique," 195, for performative aspects of indirect remonstrances and ibid., 197, on the tripartite narratological structure of tales of indirect remonstrance, which—according to Schaberg—typically consist of "(1) a violation of ritual norms on the part of the ruler, (2) a performance of an indirect remonstrance in spite of (or due to) an explicit ban on directly remonstrating with the ruler, and (3) the ruler's transformation through his decoding of the analogy drawn by the remonstrant" (as paraphrased by Christian Schwermann, review of *Text and Ritual in Early China*, ed. Martin Kern, *Monumenta Serica* 58 [2010]: 402).

88. See *Shuoyuan jiaozheng*, 209–10. Schaberg, "Playing at Critique," 201, ranks this item among the indirect remonstrances.

89. On riddles and rhetoric see Wai-yee Li, "Riddles, Concealment, and Rhetoric in Early China," in *Facing the Monarch: Modes of Advice in the Early Chinese Court*, ed. Garret P. S. Olberding, Harvard East Asian Monographs 359 (Cambridge, MA: Harvard University Press, 2013), 100–32.

90. According to Lu Yuanjun 盧元駿, *Shuoyuan jinzhu jinyi* 說苑今註今譯 (Tianjin: Tianjin Guji Chubanshe, 1988), 276n.1, Jiu Fan 咎犯 is a (deliberate?) misspelling of *jiu* Fan 舅犯, "Uncle Fan," i.e., zi Fan 子犯, grand-officer at the court of Duke Wen of Jin (i.e., Prince Chong'er, who ruled Jin under the posthumous name of Duke Wen of Jin from 636 to 628 BCE) and at the same time his maternal uncle (*jiu* 舅); see *Zuozhuan*, Xi gong 24.1 (*Chunqiu Zuozhuan zhu*, vol. 1, 412). Compare *Shiji*, *juan* 14, 593, *juan* 25, 1241, and *juan* 39, 1656–1661, 1665, which interestingly has the misspelling 咎犯, too. Since the historical *jiu* Fan flourished in the second half of the seventh century BCE, Liu Xiang's anecdote, which places him in the first half of the sixth century BCE, is clearly anachronistic.

91. See *Lienüzhuan jiaozhu* 列女傳校注, ed. Liang Duan 梁端, Sibu beiyao 四部備要 edition (Taipei: Zhonghua shuju, 1965), *juan* 6, 12a–13a. The *Hou Hanshu* 後漢書, 12 vols. (Hong Kong: Zhonghua shuju, 1971), *juan* 78, 2530, puts a fragment of Jiu Fan's remonstrance into the mouth of the legendary music master Shi Kuang 師曠. However, it would be methodologically wrong to draw the conclusion, as Xiang Zonglu did in his *Shuoyuan jiaozheng*, 210, that this shows that 咎犯 is a mistake (*e* 譌) for 師曠 and that the *Hou Hanshu*, which was compiled in the first half of the fifth century CE and thus is 450 years later than the *Shuoyuan*, retains a fragment of the "correct" or "original" version of this anecdote.

92. See section two above.

93. This is Bao Shuya 鮑叔牙, who according to *Shiji*, *juan* 62, 2131, had already served Duke Huan, i.e., *gongzi* Xiaobai 公子小白, before his accession to the throne.

94. See *Shuoyuan jiaozheng*, 219: 君直言, 臣直對.

95. See *Shuoyuan jiaozheng*, 219. Following the murder of the Duke Xiang of Qi 齊襄公 (r. 697–686 BCE), *gongzi* Xiaobai und his brother *gongzi* Jiu 公子糾, both of them sons of Duke Xi of Qi 齊僖公 (r. 730–698 BCE) and one of his concubines, competed for succession. Jiu fled to Lu 魯 und received the support of the Duke Zhuang of Lu 魯莊公 (r. 693–662 BCE). However, Xiaobai defeated Lu in the battle of Ganshi 乾時 and forced Duke Zhuang to have Jiu killed. See *Zuozhuan*, Zhuang gong 8.3, *Chunqiu*, Zhuang 9.3, 9.5, and 9.6, and *Zuozhuan*, Zhuang gong 9.3–5 (*Chunqiu Zuozhuan zhu*, vol. 1, 176–80); compare *Shiji*, *juan* 32, 1484–85.

96. As shown above (see note 81) he even does so in those cases where he does not survive.

97. See Christian Schwermann, "Schlechte Namen, Leserlenkung und Herrscherkritik in antiken chinesischen Texten," in *Auf der Suche nach der Entwicklung menschlicher Gesellschaften: Festschrift für Hans Dieter Ölschleger zu seinem sechzigsten Geburtstag von seinen Freunden und Kollegen*, ed. Günther Distelrath et al., Bonner Asienstudien 11 (Berlin: EB-Verlag, 2012), 539–94, for the function of these two figures in early Chinese criticism of rulership.

98. See *Shuoyuan jiaozheng*, 207.

99. See Schwermann, "Schlechte Namen," for the use of so-called bad names (*e ming* 惡名 or *chou ming* 醜名) as leverage in the hands of remonstrating ministers. Probably the best-known and most important representative of these names were bad posthumous names, i.e., "petty names" (*ximing* 細名), as they are called in chapter 54, "Shifa" 諡法 (Standards for [the Bestowal of] Posthumous Names) of the *Yi Zhou shu* 逸周書 (Remaining Zhou Documents); see *Yi Zhou shu*, Sibu beiyao 四部備要 edition (Taipei: Zhonghua shuju, 1965), *juan* 6, 17b. For a close parallel to the above-cited text see *Han Feizi* 10 (*Han Feizi jijie*, 72–73). Here, the remonstrance is directed at Tian Chengzi 田成子. Interestingly, the remonstrant, here named Yan Zhuoju 顏涿聚, declares: "I speak up for the sake of the country, I do not by any means speak up on behalf of my person." (I have slightly modified Christoph Harbsmeier's translation, *TLS—Thesaurus Linguae Sericae: An Historical and Comparative Encyclopaedia of Chinese Conceptual Schemes*, ed. Christoph Harbsmeier, Jiang Shaoyu 蔣紹愚, http://tls.uni-hd.de/home_en.lasso (accessed: 25 November 2013.) See *Han Feizi jijie*, 73: 臣言為國, 非為身也. This sentence is faintly echoed in the introduction to *Shuoyuan* 9 (see above): "Therefore he is concerned with [his own] country so that [his] country is not in danger, and he is concerned with [his own] person so that [his] person is not in danger" (故在國而國不危, 在身而身不殆.). For the variant spelling Yan Zhuoju 顏涿聚 see also *Zuozhuan*, Ai gong 哀公 27.3 (*Chunqiu Zuozhuan zhu*, vol. 4, 1733); compare *Shiji*, *juan* 47, 1919 and 1938, which has the spelling Yan Zhuoju 顏濁鄒, and the "Gujin renbiao" 古今仁表 (Table of People Past and Present), in *Hanshu*, *juan* 20, 931, which has Yan Zhuju 顏燭雛. See also the two related anecdotes in *Yanzi chunqiu jishi*, vol. 2, *juan* 7, 464, and *Hanshi waizhuan jishi* 韓詩外傳集釋, ed. Xu Weiyu 許維遹 (Beijing: Zhonghua shuju, 1980), *juan* 9, 314–15, which have Yan Zhuju 顏燭鄒 and Yan Zhuoju 顏斲聚, respectively. The plots of both tales differ greatly from *Shuoyuan* 9.2. Compare Oliver Weingarten, "The Figure of Yan Zhuoju 顏涿聚 in Ancient Chinese Literature," *Monumenta Serica* 63 no. 2 (2015): 229–61.

100. See *Shuoyuan jiaozheng*, 221–23.

101. See *Lüshi chunqiu* 23.2.3, in *Lüshi chunqiu jiaoshi* 呂氏春秋校釋, ed. Chen Qiyou 陳奇猷, 4 vols. (Shanghai: Xuelin chubanshe, 1984), vol. 4, 1545.

102. There are no parallels to this anecdote in the literature of the period except for some phrases in chapter 32 of the *Xunzi*; see Schaberg, "Playing at Critique," 210, 224n.65, and *Shuoyuan jiaozheng*, 219; compare *Xunzi jijie* 荀子

集解, ed. Wang Xianqian 王先謙, 2 vols., Xinbian zhuzi jicheng 新編諸子集成 edition (Beijing: Zhonghua shuju, 1997), vol. 2, 552–53.

103. I have adapted and supplemented the translation by Schaberg, "Playing at Critique," 209.

104. See *Shuoyuan jiaozheng*, 218.

105. See *Shuoyuan jiaozheng*, 217.

106. See Schaberg, "Playing at Critique," 210.

107. That Zhuyu Ji is not the simple rustic he pretends to be becomes evident from his ironic reply to his plowing partner, who doubts that Zhuyu Ji will survive his remonstrance: "When I'm plowing with you, I pit my strength against yours. But when it comes to persuading the ruler of men, I don't compare my cleverness with yours." See *Shuoyuan jiaozheng*, 218: 若與子同耕, 則比力也; 至於說人主, 則不與子比智矣. Compare the translation by Schaberg, "Playing at Critique," 209.

108. Compare the translation by Schaberg, "Playing at Critique," 209.

109. See *Shuoyuan jiaozheng*, 217.

110. One of these is Xi Fuji 僖負羈, i.e., Cao Ji 曹羈, who is also mentioned in the introduction as the incarnation of the proprietous remonstrant; see *Shuoyuan jiaozheng*, 218, compare *Shuoyuan jiaozheng*, 206–07. For Xi Fuji or Cao Ji see note 74. By mentioning him once again, Liu Xiang establishes an associative connective link between the chapter introduction and the narrative. Thus, the reference to Cao Ji seems to be a deliberate transphrastic text-structuring device. Note that according to the *Gongyangzhuan* Cao 曹 was invaded by the Rong 戎, not by Song 宋, as *Shuoyuan* 9.9 (*Shuoyuan jiaozheng*, 218) has it.

111. Compare Schaberg, "Playing at Critique," 210, who even calls it an "exemplary direct remonstrance." Considering the abovementioned rhetorical question, which serves to pretend self-restraint, and the insinuation that the exploitation of the people is conceived of as a punishment for their crimes, I would put it less strongly.

112. See *Shuoyuan jiaozheng*, 219. Compare the use of "bad names" as analyzed in Schwermann, "Schlechte Namen."

113. See Du, *Liu Xiang bianxie* Xinxu, Shuoyuan *yanjiu*, 313–21. Compare Richter, *The Embodied Text*, who analyzes these kinds of intervention in earlier manuscripts.

114. For example, compare *Shuoyuan* 9.16 (*Shuoyuan jiaozheng*, 224–25) to its more long-winded and less pointed parallel in *Yanzi chunqiu jishi*, vol. 1, *juan* 1, 90–91. Compare also the more distant parallel in *Hanshi waizhuan jishi*, *juan* 8, 298–99.

115. This is a telling name; see Schaberg, "Playing at Critique," 201. The text has Shao Ruzi *zhe* 少孺子者, i.e., the expression *shao ruzi* 少孺子, "young child, small boy; young weakling," is marked as a personal name; see *Shuoyuan jiaozheng*, 212. Compare section 9.9 (*Shuoyuan jiaozheng*, 217) for the use of the particle *zhe* 者 as a marker of a personal name: 有諸御己者, 違楚百里而耕 "There was a

certain Zhuyu Ji. He had fled a hundred *li* from Chu and ploughed." Compare the use of *zhe* in *Shiji, juan* 63, 2146: 申不害者，京人也 "Shen Buhai was a person from Jing." For evidence that the particle is also used to mark telling names, see *Liezi*, chap. 5, in *Liezi jishi* 列子集釋, ed. Yang Bojun 楊伯峻 (Beijing: Zhonghua shuju, 1985), 159: 北山愚公者，年且九十，面山而居 "Old Father Simpleton of North Mountain was nearly ninety and lived opposite the mountain."

116. The character 附, OC *boh, in the verbal phrase *qu fu* 曲附 is a loan for *fu* 跗, OC *po, "instep, foot," here referring to the forelegs of the mantis; see Gao, *Guzi tongjia huidian*, 367.

117. The text has *huangque* 黃雀, Spinus spinus (Linnaeus); see Alfred Hoffmann, *Glossar der heute gültigen chinesischen Vogelnamen*, Veröffentlichungen des Ostasien-Instituts der Ruhr-Universität Bochum 13 (Wiesbaden: Otto Harrassowitz, 1975), 65.

118. Up to this point, Shao Ruzi's reply is rhyming, the rhyme words being *shu* 樹, OC *doh (A), *chan* 蟬, OC *dan (B), *lu* 露, OC *râkh (a), *hou* 後, OC *ĥô? (A), *chan* 蟬, OC *dan (B), *pang* 傍, OC *bâŋ, bâŋh (b), *lang* 螂, OC *râŋ (b), *xia* 下, OC *grâ? (a). The rhyme serves to draw the reader's attention both to the rhymed passage, which describes what has happened in the back garden, and to the adjacent unrhymed interpretation of these events.

119. See *Shuoyuan jiaozheng*, 212–13. Compare the parallels in *Hanshi waizhuan jishi, juan* 10, 359–60, *Wu Yue Chunqiu* 吳越春秋 (Spring and Autumn Annals of Wu and Yue), Sibu beiyao 四部備要 edition (Taipei: Zhonghua shuju, 1965), *juan* 5, 8b–9a, *Zhanguoce*, vol. 2, *juan* 17, 555–61, *Xinxu jiaoshi* 新序校釋, ed. Shi Guangying 石光瑛, 2 vols. (Beijing: Zhonghua shuju, 2001), vol. 1, chap. 2, 241–68, and *Zhuangzi* 莊子 (Master Zhuang), chap. 20: "Shanmu" 山木 (Mountain Tree), in *Zhuangzi jishi* 莊子集釋, ed. Guo Qingfan 郭慶藩, 3 vols., Xinbian zhuzi jicheng 新編諸子集成 edition (Beijing: Zhonghua shuju, 2004), vol. 2, 695.

120. See Maggie Bickford, review of *Fascination of Nature: Plants and Insects in Chinese Painting and Ceramics of the Yuan Dynasty (1279–1368)*, by Roderick Whitfield, *Artibus Asiae* 58 no. 3/4 (1999), 346 and 347. Compare Schaberg, "Playing at Critique," 208, who interprets the *Zhuangzi* variant as more abstractly revealing "to Zhuang Zhou 莊周 his own entanglement (*lei* 累) in ties of exploitation" and as being "concerned with liberation from relations of dependence" and who adds that the other variants of this anecdote are "more interested in the spectacle of a ruler forced to recognize his dependence upon other states and—more important still—his dependence upon discerning critics."

121. See *Hanshi waizhuan jishi, juan* 10, 359–60. Compare the translation of this parallel in Schaberg, "Playing at Critique," 206–07.

122. For performative aspects of indirect remonstrances and for their tripartite narratological structure see Schaberg, "Playing at Critique," 195 and 197; compare note 87 above.

123. See *Hanshi waizhuan jishi*, *juan* 10, 359.

124. For the concept of author functions and its application to early Chinese literature see Steineck and Schwermann, introduction to *That Wonderful Composite Called Author*.

125. See Trauzettel, "Stellenwert," 78. Compare the chapters by Paul R. Goldin and Andrew Seth Meyer in this volume.

126. See Trauzettel, "Stellenwert," 89, for this assessment of the role of exempla in philosophical texts.

127. See *Hanshu*, *juan* 36, 1928–66, and Christian Schwermann, trans., "Ein frühes chinesisches Modell der Herrscherkritik: Die Biographie des Liú Xiàng (79–8 v.u.Z.) in der Dynastiegeschichte der Westlichen Hàn, Teil I," *Minima Sinica* 1 (2012), 67–77.

128. For the emergence of individual authorship in early imperial China see Schwermann, "Composite Authorship in Western Zhōu Bronze Inscriptions," 30–37.

6

From Villains Outwitted to Pedants Out-Wrangled

The Function of Anecdotes in the Shifting Rhetoric of the *Han Feizi*

Heng Du[1]

Anecdotes devoted to Confucius 孔子 (551–479 BCE) populate many chapters of the *Han Feizi* 韓非子 (Master Han Fei), but they paint a confusing picture. In this text attributed to Han Fei 韓非 (ca. 280–233 BCE), Confucius is at times admired as an exemplary figure,[2] while at other times he is discredited, if not fully cast off into groups blamed for society's ills.[3] How might we account for such disparate and conflicting assessments? Contradictions in early Chinese texts are too ubiquitous to be a cause for surprise, but the jury is still out on how best to interpret them. In his companion to the *Han Feizi,* for instance, Paul R. Goldin discusses a list of possible explanations, such as multiple authorship, evolving philosophical positions, or a preference for pragmatism over philosophical consistency.[4] Goldin's list suggests that this is a complex problem that must be considered from many angles. My chapter, at the broadest level, draws attention to one neglected piece of this intricate puzzle, namely the patterns and systematic distributions underlying the apparent incongruence of early texts. I will demonstrate that—similar to Sarah A. Queen's findings in her study of Confucius in the *Huainanzi* 淮南子 (The Master of Huainan)—Confucius's metamorphosis in the *Han Feizi* is not random.[5] Not only can we identify patterns among the Confucius anecdotes, these patterns can in turn help us map larger shifts throughout this text.

Stories involving Confucius, the most ubiquitous figure in the Han Feizi, are concentrated in the "anecdote chapters."[6] Clustered in the middle of the compilation, these chapters, with titles such as "Chushuo" 儲說 (Collection of Illustrative Examples), consist mostly of series of anecdotes. Even though they occupy over half of the compilation, they received far less scholarly attention than the more essay-like chapters. Such neglect partly stems from the reception history of the *Han Feizi* and other so-called Masters texts (*zishu* 子書) from the Warring States Period 戰國 (453–221 BCE), a genre of large textual compilations that began as writings attributed to various experts and teachers. Modern scholarship often sees these texts as "philosophy," and examines them through the prism of a discursive tradition that tends to relegate narratives to an auxiliary role, as mere *exempla* (stories told to illustrate a moral point) supporting philosophical argumentation.[7] In contrast, it is exactly narrative that takes center stage in the anecdote chapters of the *Han Feizi*. As heterogeneous conglomerates, they often obscure or even subvert any semblance of philosophical consistency.

Yet, as Christian Schwermann argues in his contribution to this volume, once we approach these anecdote collections on their own terms, we begin to recognize that they often function as "argumentative elements," whose complexity far exceeds simple illustrations. Confucius's predominance in the anecdote chapters already suggests the problem with reading all of these short narratives as exempla. In chapter 50, Confucius is identified as the head of the *Han Feizi*'s chief rival, the much-reviled Confucians (*ruzhe* 儒者, a term also translated as Classicists).[8] If the function of anecdotes is limited to exemplification, figures held up as model illustrations of *Han Feizi* teachings, such as the minister Shang Yang 商鞅 (d. 338 BCE), should take precedence, but they receive little attention among the anecdote collections. In contrast, even though Confucius has a tension-filled and even adversarial relationship with the *Han Feizi*, he is the favorite subject matter of the anecdote materials. What then, is the role of anecdotes in the *Han Feizi*, and why is Confucius so prominently featured? A close reading of these chapters will not only begin to tackle these questions, but also reveal the unexpected roles of anecdotes.

Most interestingly, the anecdote chapters seem to be closely tied to the emergence of the intellectual divisions between the positions represented by Shang Yang and Confucius. These divisions are not yet consistent in the *Han Feizi*, but would become solidified categories in the imagination of Han Dynasty (202 BCE–220 CE) scholars and librarians, who classified Han Fei and Shang Yang under Legalism (*fajia* 法家), and Confucius under Confucianism (*rujia* 儒家).⁹ In contrast to the clear categories of Han bibliographies, Warring States texts present a fluid picture, where universally accepted definitions of affiliations—either institutionally or conceptually—are difficult to pin down.¹⁰ Tracing Confucius's presence in the *Han Feizi* demonstrates the complexity of the Warring States context; at the same time, it also suggests an upsurge of interest in constructing intellectual identities and oppositions.

To demonstrate the systematic shifts in the *Han Feizi* compilation, and how the anecdote chapters fit into these larger patterns, I have identified the following three clusters in the 55 chapters of the *Han Feizi*:

Table 1

Cluster	*Chapters*	*Genre*
A	1–20	Expositions
B	21–23, 30–39¹¹	Anecdotes
C	40–51¹²	Expositions

This division, which is primarily based on genre characteristics, also coincides with the major changes in *rhetorical situation* (with whom the text argues) and *rhetorical strategy* (how the text argues).

Cluster A can be described as what I will call "univocal" expositions, which deliver the core *Han Feizi* doctrines, often with the ruler as the addressee, without any injection of alternative voice or perspective.¹¹ Confucius appears only once in these chapters.¹²

Cluster C is polyphonic. Its chapters either take on a dialogue form, or simulate debate with competing teachings. Only in this last cluster do we encounter the famous critiques of rivals referred to as Confucians (*ruzhe*) and Mohists (*mozhe* 墨者).¹³

The anecdote chapters of Cluster B furnish the transition between Clusters A and C, and can be divided into two (see Table 2); its first half, Cluster B1 (chapters 21–23, and 30–31), resemble Cluster A in its univocal orientation, while the second half, Cluster B2 (chapters 32–39), is more closely aligned with Cluster C, and anticipates its polyphonic characteristics. Anecdotes devoted to Confucius appear most frequently in Cluster B: 39 of the total 47 instances. In correspondence to the changes in rhetorical orientation, Confucius's role and portrayal undergoes a remarkable transformation between Clusters B1 and B2. Thus, through a close reading of these Confucius anecdotes, we will observe this pivotal transition in rhetorical situation and strategy.

Table 2

Cluster	Chapters	Rhetoric	Confucius
A	1–20	Univocal expositions of core Han Feizi teachings	1x
B1	21–23, 30–31		11x
B2	32–39	Polyphonic dialogues and debates	28x
C	40–51		7x

Cluster A and Cluster C: Villains vs. Pedants

In this section, I will give an overview of the two exposition Clusters listed in Table 1, Cluster A and Cluster C. I will begin by describing the rhetorical situation in Cluster A and how it influences this Cluster's implicit rhetorical strategies and explicit discussions of rhetoric. Then through concrete examples, I will describe the changes observed in Cluster C, its new rhetorical situation and argumentative strategies.

As I mentioned earlier, Cluster A is preoccupied with the didactic presentations of core *Han Feizi* teachings. Chapter 6, "Youdu" 有度 (Let There Be Standards), for instance, argues for the benefit of a crucial concept, *fa* 法. Often translated as "standards" or "laws," *fa* in this context denotes a code of evaluative standards that must be obeyed by all, regardless of rank and position. Like many of the Cluster A chapters, "Youdu" is addressed to the ruler, "the ruler of humankind" (*renzhu* 人主), promising him that by embodying *fa*, he can safeguard the state against the impingement of private (*si* 私) interests.[14] Chapter 5, "Zhudao" 主道 (The Way of the Sovereign), instructs the ruler in strategies for keeping his courtiers in check, such as concealing intentions in "emptiness and quietude" (*xujing* 虛靜) while verifying the courtiers' words against their actions.[15] Such an art of rulership is further elaborated in chapters such as chapter 7, "Erbing" 二柄 (Two Handles), chapter 8, "Yangquan" 揚權 (Brandishing Authority), and chapter 16, "Sanshou" 三守 (Three Precautions). A few other chapters similarly offer counsel to the ruler, but from a different angle: chapter 4, "Aichen" 愛臣 (Court Favorites) and chapter 9, "Bajian" 八姦 (Eight Kinds of Treachery), for instance, draw up taxonomies of villains, whose detailed descriptions serve as guides for uncovering malevolent courtiers.

All these chapters revolve around the power struggle between the ruler and his subjects. Addressed to the ruler, these chapters try to convince him that he is constantly under the threat of victimization by "villainous ministers" (*jianchen* 姦臣) or "influential men" (*zhongren* 重人).[16] At the same time, they recommend to his majesty the heroes of the *Han Feizi*, the "gentlemen capable of *fa*" or "*fa* specialists" (*neng fa zhi shi* 能法之士).[17] Complementing the chapters devoted to ideal rulers and archetypical villains, quite a few other chapters—such as chapter 3, "Nanyan" 難言 (Finding It Hard to Speak), chapter 11, "Gufen" 孤憤 (Solitary Indignation), chapter 12, "Shuinan" 說難 (The Difficulties of Persuasion), and chapter 13, "Heshi" 和氏 (Mr. He)—can be read as self-portraits of the *Han Feizi* protagonists, who are said to be enterprising and selfless. Overall, Cluster A characterizes court intrigues as a game between the vulnerable ruler, the threatening ministers, and the gallant *fa* specialists, a game that is reminiscent of an archetypical triangular relationship between the victim, the villain, and the hero. This is a brutal game, for the villains are said to be particularly lethal; they can manipulate the ruler into wantonly executing anyone standing in their way, nor do they shy away from committing regicide.[18]

Rhetoric, as it turns out, is the *fa* specialists' most vital tool, for the outcome of this game depends almost entirely on their ability to persuade. Cluster A does not question the teachings of the *Han Feizi*, or the efficacy of the *fa* specialists' program. According to this cluster of chapters, the only challenge lies in whether the *fa* specialist gains access to the ruler's ear. The abundance of words describing "blockages" (such as *sai* 塞 or *yong* 壅) attests to this challenge. These words refer to the villain courtiers' monopoly of the ruler's attention, as they seek to choke off any other channel of information to their lord.[19] Accordingly, the self-portraits of the protagonists all revolve around the hero who ventures to persuade, *shui* 說, the ruler without regard to threats or obstacles.[20]

This precarious court setting and the triangulated game between the ruler, the villain courtiers, and the *fa* specialists is in fact the rhetorical situation of Cluster A. Chapter 12, "Shuinan," for instance, is a set of rhetorical instructions specifically tailored for this setting. Many readers in the reception of history of the *Han Feizi* have been troubled by the manipulative rhetorical art found in "Shuinan."[21] But, as Wai-yee Li has analyzed in detail, the chapter addresses the delicate and volatile psychology specific to the court setting, where true intentions have to be circumspectly concealed, and persuasion can only be accomplished through cautious probing, suggesting, and pandering. Persuading the ruler, according to "Shuinan," is as dangerous as taming a dragon, and requires a long-term process involving careful nursing of trust.[22]

However, such a set of rhetorical strategies also generates a new challenge: these obsequious and manipulative techniques not only render the persuader-protagonists nearly indistinguishable from the villainous courtiers, they are exactly what the ruler is instructed to fend off. Indeed, how do the *fa* specialists, who are also courtiers, distinguish themselves from the alleged villains? Another interesting feature of Cluster A might in fact be designed to address this dilemma. As Michael Hunter has pointed out, the key distinction between *fa* persuaders and villainous ministers lies in their intention and character, or—in terms often used in the *Han Feizi*—whether they are "selfish" or "selfless" (*wusi* 無私).[23] This explains Cluster A's incessant praise for the *fa* specialists' upright character. But such a moral distinction is internal and subjective, especially in a setting where no one's alleged intention should be trusted.

Thus, as if to sear the unmistakable signs of selflessness onto the bodies of the *fa* specialists, a disturbing motif that graphically describes the persuaders' physical suffering haunts the protagonists' self-portraits. This is most prominently featured by an exhaustive list of wrongly punished persuaders in the "Nanyan" chapter.[24] One way to make sense of this grim motif is by borrowing the concept of "costly signaling," which entails that there is no particular reason to put stock in someone's profession of virtuous intent, since it can be made at no cost. But a speech at risk of incurring punishment comes with a cost, and therefore only those who truly care about the ruler's interest would make it. Following this logic, the willingness to face even physical punishment is a trustworthy signal of one's "selflessness," and the description of the consequent suffering is the externalization of the matyrs' internal and invisible moral qualities. The mutilated Mr. He of chapter 13 is a parable that takes this logic to its visceral extreme: like the persuader martyr, who is allegedly willing to brave the ruler's wrath to offer advice, Mr. He repeatedly presents a piece of precious jade, even though the ruler, unable to recognize the treasure, cuts off one of his limbs every time.[25] The willingness to sacrifice one's body, one might say, is a literal enactment of selflessness. Thus references to suffering are also a rhetorical strategy, which attempts to appeal to the ruler by demarcating a moral distinction between oneself and the supposed villains.

The rhetorical strategies I have discussed—be it the explicit instructions of the "Shuinan" chapter or the implicit emphasis on the signaling of the persuaders' moral character—are customized for the rhetorical situation of Cluster A, amidst the triangulated game between the ruler, the villain, and the *fa* specialists; as this setting shifts in Cluster C, a new type

From Villains Outwitted to Pedants Out-Wrangled 199

of rhetorical approach emerges. In the Cluster C chapters (40–51), a new group of antagonists, the "learned men" (*xuezhe* 學者), step onto the scene, and replace the "villainous courtiers." Even though the ruler is still at times appealed to—only nominally at best—these chapters are chiefly preoccupied with the debate with these "learned men." This in turn changes the explicit discussions of rhetoric and the implicit usage of rhetorical strategies. There is no more lengthy instruction on *how* to talk to the ruler. Discussions of the psychology of persuasion grow scarce, as do the persuaders' moral motivations. The persuader-martyr motif similarly fades away. Below, I will explore in greater detail the possible reasons for these interesting shifts.

Chapter 41, "Wenbian" 問辯 (Inquiry into Disputation), can be read as a depiction of the new rhetorical situation. As I have suggested, while Cluster A is a univocal presentation of the *Han Feizi* doctrines, Cluster C is enmeshed in polyphonic polemics. Accordingly, the "Wenbian" chapter describes the origin of *bian* 辯 (argument, disputation, or debate) as follows:

> In an age of chaos [. . .] the lord on high issues orders, but his people refute them with textual learning; the government issues laws but the people distort them in their private conduct. The ruler of humankind allows for the erosion of law and order, all the while revering the learned men's knowledge and conduct. This is why there is so much textual learning in our time. [. . .] Thus in a chaotic age, this is how speeches are received: abstruseness as a mark of insight, and verbosity as eloquence; this is how conduct is observed: eccentricity as a mark of worth, and disobedience as loftiness of spirit. Because the ruler of humankind is pleased by such "insightful" and "eloquent" speeches, and venerates such "worthy" and "lofty" conduct, he cannot be rectified by the men who create laws and methods, even as they establish examples for what to adopt or discard, and single out contentious disputations. Therefore, myriad are the people dressed in scholarly garb and wearing swords, but few are those tilling and fighting; words on "hard and white" or "without thickness" flourish, while law and order dwindle. Therefore it is said, "When a lord lacks perspicacity, debate arises."

亂世則 [. . .] 主上有令而民以文學非之, 官府有法民以私行矯之. 人主顧漸其法令而尊學者之智行, 此世之所以多文學

也 [. . .] 是以亂世之聽言也，以難知為察，以博文為辯；其觀行也，以離群為賢，以犯上為抗。人主者說辯察之言，尊賢抗之行，故夫作法術之人，立取舍之行，別辭爭之論，而莫為之正。是以儒服帶劍者眾，而耕戰之士寡；堅白無厚之詞章，而憲令之法息. 故曰：上不明則辯生焉。[26]

In this new rhetorical situation, the *fa* specialists, the "men who create laws and methods" (*zuo fa shu zhi ren* 作法術之人), remain the protagonists. The excerpt may at first appear to resemble the narratives in Cluster A, since it associates the rise of debate with a ruler's benightedness. But in Cluster A it was the rogue courtiers who were accused of obstructing the lord's ears, while here, the "learned men" are the culprits. Cluster C's characterization of the "learned men" differs strikingly from that of the "villainous ministers." Unlike the latter, they are not associated with regicidal tendencies, nor do they possess a proclivity for dismembering other fellow courtiers. Instead, they are distinguished by their predilection for disputes and their fixation on textual learning (*wenxue* 文學). Such new enemies, lacking the earlier villains' menacing presence, border on the ridiculous; they are verbose and difficult to understand, though "dressed in scholarly garb and wearing a sword" (*rufu daijian zhe* 儒服帶劍者), they cannot be counted on to engage in any real fighting. In contrast to the villains of Cluster A, who are elaborately catalogued but are almost never given a line to speak, the pedants of Cluster C are not just accused of speaking too much, their words and thoughts are now inserted into the *Han Feizi*, even if only in the form of sound bites and mischaracterizations. Through these snippets, we begin to see a certain resemblance between these new opponents and the Warring States Masters (*zhuzi* 諸子). If Cluster A chapters are the *fa* specialists' monologues *to* the ruler, the Cluster C chapters suggest scenes of debate *in front of* the ruler, against rival proponents of ideas.

Highlighting the divergence between Clusters A and C, there are major changes in the meaning and significance of key terms associated with rhetoric itself. In Cluster A, the practice of persuasion, *shui*, was central to the hero's identity; but in Cluster C, the term *shui* almost exclusively appears in negative contexts associated with figures criticized by the text.[27] Similar trends are also reflected in other lexical changes: even though *bian* as debate is a crucial concept in Cluster C, this usage is virtually absent in Cluster A, where *bian* means either astute, discerning, or, in a negative sense, sophistic.[28] Similarly, the term *wenxue* is used all but once in Cluster A, and in a neutral sense, while in Cluster C, *wenxue* as textual learning is consistently a negative concept, often—as in the passage above—declaimed as the cause of the state's downfall.²⁹ The fondness of speech and words, of *shui*, *bian*, and *wenxue*, now characteristically defines the opponent. It is the learned men who are the rhetoricians, engaged in discussions of "hard and white" (*jian bai* 堅白), i.e., meaningless arguments.³⁰ The *fa* specialists in Cluster C cannot renounce the power of speech more readily, even though in practice, as I will further discuss below, they are not immune from pedantic arguments. Despite Cluster C's avowed change of heart regarding rhetoric, debate is not only frequently mentioned, it is now the dominant discursive mode. The *fa* specialists in Cluster C rarely present their teaching without *bian*, without disputating the opponents' positions.

With the rhetorical situation entirely transformed, the focus of rhetorical strategy also shifts: from the *context* to the *content* of speeches. In the bloodstained game of Cluster A, the art of rhetoric revolves around how to create a favorable and relatively safe *context* for the delivery of the *fa* specialists' message. The three anecdotes at the end of "Shuinan," as Goldin points out, articulate this concern. They demonstrate that depending on the context, the same statement or action can lead to drastically different interpretations and consequences.³¹ Such a focus on the context of speech naturally leads to a preoccupation with pragmatics and psychology, as exemplified by the "Shuinan" chapter. But in Cluster C, for reasons still to be investigated, the presence of the ruler and the sinister courtiers fades away, and a new type of game emerges, which is far more akin to intellectual debate. Court intrigue and its dangers are no longer the looming backdrop, as the *fa* specialists now need to *demonstrate*, argumentatively, why their teaching should be preferred over other alternatives. Accordingly, the implicit rhetorical strategies of Cluster C are redirected toward dismantling the *content* of the opposing arguments, and the language, logic, and premises of the opponents' teachings are now the new targets.

The opening of chapter 50, "Xianxue," where Confucius is for the first time named the head of the Confucians, exemplifies these new rhetorical approaches:

> The prominent teachings of our time come from the Confucians and the Mohists. The foremost Confucian is Kong Qiu [Confucius], and the foremost Mohist is Mo Di [Mozi]. After the death of Confucius, there were Confucians who followed Zizhang, Confucians who followed Zisi [. . .] Thus after Confucius and Mozi, the Confucians splintered into eight factions, and the

Mohists into three. Though their tenets mutually contradict, they each call themselves the true Confucians or the true Mohists. Since Confucius and Mozi cannot come back to life, who can provide a basis for the teachings of our time? Confucius and Mozi both sought to follow Yao and Shun, and though their tenets mutually contradict, they each claimed to be the true Yao and Shun. Since Yao and Shun cannot come back to life, who can establish the truth between the Confucians and the Mohists? Even though [the transition between] the Yin [i.e., Shang; ca. 1500–1045 BCE] and Zhou [ca. 1045–256 BCE] dynasties is *only* over seven hundred years removed, and between Yu and Xia [mythical to semi-mythical reigns] over two thousand, they already cannot provide a basis for the truth of the Confucian and Mohist teachings.[32] Now, when one even wishes to scrutinize the ways of Yao and Shun from three thousand years ago, how can one ascertain whatever one imagines? Accepting certainty without corroboration of evidence is foolish; citing as authority what cannot be ascertained is fallacious. Therefore, those who take the Former Kings as clear evidence and Yao and Shun as ascertained knowledge are either foolish or fallacious. Foolish and fallacious teachings, just as disorderly and rebellious conduct, ought not to be accepted by perspicacious rulers.

世之顯學, 儒, 墨也. 儒之所至, 孔丘也. 墨之所至, 墨翟也. 自孔子之死也, 有子張之儒, 有子思之儒 [. . .] 故孔, 墨之後, 儒分為八, 墨離為三, 取舍相反不同, 而皆自謂真孔, 墨; 孔, 墨不可復生, 將誰使定後世之學乎? 孔子, 墨子俱道堯, 舜, 而取舍不同, 皆自謂真堯, 舜; 堯, 舜不復生, 將誰使定儒, 墨之誠乎? 殷, 周七百餘歲, 虞, 夏二千餘歲, 而不能定儒, 墨之真, 今乃欲審堯, 舜之道於三千歲之前, 意者其不可必乎! 無參驗而必之者, 愚也; 弗能必而據之者, 誣也. 故明據先王, 必定堯, 舜者, 非愚則誣也. 愚誣之學, 雜反之行, 明主弗受也.[33]

Kidder Smith has noted this passage's professed obsession with ascertaining claims.[34] This passage not only questions the knowability of Confucius's true teachings, it also questions Confucius's authorities, the Former Kings (*xianwang* 先王). The term "Former Kings" refers to a series of idealized ancient rulers, ranging from the mythical Yao 堯 and Shun 舜 to the founders of the Zhou dynasty, King Wen 文王 and King Wu 武王. Here, Confucius and the Former Kings are identified as the foundation upon which the Confucian camp's claim to authority rests. Thus when it casts doubt on the accessibility of these figures, it not only challenges Confucian teaching's veneration of the past, it also represents a strategic attack that pulls the rug out from under the Confucian discursive system. Other chapters in Cluster C utilize such strategies as well. Chapter 49, "Wudu" 五蠹 (Five Vermin) and chapter 51, "Zhongxiao" 忠孝 (Loyalty and Piety), for instance, offer close readings of the "Former Kings" narratives for the purpose of identifying their contradictions. Throughout Cluster C, retracing opponents' source of authority to launch a targeted attack is a recurring rhetorical strategy.

This new rhetorical approach also brings about drastic changes in the meaning and significance of words denoting Confucian virtues, such as humaneness (*ren* 仁) and righteousness (*yi* 義). While such vocabularies are innocuous and positive terms in Cluster A, Cluster C endeavors to negatively redefine them. Chapter 44, "Shuiyi" 說疑 (Suspicion of the Persuaders) and chapter 46, "Liufan" 六反 (Six Contrarieties), for instance, demonstrate how concepts such as humaneness, righteousness, and wisdom (*zhi* 智) can be the source of chaos. Chapter 47, "Bashuo" 八說 (Eight Appellations),[35] criticizes the humane men (*renren* 仁人) and the gentlemen (*junzi* 君子), portraying the positive figures of the Confucian discourse as threats against social order.[36] On the other hand, the preference in Cluster A for charitable interpretations of these moral terms finds its best illustration in, surprisingly, the exegesis of the *Laozi* 老子 (Old Master) material, chapter 20, "Jie Lao" 解老 (Explicating *Laozi*). In stark contrast to Cluster C's cynical readings, "Jie Lao" takes pains to preserve the positive meanings of terms like *ren* and *yi*, even in its interpretation of passages such as *Laozi*, chapter 38, which, literally read, disparages humaneness and propriety as the degeneration of the Way.[37] As Queen points out, "Jie Lao" seems to be interested in harmonizing these Confucian virtues with the *Laozi* text.[38]

These rhetorical shifts correlate with transformations in Confucius's appearances. There is only one single reference to Confucius in all twenty chapters of Cluster A; it is in chapter 3, "Nanyan." This chapter is styled as a memorial to the ruler by the putative author Han Fei, who conjures up a long list of suffering persuaders as his predecessors, i.e., the list of persuader-martyrs I have already discussed. Confucius is included in this list, praised for being skilled at persuasion and lamented for his detention at Kuang 匡.³⁹ Since this memorial is written in the voice of Han Fei, the text implicitly places its putative author in this tradition of persuaders, and essentially compares Han Fei to Confucius. But the *fa* specialists of Cluster C would draw a clear line between themselves and Confucius, as we have seen in the opening of "Xianxue." At the same time, it is only in this new polemical context that more references to Confucius occur, seven times in the twelve chapters of Cluster C. While Cluster A identifies with Confucius, Cluster C uses Confucius to represent alternative (and opposing) voices, eventually to represent the Confucians. In other instantiations of Confucius in this final group of chapters, he either typifies the "learned man" who speaks cleverly and is fond of debate,⁴⁰ or lends voice to the Confucian position.⁴¹ As I will further argue below, this Confucian Confucius reflects the polyphonic characteristic of the second half of the *Han Feizi* compilation.

In summary, by observing shifts in rhetorical situation and strategy, we begin to see broad and systematic changes between the first and the last groups of chapters in the *Han Feizi*. In Cluster A, persuasion occurs between the *fa* specialist and the ruler, with the other powerful courtiers as the primary antagonists. In Cluster C, argumentation takes place between *fa* specialists and proponents of competing teachings, as garrulous pedants replace the bloodthirsty ministers. Accordingly, Cluster A contains mostly speeches to the ruler, univocally expounding the *fa* specialists' teaching, while Cluster C is dominated by polemical debate. In Cluster A, explicit discussions of rhetorical strategies revolve around the psychology of the court context, but in Cluster C rhetorical strategies zoom in on the *content* of arguments.

This observation, I argue, begins to address the inconsistencies scholars have identified. Goldin, for instance, has pointed out the clashing treatments of the Former Kings: despite the vocal disdain for the "foolish" people who appeal to the ancients, the *Han Feizi* itself has also cited the Former Kings as authority, such as in chapter 6, "Youdu."⁴² Indeed, that illustrious list of suffering persuaders in chapter 3 also includes King Wen—the Former King who is the bona fide Confucian paragon—among its rank. But these inconsistencies are no longer so jarring in view of the systematic shift we have discussed. These instances all occur in Cluster A, where rhetorical conventions utilized by Confucian texts are generally accepted. They come under fire once we enter into the new polemical context of Cluster C, where nearly half of the chapters contest ideas that are identifiably Confucian.

Tracing Transition in Cluster B

In this section, I will focus on the anecdote chapters of Cluster B, divided into B1 and B2 in table 3 below. Unlike Clusters A and C, which largely resemble discursive essays, Cluster B contains thirteen chapters of different types of anecdote compilations. Chapter 21, "Yu Lao" 喻老 (Illustrating the *Laozi*), similar to chapter 20 in Cluster A, explicates *Laozi* materials, albeit not through philosophical discussions, but through anecdotes. Chapters 22 and 23, the two "Shuolin" 說林 (Forest of Illustrative Examples) chapters, pull together clever retorts as well as short tales of crafty actions.[43] Following a series of short chapters,[44] we encounter another large block of anecdote collections, the six "Chushuo" chapters. Subdivided into the inner (*nei* 內) "Chushuo," chapters 30 and 31, and the outer (*wai* 外) "Chushuo," chapters 32 through 35, these chapters conform to the same structure, beginning with the enumeration of several principles of rulership followed by a collection of illustrative anecdotes. The four chapters entitled "Nan" 難 (Critiques), which contain not only anecdotes, but also critiques or debates over the validity of the anecdote's message, follow the "Chushuo" chapters.

Table 3[45]

Cluster	Rhetoric	Chapters	Confucius
A: Expositions	*univocal*	1–20	1x
B1: Anecdotes	*expositions of core Han Feizi teachings*	21: "Yu Lao" 22–23: "Shuolin" 30–31: "Nei chushuo"	11x
B2: Anecdotes	*polyphonic dialogues and debate*	32–35: "Wai chushuo" 36–39: "Nan"	28x
C: Expositions		40–51	7x

As I have discussed, while intellectual historians and philosophers often quote the exposition chapters of Clusters A and C, the anecdote collections in the middle of the text have received far less scholarly attention. Often presumed to be carelessly compiled receptacles of raw materials, these chapters' compositional design tends to be overlooked. There is, for instance, a debate over whether the "inner" and "outer" division of the "Chushuo" chapters (shaded in grey in table 3) is meaningful. Most scholars have either denied any significance, or viewed the outer chapters as less polished and more disorderly "draft materials."[46] But if we choose to see anecdote collections as "argumentative elements," their rhetorical situations and strategies soon become apparent. This observation in turn reveals a similar development from the univocal to the polyphonic between the earlier and the later parts of Cluster B, neatly mirroring the contrasting characteristics of Clusters A and C. The moment of transition, I argue, falls exactly between the inner and outer "Chushuo" chapters, so that chapters 30 and 31, the two inner chapters, are univocal and homogeneous like Cluster A, while chapters 32 through 35, the four outer chapters, are much more polyphonic and heterogeneous, like Cluster C. Once this division is drawn, it also becomes clear that the debate scenes of the ensuing "Nan" chapters are a continuation of the polyphonic characteristic of the outer "Chushuo" chapters, and anticipate the polemic orientation of Cluster C. Thus not only is the inner-outer division of the "Chushuo" chapters meaningful, it speaks to the overall organization of the anecdote collections. Accordingly, I divide Cluster B into B1, chapters 21 through 23 and 30 and 31, and B2, chapters 32 through 39.[47]

Before demonstrating this transition in greater detail, let us first take a closer look at the distinct structure of the "Chushuo" chapters. Each of these six chapters begins with a list of teachings labeled guidelines (*jing* 經), followed by a collection of short texts meant to explain and illustrate them. The illustrative materials consist mostly of anecdotes, though aphorisms and sayings are also included. The guideline texts not only succinctly state the *fa* specialists' doctrines; they also enumerate the anecdotes associated with them in rhythmic lines that often fall into parallel couplets, possibly a form of mnemonic chant, as in the following example:

> With too much charity, laws cannot be upheld; with too little authority, the inferior encroaches on the superior. Therefore, when punishments and penalties are not a certainty, proscriptions and decrees cannot be implemented. For illustrative examples, see: "Master Dong traveling through Shiyi," and "Zichan instructing You Ji." Thus "Zhongni [Confucius] explained [a record] of frost," and the "laws of Yin [Shang dynasty] mutilated ash litterers." "The overseer took leave from Yue Chi," and "Gongsun Yang [Shang Yang] heavily punished light offenses" [. . .] Duke Si [of Wei] understood it, therefore he sold the convict.

愛多者則法不立, 威寡者則下侵上. 是以刑罰不必, 則禁令不行. 其說在董子之行石邑, 與子產之教游吉也. 故仲尼說隕霜, 而殷法刑棄灰; 將行去樂池, 而公孫鞅重輕罪 [...] 嗣公知之, 故買胥靡.[48]

In such guideline texts, the allusions to anecdotes are usually introduced by the set phrase "for illustrative examples, see . . ." (*qi shuo zai* 其說在), which seems to have prompted modern editions to add the label illustrative examples (*shuo* 說) to the ensuing sets of anecdotes.[49] Schwermann suggests that such a guideline–illustration (*jing–shuo*) structure likely reflects a "mode of writing" practiced in the Warring States Period; some of the chapters from the first century BCE compilation *Shuoyuan* 說苑 (Garden of Illustrative Examples), featured in Schwermann's contribution to this volume, follow a similar structure.

As I have already suggested, the "inner-outer" division of the "Chushuo" chapters occupies a pivotal position in the rhetorical transition outlined above. I will now demonstrate this by tracing the changing appearance of Confucius in Cluster B, in the inner "Chushuo," outer "Chushuo," and the "Nan" chapters, respectively. In the inner "Chushuo" chapters, there are a total of six anecdotes featuring Confucius, five of which utilize Confucius as a mouthpiece delivering the teachings of the *fa* specialist. For example, among the four Confucius anecdotes in chapter 30, "Nei chushuo, shang" 內儲說上 (Inner Collection of Illustrative Examples, Part One), three serve to illustrate the guideline quoted above, preaching the necessity of absolute punishment. Among them is the anecdote below, where Confucius endorses the application of heavy punishment, as he expounds an alleged Shang dynasty law:

> The laws of Yin [Shang dynasty] sentence to mutilation those who discard ashes on the street. [Confucius's disciple] Zigong thought it severe, and asked Zhongni [Confucius] about it. Zhongni said, "This shows understanding for the way to govern. Discarding ashes on the street will inevitably lead to someone covered with ashes. Covered with ashes, that person will become angry. Anger will lead to aggression. Aggression will surely result in kinsmen injuring each other. Since this is the path toward injury among kin, even punishment by mutilation is appropriate. Moreover, heavy punishment is deemed abhorrent, while refraining from discarding ashes is deemed easy. Making people do what they

deem easy so as to avoid what they deem abhorrent is the way to govern.

> 殷之法刑棄灰於街者. 子貢以為重, 問之仲尼. 仲尼曰:「知治之道也. 夫灰於街必掩人, 掩人, 人必怒, 怒則鬭, 鬭必三族相殘也. 此殘三族之道也, 雖刑之可也. 且夫重罰者, 人之所惡也; 而無棄灰, 人之所易也. 使人行之所易而無離所惡, 此治之道.」[50]

Such enthusiasm for harsh punishment can hardly pass for a Confucian stance, and the attribution of such sentiment to the sage thoroughly appalled the influential scholar Wang Yinglin 王應麟 (1223–1296).[51] At the same time, this position is indistinguishable from that of a *fa* specialist. Hence, similar to the suffering persuader *exempla* list of Cluster A, which likens Han Fei to Confucius, Cluster B1 has created a Confucius in its own image. This version of Confucius bears almost no resemblance to the Confucian Master familiar to modern readers, but is more akin to a puppet in the hands of the *Han Feizi* ventriloquist.

In fact, Confucius's comment on the mutilation laws is repeated nearly verbatim in a comment on Shang Yang's laws, also listed as an illustration for the guideline quoted above:

> The laws of Gongsun Yang [Shang Yang] are severe on light offenses. Heavy crimes are what people loath to commit, whereas small transgressions are easy to do away with. Making people do away with what is easy, so as to avoid what they loath to commit, this is the way of governance.

> 公孫鞅之法也重輕罪. 重罪者, 人之所難犯也; 而小過者, 人之所易去也. 使人去其所易, 無離其所難, 此治之道.[52]

Evidently, the same mantra, "making people do away with what is easy, so as to avoid what they loath to commit," can be associated with Confucius (the foremost Confucian) and Shang Yang (the exemplary *fa* specialist). In the remaining anecdotes of Cluster B1, Confucius identifies obstructions in the ruler's information channel, interprets a line from classical text as commending absolute punishment, and puts out a fire by threatening to punish anyone that shrinks from firefighting.[53] In all of these stories, Confucius is indistinguishable from the *fa* specialists.

How might contemporaneous readers of the *Han Feizi* have reacted to the conflation of Confucius and Shang Yang? The possibilities seem endless. Perhaps a contemporaneous reader would have seen these Confucius anecdotes as out of character, and would have, appreciating the rhetorical effect of ventriloquizing one's opponent, smiled a knowing smile. Or perhaps, the survival of such atypical Confucius anecdotes provides a precious glimpse into a world where a universally accepted image of the sage has yet to be created.[54] It is possible that just as Cluster A, which appeals to exemplary figures without regard for their (possibly later) intellectual affiliations, Cluster B1 utilizes Confucius as one among a repertoire of wisdom figures conventionally evoked to lend authority—to almost any content—not unlike Confucius's role in popular culture today. Indeed, while the intellectual content of the Confucius and the Shang Yang anecdotes are nearly identical, their difference lies in their rhetorical framework. The former places this content in the ancient time of the Shang dynasty, and suggests that its significance requires the explanation of a Master in accordance with the conventions of a "teaching scene."[55] Paired up with the Shang Yang passage, the Confucius anecdote almost appears to be a demonstration of how to adduce ancient authorities.

However we might interpret Confucius' function in Cluster B1, Cluster B2 begins to deploy the sage differently. To explain this shift, I need to first describe the overall changes in rhetorical situation and strategies, a shift detectable in the very first chapter of Cluster B2, which is also the first outer "Chushuo" chapter, chapter 32, "Wai chushuo, zuo, shang" 外儲說左上 (Outer Collection of Illustrative Examples, Part One of the Left). It is in this chapter that extensive refutations of rival teachings begin to appear. Quite a few Warring States Master figures, such as Mozi, step onto the scene for the first time, to be denounced or caricatured in ways similar to those in Cluster C.[56] Unlike the univocal presentation of the *fa* specialists' tenets in Clusters A and B1, where even Confucius serves to propagate the *fa* specialists' messages, over half of the seven guidelines from chapter 32 actually discuss aspects of the Confucian positions.

The third guideline, for instance, launches the first serious attack on the appeal to antiquity rhetoric, an important trope in Confucian and Mohist texts. As the following excerpt suggests, such attacks aim to cast doubt on the ancient texts revered by the "learned men," such as the odes and the bronze inscriptions about the "Former Kings:"

> Moreover, the Former Kings' rhapsodies and hymns, as well as their inscriptions on bells and tripods, are just like the "Imprints

on Mount Panwu" and the "Game Board on Mount Hua." If so, then what the Former Kings desired was profit, and what they employed was power. [. . .] Suppose we allow the learned men to put into practice the unfathomable [teachings] attributed to the Former Kings—perhaps it is indeed not so fitting for today?

且先王之賦頌, 鍾鼎之銘, 皆播 (番)吾之跡, 華山之博也. 然先王所期者利也, 所用者力也 [. . .] 請許學者而行宛曼於先王, 或者不宜今乎.⁵⁷

This dense passage can be slowly unpacked once we refer to the appended anecdotes: the "Imprints on Mount Panwu" and "Game board on Mount Hua" refer to the self-aggrandizing monuments supposedly built by two Warring States lords, King Zhao of Qin and King Wuling of Zhao. They are said to have sent artisans to carve up colossal footprints or game boards on the mountaintops of Mt. Panwu and Mt. Hua, with inscriptions insinuating that these rulers had encountered or even played games with immortals.⁵⁸ Chapter 32 introduces these two anecdotes to make a specific argument, namely that ancient texts can be artifacts fabricated to legitimize power, and should not be naively read as attestations of historical truth. By analogy, this guideline argues, the praises of the Former Kings, inscribed on bronze or eulogized in poems, are not necessarily evidence of a lost golden age—they could also have been propaganda no more credible than the recent kings' fabrications. In this case, there is no reason to believe that the Former Kings, unlike the rulers today, preferred virtue over profit (*li* 利) and power (*li* 力) as both means and end of their political pursuit, as the learned men would claim. Like the opening of "Xianxue," this guideline also challenges the authority of the Former Kings, but through an alternative line of reasoning that is startlingly familiar to a modern audience. By identifying a relationship between discourse and power, it complicates a historical document's relationship to historical truth, and furthermore, constructs an alternative genealogy of the Former Kings' virtues defined by their desire for profit and reliance on power.

While argument against antiquity is nearly absent before Cluster B2, it becomes a recurrent motif beginning with this passage, all the way into Cluster C. Scholars from the late nineteenth century onward have associated the *Han Feizi* with an evolutionary and progressive view of history, in contrast to the conservative attitude attributed to the Confucians. This dichotomy has been criticized as simplistic, but Yuri Pines in his recent article points out that aspects of the "changing with time" position in the *Han Feizi*, along with similar arguments in the *Shangjunshu* 商君書 (Book of Lord Shang), are indeed unique among Warring States writings, especially in their conception of history as a gradually evolving process.[59] I would add that, at least in the *Han Feizi*, the "changing with time" thesis seems to have arisen not from an interest in history *per se*, but from the desire to challenge the foundation of other Warring States teachings. The conception of history reflected in the "changing with time" argument is highly inconsistent: some passages argue that the ages of the Former Kings were too idyllic to be relevant for the degenerate present,[60] while other passages, like the one above, are altogether skeptical of the idealization of the past. What they have in common, however, is their target, for they invariably serve to discredit the antagonists of Clusters B2 and C, the learned men, or the so-called Confucians and Mohists (*ru-mo* 儒墨). The opening of chapter 49, "Wudu," for instance, famously constructs a "history of progress" chronicling ancient heroes' technological innovations;[61] but the text goes on to closely analyze the accounts of the Former Kings, pointing out in each case how "the ancient and present times differ in their custom" (*gu jin yi su* 古今異俗),[62] before culminating in an elaborate attack on the Confucians and Mohists.[63]

After the atmosphere of polemics descends upon B2, the fifth guideline of chapter 32 presents Confucius for the first time as a negative example. In this negative role, he is once again recognizable as a Confucian sage. This guideline, along with other sections of Cluster B2, suggests an ongoing debate between the Confucians and the *fa* specialists over the role of the ruler:

> As the Ode says, "If he does not labor personally, the people will have no faith in him." The commentary illustrates this with [how the King of Qi made sure that] "none dressed in purple," and it is extended to Duke Jian of Zheng and Duke Xiang of Song, instructing these highly privileged men to farm and fight.[64] But he who, instead of establishing hierarchies and demanding success, applies himself personally to the affairs of the inferiors,[65] is only behaving like [Duke Jing of Qi] "descending from chariot to run on foot," or [King Zhao of Wei] "falling asleep" [in trying to read legal codes], or those who "hid in plain clothes."[66] Kong Qiu [Confucius] did not understand this, and that is why he recommended [rulers to] be like a bowl; the Lord of Zou did not

understand this, and that is why he humiliated himself first [by cutting the tassel of his own hat].⁶⁷ The way of a perspicacious ruler emulates "Shuxiang who distributed benefits"⁶⁸ [according to merit] and "Marquis Zhao who [learned] whether to listen" [to pleas for favor].

詩曰:「不躬不親, 庶民不信.」傳說之以無衣紫, 緩之以鄭簡, 宋襄, 責尊厚以耕戰. 夫不明分, 不責誠, 而以躬親位下, 且為下走睡臥, 與夫揆弊微服. 孔丘不知, 故稱猶盂. 鄒君不知, 故先自僇. 明主之道, 如叔向賦獵, 與昭侯之奚聽也.⁶⁹

In contrast to the univocal expositions and illustrations in Clusters A and B1, this guideline resembles a dialogue. The text begins by introducing the Confucian position, namely that rulers ought to govern by example. It not only quotes a Confucian classic, a line from the *Shijing* 詩經 (Book of Odes),⁷⁰ but even cites an anecdote ostensibly from a commentary (*zhuan* 傳) associated with it, the story of "none dressed in purple" (*wu yi zi* 無衣紫). In the anecdote proper, Duke Huan of Qi succeeds in putting an end to the indulgent trend of purple cloth by eliminating it from his own attire.

But the text soon departs from the Confucian position, suggesting that the ruler's direct participation in governing is in fact inefficient and undignified. The guideline eventually critiques a quote attributed to Confucius, accusing him of ignorance ("Kong Qiu did not understand"). The *Han Feizi* position is introduced only at the end, but as the superior alternative: the last two anecdotes are about rulers implementing *fa* and carrying out rewards and punishments according to standards. This, the guideline tells us, is the way of perspicacious rulers (*mingzhu zhi dao* 明主之道).

In contrast to the earlier Confucius anecdotes from Cluster B1, which are obviously ideas of the *fa* specialists dressed in Confucius' garb, the quote attributed to Confucius here is more credibly Confucian:

Confucius says, "One who acts as the peoples' lord is like a bowl, and the people are like water. If the bowl is square, then the water is square; if the bowl is round, then the water is round."

孔子曰:「為人君者猶盂也. 民猶水也. 盂方水方; 盂圜水圜.」⁷¹

In fact, this quote has a parallel in the *Xunzi* 荀子 (Master Xun), a Warring States text commonly associated with the Confucian lineage.⁷² Unlike

Confucius's elucidation of ancient laws in the inner "Chushuo" chapter, the message here no longer directly coheres with the message of the guideline. Instead, the guideline text instructs how to interpret this illustration, which is, in this case, to reject it.

In general, Confucius in the outer "Chushuo" chapters of B2 is no longer just another puppet figure propagating *Han Feizi* doctrines. However, unlike the quote cited above, the majority of these Confucius anecdotes are still positive examples, despite the fact that they now represent the Confucian position. These cases appear to exhibit the text's deliberate attempt to appropriate Confucian teachings, or to reconcile them with its own ideas. The following anecdote from chapter 33, "Wai chushuo, zuo, xia" 外儲 說左下 (Outer Collection of Illustrative Examples, Part Two of the Left), exemplifies this point:

> Confucius was seated to attend on Duke Ai of Lu, when Duke Ai conferred on him peaches and millet. Duke Ai said, "Please help yourself." Confucius ate millet first before helping himself to the peaches, and the attendants covered their mouths and laughed. Duke Ai said, "The millet here is not to be treated as a meal, it is for cleaning the peach." Zhongni [Confucius] said, "I, Qiu [first name of Confucius], understood that very well. But cereal is the head of the Five Grains, the choicest of the sacrifices to the Former Kings. Fruits and melons are of six kinds, and peach ranks the lowest. During sacrifices to the Former Kings it cannot be brought into the temple. I have heard that a gentleman uses what is humble to clean what is privileged, but I have not heard of using the privileged to clean the humble. Now using the head of the Five Grains to clean the low ranks of fruit and melons would be like using the high to clean the low, which I consider a hindrance to righteousness. Thus I dare not to place it before the choicest of the sacrificial cereals in the ancestral temple."

> 孔子侍坐於魯哀公，哀公賜之桃與黍，哀公：「請用.」仲尼先飯黍而後啗桃，左右皆揜口而笑，哀公曰：「黍者，非飯之也，以雪桃也.」仲尼對曰：「丘知之矣. 夫黍者五穀之長也，祭先王為上盛. 果蓏有六，而桃為下，祭先王不得入廟. 丘之聞也，君子以賤雪貴，不聞以貴雪賤. 今以五穀之長雪果蓏之下，是從上雪下也，丘以為妨義，故不敢以先於宗廟之盛也.」[73]

This anecdote recalls vignettes in the *Lunyu* 論語 (Analects) that detail Confucius's exemplary ritual behaviors.[74] Indeed the Confucian position has a strong presence in the group of anecdotes surrounding this one, which, incidentally, also features the first occurrence of the term Confucians (*ruzhe*) in the *Han Feizi*;[75] it includes quite a few other anecdotes addressing the specificities of ritual prescriptions, discussing the propriety of hats, shoes, and games.[76] Nevertheless, these vaguely "Confucian" topics invariably vocalize the importance of maintaining distinction between the superior and the inferior, echoing the core teachings of the *Han Feizi*. In this context, this Confucius anecdote seems to seek a meeting ground between the Confucian notion of righteousness (*yi* 義) and the *Han Feizi* stipulation for hierarchical order. It remains to be seen whether this is a genuine attempt to synthesize the two positions.

The two guideline texts quoted above also illustrate why the outer "Chushuo" chapters might at first glance appear "draft-like" or "disorderly." The presence of polemics and added complexity, I argue, is the true difference between B1 and B2, between the inner and outer "Chushuo" chapters. In the univocal inner chapters, the guideline and illustration texts tend to have a straightforward teaching–exampla relationship. Their guideline texts tend to neatly separate the teaching and the enumeration of anecdotes with the set phrase "for illustrative examples, see . . ." (*qi shuo zai*), and the messages of the guideline and the anecdote closely adhere to each other, so that the intended messages can often be derived from reading the anecdote alone. The polyphonic outer chapters, in contrast, attempt to incorporate a more complex range of materials, as they appropriate or refute ideas from competing traditions. These heterogeneous anecdotes no longer directly illustrate the *Han Feizi* teachings, and the guideline has to instruct the readers on how to read them. Accordingly, like the B2 guidelines cited above, the allusions to anecdotes are entangled within the discursive argumentation, and the relationship between the message of the guideline and the anecdotes become convoluted.[77] Nevertheless, B2 guidelines prove to be well-crafted compositions upon closer examination. The fifth guideline from chapter 32, as I have shown, has a clear progression: it begins by stating the opponent's case and concludes by presenting its own position.

If the outer "Chushuo" guidelines are reminiscent of a dialogue, the remaining four chapters in B2, the "Nan" chapters, literally stage dialogues and debates. The "Nan" chapters also have their own distinct structure: while their anecdotes closely resemble materials in the "Chushuo" chapters, each anecdote is followed by at least one critique of its message, waged by an unidentified "someone" (*huo* 或). Confucius features prominently in these anecdotes, but now strictly as a negative figure:

> When the farmers of Mt. Li trespassed on each other's fields, [the Former King] Shun went there and tilled among them. In the course of one year, all the boundary ridges of the fields were corrected. [. . .]⁷⁸ With admiration Zhongni [Confucius] said, "Shun's office is not concerned with tilling, fishing, or pottery. The reason he travelled there was to turn around what is failing. How verily humane was he! When he placed his own person in hardship, the people followed him.⁷⁹ It is thus said, 'How the sage transforms through virtue!'"
>
> Someone (*huo*) then asked a Confucian (*ruzhe*), "At that time, where was Yao [the Former King who was Shun's predecessor]?" He replied, "Yao was the Son of Heaven." "If that were the case, why did Confucius revere Yao as a sage? When a perspicacious and observant sage sits on the throne, he purges the world of wickedness. By his orders farmers and fishermen would not quarrel and pottery would not have flaws. What then would be left for Shun to transform with his virtues? If Shun had to turn failures around, then Yao had committed negligence. To honor Shun as worthy is to do away with Yao's perspicacity and insight; to honor Yao as sagely is to do away with Shun's moral transformation. The two cannot both stand. There is a man of Chu who sells shields and spears, who praises them by saying, 'My shield is so strong that nothing can pierce through it.' He then praises the spear by saying, 'My spear is so sharp that there is nothing it does not pierce through.' Someone says, 'What happens if you try to pierce your shield with your spear?' and the man cannot answer. An invincible shield and an invincible spear cannot coexist in the same world. Now the fact that Yao and Shun cannot both be praised is illustrated (*shuo*) by the story of spear and shield."

歷山之農者侵畔, 舜往耕焉, 期年, 甽畝正. [. . .] 仲尼歎曰:「耕, 漁與陶, 非舜官也, 而舜往為之者, 所以救敗也. 舜其信仁乎! 乃躬藉處苦而民從之. 故曰: 聖人之德化乎!」

> 或問儒者曰:「方此時也, 堯安在?」其人曰:「堯為天子.」「然則, 仲尼之聖堯奈何? 聖人明察在上位, 將使天下無姦也. 今(令)耕漁不爭, 陶器不窳, 舜又何德而化? 舜之救敗也, 則是堯有失也. 賢舜, 則去堯之明察; 聖堯, 則去舜之德化, 不可兩得也. 楚人有鬻楯與矛者, 譽之曰:『吾楯之堅, 物莫能陷也.』又譽其矛曰:『吾矛之利, 於物無不陷也.』或曰:『以子之矛陷子之楯, 何如?』其人弗能應也. 夫不可陷之楯與無不陷之矛, 不可同世而立. 今堯, 舜之不可兩譽, 矛楯之說也.」[80]

As with the fifth guideline text from chapter 32, this text argues with Confucians about the ruler's proper role, though this time in a literal debate between "someone," evidently a *fa* specialist, and a Confucian. The Confucius quoted here is once again recognizably Confucian, speaking admiringly about the Former Kings, praising them with standard Confucian virtues like humaneness.

The criticism voiced by the "someone" involves a careful reading of the anecdote itself. If such Former King narratives are part of the Confucian textual learning (*wenxue*), the *fa* specialist's refutation is not any less pedantic. It is also notable that the ruler does not partake in the debates staged in these chapters, not even nominally. Moreover, unlike the rhetorical discussions in Cluster A, the outcome of this debate is no longer determined by circumstances specific to the *context* of the persuasion. Rather, the analogy in the "spear versus shield" anecdote evinces a concern for the general validity of an argument, for whether something is true anywhere in the world (*shi* 世).

Nested within the *fa* specialist's rebuttal, the "spear versus shield" story demonstrates yet another fascinating usage of anecdote: as an illustration, it is applicable not only to this argument, but is in fact reusable in other contexts, for what it demonstrates is not the truth of any proposition in particular, but the relationship between propositions. It thus resembles a *method* for testing out the validity of an argument. Indeed, it is utilized at least one other time in the *Han Feizi*, in chapter 40, "Nanshi" 難勢 (Critiquing Positional Advantage), of Cluster C.[81]

Tracing the presence of Confucius in the anecdote collection chapters reveals a shift in rhetorical situations and strategies that mirrors the overall development in the *Han Feizi*. Thus, these anecdote collections of Cluster B resemble a pivot, joining Cluster A and Cluster C, the axis of which falls right between the inner and the outer "Chushuo" chapters.

Conclusion

This essay has identified shifts in rhetorical situations and strategies within the *Han Feizi*, pointing to alternative ways to think about the contradictory appearances of Confucius. As we have seen, Cluster A presents the core teachings of the *Han Feizi*, primarily in the form of univocal expositions directed at the ruler. Cluster C, in contrast, is polyphonic and polemical in orientation, incorporating a wide range of materials, including those associated with rival traditions. Cluster B, the collections of anecdotes in the middle, bridges the transition between A and C. In Cluster B1 Confucius functions as a mouthpiece in service of *Han Feizi* teachings, while in Cluster B2 he embodies Confucian ideas that are treated in an increasingly antagonistic manner.

How might we explain this pattern, which seems to suggest the existence of an overarching organization in the *Han Feizi* compilation? Are the differences between Clusters A and C due to the formal and functional choice of an author or compiler(s), or the result of diachronic development? Underlying each of these two possible explanations is a model of authorship, since the former would attribute these patterns to an authorial design, while the latter to the accretion and sedimentation of materials. I am interested in further exploring these complex questions, but within the scope of this chapter, I can only suggest that these two possibilities are not mutually exclusive. Even when we no longer see a text as the work of a single author, we still should not ignore the human agency of the writers and compilers involved at each phase of its formation, who were likely endeavoring to impose order.

In fact, at this preliminary stage, it is often difficult to separate functional design from diachronic development. On the one hand, recent scholarship begins to uncover organizational principles within the Masters texts, showing these compilations to be more purposefully arranged than previously recognized. John Major, Sarah A. Queen, Andrew Seth Meyer, and Harold Roth's translation of the *Huainanzi*, for instance, bears out its "root-branch" structure and sheds light on its latent organization and logic.[82] Similarly, Sarah A. Queen and John Major's recent publication on the *Chunqiu fanlu* 春秋繁露 (Luxuriant Gems of the Spring and Autumn) demonstrates how the materials in that text are organized thematically.[83] In part recalling A. C. Graham's and Liu Xiaogan's works on the *Zhuangzi*, these new works continue to identify patterns and stratifications in early texts.[84] Particularly interesting in light of my findings is Queen's study of Confucius anecdotes in the *Huainanzi*. Similar to his distribution in the

Han Feizi, Confucius is only featured in the later "branch" chapters, and his presence is associated with the incorporation of alternative teachings.[85] Perhaps an implicit organization of texts comparable to the "root-branch" structure of the *Huainanzi* also shaped the *Han Feizi*, which also groups the expositions of principal teachings at the beginning, while reserving debates with rival traditions for later. On the other hand, recognizing this structural tendency does not preclude the involvement of historical factors, for it is not unlikely that the foundational texts collected at the beginning are also the oldest texts.

Similarly, it is difficult to discern whether the systematic shift in rhetorical situation is due to formal choice or diachronic change, or even both factors acting in concert. As previously discussed, Clusters A and B1 are preoccupied with the power struggle between the ruler and the ministers, while Clusters B2 and C replace the villainous ministers with figures like the "learned men," so that the task of the *fa* specialists shifts from persuading the ruler to disputing competing visions of rulership. Once again, this distribution can be attributed to formal and functional choices, namely that different parts of the *Han Feizi* were instructions intended for different purposes. At the same time, this shift of attention from conniving ministers to contentious philosophers is tantalizingly suggestive, for it mimics the generally accepted narrative of Warring States history, whose starting point is often described as being marked by the seizure of power on the part of the ministerial lineages, and whose high point featured the centralization of territorial states, the flourishing of intellectual debate, and experimentation with new methods of governing. One cannot help but wonder if time has passed between Cluster A and Cluster C, and whether they were in fact written during different stages of the Warring States Period.

Indeed, the systematic changes in vocabulary and rhetorical conventions speak more strongly for heterogeneity—either due to diachronic change or changes in sources—and seem less likely the result of the compilers' design. Between Clusters A and C, the value of Confucian moral terms is entirely inverted, as is the function served by figures like Confucius and the Former Kings; even the meaning of being a persuader fully shifts from positive to negative. These differences are contradictory, and as the *Han Feizi* might even say, they ought not to "exist in the same world" (*tong shi er li* 同世而立). But if such contradictions are puzzling, the systematic nature of their distribution also suggests possible explanations. They point to the emerging desire to construct affiliations and oppositions amidst escalating intellectual polemics. Although the causes and consequences of this desire still require much investigation, it is certainly part of the history that led to the remembrance of intellectual lineages (*jia* 家) in Han writings.

Postulating the quickening of intellectual camps could potentially account for much of the textual patterns observed. In Cluster A, the identity of the "gentlemen capable of *fa*" is defined chiefly in contrast to the villainous ministers, allegedly by the difference in their moral motivations. In this context, it seems, Confucian moral terms and rhetorical conventions are unproblematic. But in Clusters B2 and C, as the position of the *fa* specialists begins to be defined by their opposition to the Confucians and the Mohists, the once shared rhetorical conventions turn into targets of criticism.

Furthermore, the gradual solidification of intellectual camps accompanies the rise of intellectual polemics, which begins to explain Confucius's transformation. In Clusters A and B1, Confucius is a wise teacher who can lend authority to *fa* specialists' teachings, but in Clusters B2 and C, he is increasingly confined to Confucian statements and actions; and in one of the last chapters of the compilation, at the beginning of chapter 50, "Xianxue," he is named the forefather of the Confucians. In parallel to this sharpening demarcation of rival groups, the *Han Feizi* also undertakes to construct its own lineage in Cluster C. The three chapters at the beginning of Cluster C, chapter 40, "Nanshi," chapter 42, "Wen Tian" 問田 (Asking Tian), and chapter 43, "Dingfa" 定法 (Defining Standards), present a miniature refrain of Cluster A, offering renewed discussion of core concepts such as *fa*, as well as the role of the martyr persuader. But this time, these discussions are presented as words uttered by four historical figures: Shen Dao 慎到 (fl. late 4th century BCE), Shen Buhai 申不害 (d. 337 BCE), Shang Yang, and Han Fei, corresponding to four of the ten Legalist texts listed in the first-century-CE bibliography, "Yiwenzhi" 藝文志 (Treatise on Arts and Letters).[86] While these three chapters are written in the dialogue form characteristic of Cluster C, these Masters of the *fa* specialists, unlike Confucius, are praised rather than refuted.[87]

Such intellectual history narratives, which are unique to Cluster C, fundamentally change the relationship between the Master figures and their attributed teachings. In the anecdotes of earlier chapters, Confucius serves mainly as a rhetorical device. He either underscores the importance of a statement, or illustrates a teaching with his actions as an exemplary figure. But once he is named the historical founder of the Confucians, he is transformed into the progenitor (the author) of teachings. Similarly, figures like Shang Yang appear in earlier chapters as ministers who implemented and performed *fa* teachings, but in Cluster C, just as Confucius in "Xianxue," they are presented as Master figures, as authors of teachings. The "Dingfa" chapter, in its discussion of ideas attributed to Shen Buhai and Shang Yang, even employs the phrase "the words of the two experts" (*er jia zhi yan* 二家之言), a key expression in the discussions of authorship from the Han dynasty onward, but is rare in texts traditionally dated to the Warring States Period.[88]

In summary, the transition throughout the *Han Feizi* compilation likely reflects the emerging notions of intellectual identity and affiliation, so that by Cluster C, the *Han Feizi* begins to define itself horizontally in opposition to other competing groups, and vertically as the inheritor of earlier Master figures' words and ideas. Even if Shang Yang and Shen Buhai were not affiliated during their lifetime, the *Han Feizi* has brought them together. This coalescence of the *fa* founding fathers encapsulates what was possibly the goal behind the compilation of the *Han Feizi*: as Goldin points out, Han Fei is the "synthesizer of Legalism"[89] only in so far as the *Han Feizi* claims him to be so.[90] But if the historical reality of Legalism (*fajia*) was indeed tenuous, the compilation of the *Han Feizi* would be all the more an efficacious speech act that transformed the reception of this reality, be it by fleshing out of the author figure Han Fei, or creating the soon to be named Legalism.

Regardless of how one interprets these rhetorical shifts, the *Han Feizi* demonstrates that anecdotes performed a fascinating range of rhetorical functions. While studies of early Chinese rhetoric often cite the *Han Feizi*, they tend to focus on Cluster A and its explicit discussions of persuasion. G. E. R. Lloyd, for instance, cites the "Shuinan" chapter to argue for institutional differences between ancient China and Greece, identifying court audience with powerful rulers as the institutional context for rhetoric in Warring States China, in contrast to the debate among peers found in ancient Greece. This institutional difference, according to Lloyd, offers an explanation for the divergence in emphasis between the two rhetorical traditions; the former, represented by "Shuinan," was driven to focus on psychology and inter-personal pragmatics, whereas the latter to the preoccupation with the definition of "truth" as the incontrovertible rhetoric against *mere* rhetoric.[91]

My chapter contends that, even within the *Han Feizi*, polemics among peers is far from absent. It is in fact systematically reserved for the second half of the compilation, where the interest in psychology fades, and pedantic disputations over the *content* of philosophical arguments dominate. Moreover, Clusters B2 and C echo Lloyd's characterization of Greek rhetoric, be it the concern with incontrovertibility and the general validity of arguments, or even the self-righteous denunciation of rhetoric as meaningless sophistry. The convergence of Greek and Chinese rhetoric in fact lends support to Lloyd's theoretical postulation, for the difference between the rhetorical situations in Clusters A and C has indeed led to differences in rhetorical strategies. At the same time, it suggests the need to revise Lloyd's historical characterization. While the interest in the psychology of persuasion is a theme that can be traced across early Chinese texts,[92] it should be regarded as one aspect in a complex landscape, with much—such as the anecdote collections—still to be explored.

Anecdote, a type of writing often treated with suspicion in the study of philosophy, turns out to be a key element in the *Han Feizi*'s transition to philosophical debate. As I have suggested, the four outer "Chushuo" and the four "Nan" chapters of Cluster B2—in other words, the bulk of anecdote collections in the *Han Feizi*—not only initiate interaction with alternative traditions, they anticipate the intellectual polemics of Cluster C. Narratives, in contrast to discursive argumentation, are much more open to reinterpretation, and can thus perform complex rhetorical functions. While an anecdote has the capacity to quickly conjure up in the reader or listener a rich set of ideas, its interpretative flexibility also allows for the easy manipulation of these ideas, be it to modify, to appropriate, or to refute. Anecdotal writing provided an important space for polemics in late Warring States writings, for, as Andrew Seth Meyer and Ting-mien Lee demonstrate in their respective contributions to this volume, it is a textual form shared by nearly all Masters texts. To the author(s) of the *Han Feizi*, these massive anecdote collections were likely an essential ingredient of the text, providing an indispensable bridge between the exposition of its core teachings and the high-stakes battle of wits with rival persuaders.

Notes

1. This chapter is partly based on my master's thesis, "The Tapestry of Vignette Collections: A Study of the 'Chu shuo' Chapters of *Han Feizi* (MA Thesis, University of Colorado, Boulder, 2010), which would not have been possible without the inspiration and guidance of Matthias Richter. It has similarly benefited from rounds of discussions with Michael Puett, and is tremendously indebted to the extensive and insightful comments and suggestions by Wai-yee Li, Sarah A. Queen,

and Paul van Els. I must also thank the anonymous reviewers for their substantial feedback—my chapter is much improved as a result.

2. For instance, in chapter 3, "Nanyan" 難言 (Finding It Hard to Speak), see *Han Feizi jijie*, 3.22.

3. See, for example, chapter 50, "Xianxue" 顯學 (Prominent Teachings).

4. Paul R. Goldin, "Introduction: Han Fei and the *Han Feizi*," in *Dao Companion to the Philosophy of Han Fei*, ed. Paul R. Goldin (Dordrecht: Springer, 2013), 16–18.

5. Sarah A. Queen, "Representations of Confucius in the *Huainanzi*," in *The Huainanzi and Textual Production in Early China*, eds. Sarah A. Queen and Michael Puett (Leiden: Brill, 2014).

6. Confucius is mentioned about one hundred times in approximately 47 different instances, mostly by the honorific Kongzi 孔子 (Master Kong) or by his courtsy name, Zhongni 仲尼. This number can only be an estimate, since there is no unambiguous rule for defining an "instance." But some measure beyond a word count of "Kongzi" and "Zhongni" is useful. One instance here refers to either one discrete anecdote, or, in the case of discursive essays, one complete point of argument, usually corresponding to a paragraph. In the "Chushuo" chapters, the guideline (*jing* 經) and illustrative example (*shuo* 說) are counted separately, even if they refer to the same anecdote. In the "Nan" chapters, each rebuttal to the original anecdote is counted separately. These decisions are made to more accurately reflect the proportion of Confucius's presence.

7. For an historical overview of the reception of Masters texts as philosophy, see Wiebke Denecke, *The Dynamics of Masters Literature: Early Chinese Thought from Confucius to Han Feizi* (Cambridge, MA: Harvard University Asia Center, 2010), 1–31.

8. For questioning and historicization of the translation of *ru* 儒 as "Confucian," see Lionel Jensen, *Manufacturing Confucianism: Chinese Traditions and Universal Civilization* (Durham, NC: Duke University Press, 1997). For the insightful translation of *ru* as "classicism," see Michael Nylan, *The Five "Confucian" Classics* (New Haven, CT: Yale University Press, 2001). I have maintained the translation of *ru* as "Confucian" for the sake of clarity, a decision that furthermore seems justifiable in the context of this chapter, given the reference to Confucius as the founder of the *ru* in *Han Feizi* chapter 50 (see below).

9. *Hanshu* 漢書 (History of the [Former] Han Dynasty), 30.1728, 1736.

10. For the evolving reception of the Warring States polemics in the Han, see Jens Østergård Petersen, "Which Books *Did* the First Emperor of Ch'in Burn? On the Meaning of *Pai Chia* in Early Chinese Sources," *Monumenta Serica* 43 (1995): 1–52; Sarah A. Queen, "Inventories of the Past: The 'School' Affiliation of the *Huainanzi*," *Asia Major* 14, no. 1 (2001): 51–72; Mark Csikszentmihalyi and Michael Nylan, "Constructing Lineages and Inventing Traditions through Exemplary Figures in Early China," *T'oung Pao* 89, no. 1 (2003): 59–99; Kidder Smith, "Sima Tan

and the Invention of Daoism, 'Legalism,' Et Cetera," *Journal of Asian Studies* 62, no. 1 (2003): 129–56; Paul R. Goldin, "Persistent Misconceptions About Chinese 'Legalism,'" *Journal of Chinese Philosophy* 38, no. 1 (2011): 88–104.

11. Of course, nothing in early Chinese texts can actually be this neat. Chapter 20 has a close relationship with the *Laozi,* and quite a few other chapters are distinctively "Daoist," for lack of a better term. Yet if we disregard Han Dynasty classification, there is no reason to assume that the author(s) of *Han Feizi* regarded such *Laozi* elements as something external to their own tradition. In the *Han Feizi, Laozi* materials consistently serve as authority, in contrast to the treatment of the "Confucians" and the Confucian-affiliated materials. Other hints in early texts include the first-century-BCE historiography *Shiji* 史記 (Records of the Historian), which groups Laozi 老子 (Old Master) and Han Fei under the same biography (*Shiji,* 63.2139–2148). The relationship between texts later classified under "Legalism" and "Daoism" is in need of further study, for a recent publication, see Wang Xiaobo 王曉波, *Dao yu fa: fajia sixiang he Huang-Lao zhexue jiexi* 道與法: 法家思想和黃老哲學解析 (Taipei: Taiwan daxue chuban zhongxin, 2007).

12. In chapter 3, "Nanyan." *Han Feizi jijie,* 3.22.

13. Such as in chapter 50, "Xianxue." Ting-mien Lee's dissertation highlights the discrepancy between the characterization of people named *ru-mo* 儒墨 in texts like the *Han Feizi* and *Zhuangzi* versus transmitted Confucian and Mohist texts, and gathers a rich amount of evidence postulating that this term might not always refer to "Confucians and Mohists" as understood by modern scholars, but more generally (and pejoratively) to "ethical hypocrites." See: "The Blurry Boundary between Ethical Theorists and Political Strategists: The Meaning of 'Ru-Mo' in Early Chinese Texts" (PhD Diss., University of Leuven, 2015). In addition to her recommended readjustment in the reading of the term *ru-mo,* I believe what her dissertation also draws attention to is the multi-dimensionality involved in early texts' discussion of identities and affiliations, which involved competing perspectives and definitions.

14. *Han Feizi jijie,* 6.31–42. See also, Goldin, "Introduction: Han Fei and the *Han Feizi,*" 4–5.

15. *Han Feizi jijie,* 5.26–30.

16. See chapter 11, "Gufen" 孤憤 (Solitary Indignation), ibid., 11.78–85, for examples of the term *zhongren.*

17. For an example, see ibid., 11.78.

18. References to regicide and persecution of *fa* specialists can be found throughout Cluster A, such as in chapter 14, "Jian jie shi chen" 姦劫弒臣 (Treacherous, Larcenous, Murderous Ministers).

19. Chapter 5 "Zhudao," for instance, lists five types of "blockages" (*yong* 壅) orchestrated by ministers (ibid., 5.29). The beginning of chapter 11, "Gufen," similarly describes how a courtier may usurp the ruler's power by keeping him in the dark (*yongbi* 壅蔽) (ibid., 11.78–82).

20. For the etymology of *shui,* see Schwermann's chapter in this volume.

21. For a recent summary on the problems created by "Shuinan," including an overview of Han Dynasty sources and later debates on this matter, see Michael Hunter, "The Difficulty with 'The Difficulties of Persuasion' ('Shuinan' 說難)," in *Dao Companion to the Philosophy of Han Fei*, ed. Paul R. Goldin (Dordrecht: Springer, 2013), 177–82.

22. Wai-yee Li, "Riddles, Concealment, and Rhetoric in Early China," in *Facing the Monarch: Modes of Advice in the Early Chinese Court*, ed. Garret P. S. Olberding (Cambridge, MA: Harvard University Asia Center, 2013), 102–04.

23. Hunter, "Difficulty," 18.

24. *Han Feizi jijie*, 3.22–23.

25. *Han Feizi jijie*, 13.95.

26. Ibid., 41.394.

27. What complicates this analysis, as Paul van Els and Sarah A. Queen point out in the Introduction to this volume, is the fact that the graph 說 is used to write etymologically related words *shuo* (to illustrate, to explain), *shui* (to persuade), and *yue* (to please). But once we exclude the cases where 說 is unambiguously *shuo* or *yue*, the rest are almost ubiquitously associated with negative contexts. As an example, see chapter 46 "Liufan," which says: "Today, all of the learned men who try to persuade the ruler of humankind ask him to discard his interest in profit and pursue the path of mutual care. [. . .] This exhibits a naivity regarding human relations, and is both deceitful and fallacious" 今學者之說人主也, 皆去求利之心, 出相愛之道 [. . .] 此不熟於論恩詐而誣也 (ibid., 26.417).

28. For instance, in "Nanyan," "[if his speech] summarizes details and explains essentials, is direct, concise, and without ornamentations, he is seen as blunt and lacking in sophistication" 摠微說約, 徑省而不飾, 則見以為劌而不辯 (ibid., 3.21).

29. "[If his speech] disregards textual learning (*wenxue*), and he speaks with blatant frankness, he is seen as a rustic" 殊釋文學, 以質信言, 則見以為鄙 (ibid., 3.21). This is a neutral usage because among this list of missed attempts at persuasion, speaking artfully and learnedly can similarly encounter undeserved disdain from the ruler.

30. Terms like "hard and white" (*jian bai* 堅白) and "without thickness" (*wuhou* 無厚) often stand in for the paradox arguments associated with the sophists (*mingjia* 名家). Surviving evidence of these argumentations include a chapter titled "Jian bai lun" 堅白論 (On Hard and White) in *Gongsun Longzi* 公孫龍子 (Master Gongsun Long), or a paradox involving "without thickness" mentioned in the *Zhuangzi* 莊子 (Master Zhuang), chapter 33, in its discussion of Hui Shi 惠施.

31. Paul R. Goldin, "The Theme of the Primacy of the Situation in Classical Chinese Philosophy and Rhetoric," *Asia Major* 18, no. 2 (2005): 6–7. See also *Han Feizi jijie*, 12.93.

32. Chen Qiyou 陳奇猷 interprets these dates as references to the dynastic transitions, which I find preferable to emending the text (*Han Feizi jishi*, 1084).

33. *Han Feizi jijie*, 50.456–457.

34. Smith, "Sima Tan," 133.

35. Translation adopted from Lundahl, *Han Fei Zi: The Man and the Work*, 169.

36. Lee points out that the *Shiji* groups pre-Qin Masters precisely according to whether they hold a pro-*renyi* or anti-*renyi* position. Her research further suggests the centrality and touchstone quality of the debate surrounding these moral terms. See Lee, "Blurry Boundary," 91.

37. *Han Feizi jijie*, 20.132–133.

38. Sarah A. Queen, "*Han Feizi* and the Old Master: A Comparative Analysis and Translation of *Han Feizi* chapter 20, 'Jie Lao,' and chapter 21, 'Yu Lao,'" in *Dao Companion to the Philosophy of Han Fei*, ed. Paul R. Goldin (Dordrecht: Springer, 2013), 212–13.

39. *Han Feizi jijie*, 3.22.

40. See ibid., 47.425; 50.460.

41. See ibid., 49.446–447; 49.449–450; 50.457–458; 51.466–467.

42. "If *fa* is made known, the sovereign will be esteemed and not impugned [. . .] Thus the Former Kings valued *fa* and transmitted it. If the ruler of humankind relinquishes *fa* and uses his private judgment, superior and inferior will not be distinguished" 法審則上尊而不侵 [. . .] 故先王貴之而傳之. 人主釋法用私, 則上下不別 (*Han Feizi jijie*, 6.39. For translation see Goldin, "Introduction: Han Fei and the *Han Feizi*," 14).

43. As discussed earlier (in this paper, in the Introduction to this volume, and in Schwermann's contribution to this volume), the first graph in this chapter title, 說, can be read as either "explanations" *shuo*, or "persuasions" *shui*, an ambiguity difficult to resolve. I prefer the translation "illustration" to preserve a greater level of ambiguity.

44. See Lundahl, *Han Fei Zi*, 241–42.

45. The righthand column indicates the number of times each cluster of chapters mentions Confucius, with a total number of 47 occurrences.

46. The anonymous old commentary (*jiu zhu* 舊注) saw the division as meaningful, and interprets the inner "Chushuo" as the inner strategies of a lord (*Han Feizi jijie*, 30.211). But later Chinese scholars such as Chen Qiyou tend to follow the opinion of Ōta Hō 太田方, and see the inner-outer division as arbitrary. Cf. Liangshu Zheng 鄭良樹, "*Han Feizi* 'Chushuo' pian wu lun" 韓非子儲說篇五論, *Gugong xueshu jikan* 7, no. 4 (1990): 33–34. Zheng notices that more textual mistakes occur in three of the four outer chapters, and argues that the inner chapters are more polished and systematically composed (ibid., 64).

47. The inclusion of chapter 21, "Yu Lao," and chapters 22–23, i.e., the two "Shuolin" chapters, in B1 is tentative, for the agenda of these chapters requires further study to pin down. Queen points out that the majority of the "Yu Lao" anecdotes recount rulers losing their states, often despite the advices of gifted ministers

(Queen, "Han Feizi and the Old Master," 209–10). Many anecdotes in the "Shuolin" chapters, on the other hand, are about utilizing speeches to indirectly manipulate a situation to one's advantage. (For a close study and complete translation of the "Shuolin" chapters, see Michael Reeve, "Demonstrating the World: Mind and Society in the Shuo Lin Chapters of the *Han Fei Zi*." (PhD Diss., Princeton University, 2003). Therefore, the anecdotes of "Yu Lao" and "Shuolin" seem to complement well the rhetorical instructions of "Shuinan" and the court setting of Cluster A.

48. *Han Feizi jijie*, 30.212.

49. As Chen Qiyou pointed out, the *shuo* label was not present in earlier editions. The Ling edition (*Ling ben* 凌本) has the word "commentary" (*zhuan* 傳), and the Zhao edition (*Zhao ben* 趙本) has the two graphs, "commentaries to the right," (*you zhuan* 右傳) at the end of the chapter (*Han Feizi jishi*, 526).

50. *Han Feizi jijie*, 30.224. In the last line, following Wang Xianshen 王先慎, I read *zhi* 之 as *qi* 其, and *li* 離 as *li* 罹 (same below).

51. See Wang Xianshen citing *Kunxue jiwen, shi* 困學記聞十, which comments on one of these anecdotes with "the Legalist school abuses the words of the sage to this extent" 法家侮聖言至此 (*Han Feizi jijie*, 6).

52. Ibid., 30.225.

53. *Han Feizi jijie*, 30.217–218, 223–224, 226–227.

54. For a recent exploration of the diverse pre-Han portrayals of Confucius, see Michael Nylan and Thomas Wilson, *Lives of Confucius: Civilization's Greatest Sage Through the Ages* (New York: Doubleday, 2010).

55. On scenes of instruction and persuasion in early texts, see Mark Edward Lewis, *Writing and Authority in Early China* (Albany, NY: State University of New York Press, 1999), 57.

56. See, for instance, the mentioning of figures like Mozi 墨子 (Master Mo, fl. late 5th c. BCE) in chapter 32 (*Han Feizi jijie*, 32.261–262).

57. Ibid., 32.262–263.

58. Ibid., 32.276.

59. Yuri Pines, "From Historical Evolution to the End of History: Past, Present and Future from Shang Yang to the First Emperor," in *Dao Companion to the Philosophy of Han Fei*, ed. Paul R. Goldin (Dordrecht: Springer, 2013), 26–27.

60. Chapter 47 "Bashuo," for instance, describes the devolution from an ancient time of virtue (*Han Feizi jijie*, 47.426). Chapter 49 "Wudu" also presents similar arguments. See ibid., 49.443–445, and ibid., 37–38.

61. *Han Feizi jijie*, 49.442–443.

62. *Han Feizi jijie*, 49.443–445.

63. Beginning with "Now the Confucians and Mohists all praise the Former Kings for their impartial care for All under Heaven" 今儒，墨皆稱先王兼愛天下 (ibid., 49.446ff).

64. Many places in this text are difficult. I follow Gao Heng 高亨 and Chen Qiyou in emending 緩 to 援. The second phrase is changed from 責之以尊厚耕戰

following Wang Xianshen, who interprets *zunhou* 尊厚 as the "rich and privileged, thus rulers of men"; Gao Heng reads 誠 as 成 (*Han Feizi jishi*, 32.619). The Duke Xiang of Song anecdote narrates the Battle of Hongshui 泓水, where Duke Xiang led his army to defeat and ended up fatally injured. Two alternatives versions are included for the story on Duke Jian of Zheng, which praise him and his legendary minister Zichan 子產 for adhering to their respective positions and duties.

65. Following Wang Xianshen, I read 位 as 涖.

66. This phrase, *yanbi weifu* 揜弊微服, likely refers to an anecdote missing from the "illustrations" section. The previous two anecdotes feature rulers failing helplessly when trying to perform the duty of underlings, be it driving a chariot or reading legal codes. There is a metaphoric dimension to the story about Duke Jing of Qi, suggesting that ruler's direct participation in governing is as inefficient as choosing to run on foot instead of riding in a chariot.

67. This story about the Lord of Zou is nearly a repeat of Duke Huan curbing purple cloth, except that this time, the comment at the end of the story criticizes the Lord of Zou for damaging his own attire.

68. Commentators such as Ōta Hō and Chen Qiyou suggest emending *lie* 獵 to *lu* 祿, given that *fulu* 賦祿 is attested in multiple closely related contexts. See *Han Feizi jishi*, 620–21.

69. *Han Feizi jijie*, 32.264–265.

70. The *Shijing* lines are parallels to lines in "Jie nanshan" 節南山 from "Xiaoya" 小雅 (*Han Feizi jishi*, 32.619). The *Han Feizi* otherwise never quotes the *Shijing* as authority, in contrast to the Confucian-affiliated texts from the Warring States Period.

71. *Han Feizi jijie*, 32.285.

72. The parallel in *Xunzi* states "being a lord is like being a plate, when the plate is round then the water is round; being a lord is like being a bowl, if the bowl is square then the water is square" 君者, 槃也, 槃圓而水圓; 君者, 盂也, 盂方而水方 (*Xunzi jijie*, 8.234).

73. *Han Feizi jijie*, 33. 299.

74. For instance, *Lunyu*, chapter 10.

75. *Han Feizi jijie*, 33.300.

76. Ibid., 33.297–301.

77. Paul van Els's study of parallel anecdotes in *Hanshi waizhuan* 韓詩外傳 (Han's Supplementary Commentary to the Odes) and the *Huainanzi* demonstrates a similar phenomenon, namely that the attempt to incorporate more heterogeneous materials produces more complex texts, where many more of what he calls "argumentative connectives" are used. See Paul van Els, "Tilting Vessels and Collapsing Walls—On the Rhetorical Function of Anecdotes in Early Chinese Texts," *Extrême-Orient Extrême-Occident* 34 (2012): 152–54.

78. The text here offers two other examples, showing Shun transforming fishermen and potters.

79. Chen Qiyou finds this phrase nonsensical, and recommends amending 藉 to 耕, while Wang Xianshen prefers keeping the text as is. This line might indeed be a bit corrupted, but its meaning seems to be clear.

80. *Han Feizi jijie*, 36. 349.

81. Ibid., 40.391–392.

82. John S. Major et al., *The Huainanzi: A Guide to the Theory and Practice of Government in Early Han China* (New York: Columbia University Press, 2010).

83. Sarah A. Queen and John S. Major, *Luxuriant Gems of the Spring and Autumn* (New York: Columbia University Press, 2016).

84. See A. C. Graham, "How Much of Chuang Tzu Did Chuang Tzu Write?," in *Studies in Classical Chinese Thought*, ed. Henry Rosemont and Benjamin Schwartz, *Journal of the American Academy of Religion* 47, no. 3, Thematic Issue (1979), 459–501, and Xiaogan Liu, *Classifying the Zhuangzi Chapters* (Ann Arbor: University of Michigan Center for Chinese Studies, 1994).

85. Queen, "Representations of Confucius in the *Huainanzi*."

86. *Hanshu*, 30.1736.

87. The "Nanshi" and "Wen Tian" chapters both give Shen Dao and Han Fei the last word, while the "Dingfa" chapter, even as it identifies imperfections in the words attributed to Shen Buhai and Shang Yang, praises them as the *sine qua non* of the emperor's toolbox, see *Han Feizi jijie*, 43.397, 440.

88. *Han Feizi jijie*, 43.397.

89. Graham, *Disputers of the Dao: Philosophical Argument in Ancient China* (La Salle, IL: Open Court, 1989), 268.

90. Goldin, "Persistent Misconceptions about Chinese 'Legalism,'" 95–96.

91. G. E. R. Lloyd, *Adversaries and Authorities: Investigations Into Ancient Greek and Chinese Science* (Cambridge: Cambridge University Press, 1996), 79, 87–92.

92. Wai-yee Li's article traces this topic through both Masters texts and historiographies. See also Hunter, "Difficulty," 184ff.

7

The Limits of Praise and Blame
The Rhetorical Uses of Anecdotes in the *Gongyangzhuan*

Sarah A. Queen[1]

Do not on account of a father's commands reject a kingly father's commands. On account of a kingly father's commands do reject a father's commands. This is how a father should be treated by his son. Do not on account of obligations to your family neglect obligations to your king. On account of obligations to your king do neglect family obligations. This is how a superior should be treated by his subordinate.

不以父命辭王父命，以王父命辭父命，是父之行乎子也；不以家事辭王事，以王事辭家事，是上之行乎下也。[2]

Anecdotes—brief historical, quasi-historical, and legendary narratives that are embedded in a wide range of texts dating to the Warring States 戰國 (453–221 BCE) and Han 漢 (202 BCE–220 CE) periods—are an important part of the early Chinese literary tradition. Perhaps in part because of a long-standing Chinese cultural tradition that saw history as a guide to present behavior, and consequently valued the creation of written historical records, a large body of anecdotal material became widely known among members of the Chinese elite during the second half of the first millennium BCE. These anecdotes constituted a pool of material that anyone could draw upon to ornament and illustrate a speech, a commentary, or a written treatise. Their abundance is matched, moreover, by the great diversity in their rhetorical usages and in the literary genres in which they appear. For example, numerous stories appear in philosophical works such as the *Huainanzi* 淮南子 (The Master of Huainan) as persuasive tools to adopt the text's worldview; in commentarial works like the *Hanshi waizhuan* 韓詩外傳 (Han's Supplementary Commentary to the Odes) as demonstrations of the multifaceted and authoritative wisdom of the Odes; and in literary works like the *Zhuangzi* 莊子 (Master Zhuang) as vehicles for spiritual enlightenment to break through conventional ways of viewing the world.[3]

The anecdotes themselves achieved an almost proverbial status; a simple reference to Lady Boji of Song 宋伯姬 (6th c. BCE) would call to the minds of an educated audience the tale of a noble widow who chose to die in a fire rather than commit the ritual impropriety of leaving her palace without an escort, thus providing an opportunity to debate the deeper moral implications of her actions. Should Lady Boji be remembered as a misguided matron who failed to correctly prioritize conflicting moral obligations or should she be commemorated as an exemplary martyr who was willing to die to preserve her purity? In addition, a single narrative could easily generate multiple readings, emphasizing different aspects of the same basic plot. Thus, a story devoted to the well-known hegemon Duke Huan of Qi 齊桓公 (r. 685–643 BCE) could be, and was, used to depict Duke Huan as an autocrat who precipitated his own downfall through his arrogance, or as a successful and farsighted statesman whose accomplishments outweighed his faults.

While such anecdotes are well known to anyone with even a slight acquaintance with early Chinese literature, they have received surprisingly little scholarly attention as a distinctive type of writing within the *Gongyangzhuan* 公羊傳 (Gongyang Commentary), in comparison, for example, with the *Zuozhuan* 左傳 (Zuo Commentary), a roughly contemporaneous work that approaches the *Chunqiu* 春秋 (Spring and Autumn Annals) from a quite different point of view.[4] According to the *Gongyangzhuan*, Confucius 孔子 (551–479 BCE) compiled and edited the *Chunqiu* from earlier versions of the chronicle in particular ways to bequeath to posterity a hidden message of positive and negative moral judgments of the events recorded in the chronicle in the hopes that a future sage would implement his vision of reform. The *Gongyangzhuan* analyzes the wording and phrasing of the chronicle to make explicit this assumed esoteric message of world salvation.

It uses a question-and-answer format to explicate the text's laconic entries, and often uses anecdotes to enlarge on the types of royal and aristocratic behavior that Confucius supposedly singled out for praise or blame. Most scholarship on the text has focused on the supposedly esoteric language of the *Chunqiu* that conveys Confucius's judgments of people and events. In contrast, this chapter will focus on the stories that appear across the *Gongyangzhuan*, asking: When, how, and why are anecdotes deployed in the *Gongyangzhuan*? What is their rhetorical function? What ethical and political ideals do they convey? The chapter will introduce a number of exemplary tales to consider the rhetorical uses of anecdotes as an important type of writing within the *Gongyangzhuan*, distinct from other types of literary composition that comprise the work.[5]

A Typology of *Gongyang* Narratives

As this chapter will demonstrate, themes of state service and restorative justice constitute the thrust of the *Gongyang* narratives. By this I mean, they underscore the most serious affronts to intrastate and interstate harmony and delineate the norms that will enable the political elite to restore order under the guise of a return to the ritual code of King Wen of Zhou 周文王 (r. 1099/56–1050 BCE).[6] The stories articulate a decidedly statist utopian view of political justice in the manner in which they emphasize dangers and vulnerabilities that challenge the lord's power and authority. Both lord and minister must subordinate personal and familial desires and obligations to this code of justice that emphasizes the security of the state above all else. They highlight those historical agents who successfully negotiate such tensions and judge them deserving of commemoration and emulation. They highlight those ministers who exhibit exceptional courage and commitment in serving their rulers in support of this statist view of justice. They uphold worthy exemplars of these themes, and conversely condemn individuals who violated the norms of good government and social justice. The anecdotes show by means of positive and negative examples how the political elite can lead a return to the ideal society created centuries earlier by the dynastic founder King Wen of Zhou, whose virtue allowed him to rule by means of a ritual code rather than through laws and punishments. In this respect, they evince a perspective that often differs markedly from their counterparts in the *Zuozhuan*. The *Zuo* stories often exhibit the untrammeled confidence and magnificent culture of the Warring States ministerial class, marked most notably by their gracious and erudite speeches.[7] In contrast, the *Gongyang* narratives deem most praiseworthy ministers who subjugate their personal desires and concerns, demonstrating loyalty to their lords and service to their states above all other concerns. The independent and confident voice of the ministerial class, which is such a prominent feature of the *Zuozhuan*, is strikingly absent in the *Gongyangzhuan*, where instead we find a more compliant and subservient vision of service.

To understand the distinctive ethico-political ethos of these exemplary tales, this chapter will discuss some illustrative examples and explore their most prominent themes to demonstrate that they represent rhetorical sites that express the most significant and extreme political problems and tensions that the *Gongyangzhuan* seeks to address. Five types of Worthies (*xian* 賢) and their negative counterfoils constitute the focus of the anecdotes and will be examined in turn. We turn to the first group below.

Worthy Protectors

That regicide loomed large on the political horizon of the Spring and Autumn Period 春秋 (770–453 BCE) as one of the most pervasive and persistent dangers, obscuring and challenging the hierarchical order and peaceful unity the *Gongyangzhuan* sought to restore in the name of King Wen of Zhou, hardly needs to be stated. Several narratives focus on the most infamous of these instances in the state of Lu 魯.[8] Collectively they underscore the minister's first obligation to protect the life and limb of his lord. Not only was this one of the most important responsibilities of the minister, it was also unconditional: a minister was to do his utmost to preserve the ruler's life, regardless of the lord's character or his conduct. As the supreme expression of state loyalty, this responsibility required that a minister draw upon his physical, intellectual, and spiritual strengths to safeguard his lord against a spectrum of dangers from a transgression as minor as a verbal insult to the most serious of crimes, that of regicide. The *Gongyangzhuan* lavishes praise on those ministers who succeed in doing so, and it presents a number of anecdotes that evince their worthiness.

Who were these ministers and what was the nature of their worthiness? The anecdotal narratives of "Worthy Protectors," as I refer to this group, commemorate ministers' efforts to rescue their lords from peril: the righteous Kongfu Jia of Song who died defending Duke Yuyi from the Assassin Hua Du; Qiu Mu of Song who met his end while courageously attempting to confront Duke Min's assassin, Nangong Wan; Xun Xi of Jin who sacrificed his life to keep a promise to his lord; Zhaizhong of Zheng who exercised moral expediency to rescue his lord from captivity; Ji of Cao, who remonstrated thrice to save his lord from danger in an impending battle with the Rong; and Feng Choufu of Qi who doubled for his lord to free him from the enemy.[9] An analysis of the first three examples will provide an introduction to the most important themes of this group of anecdotes.

The Righteous Kongfu Jia of Song

The *Chunqiu* records the assassination of Duke Shang (Yuyi) of Song and his great officer Kongfu Jia in 709 BCE: "In the second year, in spring, in the King's first month, on the day *wushen*, Du of Song assassinated his lord Yuyi along with his great officer Kongfu." 二年春, 王正月, 戊申, 宋督弒其君與夷及其大夫孔父.[10] The *Gongyangzhuan* analyzes the exceptional wording of the record as follows:

> What does the term *ji* ("along with") denote? It denotes that [Kongfu] was involved [in the death of his lord]. Assassinations of lords were numerous. Aside from this record [of Kongfu], were there no others who were involved [in the death of their lord]? The answer is there were. Qiu Mu and Xun Xi both were involved [in the death of their lord]. Aside from Qiu Mu and Xun Xi, were there no others who were involved [in the death of their lord]? There were. If there were, then why in this case [was Kongfu] recorded? He was a Worthy.
>
> 及者何? 累也. 弒君多矣. 舍此無累者乎? 曰: 有, 仇牧, 荀息, 皆累也. 舍仇牧, 荀息, 無累者乎? 曰: 有. 有則此何以書? 賢也.[11]

The *Gongyangzhuan* presses for more information concerning the nature of Kongfu's worthiness and provides an answer as well: Kongfu's worthiness is identified with the quality of righteousness (*yi* 義) which was so refined and exemplary that it was apparent in his very demeanor.[12] But it is the narrative alone that delineates the quality of Kongfu's righteousness:

Du was plotting to assassinate Duke Shang [Yuyi]. As long as Kongfu remained alive to preserve [his lord], there would be no opportunity to apprehend and assassinate Duke Shang. Consequently Du first attacked Kongfu's home. Duke Shang realized that if Kongfu died, then he would inevitably die too. So he hastened to [Kongfu's home] to rescue him but both [Duke Shang and Kongfu] died there.

督將弒殤公，孔父生而存，則殤公不可得而弒也。故於是先攻孔父之家。殤公知孔父死，己必死，趨而救之，皆死焉。[13]

Having told the tale of how Kongfu's devotion to his lord cost him his life, the *Gongyangzhuan* concludes with a remark that underscores his moral rectitude and its generally positive influence on political life despite the exceptional actions of Hua Du: "When Kongfu took up his position in the court with his upright demeanor, no one dared to commit an offense or cause distress to his lord." 孔父正色而立於朝，則人莫敢過而致難於其君者。[14] The story provides the critical context for understanding Kongfu's worthiness through the eyes of his political peers, both superior and subordinates. It enables the reader to understand not only the precise qualities of his worthiness but also its influence in situ. How did Kongfu's worthiness influence those around him? The would-be assassin understands well the nature of Kongfu's loyalty to his ruler: he thinks nothing of dying to protect his ruler's life. Thus the assassin must attack Kongfu first, if he is to realize his ultimate plan. Kongfu's lord sees him in the same light and with the same moral appraisal, so he rushes to Kongfu's home in an effort to preserve both Kongfu's life and his own.

Dramatically and ironically, Duke Shang rushes into danger in search of the ultimate safety that only a loyal minister willing to die for his ruler can provide. Although both meet their physical deaths at the hands of the evil Du of Song, the story illustrates how Kongfu's martyrdom guaranteed that his moral demise would be forestalled forever. This *Chunqiu* entry ensured that his untimely death would live on in the public memory but the *Gongyang* narrative secured him an enduring reputation as a worthy coded as righteousness, and defined as his unwavering sense of devotion and obligation to his lord.

In describing Kongfu's worthiness, the story also highlights Du's unworthiness. Kongfu's lofty presence at court was generally sufficient to ensure social harmony and political stability. Only in the most extreme cases was that harmony and stability threatened. The *Chunqiu* hints at the exceptional qualities of Du as exemplar of evil and Kongfu as exemplar of good, but the story provides the critical detail that lends persuasive support to the judgment at hand. The story explains Kongfu's worthiness in terms of his moral rectitude, which is deemed efficacious and exemplary precisely because it defines how he serves his lord.

The Fearless Qiu Mu of Song

The second example, from 681 BCE, describes a similar case in which another great officer and his ruler are assassinated. The *Chunqiu* reports, "In Autumn, in the eighth month, on the day *jiawu*, Wan of Song assassinated his lord Jie along with his great officer Qiu Mu." 秋, 八月, 甲午, 宋萬弒其君接及其大夫仇牧.[15] In fact, the wording of this record is identical to the preceding example except for the names of the ruler, assassin, and great officer. The analysis of the terminology that follows and the ensuing judgment are also identical to the previous example, save for the names of the historical figures involved.[16]

Having judged Qiu Mu a worthy, as in the case of Kongfu before him, the *Gongyangzhuan* once again probes the nature of his worthiness, asking: "What was worthy about Qiu Mu?" 何賢乎仇牧. But in this case, it provides a different response: "Of Qiu Mu it may be said that he did not fear the powerful and recalcitrant." 仇牧可謂不畏強禦矣.[17] While Kongfu was an exemplar of righteousness, the *Gongyangzhuan* commemorates Qiu Mu for his exceptional moral courage, because he remained unruffled by powerful and unruly opponents. But what kind of moral courage did he embody? And what kind of opponent did he confront and seek to resist? Was it, for example, the moral courage of a David willing to face down a Goliath? The reader is left to wonder. The praise and blame historiography articulated in the analysis of the *Chunqiu* wording necessitates further elucidation which is provided by an illustrative story that clarifies the nature of Qiu Mu's bravery. As in the previous case, the story highlights the ethics of the lord-minister relationship under the most extreme and exceptional circumstances:

> Wan once battled with Duke Zhuang of Lu and was captured by him. After returning home from captivity, Duke Zhuang released Wan but confined him to the interior of the palace. Several months [passed] before Duke Zhuang allowed him to

return home.[18] After returning home, Wan became a great officer in Song. [On one occasion,] while playing chess with Duke Min as Min's wives all stood by his side, Wan exclaimed, "How exceptional is the goodness and virtue of the Marquis of Lu. Of all the regional lords in the world, only the Marquis of Lu is fit to be ruler!" Duke Min felt humiliated before his wives and envied such praise. Looking at [Wan] he said, "These [are the words of a former] prisoner. It is only because you were his [former] prisoner [that you speak this way]. What would you know of the virtue or evil of the Marquis of Lu?" Wan was enraged, struck Duke Min, and broke his neck. When Qiu Mu heard that the lord had been assassinated, he rushed to the scene, where he met Wan at the door, brandished his sword, and reprimanded him. Wan beat Qiu Mu with his fists and killed him, crushing his skull so that his teeth stuck in the door leaf. Of Qiu Mu it may be said, that he did not fear the strong and recalcitrant.

萬嘗與莊公戰, 獲乎莊公; 莊公歸, 散舍諸宮中, 數月, 然後歸之. 歸反為大夫於宋. 與閔公博, 婦人皆在側, 萬曰: 「甚矣, 魯侯之淑, 魯侯之美也! 天下諸侯宜為君者, 唯魯侯爾!」閔公矜此婦人, 妒其言, 顧曰: 「此虜也! 爾虜焉故, 魯侯之美惡乎至?」萬怒, 搏閔公, 絕其脰. 仇牧聞君弒, 趨而至, 遇之于門, 手劍而叱之. 萬辟殺仇牧, 碎其首, 齒著乎門闔. 仇牧可謂不畏強禦矣.[19]

The narrative transforms disembodied names in the *Chunqiu* into living agents with decided personalities. It not only describes each actor's moral character but also two distinct expressions of the lord-minister relationship. Nangong Changwan (i.e., Great Officer Wan) is clearly Qiu Mu's moral foil, and his relationship with Duke Min stands in radical opposition to Qiu Mu's. As if watching a scene in a play, the reader is drawn into the private world of Duke Min's abode, where he sits leisurely playing chess with his great officer, while his harem looks on at his side.

With these simple props, the narrative sets the scene to explore the moral characters of this lord and his minister. The dialogue that unfolds between them leaves no doubt that both suffer from arrogance and pride. For his part, Great Officer Wan exhibits extreme disrespect as he openly and unabashedly brags about another ruler to Duke Min. Though the manner in which he delivers his message is problematic, the message seems less so. After all, he is praising Duke Zhuang of Lu for his goodness and virtue. This is potentially an opportunity for transformational learning on the part of Duke Min: the possibility of a positive outcome is not precluded a priori by Wan's recognition of Duke Zhuang's goodness. But it does seem to be preempted by Duke Min's character; wanting to look desirable to his harem, he feels annoyed and envious when his subordinate chooses to praise another lord in his stead. Or perhaps the compliment amounts to a form of insubordination, belying Wan's deeper loyalty to a ruler not his own.

Whatever the explanation, Duke Min returns the perceived insult with another, suggesting that Wan's high estimation of Duke Zhuang amounts to nothing other than a sycophantic gratitude for having been set free by the lord. Infuriated by the insult, Wan kills Duke Min in a rage exhibiting the most extreme kind of disloyalty a minister can demonstrate to his lord: the act of regicide. Having learned of the assassination, Qiu Mu's response is both immediate and unpremeditated: he rushes to the scene to confront, upbraid, and punish Wan, without any thought for his personal safety or consideration for the strength of the opponent at hand. Like David, Qiu Mu wields his sword against his Goliath, for he is fueled by a rage of a wholly different quality and kind than the anger that led Wan to murder his lord. What kind of rage enables one to muster the courage to face down a powerful and headstrong killer? Indeed, the grisly details of Qiu Mu's death underscores the exceptional strength of his bravery and his bond of fealty to his lord. Commemorated as a Worthy and singled out as a model of emulation, Qiu Mu's faithfulness to his lord is called forth in vivid terms each time the story is read anew.

The Trustworthy Xun Xi of Jin

The third example recounts the assassination of the ruler Zhuozi of Jin and his great officer Xun Xi by the hand of the official Li Ke in the year 650 BCE.[20] The record of the assassination, the discussion of terminology, and the ensuing judgment are also identical to the last two examples except for the proper names listed.[21] Moreover, as in the previous examples, a minister is judged a "Worthy," and the *Gongyangzhuan* asks once again: "What was worthy about Xun Xi?" 何賢乎荀息. At this point, the singularity of this historical figure comes to the fore, as Xun Xi's worthiness is identified with his ability to keep his word: "Of Xun Xi it may be said that he did not swallow his words." 荀息可謂不食其言矣. The narrative that follows develops this theme further, identifying Xun Xi's worthiness with the quality of trustworthiness (*xin* 信).

The *Gongyang* tale begins with a brief account of the amorous affair between Duke Xian of Jin and his favorite consort Li Ji. Driven by his passion, Duke Xian kills the rightful heir to the throne, in his desire to establish her son as his successor.[22] Worried about whether his plans to establish Li Ji's son on the throne will come to fruition after his death, and painfully aware that his only assurance lies with his great officer, Xun Xi, Duke Xian summons him for a final deathbed conversation, in which he tellingly questions him about the meaning of trustworthiness:

> When Duke Xian was ill and about to die, he spoke to Xun Xi saying, "What kind of officer can be called trustworthy?" Xun Xi replied, "When those who have died are brought back to life, and those who are living feel no shame for what they promised [the deceased in the past], then they can be called trustworthy.
>
> 獻公病將死, 謂荀息曰:「士何如則可謂之信矣?」荀息對曰:「使死者反生, 生者不愧乎其言, 則可謂信矣.」[23]

Xun Xi assures his lord that he understands well the meaning of trustworthiness, and by implication, that he will not waver in his promise to execute his lord's request to install his designated, though wrongful, heir.

In the next leg of the story, Duke Xian has passed and Xi Qi has been successfully installed as the new ruler, but all is not settled in the state of Jin. Li Ke, the powerful official and former tutor of the rightful heir Shen Sheng determines to reestablish the rightful line of succession. In search of supporters, he approaches Xun Xi and endeavors to persuade him to join the assassination plot, but Xun Xi declines to participate. The narrative recounts:

> Duke Xian died and Xi Qi was established as his successor. Li Ke spoke to Xun Xi, saying, "Our lord murdered the legitimate heir and established the illegitimate heir [in his stead], abandoning the elder to establish the younger. What will you do about this?" Xun Xi replied, "When our lord once questioned his subject [about trustworthiness], I replied: 'When those who have died are brought back to life, and those who are living feel no shame for what they promised [the deceased in the past], then they can be called trustworthy.'" Li Ke understood that

Xun Xi would have no part in his plot and he withdrew. [Subsequently Li Ke] assassinated Xi Qi. Xun Xi [then] established Zhuozi as his successor. When Li Ke assassinated Zhuozi, Xun Xi gave his life for him. Of Xun Xi it may be said that he did not swallow his words.

獻公死, 奚齊立. 里克謂荀息, 曰:「君殺正而立不正, 廢長而立幼, 如之何? 願與子慮之.」荀息曰:「君嘗訊臣矣, 臣對曰: 使死者反生, 生者不愧乎其言, 則可謂信矣.」里克知其不可與謀, 退, 弑奚齊. 荀息立卓子, 里克弑卓子, 荀息死之. 荀息可謂不食其言矣![24]

Xun Xi and Li Ke embody and exemplify the moral dilemmas raised by Duke Xian's conduct: When a ruler murders his own son to bypass the norms of succession and appoints an illegitimate heir in his stead, what, if anything should be done? What is the highest source of authority to whom a minister owes his allegiance: the ritual norms of governance or the ruler who ideally embodies these norms? When the ruler fails to do so, what kinds of actions does the *Gongyangzhuan* condone? Li Ke feels duty-bound to restore the norms of succession abandoned by his former lord but doing so involves regicide. Xun Xi opts out of the plot to reestablish a legitimate line of succession, preferring instead to keep his promise to his former lord, despite the lord's misguided decision to disregard the norms of succession and follow his personal desires to appoint Xi Qi as heir. Though Xun Xi will have no part in Li Ke's efforts to rectify the norms of succession, Li Ke presses on, dispensing first with Xi Qi, then with his brother Zhuozi after each is installed as ruler. Along the way, he takes down Xun Xi, who sacrifices his life rather than go back on his word to his lord. It is difficult to fathom why the *Gongyangzhuan* would valorize what appears at first glance to be Xun Xi's utterly obsequious behavior toward his lord, particularly when it meant flouting one of the mainstays of a state's stability, the norms dictating succession. But here as in the last few cases, the *Gongyangzhuan* appears to define ministerial worthiness with the decided intent to limit the powers of the ministerial class and enhance those of the ruler. Since the lord was synonymous with the state, it is little wonder Xun Xi earns a worthy reputation for not eating his words!

The remaining tales of worthy protectors that constitute this first group of narratives describe how ministers' obligations to protect their lords often brought them into conflict with other norms that required equally difficult choices. Many of the stories address these normative conflicts and clarify how they ought to be prioritized but a central theme unites all of them: saving one's lord was to be given the highest priority even if it meant that the minister abrogate other rules of conduct and pay with his life. Thus, for example, to rescue his ruler from captivity, Feng Choufu assumed his lord's identity, an act typically judged treasonous but the *Gongyangzhuan* judges him a Worthy nonetheless, because his actions served the higher good of saving his lord from death. Having done so, however, Feng Choufu quickly meets his own death when Xi Ke, the commander of the opposing army decapitates him for his ruse.[25]

Under threat from Song, Zhaizhong of Zheng expels his lord Hu and installs Du, a contender for the throne backed by Song. He risks punishment for the crime of treason, but the story ultimately justifies his actions as a temporary expedient to save his lord's life and preserve an opportunity to reinstall him in the future.[26] Though the risks of punishment Zhaizhong shoulders are no less perilous than those of Feng Choufu, Zhaizhong's actions are ultimately sanctioned, and he survives to see his ruler reinstalled and the state of Zheng temporarily preserved. How so? The *Gongyangzhuan* mediates Zhaizhong's moral dilemma—exiling his lord to save his life—by offering the following definition of the principle of "expedient assessment" (*quan* 權)[27] and its proper application:

> What does "expedient assessment" mean? Expedient assessment is contrary to the constant norms but ultimately achieves some good. As for the implementation of expedient assessment, unless the death [of a lord] or the annihilation [of a state] is at stake, it cannot be implemented. These are principles governing the implementation of expedient assessment: The one who implements expedient assessment may personally suffer degradation and harm, but no harm must come to others. To kill others to save one's own life, or annihilate other states to preserve one's own state are actions the Gentleman does not take.
>
> 權者何? 權者反於經, 然後有善者也. 權之所設, 舍死亡無所設. 行權有道, 自貶損以行權, 不害人以行權. 殺人以自生, 亡人 [國] 以自存, 君子不為也.[28]

One may violate constant norms and exercise expedient assessment only when the life of one's lord or the survival of the state is in question. But in doing so, no harm may come to other people or states. The *Gongyangzhuan* does not sanction violence toward other people and states, even on grounds of self-defense. Such extreme pacifism appears to be one of the hallmarks of the ritual code of justice the *Gongyangzhuan* promotes. Most importantly, in exercising expedient assessment, Zhaizhong has sorted his priorities correctly and accomplished the highest good: he has preserved his ruler's life to ultimately reestablish him on the throne.

The anecdotes describing worthy protectors demonstrate that the obligations of a minister to protect his lord included a diverse array of activities. Offering protection to one's lord came in many guises—whether by deterring or attempting to deter a lord's would-be assassin; freeing a lord from captivity; remonstrating with a lord to dissuade him from following a perilous course of action; or keeping a promise to protect a lord's final death-bed request—such actions were the stuff of worthy ministers and they often involved great risk. A minister was to do everything possible to preserve the life of his lord as the highest source of authority and focus of loyalty to the state.

Worthy Avengers

Though ministers ideally stepped forward to rescue their lords and preserve their states, that those ministers who did so were judged Worthies and commemorated in story suggests that such ministers constituted the exception rather than the rule. Holding them up as models of emulation was one decided strategy to mitigate the political mayhem caused by endemic regicides and restore the lost fealty between minister and ruler identified with the halcyon age of King Wen's unified rule.

A second strategy was to commemorate as Worthies those ministers who avenged their lords' wrongful deaths by executing their assassins. This second group of anecdotal narratives that portray historical personalities as "Worthy Avengers" illustrates how the principle of revenge was ideally to inform a ministers' conduct: one in which public/state considerations were to take precedence over private/familial concerns. The *Gongyangzhuan* delineates a minister's obligation to punish his lord's assassin and its familial correlate, a son's responsibility to avenge his father's wrongful death, following the *Chunqiu* record of Duke Yin's death. It considers that Confucius composed this exceptional record, which omits the lord's burial, to express his sympathy for Duke Yin who has died at the hands of an assassin who has yet to be punished for committing regicide.[29] The *Gongyangzhuan* explains further:

> When a lord is assassinated and his ministers do not punish the assassin they are not true ministers. When sons do not avenge a father's grievance, they are not true sons. Burials constitute the obligations of the living [toward the dead]. In the *Chunqiu*, if the lord is assassinated and the assassin is not punished, it does not record the burial because it considers that the burial cannot be related to true ministers or sons.
>
> 君弒, 臣不討賊, 非臣也. 子不復讎, 非子也. 葬, 生者之事也. 《春秋》君弒, 賊不討, 不書葬, 以為不繫乎臣子也.[30]

Five colorful parables explore these obligations binding ministers and sons to their lords and fathers, elucidating how these two obligations—one toward the family and one toward the ruler—are to be prioritized. The stories of Duke Xiang of Qi who annihilates Ji to avenge the wrongful death of the former Duke Ai;[31] Wu Zixu who avenges the wrongful death of his father;[32] and Prince You (Ji You) of Lu who punishes with death not only his brother Shu Ya for plotting to assassinate the future Duke Min[33] but also his brother Qing Fu for assassinating Zi Ban after being installed as Duke Min,[34] provide positive instantiations of the principle of revenge. The story of the eminent Zhao Dun of Jin who fails to punish Duke Ling's assassin, his cousin Zhao Chuan, constitutes the sole negative example of this principle.[35] Each of these stories argues persuasively for the importance of revenge as a principle of public and state justice that must take priority over private and familial concerns. They do so by telling the stories of those who resolve these very conflicts in their efforts to avenge the wrongful death of a lord.

As in other anecdotes, moral choices are never simple and straightforward: an underling committed to punish his lord's assassin—or its corollary, to avenge the wrongful death of a past lord generations removed—must contend with conflicting norms to accomplish this moral end. Once again, the anecdotes illustrate the choices involved, heightening the reader's awareness that ethical choices always seem to fall somewhere on the spectrum between absolute good and evil. Moreover, they often subvert the conventional readings of stock characters, as evil rulers are deemed worthy while upright ministers are criticized. For example, the incestuous Duke Xiang of Qi is praised as a worthy for avenging the wrongful death of Duke Ai, while the commendable minister Zhao Dun is denigrated for failing to punish

Duke Ling's assassin despite his unruly and despicable character. The Worthy Ji You of Lu and his negative counterfoil Zhao Dun of Jin illustrate well how the *Gongyangzhuan* endeavors to elevate obligations to the ruler/state above those of the father/family when it comes to the principle of revenge.

Ji You of Lu

In the two anecdotes devoted to Ji You of Lu, also known as Jizi, the prince demonstrates his loyalty to the state under the most extreme of circumstances; avenging the wrongful death of his lord compels Ji You to execute his two brothers. The first story describes how he pursues and punishes his brother Shu Ya for plotting to assassinate the heir apparent Zi Ban and future Duke Min. Such actions necessitate that he resolve conflicting obligations to his state and to his family. Several principles come into play that the narrative seeks to mediate. The first principle makes clear that when it comes to rebellion initiated by relatives of a lord or an heir apparent there is no distinction between the intent and the act:

> Prince Ya on this occasion only plotted [to assassinate Zi Ban]. Why does the wording represent Jizi as having personally assassinated [Shu] Ya? The relatives of a lord must not plot. If they do so they must be punished with execution. Then [punishment by execution] was condoned? The answer is yes. When an heir apparent who is a younger brother of the same mother is killed, [the *Chunqiu*] directly refers to him as lord to indicate the seriousness [of the offence].

> 公子牙今將爾, 辭曷為與親弒者同? 君親無將, 將而誅焉. 然則善之與? 曰: 然. 殺世子母弟, 直稱君者, 甚之也.³⁶

But for Ji You, punishing a would-be assassin, involves killing his own brother. How does Ji You resolve such conflicting demands on his loyalty? The story explains that having caught wind of his brother's rebellious plot, Ji You waits patiently until Shu Ya finalizes his assassination plans. He then mixes a poisonous concoction, presents it to his brother, and urges him to drink it to spare him the disgrace of regicide, so that his descendants will avoid the death penalty and live on in the state of Lu.³⁷ This show of compassion is critical, as the *Gongyangzhuan* concludes:

What is condoned in the case of Jizi, who killed his elder brother by the same mother? In accordance with the righteous principles governing the relations between lord and minister, one cannot exclude one's elder brother from a justified execution. Then why did Jizi not simply execute Ya instead of poisoning him? The execution was to be carried out on his older brother so he wanted to conceal it and allow his brother to escape the disgrace of execution, making it appear as if he had died from illness. This is the principle of treating relatives with affection.

季子殺母兄, 何善爾? 誅不得辟兄, 君臣之義也. 然則曷為不直誅, 而酖之? 行諸乎兄, 隱而逃之, 使托若以疾死然, 親親之道也.[38]

The second tale depicts an equally uncompromising Ji You. Having assassinated Duke Min, Ji You's brother Qing Fu flees to the nearby state of Ju but is expelled. He then attempts to enter Qi but he is also refused sanctuary. Bereft of options, the fugitive brother returns to his camp on the borderlands along the Wen River and sends a messenger to Ji You to plead on his behalf to be allowed to return home. Ji You refuses unequivocally, stating: "The prince must not re-enter [Qi]. If he does, he will be killed!" 公子不可以入, 入則殺矣.[39] When he hears his messenger wailing, Qing Fu recognizes he will be forced to live as an exile until death. In utter desperation, he then raises a carriage pole and hangs himself.[40]

The stories of Ji You who is responsible for the death of two of his brothers implicated in Duke Min's assassination provides a compelling contrast to that of Zhao Dun of Jin, who tarnishes his fine reputation as an upright minister because he fails to punish his relative Zhao Chuan for the assassination of Duke Ling and thus is also held responsible for it.[41] Though this long and detailed anecdote depicts the many facets of Duke Ling's treacherous behavior and his consequent lack of support among his ministers and people alike, suggesting that Zhao Chuan's decision to assassinate the lord was closer to righteous rebellion than regicide, the story does not make such explicit claims. Indeed, the depths of Duke Ling's evil and Zhao Dun's uprightness, serves to underscore a norm that appears to brook no compromise: ministers are obligated to punish a lord's assassin regardless of how loathsome the personal character or conduct of the lord might be.[42] Why is such an upright minister as Zhao Dun held responsible for failing to punish his lord's assassin when his lord's ignominious conduct presumably calls forth his own demise? Perhaps with these ironic twists of fate, the story seeks to disaggregate the monarchy as an institution from the various rogues who might occupy the throne at any given moment. The institution of the monarchy must be preserved at all costs. This is tantamount to a requirement that a minister put to death his lord's assassin regardless of that lord's individual character or conduct and regardless of the minister's familial relation to the assassin. This, then, is another expression of the *Gongyangzhuan*'s strategy to articulate, resolve, and prioritize a statist, as opposed to a familial, view of justice.[43]

Worthy Regents

Not only was the lord's person vulnerable to attack, but also his ability to pass on his authority and power to a legitimate heir was also fraught with challenges. Undoubtedly one of the most precarious moments in the political life of the various states that populated the Spring and Autumn landscape, was the transfer of political power to an heir apparent after the death of his father and lord. More often than not, the death of a lord was followed by succession struggles that might take generations to resolve, despite the observance of correct norms of succession. To alleviate succession struggles, the *Gongyangzhuan* upholds two strategies as normative: regency and abdication. The next group of anecdotes, which depict "Worthy Regents" and "Worthy Abdicators," praise those who prevent succession struggles by becoming regents or abdicating rule. Thus, when Duke Yin of Lu assumes the regency until his brother, the future Duke Huan, is old enough to take over the reigns of government, he is praised for his actions. So, too, is Prince Muyi of Song, who returns home, to defend Song and preserve the state by ascending the throne until Duke Xiang is freed from captivity.[44] The regency of Duke Yin, perhaps the most famous example, illuminates how the *Gongyangzhuan* once again articulates its statist vision of justice, in which preserving the ruler is given the highest priority.

Duke Yin's Regency

The opening passage of the *Gongyangzhuan* for the year 722 BCE addresses the first of many succession crises documented in the *Chunqiu*: Duke Hui of Lu has passed away, but failed to sire a son with his principal wife. Thus a successor among the sons of his consorts must be designated as the new lord and the choice comes down to one of two sons by different consorts. Duke Yin is installed as the new lord but is his bid for power legitimate?

The *Gongyangzhuan* insists that the ascension is legitimate because Duke Yin intends to assume the throne only as a regent, to restore peace to the state and preserve the throne for his brother Huan until he grows old enough to assume power. The *Gongyangzhuan* claims that the *Chunqiu* does not employ the usual phrase for the ascension of a new lord (*ji wei* 即位) to indicate Duke Yin's intention to serve as regent. The *Gongyangzhuan* explains the mitigating circumstances as follows:

> The lord intended to bring peace to the state and then return it to Huan. Why return it to Huan? Huan was younger but of nobler rank. Yin was older but of humbler rank. The difference between their relative statuses was slight. Among the people of the state there was no one who knew this. Yin was older and moreover he was a worthy man and so various great officers supported Yin and established him as lord. Under such conditions, if Yin declined to be established as lord, then he would have no way to assure that Huan would later be established as lord. Moreover, if Huan was established as lord, he feared that the various great officers would not be able to minister to such a young lord. Thus in all cases, Yin's ascension was to assure Huan's ascension. Yin was older and moreover a worthy man. Why was it not fitting for him to be established as lord? The establishment of the sons of the principal wife is based on seniority and not on considerations of their worthiness; the establishment of sons by secondary wives [viz. the lord's consorts] is based on nobility and not on seniority. In what respect was Huan of higher noble rank than Yin? His mother was of higher noble rank than Yin's mother. Why if the mother was of higher noble rank should the son be considered of higher noble rank? A son shares the nobility of his mother and a mother shares the nobility of her son.

> 公將平國而反之桓. 曷為反之桓? 桓幼而貴, 隱長而卑, 其為尊卑也微, 國人莫知. 隱長又賢, 諸大夫扳隱而立之. 隱於是焉而辭立, 則未知桓之將必得立也. 且如桓立, 則恐諸大夫之不能相幼君也, 故凡隱之立為桓立也. 隱長又賢, 何以不宜立? 立適以長不以賢, 立子以貴不以長. 桓何以貴? 母貴也. 母貴則子何以貴? 子以母貴, 母以子貴.⁴⁵

The discussion clarifies that based on the norms of succession, the future Duke Huan stands as the legitimate heir, for he is of nobler rank than his brother Duke Yin. This first discussion of succession is pertinent to all subsequent discussions of succession as it articulates the norms that constitute the basis for all future judgments of this type. It is the seminal judgment that defines the legitimacy or illegitimacy of every succession that follows. Since Duke Yin is of lower noble rank than his brother [the future] Duke Huan, Duke Yin's ascension would otherwise raise serious questions concerning the legitimacy of his reign. But his ascension is nonetheless defended on another principle: the principle of guardianship or regency, which maintains that Duke Yin took up the reins of the state to establish peace and so preserve the state so that in the future it could be passed to Huan.

The passage identifies a number of factors that lend legitimacy to the notion of a state guardianship on the part of Yin: Huan's youth contributes to the precariousness of the situation; Yin's experience and worthiness have won him support among the great officers of Lu; the slight difference in their relative status though small was significant; and the fact that the people of Lu were not generally aware of their differences in noble rank. Given all these factors, the *Gongyangzhuan* argues, if Yin did not assume the throne, he might unwittingly contribute to further instability in Lu, because though the great officers support Yin, it is not clear that they would lend their support to Huan. Thus Duke Yin, as the argument seems to go, has no other choice but to assume the throne as regent, if he is to preserve the state so that later the legitimate heir can establish his rightful claim as ruler.[46]

Failure to sire a son with a principal wife leading to struggles among the various sons of a lord's consorts was but one source of succession struggle upon the death of a lord. Three narratives address other sources of succession struggles: lords who violate the norms of succession by disregarding legitimate heirs and designating personal favorites in their place and princes who challenge an heir apparent's claim to the throne. As the mirror image or foil to the stories devoted to "Worthy Regents," these stories chastise rulers for placing private pleasures and concerns ahead of their public responsibilities as lords of states, demonstrating all too clearly the chaos and violence that follows in the wake of such disastrous choices.[47]

Worthy Abdicators

Four stories highlight legitimate heirs to the throne, who nonetheless yield the state to avoid intrastate or interstate conflicts and are judged to be Worthies: Shu Wu of Wei yields the state to his brother, the Duke of Wei;[48] Prince Zha of Wu abdicates to his half-brother Liao;[49] Prince Xishi turns over the state to Prince Fuchai of Cao;[50] and Shushu of Zhulou relinquishes power to his stepson Xiafu.[51] The story of Prince Zha of Wu provides a particularly compelling example of stories devoted to this theme as a succession of three brothers agree to act as regent to preserve the throne for their youngest brother.

Ji Zha of Wu

The story of Prince Zha of Wu (a.k.a. Jizi or Ji Zha) combines the themes of regency and abdication into a single story, to ponder a succession crisis involving the oft-repeated crime of fratricide. The lord's three brothers dissuade the ruler from passing the throne to his eldest son with the promise that they will act as regents and eventually pass the state on to their young brother Jizi who they believe to be most competent to rule. The following description of their conduct upon assuming the reins of governance evinces the brothers' sincere desire to act as state guardians:

> Therefore when they served as lord, they disregarded death and performed brave deeds. Whenever they took sustenance, they always invoked a prayer, saying, "If Heaven indeed has regard for the state of Wu, quickly bring down a curse upon my body [so that I will die, thus hastening the handing over of the state to Jizi]." Subsequently, Ye died, and Yu Ji was installed as ruler; Yu Ji died and Yi Mei was installed as ruler; Yi Mei died and so the state properly belonged to Jizi.
>
> 故諸為君者，皆輕死為勇，飲食必祝，曰：「天苟有吳國，尚速有悔於予身。」故謁也死，餘祭也立。餘祭也死，夷昧也立。夷昧也死，則國宜之季子者也.[52]

As fate would have it, when Yi Mei passes away, the rightful heir, Jizi, who is next in line to succeed him, is on a mission abroad. The eldest son of a concubine named Liao is appointed ruler in his absence. Upon his return home, Jizi simply accepts Liao as Wu's rightful ruler, a decision that does not sit well with Helu, the eldest son of the late lord Yi Mei, who also has a legitimate claim to the throne as the eldest son of the former lord. As Helu explains to Jizi:

> That our former lords did not hand the state to their sons but instead handed it to their younger brothers, was entirely on

account of you, Jizi. Shall we follow the instructions given by our former lords? If so, the state should properly belong to you, Jizi. Or shall we disobey the instructions of our former lords? If so, I am the one who should properly be set up as ruler. How can Liao [the son of a concubine] possibly have any claim to the title?

先君之所以不與子國而與弟者, 凡為季子故也. 將從先君之命與, 則國宜之季子者也; 如不從先君之命與, 則我宜立者也, 僚惡得為君乎?[53]

How should the dilemma be resolved? According to the norms of succession, Helu has a claim to the throne as the eldest son of the former lord. However, his father received the throne as the last of a fraternal regency, to preserve the throne until Jizi, having recovered from his physical ailments and reached maturity, could assume the throne. To honor his former lord and father, Helu recognizes that he is duty bound to defer to Jizi. But Jizi was passed over, when Liao, the weakest claimant to the throne, was established as Wu's reigning lord. Helu resolves the dilemma by killing Liao with the intention of handing over the state to Jizi.

Helu then approaches Jizi in the hopes of installing him on the throne, but Jizi will not accept the offer. He explains his reasons to Helu, stating:

You assassinated my lord. If I were to receive the state as a gift from you, then I would become an accomplice in your rebellion. You killed my elder brother. If I in turn were to kill you, then fathers and sons, elder brothers and younger brothers, would continue to kill one another in an endless sequence.

爾弒吾君, 吾受爾國, 是吾與爾為篡也. 爾殺吾兄, 吾又殺爾, 是父子兄弟相殺, 終身無已也.[54]

Caught in the horns of a regicidal and fratricidal dilemma, Jizi opts to leave the state of Wu never to return home. The story concludes: "Therefore the Gentleman regarded Jizi's declining to accept the state as a righteous deed, and the fact he did not kill [Helu] as a humane act." 故君子以其不受為義, 以其不殺為仁.[55] On the one hand, Jizi will not assume a throne having been vacated as the consequence of a regicidal act that would implicate him in a rebellion. On the other hand, he cannot bring himself to punish his brother for the assassination of his lord. And so he exercises the only option left to him: he leaves the state and absolves himself of this responsibility altogether. In contrast to Zhao Dun who returns to his state but fails to punish the lord's assassin and thus is judged harshly by the *Gongyangzhuan*, Jizi's self-inflicted exile is recognized as one strategy enabling him to treat a relative humanely without transgressing the statist norm that obligates him to punish his lord's assassin, had he remained a subject of Wu.

Devotees of Ritual Propriety and Trustworthiness

The last category consists of a series of anecdotes that focus on fidelity to ritual propriety (*li* 禮) and trustworthiness (*xin* 信). Four stories denigrate historical figures as blameworthy due to their utter lack of decorum and deceptive speech. They illustrate how seemingly insignificant lapses of ritual propriety and trustworthiness can all too readily precipitate significant interstate and intrastate conflicts.[56] In contrast to these tales of ritual woe, six narratives describe positive instantiations of ritual propriety and trustworthiness in speech, maintaining that these ethical values must be maintained at all cost, even to the point of death. Perhaps the most striking example of this uncompromising ethos is the story of Song Boji (a.k.a. Song Gongji), the only female commemorated as a Worthy in the *Gongyangzhuan*, who willingly sacrifices her life to uphold a point of ritual protocol. Though encouraged by her attendants to vacate her palace to escape an approaching fire that promises to engulf her in flames, Boji refuses to leave. She explains that she cannot leave because ritual propriety demands that a woman must be accompanied by her governess and guardian when leaving her home, and her guardian has yet to arrive.[57] Equally illustrative is the story that praises Duke Huan of Qi for the trustworthiness he exhibits during the critical interstate meeting at Ke with Duke Zhuang of Lu in 681 BCE. It recounts how the leader of the Lu forces threatened Duke Huan with a sword and demanded that Qi return lands that they had previously acquired. Although it was permissible to violate covenants concluded under threat, Duke Huan does not violate his promise, respects the covenant, and returns the occupied territories to Lu.[58] As the *Chunqiu fanlu* 春秋繁露 (Luxuriant Gems of the Spring and Autumn) notes in recalling these two stories, propriety and trustworthiness are to inform all aspects of court life:

> The *Chunqiu* honors propriety and values trustworthiness. Trustworthiness is more valuable than one's territory; propriety is more venerable than one's life. How do we know that this is

so? Lady Boji of Song perished in a fire [to forestall] doubt of her propriety. Duke Huan of Qi gave up territory [to forestall] doubts of his trustworthiness. In the *Chunqiu*, worthies are raised up and taken as models for the world. This is to say regarding trustworthiness and propriety, there is nothing to which propriety does not respond, there is nothing which trustworthiness cannot repay. This is Heaven's calculation.

《春秋》尊禮而重信. 信重於地, 禮尊於身. 何以知其然也? 宋伯姬疑禮而死於火, 齊桓公疑信而虧其地, 《春秋》賢而舉之, 以為天下法, 曰禮而信, 不答, 施無不報, 天之數也.[59]

A third story consists of a long and moving exchange between the exiled Duke Zhao of Lu and Duke Jing of Qi. Having usurped several ritual prerogatives of the Son of Heaven while ruling the state of Lu and having failed to perform those rituals appropriate to his position, the exiled Duke Zhao expresses his sincere remorse and shame for his past ritual failings that he now recognizes cost him his state. The anecdote depicts a transformed Duke Zhao who appears as a humble devotee of ritual propriety, hoping to preserve the purity of several rituals by refusing to participate when Duke Jing of Qi solicits him to do so. As Duke Zhao explains:

> A man who mourns [the loss of his state] is not wise. I have been unable to guard the spirits of the state of Lu and I have managed my office to my own disgrace. I dare not disgrace this great ritual [with my participation]. I dare to presume to decline your offer.

喪人不佞. 失守魯國之社稷, 執事以羞, 敢辱大禮? 敢辭.[60]

The sense of loss and remorse is underscored in the final scene of the narrative when, after wailing and weeping with his small band of followers, Duke Zhao determines to perform the Rite of a Chance Meeting (*yuli* 遇禮) to ensure that his encounter with Duke Jing is honored with the appropriate ritual observance. Significantly, Duke Zhao's new found humility is reflected in the humble accouterments he musters to perform the ritual:

> When his [viz. Duke Zhao] weeping had subsided, he used his men to clear away the grasses, used a chariot cover to serve as a mat, and used a saddle to serve as a table to mark the mutual

encounter [between Duke Zhao and Duke Jing] with the Rite of a Chance Meeting.

既哭以人為菑側, 以幦為席, 以鞍為几, 以遇禮相見.⁶¹

The passage concludes with Confucius's telling appraisal which confirms Duke Zhao's transformation to an exemplar of ritual propriety despite his past record: "His ritual propriety and his ceremonial speech are sufficient to be observed!" 其禮與其辭足觀矣.⁶²

The next two stories are set within the context of famous battles of the period, the Battle of Hong (638 BCE) and the Battle of Bi (597 BCE). The *Gongyang* version of the Battle of Hong narrative, in contrast with its *Zuo* counterpart that derides Duke Xiang of Song for his devotion to an outmoded code of chivalry that costs him his life, commemorates this lord as a Worthy for his rectitude (*zheng* 正) in battle.⁶³ Rectitude in this context denotes willingness to adopt an uncompromising commitment to uphold the ritual protocols of battle; this is all the more praiseworthy in the eyes of the *Gongyang* commentators, because his unwavering commitment brought life-threatening disadvantages to Duke Xiang.⁶⁴ In the story of the Battle of Bi between Chu and Jin, King Zhuang of Chu, the lord of a state generally relegated to the category of "uncivilized," is praised for "acting out of a sense of ritual propriety" (*wei li* 為禮) during a military conflict.⁶⁵ The last story in this group is set amidst the famous Chu blockade of Song in 594 BCE. It celebrates the efforts of two officers whose respective commitments to humanitarian concerns inspire them to speak truthfully of their wartime conditions. This honest exchange of words between Hua Yuan of Song and Sima Zifan of Chu brings peace to Song and Chu. While the *Gongyangzhuan* criticizes them for overstepping the responsibilities of their official station, the narrative ultimately deems them praiseworthy for bringing peace to these war-torn states. Eschewing the strategy of wartime deception, two officers choose to speak honestly with one another because they recognize a mutual code of shared humanitarian values and seek to end the violence and bloodshed between the states of Song and Chu.⁶⁶

Conclusion: Anecdote as Historiographical Muse

What can we conclude from these examples that demonstrate how the *Gongyangzhuan* deployed anecdotes as a decided and indispensible exegetical tool? Clearly the assumption that the *Chunqiu* encompassed grand moral principles embodied in the many judgments left by Confucius required proof, not only at the level of terminology, but at the level of history. It was one thing to claim that Confucius praised a particular historical actor for his good intentions or actions, or condemned another for his evil desires or acts, but how was that to be demonstrated?

By telling the stories behind the judgments, the *Gongyangzhuan* clarified the circumstances under which men chose to make particular moral choices and what those conflicting moral choices were. In doing so, the stories imbued the judgments with persuasive power. The judgments delineated the abstract moral principles allegedly conceived by Confucius, but the stories demonstrated their efficacy in affecting social transformation. In other words, the historical narratives added flesh to the bones of Confucius's judgments, leaving no doubt of their didactic message. They provided the needed context to illustrate how different kinds of virtue could transform and ameliorate a situation and how its converse could fuel the flames of corruption and decline.

As we have seen, these narratives accomplish indispensable interpretive work for the *Gongyangzhuan* as a whole. They appear when the predominant praise and blame mode of explication tied exclusively to the wording of a given entry cannot fully disclose the ethical nuances of the judgment at hand. The narratives represent a distinctive mode of explication that addresses the most critical flashpoints, arenas of greatest significance, ambiguity, and contestation in the imagined community of King Wen's unitary rule (*da yitong* 大一統) that the *Gongyangzhuan* glorifies in its opening passage. Thus, the narratives are neither an afterthought, nor are they later interpolations that accidentally or haphazardly found their way into the *Gongyangzhuan*. Rather, they appear to be the consequence of deliberate choices on the part of the compiler to commemorate the most extreme exemplars of good and evil within this graded context of moral ambiguity and contestation.[67]

Against the terse and bleak catalogue of political crises and power abuses that constitutes the *Chunqiu*, the narratives express an ethos of restorative justice and state service. As we have seen, the path of return is not always straightforward; it is fraught with conflicting loyalties and competing norms that the narratives serve to arbitrate, as they relate the most egregious sources of intrastate chaos and interstate conflict involving crimes of regicide, fratricide, matricide, rebellion, and usurpation, as well as their proposed prescriptions: trustworthy, courageous, and upright ministers who would die to protect their lords from assassination and their states from annihilation.

The narratives do not, however, simply express nostalgia for a bygone era, where aristocratic notions of fealty and chivalry reigned supreme. They seek to repurpose these older values to the new realities that resulted from the breakdown of Zhou ritual order. Collectively they articulate a reformist agenda which sought to mediate the conflicting obligations between one's familial obligations as a son and a father and one's statist commitments as a minister and lord. They suggest strategies to subsume and subordinate family and clan loyalties to a public, institutionalized vision of monarchical rule. This would potentially liberate the ruling elite from familial loyalties and concerns to become true statesmen who are informed and inspired by a statist view of justice. Endeavoring to put the state before the family would prove to be an eternal and nettlesome challenge for centuries to come, as the disunity and strife of the Warring States Period gave way to the unified empire of the Qin and Han and the many imperial dynasties that followed.

Notes

1. I would like to thank Paul van Els for organizing one of the most productive and enjoyable workshops I have had the good fortune to attend. I would also like to thank Paul van Els, Joachim Gentz, Yuri Pines, and John Major for their thoughtful reading and constructive criticisms of earlier drafts of this essay. Thanks also to the anonymous reviewers for their feedback.

2. Ai 12.3.1.

3. For further discussions of the rhetorical uses of anecdotes see Sarah A. Queen, "The Creation and Domestication of the Techniques of Lao-Zhuang: Anecdotal Narrative and Philosophical Argumentation in *Huainanzi* 12, *Asia Major* 21, no. 1 (2008); "*Han Feizi* and the Old Master: A Comparative Analysis and Translation of *Han Feizi* chapter 20, 'Jie Lao,' and chapter 21, 'Yu Lao,' in *Dao Companion to the Philosophy of Han Feizi*," ed. Paul R. Goldin (Dordrecht: Springer, 2013); "Beyond Liu Xiang's Gaze: Debating Womanly Virtue in Ancient China," *Asia Major* Third Series, 20, no. 2 (2016): 7–46; and Paul van Els, "Tilting Vessels and Collapsing Walls—On the Rhetorical Function of Anecdotes in Early Chinese Texts," *Extreme-Orient, Extreme-Occident* 34 (2012): 141–66.

4. The origins and authors of the *Gongyangzhuan* are shrouded in mystery to this very day, though several masters are cited in its pages. By the Han Dynasty the authorship and transmission of the *Gongyangzhuan* had become associated with the Gongyang family, but this account is likely hagiographical. Despite the unknown

origins of the *Gongyangzhuan* and the manner in which it was transmitted in the pre-imperial period, the content and concerns of the *Gongyangzhuan* indicate that its authors were clearly working in a late Warring States context, not in the post-unification political context of the Han dynasty.

5. The thirty-odd narratives of the *Gongyangzhuan* are but one of several genres of literary composition that appear alongside of other forms of writing such as administrative rules, ritual norms, word glosses, and exegetical principles. Each accomplished different kinds of work for the *Gongyangzhuan*. For discussions of this topic see Joachim Gentz, "Long Live the King! The Ideology of Power Between Ritual and Morality in the *Gongyang Zhuan*," in *Ideology of Power and Power of Ideology in Early China*, eds. Yuri Pines, Paul R. Goldin, and Martin Kern (Leiden: Brill, 2014), 69–117.

6. Gentz, "Long Live the King," has come to similar conclusions working independently on other aspects of the *Gongyangzhuan*.

7. For three thoughtful discussions of the *Zuo* narratives, see Wai-yee Li, *The Readability of the Past in Early Chinese Historiography* (Cambridge, MA: Harvard University Press, 2008); Yuri Pines, *Foundations of Confucian Thought: Intellectual Life in the Chunqiu Period 722–453 B.C.E.* (Honolulu: University of Hawai'i Press, 2002); and David Schaberg, *A Patterned Past: Form and Thought in Early Chinese Historiography* (Cambridge, MA: Harvard University Press, 2002).

8. Four tales recount assassinations of regional lords or designated heirs and roundly condemns them as heinous crimes. See Yin 1.4.5 for Prince Hui's participation in the killing of Duke Yin of Lu; Zhuang 3.1.2 for Wen Jiang's involvement in the assassination of Duke Huan of Lu; Cheng 8.15.2 for Prince Sui's murder of the heir apparent Prince Zi Chi of Lu and his loyal tutor Earl Shuzhong Hui to install Prince Sui as Duke Xuan of Lu; and Xiang 9.7.9 for the Great Officer Zi Si's assassination of Duke Xi of Zheng on route to the interstate meeting in Wei. All references to the *Gongyangzhuan* are keyed to the ICS Ancient Chinese Text Concordance Series' *Gongyangzhuan zhuzi suoyin* 公羊傳逐字索引, ed. D. C. Lau (Hong Kong: Commercial Press, 1995). My translations of the *Gongyangzhuan* build on the fine work of Goran Malmqvist, "Studies on the *Gongyang* and *Guuliang* Commentaries I," *Bulletin of the Museum of Far Eastern Antiquities* 43 (1971): 67–222.

9. For these narrative accounts, see respectively Huan 2.2.1; Zhuang 3.12.3; Xi 5.10.4; Huan 2.11.4; Zhuang 3.24.6; and Cheng 8.2.4.

10. Huan 2.2.1.

11. Huan 2.2.1.

12. The *Gongyangzhuan* explains, "What was worthy about Kongfu? Of Kongfu it may be said that his righteousness manifest itself in his demeanor. Under what circumstances did his righteousness manifest itself in his demeanor?" 何賢乎孔父? 孔父可謂義形於色矣. 其義形於色奈何? (Huan 2.2.1).

13. Kongfu Jia is mentioned numerous times in the *Gongyangzhuan*, *Guliangzhuan*, and *Zuozhuan*. All treat him as a courageous man who died with valor though the *Zuo* discussion at Huan 2.2.19 differs considerably from the *Gongyang*

narrative, focusing on Hua Du's reprehensible nature rather than Kongfu Jia's exemplary character. It explains: "In the second year, in spring, Du attacked the Kong clan, murdered Kongfu and carried off his wife. Duke Shang was enraged [by these actions] and Du, in utter dread, subsequently murdered him. The Gentleman considered that Du was one who possessed a heart devoid of regard for his lord and so proceeded to commit this evil. Therefore he first recorded the assassination of the ruler [when it was second in point of fact]." 二年, 春, 宋督攻孔氏, 殺孔父而取其妻, 公怒, 督懼, 遂弒殤公, 君子以督為有無君之心, 而後動於惡, 故先書弒其君.

14. Huan 2.2.1.

15. Zhuang 3.12.3. Wan of Song is Nangong Changwan 南宮長萬.

16. Zhuang 3.12.3: "What does the term *ji* ("along with") denote? It denotes that [Qiu Mu] was involved [in the death of his lord]. Assassinations of lords were numerous, aside from this record [of Qiu Mu], were there no others who were involved [in the death of his lord]? Kongfu and Xunxi both were involved [in the deaths of their lord]. Aside from Kongfu and Xunxi, were there no others who were involved [in the deaths of their lord]? There were. If there were, then why in this case was [Qiu Mu] recorded? He was a Worthy." 及者何? 累也. 弒君多矣. 舍此無累者乎? 孔父, 荀息皆累也. 舍孔父, 荀息, 無累者乎? 曰: 有. 有則此何以書? 賢也.

17. Zhuang 3.12.3. For the expression *bu wei qiang yu* 不畏強禦 see *Shijing* "Zheng Min," Mao 260.

18. The *Zuozhuan* at Zhuang 3.12.3 explains this event rather differently: "Duke [Zhuang] availed himself of an [arrow called] "Gold Servant Lady" to shoot Nangong Changwan and his Spearman to the Right, Sun Sheng took him captive. The people of Song requested his release and he was subsequently let go. But Duke Zhuang ridiculed him saying, "Formerly I respected you but since you have become a captive of Lu, I respect you no longer." [Nangong Changwan] was annoyed by this."

19. Zhuang 3.12.3.

20. "Li Ke of Jin assassinated his lord Zhuozi and his great officer Xun Xi." 晉里克弒其君卓子及其大夫荀息 (Xi 5.10.4).

21. "What does the term *ji* ("along with") denote? It denotes that [Xun Xi] was involved [in the death of his lord]. Assassinations of lords were numerous. Aside from this record [of Xun Xi], were there no others who died for their lord? The answer is: there were. Kongfu and Qiu Mu both were involved in the death of their lords. Aside from Kongfu and Qiu Mu, were there no others who were involved in the deaths of their lord? There were. If there were, then why was a record made here? He was a Worthy." 及者何? 累也. 弒君多矣. 舍此無累者乎? 曰: 有. 孔父, 仇牧皆累也. 舍孔父, 仇牧無累者乎? 曰: 有. 有則此何以書? 賢也 (Xi 5.10.4).

22. Xi 5.10.4. The *Gongyang* version of the story begins: "Xi Qi and Zhuozi were Li Ji's sons. Xun Xi was their tutor. Li Ji was the most beautiful woman in the

state. Duke Xian loved her deeply and hoped to establish her sons on the throne, and so he killed the heir apparent, Shen Sheng. Li Ke had been Shen Sheng's tutor." 奚齊, 卓子者, 驪姬之子也, 荀息傅焉. 驪姬者, 國色也. 獻公愛之甚, 欲立其子, 於是殺世子申生. 申生者, 里克傅之. In contrast, the *Zuo* account makes much of Duke Xian's infatuation with Li Ji and describes in great detail how he falls victim to her plot to assassinate the rightful heir Shen Sheng and set her own sons up in his stead. The *Zuo* tale also differs in emphasizing Shen Sheng's filial piety. See Zhuang 28.1 to Xi 4.6. For a robust discussion of the *Zuo* account see Li, *Readability of the Past*, 166–68, 208, 212–13, and 249–54.

23. Interestingly the *Zuozhuan* at Xi 9.5.1 relates a similar deathbed conversation between Duke Xian and Xun Xi in which Duke Xian also seeks confirmation that this minister will install his designated heir after his death. Here, however, Duke Xian queries Xun Xi on the meaning of loyalty and faithfulness (*zhongzhen* 忠真) rather than the trustworthiness (*xin* 信) of the *Gongyang* discussion. For insightful discussions of the *Zuo* version of this story, see Pines, *Foundations*, 151; and Eric Henry, "'Junzi yue' versus 'Zhongni yue' in *Zuozhuan*," *Harvard Journal of Asiatic Studies* 59, no. 1 (1999): 146.

24. Xi 5.10.4.

25. Cheng 8.2.4. Significantly, the *Zuo* narrative of Feng Choufu ends quite differently. Feng pleads for his life and Xi Ke pardons him, stating: "It would be inauspicious for me to execute a man who does not find it hard to die for his lord's safety. I will pardon him to encourage those who serve their lords." Schaberg, *A Patterned Past*, 248.

26. See Huan 2.11.4.

27. The term *quan* is typically rendered "to weigh." Here it refers to weighing moral choices under pressing or unusual circumstances that demand an expedient assessment of the situation involving a choice between following ritual protocol or violating it to achieve a greater or more lasting good. This use of *quan* conforms to what Griet Vankeerberghen calls "achieving balance." See her most thoughtful essay entitled "Choosing Balance: Weighing (權) as a Metaphor for Action in Early Chinese Texts," *Early China* 30 (2005–2006), 47–89.

28. The *Zuozhuan* at this same entry explains: "An officer Yong of Song had married his daughter to Duke Zhuang of Zheng and she was called Yong Ji. She gave birth to Duke Li [a.k.a. Tu]. The Yong clan was favored by Duke Zhuang of Song. Thus they beguiled Zhaizhong, seized him, and said, 'If you do not install Tu, you will die.' They also seized Duke Li [Tu] and sought bribes from him. Zhaizhong made a covenant with men from Song and so returned home with Duke Li and installed him as ruler." 宋雍氏女於鄭莊公, 曰雍姞, 生厲公, 雍氏宗有寵於宋莊公, 故誘祭仲而執之, 曰:「不立突, 將死.」亦執厲公而求賂焉. 祭仲與宋人盟, 以厲公歸而立之.

29. "Why is the burial not recorded? In order to commiserate? What was there to commiserate? He was assassinated" 何以不書葬? 隱之也. 何隱爾? 弒也 (Yin 1.11.4).

30. Yin 1.11.4.
31. Zhuang 3.4.4. For a detailed discussion of this story see Sarah A. Queen, "The Gentleman's Views on Warfare According to the *Gongyang Commentary*," in *A Concise Companion to Confucius*, ed. Paul R. Goldin (Malden, MA: Wiley, forthcoming).
32. Queen, "The Gentleman's Views on Warfare."
33. Zhuang 3.32.3.
34. Xi 5.1.9.
35. Xuan 7.6.1.
36. Zhuang 3.32.3.
37. See Zhuang 3.32.3.
38. Zhuang 3.32.3.
39. Xi 5.1.9.
40. Xi 5.1.9.
41. Xuan 7.2.4 states "Autumn, the ninth month, *yi chou*, Zhao Dun of Jin assassinated his lord Yigao" 秋, 九月乙丑, 晉趙盾弒其君夷皋.
42. For the story of Zhao Dun see Xuan 7.6.1.
43. This is an interesting case. Xuan 7.2.4 states that Zhao Dun assassinated his ruler Yi Gao. But his reappearance at Xuan 7.2.6 must be explained since the *Gongyangzhuan* claims elsewhere that assassins do not reappear in later entries after they have committed the crime of regicide. The *Gongyangzhuan* at Xuan 7.6.1 discuses the contradiction as follows: "Zhao Dun assassinated his lord. Why does he reappear here? The one who personally assassinated the lord was Zhao Chuan. If the one who personally assassinated the lord was Zhao Chuan, why then does the *Chunqiu* implicate Zhao Dun? [Zhao Dun] did not punish the assassin." 趙盾弒君, 此其復見何? 親弒君者趙穿也. 親弒君者趙穿, 則曷為加之趙盾? 不討賊也. The narrative supports the assertion that Zhao Chuan was guilty of assassinating Lord Ling but Zhao Dun failed to punish his assassin by (1) depicting Zhao Dun as proclaiming his innocence to Heaven; (2) claiming that Zhao Chuan took advantage of the people's discontent to rise up and assassinate Lord Ling; and (3) demonstrating that Zhao Dun did not punish Zhao Chuan when he reentered the capital after the assassination. The *Chunqiu fanlu* develops a different and more complicated reading of Zhao Dun. It argues that precisely because he was a worthy who failed to adhere to the principle of punishing the lord's assassin, the *Chunqiu* "expressly associates him with this great evil and implicates him with strong criticism to cause people to think deeply and look into themselves, reflecting on the Way, so that they say, "Oh! The great duty of the ruler and minister, and the Way of father and son indeed extend this far!" This is why the lesser wrong is criticized more heavily." See *Chunqiu fanlu zhuzi suoyin* 春秋繁露逐子索引, ICS Ancient Chinese Text Concordance Series (Hong Kong: Commercial Press, 1992), 2/5/1–31.
44. Xi 5.21.6
45. Yin 1.1.1.

46. For a similar reading of this topic see Michael Nylan, *The Five "Confucian" Classics* (New Haven, CT: Yale University Press, 2001), 259–61.

47. One such story denigrates Duke Xuan of Song for disregarding the legitimate heir apparent to designate his favored brother Yuyi as his successor. After becoming enthroned, Duke Miu [also known as Mu] reinstalls Yuyi as rightful heir but this is not sufficient to stave off generations of discord in Song. Thus the narrative concludes: "the Gentleman glorified those who conformed to correct norms, for the [succession] disasters in Song were Duke Xuan's creation." See Yin 1.3.7. Another story about Duke Jing of Qi relates how he passed over his rightful heir, Yang Sheng, to install She and how his officer Chen Qi murders She and reinstates Yang Sheng as lord. See Ai 12.6.8. A third anecdote describes how Prince Sui assassinates the heir apparent Prince Zi Chi of Lu and his loyal tutor Earl Shuzhong Hui to install the future Duke Xuan of Lu. See Cheng 8.15.2.

48. Xi 5. 28.18.
49. Xiang 9.29.8.
50. Zhao 10.20.2.
51. Zhao 10.31.6.
52. Xiang 9.29.8.
53. Ibid.
54. Ibid.
55. Ibid.

56. One narrative traces the origins of the Battle of An to the lack of ritual decorum on the part of Duke Qing of Qi's mother, Xiao Tong Zhizi, toward the Jin envoys, Xi Ke and Zangsun Xu. (Cheng 8.2.4.). Another anecdote holds Lord Ling of Jin responsible for the death of his minister Yang Chufu when he betrays Yang's confidence, by sharing his negative assessment of He Shegu with this candidate for promotion to Commander of the Army. Infuriated by Yang's attempt to dissuade the lord from promoting him, He Shegu murders Yang Chufu (Wen 6.6.8.). See also the story in which the Lord of Yu accepts bribes, bringing on the annihilation of Guo and his own state of Yu (Xi 5.2.1) and the parable in which the Lord of Qin is judged uncivilized for launching a surprise attack on Jin (Xi 5.33.3).

57. Xiang 9.30.6. Once again, in contrast to the positive assessment of the *Gongyang*, the *Zuo* judges Boji's conduct negatively. For a comparative analysis of the Song Boji narratives in the *Gongyang, Zuo,* and *Guliang* commentaries, see Queen, "Beyond Liu Xiang's Gaze."

58. Zhuang 3.13.4.
59. *Chunqiu fanlu zhuzi suoyin* 1/1/15–22.
60. Zhao 10.25.6.
61. Ibid.
62. Ibid.

63. For a compelling analysis of the *Zuo* version of this story see Schaberg, *Patterned Past*, 1–4.

64. Queen, "The Gentleman's Views on Warfare."
65. Xuan 7.12.3.
66. Queen, "The Gentleman's Views on Warfare."
67. Given that some of these choices, as we have seen, appear rather unorthodox, particularly vis-à-vis other commentators in the *Chunqiu*, the identity of the compiler and the world he lived in, remains an important but unanswered question beyond the scope of this essay.

Part III

Anecdotes and History

8

History without Anecdotes
Between the *Zuozhuan* and the *Xinian* Manuscript

Yuri Pines[1]

The importance of anecdotes in pre-imperial and early imperial historiography is self-evident. They permeate most of the texts later classified as histories (*shi* 史), such as *Guoyu* 國語 (Discourses of the States) and *Zhanguoce* 戰國策 (Stratagems of the Warring States), as well as many of the masters (*zi* 子) texts, such as *Yanzi chunqiu* 晏子春秋 (Spring and Autumn Annals of Master Yan), *Lüshi chunqiu* 呂氏春秋 (Spring and Autumn Annals of Mr. Lü), or significant portions of *Han Feizi* 韓非子 (Master Han Fei); and they dominate even some of the canons (*jing* 經), e.g., the *Zuozhuan* 左傳 (Zuo Commentary). In addition, anecdotes frequently surface in collections of unearthed manuscripts, most notably that of the Shanghai Museum.[2] Indeed, David Schaberg may be close to the point in his assertion that the anecdotes formed "the basic form of historical narrative—and therefore the basic stuff of historical knowledge itself."[3] The recent spur in the interest in anecdotes, demonstrated by the present volume, comes then as no surprise.

That said, a word of caution is needed. Our understanding of early Chinese historiography may be significantly skewed due to the low rate of survival of pre-imperial historical texts. Sima Qian司馬遷 (ca. 145–90 BCE) famously lamented the destruction of scribal records (*shiji* 史記) of the Warring States Period 戰國 (453–221 BCE) by the Qin Dynasty 秦 (221–206 BCE).[4] Yet Qin biblioclasm aside, more texts might have been lost due to the lackluster interest in their content by members of educated elite. It may be plausibly assumed that as for those historical texts that were purely informative, and lacked either entertaining or didactic qualities, or, alternatively, canonical status (as did the *Chunqiu* 春秋 [Spring and Autumn Annals] of the state of Lu 魯 and its commentaries), the possibility that they would be cherished enough to be transmitted for generations was minuscule indeed.⁵

In this chapter I want to explore the somewhat neglected non-anecdotal strand of early Chinese historiography. I believe that only through proper understanding of this strand will we be able to contextualize the anecdotes within the corpus of pre-imperial and early imperial historical and quasi-historical writings. By speaking of non-anecdotal historiography, I plan to focus not on the laconic annalistic tradition represented by the Lu *Chunqiu* (and, possibly, a few related texts, such as the *Zhushu jinian* 竹書紀年 [*Bamboo Annals*]),⁶ but rather on longer narratives which lack the essential characteristics of the anecdotes, as depicted by Schaberg in his seminal paper. I shall start my discussion with the *Zuozhuan*, which may be considered a fountainhead of many of the historical anecdotes scattered in the texts from the Warring States and well into the Western Han Dynasty 西漢 (202 BCE–9 CE). I want to demonstrate that aside from individual anecdotes or "chains of anecdotes," insightfully analyzed by Schaberg,⁷ the *Zuozhuan* contains lengthy narratives that are more informative and much less entertaining or moralistic than the anecdotes, and that these narratives and the anecdotes may have targeted different audiences. Then, I shall shift to the newly published historical text from the Qinghua (Tsinghua) University 清華大學 collection, named *Xinian* 繫年 (Sequence of Years) by its present-day editors. I shall show that, like significant segments of the *Zuozhuan*, the *Xinian* does not target the educated elite as a whole but provides working historical knowledge for policymakers, and that it may be representative of an important yet neglected genre of informative and non-didactic history. By analyzing the *Xinian*, its possible audience, and the reasons for its disappearance, I hope to highlight the diversity of early Chinese historiographic traditions, and to fine-tune our understanding of the anecdotes and their role in pre-imperial historical lore.

The Riddle of Boredom: Non-anecdotal Narratives in the *Zuozhuan*

The *Zuozhuan* is the single largest pre-imperial historical text, and it can be rightly considered the fountainhead of traditional Chinese historiography. The text purportedly comments on the canonical *Chunqiu* annals, but instead of focusing on discerning the "subtle message" of the *Chunqiu*, it aims to provide a broader historical context for the laconic entries of the latter. There is no doubt that the *Zuozhuan* incorporated abundant materials from earlier historical texts prepared in the major polities of the Spring and Autumn Period 春秋 (770–453 BCE); but the precise nature of these early texts and the degree of the editorial intervention by the *Zuozhuan* author(s) are still very much debated.[8] My goal here is to not to address these debates (in which I have taken part in the past), but to focus on some of the less frequently discussed segments of the *Zuozhuan*.

As is well known, the *Zuozhuan* comprises many hundreds of narrative segments: some are very brief (just a few dozen graphs), while others are quite complex and span many years of the narrative.[9] These building blocks of the *Zuozhuan* had a highly different afterlife. Some were incorporated into later collections of anecdotes and retold many times; others were all but forgotten. One of the possible reasons for the marked differences in their circulation, is the literary qualities of these narratives. Some are highly engaging and easily catch the eye of either the traditional or modern reader;[10] others are quite boring and, except for a few experts and professional exegetes, are rarely noticed at all. Yet it is to these boring stories I want to turn now, as I believe that they can provide more clues about early Chinese historiography.

Let us take, for instance, the story of the rebellion of Hua 華 and Xiang 向, two major ministerial lineages from the state of Song 宋. Both were branch lines of the Song ruling lineage; yet as it often happened in the Spring and Autumn Period, the increasing tension between them and Duke Yuan of Song 宋元公 (r. 531–517 BCE) pushed them to a violent insurrection. The rebellion spanned three years (522–520 BCE), and became one of the most spectacular events in the history of the late Spring and Autumn Period. First, it profoundly shattered the state of Song, starting with the massacre of many of its princes, and ending with the partial extermination and partial expulsion of both rebellious lineages, the members of which for generations constituted the crème de la crème of the Song elite. Second, this rebellion had strong ramifications across the borders of Song, causing military or diplomatic intervention from most of the powerful states of that age, including Jin 晉, Chu 楚, Qi 齊, and Wu 吳, in addition to Song's tiny neighbors, Cao 曹 and Wei 衛. Third, the rebellion had a fascinating plot, with intermittent successes of each of the fighting parties and spectacular displays of largesse and treachery, cowardice and courage. Fourth, it generated immense personal dramas, including most notably that of Hua Feisui 華費遂, the Grand Marshal of Song who first assisted Duke Yuan in quelling the rebellion, driving one of his own sons into exile, but then was forced to join the rebels almost against his will, because of a fratricidal struggle between two of his remaining sons. In short, the story of the Hua and Xiang rebellion could easily become a literary masterpiece of—let me exaggerate a little—quasi-Shakespearean proportions.

In light of all this, it is perplexing to discover how indifferent the authors of later texts appear to the turmoil in Song. I have not discovered a single reference to the Hua and Xiang revolt in any of the collections of anecdotes from the Warring States and Han periods. The drama seems to have been lost almost completely, never evoking much interest. Why? Was it because of Song's relative marginality in the late Spring and Autumn Period and thereafter? I doubt this: after all, numerous anecdotes from the lives of comparable polities, such as Zheng 鄭 and Wei 衛, permeate contemporaneous texts. Was it perhaps because the Song events lacked a clear didactic value? I doubt this too. The *Zuozhuan* carefully conveys its negative judgment of both parties: the future head of Hua rebels is derided, eight years before the rebellion, for his lack of decorum, whereas the lord of Song is criticized as "lacking trustworthiness and abundantly relying on his private [henchmen]."[11] While the narrative is too complex to be reduced to the simplistic "good guys vs. bad guys" dichotomy, this is a feature of many other stories in the *Zuozhuan*, as Wai-yee Li has shown.[12] Then why was the story of the Song rebellion all but forgotten?

I think the answer should be sought in certain features of the *Zuozhuan* narrative. Despite my praise of the story's plot, one cannot but feel that in purely literary terms it is not sufficiently engaging. The reason is not just its dispersal among other contemporaneous dramas, which are thickly covered in the Duke Zhao of Lu 魯昭公 (r. 541–510 BCE) section of the *Zuozhuan*, but primarily the abundance of minor details that do not help the reader to focus on the narrative and come at the expense of other, more engaging stories. Much of the narrative is dedicated to information that, for a later reader, might have been all but irrelevant: the date of every major encounter between the rebels and the loyalists is recorded, and so are the names of the otherwise unknown persons who participated in related intrigues and battles; we are also told of every minor location in or near the Song capital which was attacked, besieged, or conquered by one side or the other. What we miss are thicker depictions of the drama. The mass murder of the lord's closest kin at the start of the rebellion and the subsequent murder of the

Hua and Xiang hostages by the treacherous Duke Yuan are reported, but there are no traces of intense feelings that these actions could have enticed; Hua Feisui's willingness to sacrifice his kin out of political loyalty is narrated, but the reasons for his ultimate siding with his fratricidal son against the lord a year later are not given; we are duly informed of the names of military leaders of different polities who intervened on Song's behalf, but so little additional information is given that we cannot really estimate how important this intervention was from the point of view of contemporaneous interstate order. The lack of any summary—by a participant, a wise observer, or the *Zuozhuan* narrator (the gentleman [*junzi* 君子])—makes us feel that the story is "incomplete," that it was not sufficiently polished when incorporated into the *Zuozhuan*. Perhaps for this reason it was abandoned by later anecdote-seekers for the sake of other, less dramatic but better narrated events.

A very similar feeling of a "missed drama" is generated by the *Zuozhuan* account of another major turmoil, the rebellion of Prince Zhao 王子朝 in the Zhou 周 royal domain from 521 to 516 BCE (incidentally, the narration of this rebellion starts immediately after the last entry related to the Song revolt). Once again we find all the components of a good drama: a major turmoil which devastated the already crippled royal domain and was quelled only thanks to the intervention by the principal power of that age (Jin); bloody rivalry among royal scions; coalitions of nobles who supported each of the candidates; the murder of an incumbent king; multiple intrigues, treachery, and assassinations; and many others. Prince Zhao's rebellion is duly preceded by several predictions and omens; speeches by participants and foreign observers allow us to assess the reasons for Zhao's failure, and the story ends with a lengthy and eloquently written letter from Prince Zhao, in which he complains bitterly against Jin's decision to support his rivals, and which, in turn, is dismissed by a wise observer from Lu.[13] Yet once again, the story remains largely unnoticed in later texts, and, most oddly, even the Zhou sections of the *Guoyu*, which narrate events from the life of the royal domain in great detail, omit it entirely.[14] And, again, the reason may be the very non-engaging form of much of the *Zuozhuan* narration. To illustrate my point, below is a section from the narrative of the rebellion from its last year, 516:

> Fourth month. The Duke of Shan arrived at Jin to report urgency. The fifth month, on *wuwu* [day 5 of the *ganzhi* cycle],[15] forces of the Liu [lineage] defeated the army of Wangcheng [of Prince

Zhao] at the [settlement of the] Shi lineage. On *wuchen* [day 15], the forces of Wangcheng encountered the forces of Liu at Shigu, the forces of Liu were utterly defeated. [. . .] Seventh month, on *jisi* [day 17], the Duke of Liu fled together with the [incumbent] king. On *gengwu* [day 18], [they] camped at Qu. Forces of Wangcheng burned down [the settlement of] Liu. On *bingzi* [day 24], the king stayed at the [settlement of the] Chu lineage. On *dingchou* [day 25], the king camped at Wangu. On *gengchen* [day 28], the king entered [his territory] from Xuma. On *xinsi* [day 29], the king camped at Hua. Zhi Li and Zhao Yang of Jin led the army to reinstate the king. They ordered Nü Kuan to guard the Que Pass.

四月, 單子如晉告急. 五月戊午, 劉人敗王城之師于尸氏. 戊辰, 王城人, 劉人戰于施穀, 劉師敗績. [. . .] 七月己巳, 劉子以王出. 庚午, 次于渠. 王城人焚劉. 丙子, 王宿于褚氏. 丁丑, 王次于萑穀. 庚辰, 王入于胥靡. 辛巳, 王次于滑. 晉知躒, 趙鞅帥師納王, 使汝寬守闕塞.¹⁶

This narrative has no identifiable didactic or literary value; actually, it is extremely boring and reading it is no more intellectually or esthetically engaging than reading a telephone book. Like the latter, the *Zuozhuan* narrative is highly informative, and may benefit a reader with a good working knowledge of the geography of the Luoyang region and of multiple lineages in the Zhou royal domain. Yet for anybody else—and I assume that this includes the overwhelming majority of thinkers and statesmen from the Warring States period on—this sort of narration can serve at best as a remedy for insomnia. Those used to look at the past as a mirror for the present may well bemoan the abundance of minor details that obscure rather than highlight the potential didactic message of the narrative. Taken from this perspective, and given the absence of alternative, more literarily appealing versions of Prince Zhao's rebellion, we find the subsequent neglect of this event not very surprising indeed.

The question to be asked now is: Who were the addressees of the many lengthy, extraordinarily detailed, and, let us say frankly, quite boring stories from the *Zuozhuan*? Were they the "rulers, thinkers, and their students" identified by Schaberg (entirely correctly in my view) as the main audience of the anecdotes?¹⁷ I doubt it. The very fact that the *Zuozhuan* way of presentation remains exceptional in the entire lore of pre-imperial historical or quasi-historical texts, is not trivial. It indicates a different kind of audience from that of the rest of the anecdotes.

In my eyes, the identity of this audience is not difficult to guess. Only one group would be really interested in these intense details: statesmen from the polity whose history is narrated. For Song aristocrats, any information about the downfall of the Hua and Xiang lineages and their replacement by the members of the Yue 樂 lineage and by others of Duke Yuan's relatives would have been highly meaningful; ditto for the successors of the Liu 劉, Shan 單, and other noble lineages of the Zhou royal domain, who participated in quelling Prince Zhao's revolt. For outsiders in need of a short résumé of the drama, these details are meaningless, but for insiders they are highly valuable. For the sake of comparison we may look at domestic and foreign accounts of parliamentary elections in country X. For a foreign audience, the main issue would be that party A defeated party B, because B was corrupt, detached from the masses, and full of mediocrities, while A was young, determined to improve the people's standard of living, and so on. For insiders, it may be much more important that A received more votes in district Y because of local grievances against the B party representative, while in district Z the B party lost just because of the switch of a local power-holder from one party to another. These details, which would bore the average newspaper reader, are of vital importance to local political analysts who want to gain an in-depth understanding of the political processes in the immediate past of their country.

If my guess is correct, that many of the *Zuozhuan* narratives were initially prepared for local consumption (i.e., for a small group of hereditary political practitioners) and only later incorporated into the *Zuozhuan* and immortalized there, this would also explain the ambiguity of the moral message of many of these stories. For an outsider, what is needed from an anecdote is some didactic content: in Schaberg's definition, "substantiating arguments about the workings of the world, particularly the political world." For an insider, the accumulation of details may make a simplistic "good-bad" dichotomy less feasible. For an outsider, historical details matter only "as a complement to rhetorical aims."[18] For an insider they are much more important because they provide crucial clues as to what (supposedly) really happened. Yet an abundance of details dilutes the moral message of an anecdote, just as detailed knowledge of political events in the contemporary world may undermine some of the political clichés promulgated in the mass media. I think this is the major reason why the *Zuozhuan* anecdotes are amenable to multiple interpretations, as noticed by Li Wai-yee.

It should be clarified here that an "informative history" as represented in the above narratives was not necessarily devoid of didactic goals. Its authors could manipulate their information through omissions or embellishments, through tendentious arrangement of the sequence of events or through highlighting certain personages at the expense of others. Moreover, as readers of the dullest annalistic history—the *Chunqiu*—know, even a smallest substitution of a word may well be indicative of hidden "praise or blame." Yet these subtle means of delivering one's message differ fundamentally from those used in the historical anecdotes. The message of the latter is explicit and it can be grasped by an educated person even centuries after the historical context of an anecdote lost its importance. Messages hidden in informative non-anecdotal histories, in distinction, can be fully appreciated only by an insider: a person with intimate knowledge of narrated events. As such an "informative history" has much shorter life span than an anecdotal one, as I shall clarify below.

Going back to the *Zuozhuan*, the above examples suffice to show how some of the *Zuozhuan* narratives differ from the moralizing histories of the Warring States and later periods. Being detailed to the point of boredom on the one hand, and lacking a clear-cut moral message on the other, these narratives make sense only insofar as they were written for the immediate use of local statesmen, and that their incidental incorporation into the *Zuozhuan* dislocated them from their normal surroundings, affording the reader a glimpse of the long-gone genre of early historical works, works of the age when the confluence of history and philosophy was much less evident than in the Warring States period.

Until recently, my argument about the need to look beyond the pure didacticism of the Warring States period anecdotes and to analyze early sources of the *Zuozhuan* as reflecting an "informative" and not just a "moralizing" trend in early Chinese historiography faced the impediment of having to demonstrate examples of such an informative history outside the *Zuozhuan* narrative. Now, although I still lack direct evidence for the primary sources of the *Zuozhuan*, fortunately there exists an example of another piece of non-moralizing history that possibly dates from a time not far removed from that of the *Zuozhuan*'s compilation (ca. fifth c. BCE?).[19] In what follows, by analyzing the *Xinian* narrative, I hope to demonstrate the significance of non-moralizing historiography in early China.

The *Xinian*: Introduction[20]

The *Xinian* is one of the dozens of allegedly Warring States Period manuscripts, which were purchased by Qinghua University at the Hong Kong antiquity market. In its published form the *Xinian* occupies the entire second volume of the Qinghua bamboo manuscript collection.[21] With just over 5,000 graphs, the *Xinian* is a relatively short text. It is divided into twenty-three sections (*zhang* 章) and written on 138 bamboo slips of 44.6 cm to 45 cm in length. Each slip is numbered on its verso, and every section starts on a new slip (that is to say: if a section ends before the end of a bamboo slip, the remainder of that slip is left empty). The slips are generally well-preserved; only in section thirteen parts of slips 63 through 65 are missing. Unfortunately, we have no idea of the text's original mortuary setting: like all Qinghua manuscripts that had supposedly been looted from the mainland, it lacks clear provenance. Conventional wisdom assumes that since all Qinghua texts are written in what is usually called a "Chu script," they might have been looted from a Chu tomb; both the orthography and the radiocarbon analysis of one of the Qinghua slips suggest a date of around 300 BCE, which would make it roughly contemporaneous with the hoard of manuscripts discovered in 1993 at Tomb 1, Guodian 郭店 (Hubei) and the manuscripts in the possession of Shanghai Museum.[22]

The twenty-three sections of the *Xinian* can be divided into three groups according to the different chronologies employed. The first four sections (most of which deal with the Western Zhou 西周 [ca. 1045–771 BCE] period) employ the chronology of the Zhou kings. Of the later nineteen sections, which cover the events from the seventh to the early fourth century BCE, eight date events according to the reigning years of the lords of Jin, ten use the chronology based on the reigning years of the kings of Chu, and one uses both Jin and Chu chronology.[23] Conceivably, these sections came from, respectively, Zhou, Jin, and Chu local histories. That is, like *Zuozhuan* and *Guoyu*, the *Xinian* is based on incorporation of earlier materials; it was not written from scratch.

Scrutiny of the *Xinian*'s language strengthens the above observation. While the editors probably unified the language of their sources, they may have left it unchanged whenever two or more usages were acceptable. For instance, the preposition "with" or "and" can be transcribed as either *ji* 及 or *yu* 與. The former appears ten times in the Zhou and Jin sections, and only once in a Chu section. The latter appears eleven times in Chu sections and only four in those of Zhou and Jin. This geographic difference corresponds to the preponderance of *yu* in Chu manuscripts, which almost never employ *ji*;²⁴ clearly it reflects the original linguistic differences in the source materials. Elsewhere, the differences are not geographic but temporal. Thus, the *Xinian* transcribes the locative *yu* ("at") particle both with the "solemn" graph 于 (which is more common in early Zhou texts) and with the more "colloquial" graph 於 (which predominates the texts of the Warring States period). In the *Xinian* temporal distribution of both particles is highly visible: the "older" *yu* 于 predominates in earlier sections (28 *yu* 于 versus 1 *yu* 於 in the first four sections, that deal with the Western Zhou, 22 slips), while the "newer" *yu* 於 is much more frequently used in the later part of the text (19 *yu* 於 versus 5 *yu* 于 in the last three sections, 25 slips). This latter pattern strongly resembles the *Zuozhuan*, which also evidently incorporated different *yu* particles from its original sources without unifying their transcription.²⁵

These linguistic differences between different sections of the *Xinian*²⁶ allow two major conclusions. First, they corroborate our earlier suggestion that the *Xinian* is based on incorporation of earlier sources, and these were clearly written sources (otherwise such differences as in transcription of *yu* 于/於 particles would be difficult to explain). Second, it seems highly likely that the *Xinian* is not a forgery but an authentic text. It is inconceivable that forgers—sophisticated as they may be—would be able to reconstruct linguistic changes or barely noticeable geographic differences in the Zhou language. This, in addition to the abundance of new historical information, which is also unlikely to come from a forger's hands, convinces me of the authenticity of the *Xinian*.²⁷

Differences in its source materials aside, it is clear that the *Xinian* was composed (and not just transcribed) in the state of Chu. Several features of the text demonstrate its Chu origins with certainty. First, each section of the text (except for the first section, which narrates exclusively Western Zhou affairs) deals with the state of Chu either directly or indirectly, through discussing its primary rivals or allies. Most notable is the state of Jin, whose struggle with Chu occupies the core of the *Xinian*. Second, the geographical perspective of the *Xinian* is obviously biased toward the western part of the Zhou world. For instance, the state of Qin 秦 (an important ally of Chu during much of the period under discussion) is covered much more "thickly" than in other contemporaneous texts,²⁸ while eastern states, such as Qi and Lu (which played a lesser role in Chu history) are less prominent. The exploits of Duke Huan of Qi 齊桓公 (r. 685–643 BCE) in particular, which occupy pride of place in the *Zuozhuan*, are all but ignored. Third, the Chu affiliation becomes more pronounced in the last sections of the text. For instance, while in earlier sections years are counted intermittently by the reign years of the rulers of Zhou, Chu, or Jin, in the last three sections only Chu dating is employed, even when the narrative deals with Jin. Fourth, while the text readily acknowledges Chu military defeats (see below), it avoids any direct reference to domestic turmoil in the state of Chu, such as the coups that first catapulted King Ling 楚靈王 (r. 540–529 BCE) to the throne and then accompanied his downfall.[29] Fifth, there are ritual indications of the text's respect toward the Chu kings: their deaths are invariably recorded as "passing away" (*jishi* 即世), while this courtesy is not observed with regard to other regional lords.[30] All this suggests that the text was produced in Chu, although it clearly incorporates non-Chu materials.

As for the dating of the text, here the majority view is that it was produced slightly after the reign of King Dao of Chu 楚悼王 (r. 401–381 BCE), whose posthumous name is recorded in section 23, and whose early years on the throne are the last to be narrated.[31] There are further indications of an early fourth century BCE date: e.g., employment of the personal name (*ming* 名) rather than the posthumous name (*shi* 諡) for several rulers mentioned in the last two sections, which suggests that these sections were composed either during those rulers' lifetime or shortly after they passed away, when their private name had not yet been obliterated by the posthumous one (see further below). As a working hypothesis, I shall treat the text, then, as a Chu product of circa 370 BCE.[32]

The publication of the *Xinian* excited scholars and led to an explosion of studies of the text in China and to a lesser extent in Japan.[33] Many focused on the information that the *Xinian* provides regarding different lacunae in the Zhou history; others explored the text's genre affiliation. With regard to the latter, Li Xueqin's 李學勤 initial assessment that the *Xinian* is "very close to the *Zhushu jinian*"[34] has been rejected by scholars who have pointed out the *Xinian*'s non-chronological structure, which clearly distinguishes it from the annalistic tradition. The twenty-three sections of the *Xinian* are arranged in a roughly chronological order, yet since the narrative in some of them spans a few generations and even a few centuries, the narration in the text runs back and forth in time, which would not be the case in an annalist text. Actually, the genre of the *Xinian* has no ready parallels among the pre-imperial historical texts. Curiously, it most closely resembles the "topical arrangement" style (*jishi benmo* 紀事本末) texts from the late imperial era. Each of the *Xinian*'s twenty-three sections deals with a sequence of events that shaped the "geopolitical" situation in the Zhou world, and each is a narrative unit in its own right.³⁵ As I shall try to demonstrate, this topical arrangement of the *Xinian* not only distinguishes it from other pre-imperial historical texts but is also directly related to its non-anecdotal nature.

Non-moralizing History: The *Xinian* vs. *Zuozhuan* Narratives

Of the twenty-three sections of the *Xinian*, the narrative in seventeen sections (from the second part of section 4 to the first part of section 20) overlaps partly or fully with that in the *Zuozhuan*. What is the precise relation between the two texts? One scenario that can be easily ruled out is that *Zuozhuan* is secondary to the *Xinian*. It would be highly implausible that its authors relied on the *Xinian*'s brief accounts so as to create a detailed narrative with hundreds of dates, personal names, place names, official titles, and so on, none of which exist in the *Xinian*. An alternative scenario—that the *Xinian*, conversely, abridges the *Zuozhuan* narrative—is what the first impression suggests; but I think this is wrong too. Despite considerable overlap between the two texts, the *Xinian*—as I shall demonstrate below—contains enough independent information to rule out its being merely a *Zuozhuan* abridgement. Moreover, the fact that the *Xinian* never employs the chronology of the state of Lu, which dominates the *Zuozhuan*, is further suggestive of its independent origin. In what follows my working hypothesis is that the both texts shared common primary sources, which I tentatively identify as "scribal records" prepared by Jin and Chu scribes.³⁶ By comparing the utilization of these sources in both texts, I hope to show that the *Xinian* deliberately omitted moralizing and entertaining aspects of the narratives, while preserving the essence of historical information. This selection distinguishes it not only from the *Zuozhuan*, but, more essentially, from later historical anecdotes. For the sake of comparison, I have selected one short section of the *Xinian*, section 5 which deals with events of 684–680 BCE, and a lengthy section 15, the narrative of which spans the entire sixth century BCE.

Section 5

Marquis Ai of Cai took a wife from Chen; the Marquis of Xi also took a wife from Chen, who was Xi Gui. When Xi Gui was en route back to Xi, she passed through Cai. Marquis Ai of Cai ordered her to be stopped, saying, "Since she is from the same family [as my wife], she must enter [the city]." Xi Gui then entered into Cai, and Marquis Ai of Cai "wived" her.[37] The Marquis of Xi considered [Marquis Ai] incompliant;[38] then he sent a messenger to King Wen of Chu, saying, "My lord should come and attack us; we shall seek help from Cai, and you can thereupon defeat them." King Wen raised an army and attacked Xi, and Marquis Ai of Cai led his army to save Xi. King Wen defeated him at Shen, and captured Marquis Ai of Cai, returning with him.

King Wen was a guest at Xi, and the Marquis of Cai accompanied him. The Marquis of Xi was serving ale to King Wen. The Marquis of Cai knew that he had been lured by the Marquis of Xi; hence he told King Wen, "The wife of the Marquis of Xi is extraordinarily beautiful; my lord must command to see her." King Wen ordered to see her. The Marquis of Xi refused, but the King insistently ordered to see her. Having seen her, he went back [to Chu]. The next year, he raised an army and invaded Xi. He overpowered it, killed the Marquis of Xi, and took Xi Gui with him to return. She [eventually] gave birth to Du'ao and [the future] King Cheng.

Thanks to this, King Wen opened lands northward beyond Fangcheng, expanded to the Ru River, trained his armies near Chen and thereupon acquired Dun so as to frighten the Marquis of Chen.

蔡哀侯取妻於陳，息侯亦取妻於陳，是息媯．息媯將歸于息，過蔡，蔡哀侯命止之，【23】曰：「以同姓之故，必入．」息媯乃入于蔡，蔡哀侯妻之．息侯弗順，乃使人于楚文王【24】曰：「君來伐我，我將求救於蔡，君焉敗之．」文王起師伐息，息侯求救於蔡，蔡哀侯率師【25】以救息，文王敗之於莘，獲哀侯以歸．文王爲客於息，蔡侯與從，息侯以文【26】王飲酒，蔡侯知息侯之誘己也，亦告文王曰：「息侯之妻甚美，君必命見之．」文【27】王命見之，息侯辭，王固命見之．既見之，還．明歲，起師伐息，克之，殺息侯，取【28】息媯以歸，是生堵敖及成王．文王以北啓出方城，圾（立）肆（肆?）於汝，改(治?)旅於陳，焉【29】取頓以贛（恐?）陳侯．【30】[39]

The narrative of the *Xinian* is very close to that of the *Zuozhuan*, where it is divided into two separate anecdotes recorded under the years 684 and

680 BCE. The first of these appears as a comment on the entry in the *Chunqiu*, which records Chu's victory over Cai.⁴⁰ This anecdote is reproduced in the *Xinian* very closely, except for a clearer indication that the Duke of Cai "wived," i.e., committed adultery with his sister-in-law (in the *Zuozhuan* it is substituted with a euphemism that the Duke of Cai "did not treat her appropriately as a guest" [*fu bin* 弗賓]). The second anecdote in the *Zuozhuan* is related to another entry of the *Chunqiu*, according to which the Chu army entered the Cai capital in the seventh month of 680 BCE.⁴¹ This anecdote is relatively sophisticated. It starts with the story of the Duke of Cai instigating the Chu attack against Xi, enticing King Wen with the intention of obtaining Xi Gui. Then comes another mini-anecdote (later embellished and modified in the *Lienüzhuan* 列女傳 [Biographies of Exemplary Women]), about the tragic life of Xi Gui as a Chu captive: despite winning King Wen's favor, she refused to speak as a self-imposed punishment for serving two husbands. Then, the *Zuozhuan* explains that after King Wen heeded the suggestion of the Duke of Cai and invaded Xi, he followed with an attack on Cai itself. Finally, the concluding remark by the "gentleman" criticizes Duke Ai of Cai for his malevolent manipulations that brought disaster to his own state.

It is with regard to this second anecdote that the difference between the *Xinian* and the *Zuozhuan* becomes more pronounced. First, the sequence of events in the *Xinian* differs slightly: the elimination of Xi occurs one year after the first intervention of King Wen against Cai, which means that (adopting the *Chunqiu* chronology), Xi was eliminated in 683 BCE, three years before the Chu incursion into Cai in 680 BCE. This slight change—if not a mistake—may suggest that the *Xinian* author(s) were better informed about the annihilation of Xi than the *Zuozhuan* author(s). Alternatively, it is possible that the *Zuozhuan* transmitted the story of the elimination of Xi to the year 680 so as to strengthen the connection between it and the incursion into Cai on that year, making the two events closely related and thereby strengthening the didactic message, which criticized the lord of Cai's perfidy. These differences are of little importance, but there is a second and more substantial one. The *Xinian* authors eliminate all the moralizing aspects of the *Zuozhuan* story: Xi Gui's chastity, or the lack thereof, is of no interest to them; the machinations of the rulers of Xi and Cai do not merit praise or blame; the focus of the narration clearly lies elsewhere. This focus is fully revealed in the last phrase of the story (which does not exist in the *Zuozhuan* and evidently reflects a distinctive Chu perspective): the Cai-Xi intrigue served as a springboard for Chu's expansion beyond the

Fangcheng 方城 line into the Ru 汝 river valley.[42] It is this aspect—and only this aspect—that matters to the *Xinian* authors.

Section 5 may be illustrative of most of the entries in the *Xinian*. An event—or a chain of events, as shown below—is discussed primarily as background material to explain changes in Chu's geostrategic situation. The emphasis may shift from Chu's own actions to that of its rivals and allies (Qin, Jin, Qi, Wu 吳, and Yue 越), but the focus always remains on the changing balance of power. The authors appear to be indifferent with regard to other didactic messages that could be deduced from their narrative. The anecdotal nature of the narrative is not obscured entirely, but it becomes much less pronounced than in the *Zuozhuan*, not to say in later texts that reproduce the same anecdote, such as, in the case of section 5, the *Lüshi chunqiu* and *Lienüzhuan*.[43]

Let us now move to a longer narrative which incorporates several series of anecdote chains that appear in the *Zuozhuan*, namely section 15. In view of its length, I have divided it into two parts. The section states:

> When King Zhuang of Chu ascended the throne [613 BCE], Wu was submissive to Chu. Prince Zhengshu of Chen took as wife a daughter of Duke Mu of Zheng named Shao Kong.[44] In the fifteenth year of King Zhuang [599 BCE], Prince Zhengshu of Chen killed his lord, Duke Ling. King Zhuang led an army and laid siege to Chen. The King ordered the Duke of Shen, Qu Wu, to go to Qin and ask for troops, and getting the troops [Qu Wu] returned. The King entered the Chen [capital], killed Zhengshu, took his wife and gave her to the Duke of Shen. *Lianyin* Xiang the Elder contended with [the Duke of Shen] and seized Shao Kong.[45] When *lianyin* Xiang the Elder was captured at Heyong,[46] his son, Heiyao, also married Shao Kong. When King Zhuang passed away and King Gong ascended the throne [590 BCE], Heiyao died, and Marshal Zifan contended with the Duke of Shen for Shao Kong.[47] The Duke of Shen said: "this is the wife I was given [by King Zhuang]," and married her. The Marshal considered the Duke of Shen incompliant.[48] When the king ordered the Duke of Shen to go to a visit to Qi, the Duke of Shen secretly carried Shao Kong off and left. From Qi he thereupon escaped to Jin, from Jin he went to Wu, thereby facilitating routes of communication between Wu and Jin, and teaching the men of Wu to oppose Chu.

楚莊王立，吳人服于楚．陳公子徵舒取妻于鄭穆公，是少𡠗．莊王立十又五年，【74】陳公子徵舒殺其君靈公，莊王率師圍陳．王命申公屈巫蹠秦求師，得師以【75】來．王入陳，殺徵舒，取其室以予申公．連尹襄老與之爭，抯（奪）之少𡠗．連尹戠（捷）⁴⁹於河【76】𤄒，其子黑要也或（又）室少𡠗．莊王即世，共王即位．黑要也死，司馬子反與申【77】公爭少𡠗，申公曰：「是余受妻也．」取以爲妻．司馬不順申公．王命申公聘於齊，申【78】公竊載少𡠗以行，自齊遂逃蹠晉，自晉蹠吳，焉始通吳晉之路，教吳人反楚．【79】⁵⁰

This lengthy narrative incorporates several accounts, the detailed version of which is present in the *Zuozhuan*. The first section deals with the ultimate *femme fatale* of the *Zuozhuan*, Xia Ji (in the *Xinian* she is named Shao Kong, as explained in the relevant note above), who "has killed three husbands, one ruler, and one son, and has brought one state and two high ministers to their destruction."⁵¹ According to the *Zuozhuan* account, Xia Ji had illicit relations with Duke Ling of Chen and with two of his high ministers, which infuriated her son (or, in the *Xinian*'s version, her husband), Xia Zhengshu, who then assassinated his ruler, causing the subsequent Chu invasion. Xia Ji remained an apple of discord among the leading Chu ministers; their struggle caused one of the most gifted Chu statesmen, Qu Wu (or Wuchen 巫臣), the Duke of Shen, to flee his state; later, as his enemies massacred his family, Qu Wu avenged their death by fostering the Jin-Wu alliance directed against Chu. These complex stories, full of didactic digressions, are compressed in the *Xinian* into slightly more than two hundred words, diminishing thereby their dramatic effect, cutting off substantial details (such as Xia Ji's adultery or the massacre of Qu Wu's family), omitting speeches, and undermining the potential didactic—or entertaining—value of each of the anecdotes involved. What remains is a factual skeleton focusing on a single significant issue: how the course of events turned a member of a Chu royal lineage, Qu Wu, into an arch-enemy of his native state, contributing to a major setback in Chu's strategic position. Yet the true significance for the authors is clearly not Qu Wu's personal case (hence, the story of the massacre of his family is omitted), but, rather the consequences of his actions: the rise of Wu, which becomes the main subject of the narrative in its second part:

> Coming to time of King Ling [of Chu], King Ling invaded Wu. He made the Nanhuai expedition, seized Prince Jueyou of Wu,

and thereafter Wu again submitted to Chu.[52] When King Ling passed away, King Jingping [aka King Ping, r. 528–516 BCE] ascended the throne [528 BCE].[53] Junior Preceptor [Fei] Wuji slandered *lianyin* [Wu 伍] She and had him killed. She's sons, Wu Yun and Ji of Wu [Wu Ji] fled and submitted to Wu 吳.[54] Wu Ji led the men of Wu to lay siege to Zhoulai, digging a lengthy moat and filling it with water so as to defeat the Chu army; this is the Moat of Ji's Father.[55] When King Jingping passed away, King Zhao ascended the throne [516 BCE]. Wu Yun became the chief minister (*taizai* 太宰) of Wu; he taught Wu how to cause uprisings among the regional lords [allied with] Chu; thus he defeated the Chu army at Boju and thereupon entered Ying, [the Chu capital].[56] King Zhao returned to Sui; and he fought the Wu forces at Xi (Yi). Prince Zhen of Wu was about to rebel and make trouble for Wu: King Helu of Wu then had to return, and King Zhao thus recovered his state.

以至靈王, 靈王伐吳, 爲南懷 (淮?) 之行, 執吳王子蹶由, 吳人焉或 (又) 服於楚. 靈王即世,【80】景平王即位. 少師無極讒連尹奢而殺之, 其子伍員與伍之雞逃歸吳. 伍雞將【81】吳人以圍州來, 爲長壑而洍之, 以敗楚師, 是雞父之洍. 景平王即世, 昭王即【82】位. 伍員爲吳太宰, 是教吳人反楚邦之諸侯, 以敗楚師于柏舉, 遂入郢. 昭王歸【83】隨, 與吳人戰于析 (沂). 吳王子晨將起禍於吳, 吳王闔盧乃歸, 昭王焉復邦.【84】[57]

The *Zuozhuan* tells in great detail about the brief hegemony of King Ling of Chu 楚靈王 (r. 540–529 BCE), who overawed his neighbors and humiliated Wu by repeated incursions; about the coup against King Ling, the ensuing turmoil, and the subsequent decline in Chu's prestige; about the intrigues of the infamous Chu plotter, Fei Wuji, who caused the downfall of the Wu 伍 lineage; and about Wu Yun's (i.e., Wu Zixu's 伍子胥) subsequent flight to Wu, where he started preparing revenge against Chu, eventually bringing his native country to the verge of annihilation. All these affairs, in addition to the dramatic flight of King Zhao from his capital in 506 BCE and the no less dramatic recovery of his fortunes, are absent from the *Xinian* or shortened to a few words. Gone are individual dramas, moral dilemmas, malevolence and benevolence of rulers and ministers. Nothing should distract the reader from the single thread of the narrative: explaining how the

Wu-Chu conflict unfolded until it peaked with the stunning occupation of the Chu capital by the invading Wu armies in 506 BCE.

Each segment of the *Xinian* narrative is paralleled in the *Zuozhuan*, with two exceptions: the story of Qu Wu's mission to Qin to seek support against Chen in 598 BCE, and the exploits of Wu Zixu's brother, Wu Ji (or, as he is named in the text, Ji of Wu 伍之雞).⁵⁸ In both cases I believe, *pace* the editors of Volume 2 of the Qinghua bamboo slips (hereafter: *Qinghua 2*), that this information is wrong and is based on the *Xinian* authors' carelessness. In the first case, it is highly improbable that Chu would seek Qin's assistance against Chen, not only because Chen's location is distant from Qin, but mostly because Chu's invasion of Chen was ultimately unopposed and did not require significant coalition-building. In my eyes, it is likely that the *Xinian* authors conflated this event with a real request of support from Qin by a Chu messenger, Shen Baoxu 申包胥, against Wu in 506 BCE.⁵⁹ Perhaps they were misled by the identity between Shen Baoxu's lineage name (Shen 申) and Qu Wu's fief of Shen 申, and transposed the story a century backward in time. As for Ji of Wu, I fully accept Ziju's 子居 assertion that this name is based on a popular etymology of the name of the battlefield where Chu armies were defeated by their Wu adversaries in 519 BCE, Jifu 雞父, which literally means Rooster's (or Ji's) Father.⁶⁰ The place name, recorded in the *Chunqiu*, should have existed before the battle of Wu against Chu, but later it might have become associated with Wu Zixu's revenge for his father's death in Chu custody.⁶¹ Since the place name could not be meaningfully associated with Zixu himself, his new brother was invented. It is highly unlikely that such an important personage, if he ever existed, would have evaded the attention of countless historians and literati who retold Wu Zixu's story, turning it into one of the best-known narratives from the late Spring and Autumn Period.⁶² Similar carelessness may explain other lapses in the *Xinian*'s narrative, such as misidentification of Xia Ji's son, Xia Zhengshu, as her husband and as a prince (*gongzi* 公子, i.e., a son of one of Chen's rulers). On the other hand, it is possible that the *Xinian* is more accurate than *Zuozhuan* in identifying Xia Zhengshu as Xia Ji's husband and not son, because in terms of Xia Ji's age it is highly improbable that back in 598 she already had an adult son.⁶³

Let us leave aside for a moment the issue of the *Xinian*'s historical accuracy and try to understand how the authors utilized their primary sources. As mentioned above, I believe that discrepancies between *Xinian* and *Zuozhuan* rule out direct borrowing of the former from the latter (and, of course, vice versa): no [mis]reading of the *Zuozhuan* would yield such a story as invention of Wu Ji, for instance.⁶⁴ On the other hand, the overlap between the two texts is still overwhelming. An easiest explanation would be that both texts shared a common third source, which their authors modified in accordance with their ideological, esthetic, or other needs. It seems probable that a detailed *Zuozhuan* narrative retained more of the original source material, while the *Xinian* authors were more prone to introduce abridgements.

From comparing both versions we can understand how the *Xinian* authors treated their sources. They compressed the original account, omitted unnecessary details, and also possibly supplemented it with additional information that could have derived from other sources or from oral lore (such as the invention of Wu Ji). In the process, many minor details, such as dates, place names, and official titles, which permeate the *Zuozhuan* narrative, were reduced to an absolute minimum, with reign periods of the Chu kings serving as the primary chronological tool. Moreover, the *Xinian* narration lost most of what should be expected of a chain of anecdotes as analyzed by Schaberg.[65] Because of this compression, the narrative cannot be divided into "single events" with a clear "beginning, middle and end"; gone are the speeches; and no clear means of conveying didactic message are discernible. What remains is a brief and energetic political history. Carelessness regarding minor details should not mislead us: on important matters, the text appears clear and unequivocal. In a few hundred graphs it tells in a nutshell the story of Chu's conflict with Wu; this story is told not for its moral or entertaining qualities but in order to provide working knowledge for a reader who wants to be briefly informed about historical changes in Chu's geostrategic situation. This account is highly informative, and, insofar as we can judge from other sources, fairly accurate.

Many anecdotal collections of the Warring States Period and beyond utilized the *Zuozhuan* or its sources, detaching moralizing anecdotes from lengthier annalistic accounts. The *Xinian* authors likewise abridged the source histories utilized in the *Zuozhuan*, but in marked distinction from other texts, they omitted most of the didactically important aspects of the *Zuozhuan* narrative, retaining primarily the factual skeleton of political history. Readers of the *Xinian* were expected to learn from the text not how to behave, but about what happened in the preceding century or two, and how the past events shape the world in which they are living.

The *Xinian* and Chu Historiography

Let us move now beyond the temporal span covered by the *Zuozhuan*, to those *Xinian* sections which derive in all likelihood from fifth to fourth century BCE Chu historical sources. Sections 20 through 23 are particularly valuable for a historian of early China, because, except for a few opening sentences in section 20, they cover the period from 453 to ca. 396 BCE, which remains a *terra incognita* due to dearth of reliable historical information.[66] A detailed analysis of their rich content deserves a separate discussion; here I shall focus only on what we can glean from these sections about aspects of indigenous Chu historiography. Especially the two last sections are very promising in this regard. As they narrate the events of what was for the *Xinian* authors a recent past, it may be assumed that they are closer in their outlook to the original records done by Chu scribes. For my analysis I have chosen the last section, *Xinian* 23, which narrates Chu's conflicts with Jin (or more precisely with the three successor states of Jin, namely Wei 魏, Han 韓, and Zhao 趙), between 404 and 396 BCE. I have divided this lengthy section into three parts:

> In the fourth year of King Shenghuan of Chu [a.k.a. King Sheng, r. ca. 407–402 BCE],[67] Tian, the Duke of Song, and Tai, the Earl of Zheng, attended the Chu court. The king ordered the Duke of Song to fortify the Yu Pass, and establish Wuyang [fortress?].[68] Qin forces defeated the Jin army at Luoyin in order to help Chu.[69] When King Sheng passed away, King Daozhe [a.k.a. King Dao, r. ca. 401–381 BCE] ascended the throne.[70] The Zheng forces assaulted the Yu Pass, and Lord Huanding of Yangcheng[71] led the forces of the Yu Pass and of the upper parts of the country[72] to repel them. He fought the [invaders] at Guiling, but the Chu armies did not succeed.[73] Jia of Jing (i.e. Jing Jia) and Shuzi Gong were captured and died [there]. In the next year [400 BCE?], Fu[74] Yu of Jin led the Jin and Zheng armies to install Prince Ding.[75] The Duke of Luyang led an army to combat the Jin forces; the Jin forces returned, having failed to install the Prince.

> 楚聲桓王立四年, 宋公田, 鄭伯駘皆朝于楚. 王率宋公以城榆關, 是 (寔) 武陽. 秦人【126】敗晉師於洛陰, 以爲楚援. 聲王即世, 悼哲王即位. 鄭人侵榆關, 陽城桓定君率【127】榆關之師與上國之師以交之, 與之戰於桂陵, 楚師無功. 景之賈與舒子共戠(捷)而死. 明【128】歲, 晉 (貝+甫) 余率晉師與鄭師以入王子定. 魯陽公率師以交晉人, 晉人還, 不果入王子.[76]

The story starts with depicting the epochal struggle of the late fifth century, which engulfed most of contemporaneous polities and which shaped to a large extent the political map of the Warring States era. It continues the narrative in sections 21 and 22, which narrate the formation of two competing axes: Jin's alliance with southeastern state of Yue, directed primarily against Qi, and Qi's alliance with Chu, directed primarily against Jin. In 403 BCE, Qi suffered a major defeat, in the aftermath of which the three de facto rulers of Jin, heads of the Wei, Han, and Zhao lineages, were officially granted the position of regional lords by the king of Zhou. The narrative in section 23 starts in the immediate aftermath of this event: the attempt of Chu to solicit support of intermediate states of Song and Zheng; Qin's supportive (but inconsequential) assault on Jin in the far west, and the formation of Jin-Zheng alliance directed against Chu. In the background of these events stands domestic struggle in the state of Chu, due to which King Sheng was murdered and succeeded by King Dao; the latter had to fight against his brother (or uncle?), Prince Ding. Yet, as is common in the *Xinian*, domestic troubles of the state of Chu are not narrated in full, and the text's focus remains purely on the state's foreign relations.

Let us turn now at the first sentence of section 23. Here (as also in a few phrases of section 22 that narrate the events of 404–403 BCE) the *Xinian* authors dispense with their convention of identifying rulers of the Zhou polities by their posthumous names added to the ducal (*gong* 公) title. Rather, the visiting Song and Zheng leaders (Duke Xiu of Song 宋休公 [r. ca. 403–385 BCE], and Duke Xu of Zheng 鄭繻公 [r. ca. 422–396 BCE]) are identified by their private names and by their ranks in the Zhou system (duke [*gong* 公] for the ruler of Song, earl [*bo* 伯] for the ruler of Zheng).[77] This usage unmistakably resembles the Lu *Chunqiu* and may reflect a common annalistic tradition that was apparently shared by the Chu court scribes. Yet since this is the one of only a very few unmistakably annalistic records in the *Xinian* (others are in section 22), it is likely that it was not directly incorporated from the Chu court annals, but from a more detailed historical source that used the annals and expanded upon them, much as the *Zuozhuan* did to the Lu *Chunqiu*.[78] Editorial efforts of the *Xinian* editors in this case were minimal. They did change the original language from what should have been "The Duke of Song and the Earl of Zheng *attended our court*" (來朝) to "attended the Chu court" (朝于楚), but did not update the names of the visiting leaders, despite the fact that the compilation had obviously been finished *after* the deaths of both rulers of Song and Zheng, when their posthumous names should have been known.⁷⁹ Careless editing aside, the record does suggest the existence of an indigenous Chu annalistic tradition, akin to the *Chunqiu* of Lu, as is hinted at in the *Mengzi* 孟子 (Mencius).⁸⁰ The *Xinian* continues with narration of the evolution of the Chu-Jin conflict:

> In the next year [399 BCE], Lord Zhuangping of Liang led an army to invade Zheng.⁸¹ Four generals of Zheng—Huangzi, Zima, Zichi, and Zifengzi—led an army to combat the Chu forces. The Chu forces crossed the Fan River and prepared to fight; and the Zheng army fled, entering [the city of] Mie. The Chu army laid siege to Mie, and completely subdued the Zheng army and its four generals, returning with them to [Chu's capital] Ying. Moreover, Chief Minister (*taizai*) Xin of Zheng made trouble in Zheng: Ziyang of Zheng was eliminated, leaving no posterity in Zheng.⁸² In the next year [398 BCE], Chu returned the four Zheng generals and their myriad people to Zheng. The Jin forces encircled Lü and Changling, and overpowered these cities.⁸³ The King [of Chu] ordered Lord Daowu of Pingye to lead an army and invade Jin.⁸⁴ He subdued Gao, captured Duke Shejian of Teng⁸⁵ and returned to repay the invasion of Changling.

> 明歲, 【129】郎 (梁?) 莊平君率師侵鄭, 鄭皇子, 子馬, 子池, 子封子率師以交楚人, 楚人涉氾, 將與之戰, 鄭師逃 【130】入於蔑. 楚師圍之於蔑, 盡逾 (降) 鄭師與其四將軍, 以歸於郢. 鄭太宰欣亦起禍於 【131】鄭, 鄭子陽用滅, 無後於鄭. 明歲, 楚人歸鄭之四將軍與其萬民於鄭. 晉人圍津, 長陵, 【132】克之. 王命平夜悼武君率師侵晉, 逾 (降) 郜, 馘捷)滕公涉澗以歸, 以復長陵之師.⁸⁶

The story depicts Chu's impressive success in its struggle against Zheng: capture of the entire Zheng army led by Zheng's leading nobles. This success, attained around 399 BCE, did not benefit Chu, though. For whatever reasons, the Chu leaders decided to release their captives and make peace with Zheng, which was then preoccupied with domestic turmoil. The text remains silent as for the reasons for this sudden leniency; but the disappearance of Zheng from subsequent narrative indicates that it was pacified and stopped invasions of Chu. For Chu, however, this did not bring respite.

The tit-for-tat attacks between Jin and Chu continued, culminating in the major conflict between the two states circa 396 BCE, the Wuyang campaign:

> After two years [396 BCE?],[87] Han Qu and Wei Ji led an army and laid siege to Wuyang, to repay the incursion of Gao.[88] The Duke of Luyang led an army to help Wuyang, and fought the Jin army below the Wuyang walls. The Chu army was greatly defeated. Three lords-possessors of the *gui* tablet, the Duke of Luyang, Lord Daowu of Pingye and Lord Huanding of Yangcheng, as well as *youyin* Si of Zhao (Zhao Si) died in that battle;[89] the Chu forces threw away their banners, tents, chariots and weapons, and returned, running like fleeing dogs. The Chen people thereupon rebelled and let Prince Ding back to Chen.[90] Thus the state of Chu lost a lot of walled cities.
>
> When the Chu army was planning to go to rescue Wuyang, the King ordered Lord Daowu of Pingye to dispatch somebody to Chen Hao of Qi to request military help.[91] Chen Jimu [of Qi] led one thousand chariots and followed the Chu army to Wuyang. On the day *jiaxu* [day 11], Jin fought with Chu; on *bingzi* [day 13], the Qi army arrived at Yi and then turned back.

厭（薦?）年，韓【133】取，魏擊率師圍武陽，以復鄩之師. 魯陽公率師救武陽，與晉師戰於武陽之城【134】下，楚師大敗，魯陽公，平夜悼武君，陽城桓定君，三執珪之君與右尹昭之竢死焉，楚人盡棄其【135】旃幕車兵，犬逸而還. 陳人焉反而入王子定於陳. 楚邦以多亡城. 楚師將救武陽，【136】王命平夜悼武君李(使)人於齊陳淏求師. 陳疾目率車千乘，以從楚師於武陽. 甲戌，晉楚以【137】戰. 丙子，齊師至喦，遂還. 【138】[92]

The lengthy struggle with the successor states of Jin ended in a disaster for Chu. Around 396 BCE its army suffered a crushing defeat, which was aggravated by the domestic rebellion of supporters of the ousted Prince Ding of Chu. The text does not conceal the scope of the defeat, nor does it display any lenience toward Chu's international prestige, adding that the "Chu forces threw away their banners, tents, chariots and weapons, and returned, running like fleeing dogs." This frank acknowledgment of Chu's humiliation stays in sharp contrast to the continuous concealment of domestic troubles, such as the regicide of King Sheng and details of Prince Ding's rebellion. It seems that the *Xinian* was not much concerned with Chu's "national" pride.

The ending sentences of section 23 are quite exceptional in the text. This appendix breaks the chronological framework of the narrative and goes back to the events that directly preceded the crushing defeat of the Chu armies at Wuyang. The addition might have been done to avoid a pessimistic ending of the text with a defeat that caused Chu soldiers to flee "like dogs" from the battlefield, and which resulted in the "loss of many walled cities" by the Chu side. Yet the appendix was not properly edited; hence it contains two dates of the sexagenary *ganzhi* 干支 (Stems and Branches) cycle, which appear to be transmitted from a lengthier Chu history without being properly edited. Normally, as is well demonstrable in the *Zuozhuan*, the *ganzhi* dates are meaningful only when a month is provided; otherwise they do not allow to date an event.[93] It is technically possible of course that the two dates in the final slip were meant to show that the Qi army missed the battle by two days, but this goal could easily have been achieved without adding the *ganzhi* dating. It is more likely that the editors just transposed the dating from a Chu historical source without modifying it (in that case, the month could have been mentioned in one of the earlier phrases, abridged by the *Xinian* author[s]). This carelessness is a blessing for us: it shows that meticulous dating of events, characteristic of the *Zuozhuan* and its sources, was the rule in Chu court histories as well.[94]

Let us summarize now section 23 of the *Xinian*. The discussion here (as in the preceding section 22) differs from most of the early sections, as it is much more intensive. Almost every year in the ca. 403–396 BCE span covered in this section merits a special entry,[95] and while the dating remains very rough (no months or days are provided), we have more details about the names of the participants and places than is usual in the *Xinian*. Clearly, the abridgment of the original sources was less radical in this case than in earlier sections of the text, perhaps because the events were not too far removed from the date of the *Xinian*'s composition, and details still mattered.

Section 23 in the *Xinian* provides abundant information about battles, alliances, and movements of forces; but it does not contain anything akin to an anecdote. No speeches, no evaluation of the participants' motivations, of their mistakes, of heroism or cowardice, wisdom or folly. Having no *Zuozhuan*-style background, we lack any clue about the reasons for Zheng's break with Chu around 403 BCE or about the role of the fugitive Prince Ding of Chu in this country's conflicts with its neighbors; we know nothing about the reasons for Chu's lenient treatment of Zheng captives; we do not even know who—if anyone at all—should be blamed for Chu's eventual defeat. This kind of information would be promptly supplied in the majority of the *Zuozhuan* narratives, and it would be essential in any of the later anecdotes. In the *Xinian* it is simply omitted. The authors wanted to inform their readers of military and diplomatic developments that resulted in Chu's debacle, but they were interested neither in teaching a moral lesson, nor in entertaining the reader. If the text contains didactic messages, these are so well hidden that I could not discover them. In my eyes, the text aims simply at providing essential information about events that changed the balance of power between Chu and its adversaries. This is achieved without any visible didacticism.

Summary: Non-anecdotal Historiography

The *Xinian* differs in form from the *Zuozhuan*; it differs from the narrative histories that evidently served as the building blocks of the *Zuozhuan*; and it also differs from collections of anecdotes from the pre-imperial and early imperial ages, which often borrow from the *Zuozhuan* or from its source histories. It represents a different type of history: a narrative devoid of moralizing stories, a narrative with much less pronounced didacticism, a narrative the focus of which is on informing the reader of the evolution of interstate relations in recent centuries.

Who was the audience of the *Xinian*? I would imagine a very limited group of persons: probably leading policymakers, the ruler and his closest advisors, who were in need of working knowledge of the historical background for the current balance of power. This material could particularly benefit them during diplomatic encounters with representatives of other states. In a recent study David Schaberg explored the speeches of the messengers (*shi* 使) and disclosed their common ground with the scribes (*shi* 史): both shared similar training, which "encompassed both ritual formulas and more substantial knowledge of history and official practice."[96] How was "substantial knowledge of history" attained? Some might have studied history in earnest; but many others might have been in need of a brief résumé of major geopolitical shifts in the past rather than of detailed narrative. Such résumés can be compared to modern briefings for a traveling head of the state: not an extensive narrative with plenty of dates, names and events, but a brief summary which presents the most essential information that can be utilized during the diplomatic encounter. I suppose such a summary prepared nowadays may be similar to the *Xinian*.[97]

Following Schaberg's parallel, I may assert that the *Xinian* was a useful asset for a Chu messenger (*shi* 使), but it was probably prepared by professional scribes (*shi* 史). Evidently, the authors extracted their information from much longer narrative histories, which might have been utilized by the *Zuozhuan* composers as well. Judging from the *Zuozhuan*, these histories tried both to inform and to educate or entertain; they probably comprised both detailed accounts of events and moralizing digressions. These latter became particularly significant for later readers, who valued the didactic potential of historical narratives rather than pure information; hence, didactic segments were extracted from earlier narratives and became the core of the anecdote genre. In the age of intense intellectual polemics of the Warring States Period, historical anecdotes became indispensable for ideological manipulation: through tendentious accounts of history, authors could convince the audience of the advantages of their political recipes. Didacticism prevailed, details were sacrificed, and obvious distortions of history became the rule throughout the Warring States Period and well into the early Han.[98]

Informative histories had a much shorter life-span than moralizing anecdotes. As time passed, details of struggles and intrigues among the bygone polities and lineages became increasingly irrelevant for the educated audience. The *Xinian* itself, for instance, would surely be considered anachronistic by about 300 BCE, as the state of Jin became a distant memory akin to the Austro-Hungarian Empire in our days, while Chu became engaged in a bitter struggle with its erstwhile ally, the state of Qin. Perhaps long before the Qin biblioclasm of 213 BCE delivered a coup de grâce to the historical narratives of the vanquished Warring States, such documents as the *Xinian* were already out of circulation. Having outlived their usefulness, they perished from memory, or, what is more likely, were replaced by newer, updated texts, which also disappeared in due time. It took the grand project of the Sima 司馬 family under Emperor Wu of the Han Dynasty 漢武帝 (r. 141–87 BCE) to revive intellectual interest in informative history, restoring the glory of the historical genre. Their success, like the success of the *Zuozhuan* before, derived in no small measure from their ability to use historical narrative simultaneously for ideological and informative purposes.

The pervasive position of anecdotes in the historical and quasi-historical lore of the Warring States period has created a wrong impression that they are the "all" in early Chinese history writing. Recent discoveries require a reconsideration of this assertion. Thus, another major quasi-historical work from the Shanghai Museum collection, the *Rongchengshi* 容成氏, demonstrates that an ideological agenda could be served not only by anecdotes but by preparing a "comprehensive" history of the ruling dynasties of legendary and semi-legendary past.[99] The *Xinian* presents another alternative: a brief informative history with minimal, if any, didactic or ideological emphases. Future discoveries may reveal more filiations of early historical genres. Events of the past were recorded, memorized, narrated, embellished, or invented for a variety of political, ideological, and esthetic needs. New discoveries liberate us from the excessive dependence on the ideological production of the Warring States thinkers and from the narrow prism of Han redactors, and allow us to come to terms gradually with immense variety of early Chinese historiography.

Notes

1. This research was supported by the Israel Science Foundation (grant No. 240/15) and by the Michael William Lipson Chair in Chinese Studies. I am grateful to the participants of the Anecdotes Workshop in Leiden (2013), in particular to Paul R. Goldin, and to the volume's editors and anonymous reviewers for their comments and suggestions.

2. The Shanghai Museum collection comprises several dozen manuscripts allegedly smuggled from the Mainland to Hong Kong antiquities market and purchased by Shanghai Museum in 1994. To date nine volumes have been published; these include more than two dozen individual anecdotes.

3. David Schaberg, "Chinese History and Philosophy," in *The Oxford History of Historical Writing*, vol. I: *Beginnings to AD 600*, eds. Andrew Feldherr and Grant Hardy (Oxford: Oxford University Press, 2011), 394.

4. See *Shiji* 史記 (Beijing: Zhonghua shuju, 1997) 15.686. From Sima Qian's lamentation it is clear that historical texts suffered most from the book burning. For different interpretations of Qin's biblioclasm, see Jens Østergård Petersen, "Which Books Did the First Emperor of Ch'in Burn? On the Meaning of *Pai Chia* in Early Chinese Sources," *Monumenta Serica* 43 (1995): 1–52; Martin Kern, *The Stele Inscriptions of Ch'in Shih-huang: Text and Ritual in Early Chinese Imperial Representation* (New Haven, CT: American Oriental Society, 2000), 183–96; Yuri Pines, *Envisioning Eternal Empire: Chinese Political Thought of the Warring States Era* (Honolulu: University of Hawai'i Press, 2009), 180–83.

5. Sima Qian indeed notices that, in distinction from canonical "odes" (*shi* 詩) and "documents" (*shu* 書), "scribal records" were not stored by private individuals (*Shiji* 15.686).

6. For my treatment of the Lu *Annals*, see Yuri Pines, "Chinese history-writing between the sacred and the secular," in *Early Chinese Religion: Part One: Shang through Han (1250 BC–220 AD)*, eds. John Lagerwey and Marc Kalinowski (Leiden: Brill, 2009), 318–23. For the nature of the *Zhushu jinian*, see relevant sections of Edward L. Shaughnessy, *Rewriting Early Chinese Texts* (Albany, NY: State University of New York Press, 2006); cf. David S. Nivison, *The Riddle of the Bamboo Annals* (Taipei: Airiti, 2009).

7. For Schaberg's detailed treatment of the *Zuozhuan* anecdotes and chains of anecdotes, see his *A Patterned Past: Form and Thought in Early Chinese Historiography* (Cambridge, MA: Harvard University Asia Center, 2001).

8. See Schaberg, *A Patterned Past*; Yuri Pines, *Foundations of Confucian Thought: Intellectual Life in the Chunqiu Period, 722–453 B.C.E.* (Honolulu: University of Hawai'i Press, 2002); and Wai-yee Li, *The Readability of the Past in Early Chinese Historiography* (Cambridge, MA: Harvard University Press, 2007).

9. A very convenient tool of tracing these large segments is the topical arrangement of the *Zuozhuan*, undertaken by Gao Shiqi 高士奇 (1645–1704) in *Zuozhuan jishi benmo* 左傳紀事本末 (Beijing: Zhonghua shuju, 1979).

10. The appeal of the *Zuozhuan* anecdotes is visible in Burton Watson's focus on these in his *The Tso chuan: Selections from China's Oldest Narrative History* (New York: Columbia University Press, 1989). Watson's translation serves, due to its high readability, as the basic introduction to the *Zuozhuan* for undergraduate students throughout the Anglophone world. I expect that the new translation of the *Zuozhuan* by Stephen Durrant, Wai-yee Li, and David Schaberg (Seattle: University of Washington Press, 2016) will profoundly change the situation in the field.

11. *Chunqiu Zuozhuan zhu* 春秋左傳注; ed. Yang Bojun 楊伯峻 (Beijing: Zhonghua shuju, rev. ed. 1990, hereafter *Zuo*), Zhao 12.3: 1332; Zhao 20.3: 1409.

12. Li, *The Readability*.

13. *Zuo*, Zhao 26.9: 1475–79.

14. *Guoyu* is a heterogeneous compilation of anecdotes, some of which may derive from the same sources that served the compiler of the *Zuozhuan*. There are several indications that *Guoyu* in general was composed later than the *Zuozhuan*, and underwent heavier editorial intervention. See Yuri Pines, "Speeches and the Question of Authenticity in Ancient Chinese Historical Records," in *Historical Truth, Historical Criticism and Ideology: Chinese Historiography and Historical Culture from a New Comparative Perspective*, ed. Helwig Schmidt-Glintzer, Achim Mittag, and Jörn Rüsen (Leiden: Brill, 2005), 207–13.

15. The *ganzhi* cycle will be explained below.

16. *Zuo*, Zhao 26.5 and 26.7: 1473–74.

17. Schaberg, "Chinese History and Philosophy," 396.

18. Schaberg, "Chinese History and Philosophy," 398 for both citations.

19. The dating of the *Zuozhuan* composition is very much disputed, particularly because of a lengthy time that may have passed between its initial compilation

and the text's fixation in a form close to the current version. In Pines, *Foundations*, I discuss various approaches toward the text's dating and the problem of manifold interpolations into the text during the lengthy period of its transmission.

20. Much of the discussion in this section is based on Yuri Pines, "Zhou History and Historiography: Introducing the Bamboo *Xinian*," *T'oung Pao* 100, no. 4–5 (2014): 287–324, esp. 290–98.

21. Li Xueqin 李學勤, ed., *Qinghua daxue cang Zhanguo zhujian* 清華大學藏戰國竹簡 Vol. 2 (Shanghai: Shanghai wenyi, 2011), hereafter *Qinghua 2*. For an introduction to the *Xinian*, see Li Xueqin 李學勤, "Qinghua jian *Xinian* ji youguan gushi wenti" 清華簡《繫年》及有關古史問題, *Wenwu* 文物 no. 3 (2011): 70–74.

22. For an introduction to Guodian discovery, see e.g., Sarah Allan and Crispin Williams, eds., *The Guodian Laozi: Proceedings of the International Conference, Dartmouth College May 1998* (Berkeley: The Society for the Study of Early China and the Institute of Asian Studies, University of California, 2000). For the Shanghai Museum collection see note 2 above.

23. The three groups mentioned in this paragraph are those that use Zhou chronology, Jin chronology, and Chu chronology. As is clear from this paragraph, an additional subgroup uses a mixture of Jin and Chu chronology.

24. In Chu manuscripts *ji* appears as "with" only in six cases while *yu* in 99 cases (or 127 cases if Zeng 曾 manuscripts are added); in Qin manuscripts, by contrast, *yu* is used only four times, while *ji* appears 313 times; see Zhang Yujin 張玉金, *Chutu Zhanguo wenxian xuci yanjiu* 出土戰國文獻虛詞研究 (Beijing: Renmin chubanshe 2011), 251–81. For a recent study of the *ji* particle in the *Chunqiu* and its commentaries, and the commentators' difficulty to understand *ji* in its meaning as "with," "and," see Newell Ann Van Auken, "*Spring and Autumn* Use of *Jí* 及 and Its Interpretation in the *Gōngyáng* and *Gŭliáng* Commentaries," in *Studies in Chinese and Sino-Tibetan Linguistics: Dialect, Phonology, Transcription and Text*, eds. Richard VanNess Simmons and Newell Ann Van Auken (Taipei: Institute of Linguistics, Academia Sinica, 2014), 429–56. For a detailed discussion of *ji* and *yu* in the *Xinian*, see Chen Minzhen 陳民鎮, "Qinghua jian *Xinian* xuci chutan" 清華簡《繫年》虛詞初探, *Chutu wenxian yuyan yanjiu* 出土文獻語言研究 2 (2015), 50–51.

25. For the usage of *yu* 于/於 particles in *Zuozhuan* and comparison to other pre-imperial texts, see He Leshi 何樂士, *Zuozhuan xuci yanjiu* 左傳虛詞研究 (Beijing: Shangwu chubanshe, rev. ed. 2004), 81–122; cf. Zhao Daming 趙大明, *Zuozhuan jieci yanjiu* 《左傳》介詞研究 (Beijing: Shoudu shifan daxue chubanshe, 2007), 34–158; Pines, *Foundations*, 217–20; for their usage in paleographic materials from the Warring States period, see Zhang Yujin, *Chutu Zhanguo wenxian*, 61–106. For the observation that Warring States Period copyists were careful in reproducing distinct *yu* particles even when their grammatical usage was identical, see Olivier Venture (Feng Yicheng 馮儀誠), "Zhanguo liang Han 'yu,' 'yu' er zi de

yongfa yu gushu de chuanxie xiguan" 戰國兩漢 '于', '於' 二字的用法與古書的傳寫習慣, *Jianbo* 2 (2007): 81–95.

26. For yet another example of these differences (possible substitution of *nai* 乃 particle in the meaning of "then," "thereupon" with *sui* 隨), see Pines, "Zhou History and Historiography," 295.

27. One notable piece of previously unknown and highly reliable information provided by the *Xinian* concerns the origins of the Qin ruling lineage (see detailed discussion in Pines, "Zhou History and Historiography," 299–303). Another potential indication of the reliability of the *Xinian* is its reference (section 18, slip 100) to Tuo (佗=佗) (r. until 504 BCE), the ruler of a tiny polity of Xu 許. In the *Chunqiu* and the *Zuozhuan* this ruler is identified as Si 斯. However, a Xu Zi Tuo-zhǎn 許子佗盞 vessel unearthed in 2003 at Nanyang, Henan, in the vicinity of Tuo's new capital, Rongcheng 榮成, identifies this ruler by the same name (佗=佗) as recorded in the *Xinian*. Since the identification of the Xu ruler's name as Tuo was tentative and was not widely known in the scholarly community, it is almost unbelievable that a forger would use this graph instead of the name Si recorded in the canonical work. See detailed discussion in Huang Jinqian 黃錦前, " 'Xu Zi Tuo' yu 'Xu Gong Tuo'—jian tan Qinghua jian *Xinian* de kekaoxing" 許子佗與許公佗: 兼談清華簡《繫年》的可靠性, http://www.bsm.org.cn/show_article.php?id=1756 (accessed: July 29, 2016).

28. See Yuri Pines, "Reassessing Textual Sources for Pre-Imperial Qin History," in *Sinologi Mira k iubileiu Stanislava Kuczery: Sobranie Trudov*, eds. Sergej Dmitriev and Maxim Korolkov (Moscow: Institut Vostokovedeniia RAN, 2013), 236–63.

29. The *Xinian* routinely reports about every slain Chu king that he had simply "passed away"; only in section 18 (slip 99) King Ling's death is referred to as having "encountered misfortune" 見禍 (*Qinghua 2*: 180).

30. See Chen Wei 陳偉, "Qinghua daxue cang zhushu *Xinian* de wenxianxue kaocha" 清華大學藏竹書《繫年》的文獻學考察, *Shilin* 史林 1 (2013): 44–45.

31. A major exception to this view is Yoshimoto Michimasa's 吉本道雅, "Seika kan keinen ko" 清華簡繫年考, *Kyōtō daigaku bungakubu kenkyū kiyō* 京都大學文學部研究紀要 52 (2013): 1–94. Yoshimoto dates the *Xinian* to the latter half of the fourth century BCE, because he presupposes that this text is based on the *Zuozhuan*, and because his earlier research postulated the mid-fourth-century dating of the latter. Recently Guo Yongbing 郭永秉 put forward additional evidence in favor of the *Xinian*'s dating to the early decades of the fourth century BCE on the basis of the shape of some of its characters in the context of the evolution of the so-called Chu script. See Guo's "Qinghua jian *Xinian* chaoxie shidai zhi guce: jian cong wenzi xingti jiaodu kan Zhanguo Chu wenzi quyuxing tezheng xingcheng de fuza guocheng" 清華簡《繫年》抄寫時代之估測: 兼從文字形體角度看戰國楚文字區域性特徵形成的複雜過程, *Wen shi* 文史 3 (2016): 5–42. I am not in a position to judge the validity of Guo's analysis.

32. This dating makes the *Xinian* roughly contemporary with another Chu quasi-historical text from the Qinghua collection, *Chuju* 楚居, for which see a brief introduction by Asano Yūichi 淺野裕一, "Qinghua jian *Chuju* chutan" 清華簡《楚居》初探, *Qinghua jian yanjiu* 清華簡研究 1 (2012): 242–47.

33. For a good, albeit incomplete summary of 2011–2012 studies, see Chen Minzhen 陳民鎮, "Qinghua jian *Xinjian* zhounian zongshu" 清華簡《繫年》週年綜述, http://www.gwz.fudan.edu.cn/SrcShow.asp?Src_ID=1977 (accessed: July 29, 2016). In 2015, no fewer than ten monographs on the *Xinian* (of very uneven quality) were published by the Zhongxi shudian publishing house, Shanghai.

34. Li Xueqin, "Qinghua jian *Xinian*," 70.

35. The "topical arrangement" style started under the Song dynasty (960–1279) when Yuan Shu 袁樞 (1130–1205) prepared a topically arranged version of *Zizhi tongjian* 資治通鑒; this style became very popular in under the Ming and Qing dynasties. For a very good analysis of the *jishi benmo* style of the *Xinian*, see Xu Zhaochang 許兆昌 and Qi Dandan 齊丹丹, "Shilun Qinghua jian *Xinian* de bianzuan tedian" 試論清華簡《繫年》的編纂特點, *Gudai wenming* 古代文明 6, no. 2 (2012): 60–66; for a similar assessment, see Liao Mingchun 廖名春, "Qinghua jian *Xinian* guankui" 清華簡《繫年》管窺, *Shenzhen daxue xuebao (renwen shehuikexue ban)* 深圳大學學報（人文社會科學版）no. 3 (2012): 51. Other scholars propose alternative identification of the *Xinian*'s genre: Chen Minzhen 陳民鎮 ("*Xinian* 'gu zhi' shuo—Qinghua jian *Xinian* xingzhi ji zhuanzuo beijing chuyi" 《繫年》"故志"說——清華簡《繫年》性質及撰作背景芻議, *Handan xueyuan xuebao* 邯鄲學院學報 no. 2 [2012]: 49–57, 100) affiliates it with the so-called *zhi* 志 histories; Chen Wei 陳偉 speculates that it may be related to the now lost *Duoshiwei* 鐸氏微 (Subtleties of Mr. Duo), a circa 340 BCE text by Duo Jiao 鐸椒 ("Qinghua daxue," 48). Li Xueqin defends his argument in favor of the *Xinian*'s similarity with the *Zhushu jinian* in his "You Qinghua jian *Xinian* lun *Jinian* de tili" 由清華簡《繫年》論《紀年》的體例, *Shenzhen daxue xuebao (renwen shehuikexue ban)* 深圳大學學報（人文社會科學版）no. 2 (2012): 42–44. For a recent study which largely shares my views of the *Xinian*, see note 97 below.

36. For a preliminary analysis of these "scribal records," see Pines, *Foundations*, 14–26.

37. "To wife" 妻 is glossed by Hu Sanxing 胡三省 (1230–1302) as "to commit adultery with a married woman" (私他人婦女), and this gloss fits perfectly here. See Cheng Wei 程薇, "Qinghua jian *Xinian* yu Xi Gui shiji" 清華簡《繫年》與息媯事跡, *Wenshi zhishi* 文史知識 4 (2012): 45–48 on p. 47; cf. Chen Wei 陳偉, "Du Qinghua jian *Xinian* zhaji" 讀清華簡《繫年》札記, *Jianghan kaogu* 江漢考古 3 (2012), 117–21 on p. 18. See also *Qinghua er*, 276–77.

38. I read *shun* 順 in 弗順 as a transitive verb; this usage ("to consider somebody incompliant," or, more precisely, "to bear a grudge against somebody") is peculiar to the *Xinian* (see also section 15 and note 48 below).

39. *Qinghua 2*: 147; slip numbers appear in Chinese in bold square brackets. In working on the *Xinian* text I have utilized, aside from *Qinghua 2* volume, also annotations by Xiaohu 小狐, "Du *Xinian* yizha" 讀《繫年》臆札, published on Fudan University site, http://www.gwz.fudan.edu.cn/SrcShow.asp?Src_ID=1766 (accessed: July 29, 2016); notes by Ziju 子居 published on the Qinghua University site, http://www.confucius2000.com/admin/lanmu2/jianbo.htm (accessed: July 29, 2016); and the partial annotation by The Huadong Normal University Small Group of Reading Warring States Period Bamboo Documents 華東師範大學中文系戰國簡讀書小組 published on the Wuhan University site, http://www.bsm.org.cn/show_article.php?id=1609 (accessed: July 29, 2016). When revising this article, I have consulted also the *magnum opus* by Su Jianzhou 蘇建洲, Wu Wenwen 吳雯雯, and Lai Yixuan 賴怡璇, *Qinghua er 'Xinian' jijie* 清華二《繫年》集解 (Taibei: Wanjuan lou, 2013; hereafter *Qinghua er*). For additional sources, see notes below.

40. *Zuo*, Zhuang 10.3: 184. The *Chunqiu* record (*Zuo*, Zhuang 10.5: 181) is the first appearance of Chu (which is then named Jing 荊) in the *Chunqiu*.

41. *Zuo*, Zhuang 14.3: 198–99.

42. The precise location of Fangcheng is disputed: it is likely that initially the term referred to the mountain ranges going from Funiu Mountains 伏牛山 eastward, which served as a natural boundary of the state of Chu; by the fifth century BCE a long protective wall was built in the area, and Fangcheng became identified with it. See Wu Wenwen's discussion in *Qinghua er*, 298–302.

43. For the *Lüshi chunqiu* version see Chen Qiyou 陳奇猷, *Lüshi chunqiu jiaoshi* 呂氏春秋校釋 (Shanghai: Xuelin, 1990), "Chang gong" 長攻 14.5: 991–92; for the *Lienüzhuan* version, see *Gu Lienüzhuan* 古列女傳, composed by Liu Xiang 劉向, "Zhen shun zhuan" 貞順傳, e-*Siku quanshu* edition, 4: 6–7.

44. From the *Zuozhuan* and *Guoyu* it is clear that Zhengshu was not a prince; here the *Xinian* is obviously mistaken. Shao Kong is known in other texts as Xia Ji 夏姬; Shao may be the lineage name of her husband, Yushu 御叔, Kong is her private name (*Qinghua 2*: 171n.2). According to the *Zuozhuan*, she was Zhengshu's mother and not wife.

45. *Lianyin* 連尹 is an official title in Chu hierarchy. The precise function of the *lianyin* is unknown, and the title is therefore left untranslated.

46. "Captured at Heyong" apparently refers to capturing Xiang's body after his death in action during the Bi 邲 battle between Chu and Jin in 597 (see *Zuo*, Xuan 12.2: 743); for Heyong's proximity to Bi, see Wu Wenwen's gloss in *Qinghua er*, 555–56.

47. In the *Zuozhuan*, the sequence of events differ: Hciyao was murdered by Marshal Zifan and his accomplices at the same time that Qu Wu's family was massacred; already before that Qu Wu had smuggled Xia Ji (viz. Shao Kong) out of Chu.

48. See note 38 above for *shun* 順 in the context of 弗順 as a transitive verb: "to consider somebody incompliant," i.e., to bear a grudge against him.

49. For reading the graph here as *jie* 捷 (to capture), see Chen Jian's 陳劍 explanations, as cited in *Qinghua er*, 554–55.

50. *Qinghua 2*: 170.

51. *Zuo*, Zhao 28.2: 1492.

52. For the invasion of Wu in 537 BCE and the capture of Prince Jueyou, see *Zuo*, Zhao 5.8: 1270–72; from the *Zuozhuan* it is clear that Wu did not submit to Chu in the aftermath of this invasion.

53. In other texts, this king is known by just one posthumous name, King Ping 楚平王 (r. 528–516 BCE).

54. Wu Yun is the famous Wu Zixu 伍子胥 (d. 484 BCE), for the evolution of whose story see David Johnson, "Epic and History in Early China: The Matter of Wu Tzu-Hsü," *Journal of Asian Studies* 40, no. 2 (1981): 255–71. There is no evidence for Wu She's another son, Ji of Wu, in any other historical source.

55. The *Chunqiu* records Wu's defeat of Chu and its allies in 519 BCE at the location named Ji's Father (or Rooster's Father? 雞父).

56. These are dramatic events of 506 BCE, when the state of Chu was on the verge of extinction; see *Zuo*, Ding 4.3: 1542–49.

57. *Qinghua 2*: 170.

58. The *Xinian* often adds possessive particle *zhi* 之 between an individual's lineage name (surname) and his personal name. This feature figures prominently also in the Warring States Period Chu extract from the *Zuozhuan*, a part of the Zhejiang University collection.

59. For Shen Baoxu's heroic mission to Qin to request assistance against Wu, see *Zuo*, Ding 4.3: 1547–49; Ding 5.5: 1551. This mission is referred to (without mentioning Shen's name) in section 19 of the *Xinian*.

60. See Ziju, "Qinghua jian *Xinian* 12–15 zhang jiexi" 清華簡《繫年》12～15 章解析, http://www.confucius2000.com/admin/list.asp?id=5413 (accessed: July 29, 2016). "Rooster" may be just a river's name (Ji 雞).

61. *Zuo*, Zhao 23.7: 1440.

62. See Johnson, "Epic and History."

63. See Wei Cide 魏慈德, "Qinghua jian *Xinian* yu *Zuozhuan* de Chu shi yitong" 《清華簡・繫年》與《左傳》中的楚史異同, *Donghua Hanxue* 東華漢學 17 (2013): 25. If the manipulation was performed in the *Zuozhuan*, then making Xia Ji into a mother rather than wife of Xia Zhengshu could have been done to stress her role as an ultimate age-defying femme fatale. I am grateful to Wai-yee Li for this observation.

64. It may worth reminding at this point that seven *Xinian* sections do not overlap with the *Zuozhuan* at all, and that even overlapping sections may propose radically different interpretation of certain events; see more in Pines, "Zhou History and Historiography," 315–21.

65. Schaberg, "Chinese History and Philosophy," 395–96.

66. This period is covered neither in the *Zuozhuan* nor in *Guoyu* (both end their narrative with the year 453 BCE); while the *Shiji* account for ca. 450–380 BCE is sketchy and fairly inaccurate. Heretofore, the only significant additional source for the second half of the fifth century BCE history was the *Zhushu jinian*, fragments of which survived in manifold early citations; in addition a few pieces of information are found in the *Mozi* 墨子 and in several bronze inscriptions, such as the Piaoqiang-*zhong* [厂+扁] 羌鐘.

67. The dates of the late fifth century BCE Chu kings are not entirely clear; according to the reconstruction proposed by Li Rui 李銳 ("You Qinghua jian *Xinian* tan Zhanguo chu Chu shi niandai de wenti" 由清華簡《繫年》談戰國初楚史年代的問題, *Shixueshi yanjiu* 史學史研究 no. 2 [2013], 100–104), King Sheng reigned between 404–401, and King Dao ascended the throne in the year 400. Yet since this reconstruction remains somewhat speculative, I do not adopt it here.

68. Yu Pass 榆關 is a strategic point halfway between the capital of Zheng and Daliang 大梁 (now Kaifeng), the would-be capital of the state of Wei 魏. The location of Wuyang is disputed, but it is likely to be located not far from Yu Pass and not far from the Song territory, perhaps in the borders of the current Henan and Shandong provinces.

69. Luoyin is located to the west of the Yellow River near its conflation with the Wei 渭 River; during the period under discussion it was the westernmost part of Jin territory.

70. According to the *Shiji* 40: 1720, King Sheng was assassinated. As is common in the *Xinian*, dramas from the domestic life of Chu are glossed over.

71. Lord of Yangcheng, just as lords of Luyang, Liang, and Pingye mentioned below were senior enfeoffed nobles of Chu, whose fiefs were located in the Huai 淮 River valley. See more about Chu enfeoffed lords in note 89 below.

72. *Shang guo* 上國, "upper parts of the country" (i.e., of Chu) refer to western areas of Chu which were upstream the rivers that flow through the country. See Du Yu's 杜預 (222–85) gloss on this term in the *Zuozhuan* (*Zuo*, Zhao 14.3: 1365).

73. Guiling is located to the north of the Yellow River, in present day Changyuan 長垣 County, Henan. That the battle was waged there means that the Chu armies invaded deeply into the Jin territory.

74. For reading the surname of a Jin commander as Fu [貝+甫], see Su Jianzhou 蘇建洲, "*Qinghua daxue cang Zhanguo zhujian (er)-Xinian* kaoshi si ze" 《清華大學藏戰國竹簡 (貳)·繫年》考釋四則, *Jianbo* 簡帛 7 (2012): 73–74.

75. Prince Ding, possibly King Sheng's son, fled Chu and contested the throne from King Dao.

76. *Qinghua 2*: 196.

77. It is not my intention here to discuss the appropriateness of European aristocratic nomenclature to the Zhou China; I apply European ranks just as a matter of heuristic convenience.

78. The annalistic source of this sentence is further buttressed by its usage of an older and more "respected" *yu* 于 particle, while elsewhere section 23 invariably uses 於. See more in You Rui 尤銳 (Yuri Pines), "Cong *Xinian* xuci de yongfa lun qi wenben de kekaoxing: jian chutan *Xinian* yuanshi ziliao de laiyuan" 從《繫年》虛詞的用法重審其文本的可靠性—兼初探《繫年》原始資料的來源, *Qinghua jian Xinian yu gushi xintan* 清華簡《繫年》與古史新談, ed. Li Shoukui 李守奎 (Shanghai: Zhongxi shuju, 2016), 224–27.

79. There is much uncertainty regarding precise dates of the rulers of Chu and Song at the turn of the fifth century (see Li Rui, "You Qinghua jian"), but it is sure that King Dao of Chu, whose posthumous name is mentioned in the last section of the *Xinian* died in 381 BCE, and this date should be later than the deaths of Duke Xiu of Song (r. ca. 403–385 BCE) and Lord Xu of Zheng (ca. 396 BCE). For the complexity of the usage of rulers' names in the annalistic sections of the *Xinian*, see You Rui (Yuri Pines), "Cong *Xinian* xuci," 227-28.

80. Mengzi mentions the *Sheng* of Jin and *Taowu* of Chu as identical with the Lu *Chunqiu*. See *Mengzi yizhu* 孟子譯注, ed. Yang Bojun 楊伯峻 (Beijing: Zhonghua shuju, [1960] 1988), "Li lou, xia" 8.21: 192. See also the Introduction to this volume.

81. Lang 朗 was identified by Dong Shan 董珊 as Liang 梁, a city in the Ru River valley, on Chu's northern frontier. See Ma Nan 馬楠, *Qinghua jian 'Xinian' jizheng* 清華簡《繫年》輯證 (Shanghai: Zhongxi shuju, 2015), 472n.4.

82. Ziyang 子陽 was the most powerful Zheng statesman of the time; his elimination by *taizai* Xin appears to be a critical step toward Zheng's weakening en route to its elimination at the hands of the state of Han in 375 BCE. For debates about Ziyang's death and its consequences, see *Qinghua er*, 903–07.

83. The location of both these fortresses is unclear; the identification proposed by the editors of *Qinghua 2* (p. 199, n. 19) does not make sense geographically, placing Lü in the westernmost part of Chu, while Changling in the Huai 淮 River valley. As Su Jianzhou correctly notices, it is highly unlikely that the Jin armies would penetrate so deeply into Chu's hinterland (*Qinghua er*, 908).

84. Lords of Pingye belonged to a collateral branch of the Chu royal lineage, enfeoffed at Pingye in southern Ru 汝 River valley. Su Jianzhou (*Qinghua er*, 908–09) identifies Lord Daowu as a son of another lord of Pingye, who was the occupant of Xincai Geling 新蔡葛陵 Tomb, excavated in 1994. For lords of Pingye, see more in Zheng Wei 鄭威, *Chuguo fengjun yanjiu* 楚國封君研究 (Wuhan: Hubei jiaoyu chubanshe 2012), 115–18.

85. The state of Teng 滕 was conquered by Yue 越 ca. 420 BCE (see *Zhushu jinian* information from the gloss to *Shiji* 41: 1747); it is not clear whether by 398 BCE it had already regained its independence, or whether Lord Shejian was a Yue governor of Teng.

86. *Qinghua 2*: 196.

87. The precise reading of 厭年 is contested; it may refer to "the next year" or "after two years." See more in *Qinghua er*, 912–16.

88. Han Qu is Marquis Lie of Han 韓烈侯 (r. 399–387 BCE), Wei Ji is Marquis Wu of Wei 魏武侯 (r. 395–370 BCE). It is not clear whether at the time of the incursion Marquis Wu had already ascended the throne or did he act on behalf of his ailing father, Marquis Wen of Wei 魏文侯 (r. 445–396 BCE). Notably, despite the official elevation of the marquises of Han and Wei to the status of regional lords (*zhuhou* 諸侯) in 403 BCE, the *Xinian* treats them here as military leaders of the unified state of Jin. This is not a consistent ideological stance, though: section 22 does recognize the "marquis" (*hou* 侯) title of Marquis Wen of Wei.

89. Possession of the *gui* 珪 tablet marked the highest degree of authority in Chu: the ducal position of an enfeoffed noble. See Chen Yingfei 陳穎飛, "Chu Daowang chuqi de da zhan yu Chu fengjun: Qinghua jian *Xinian* zhaji zhi yi" 楚悼王初期的大戰與楚封君：清華簡《繫年》札記之一, *Wenshi zhishi* 文史知識 5 (2012): 106. For the exceptional power of the group of enfeoffed nobles in Chu, see Zheng Wei, *Chuguo fengjun yanjiu*. Zhao Si 昭竢 was another important noble; probably a descendant of King Zhao of Chu 楚昭王 (r. 516–489 BCE).

90. Originally, the text's editors identified Chen in this sentence as a reference to the state of Qi, which was already ruled (de facto if not de jure) by the Chen 陳 (Tian 田) lineage (*Qinghua 2*: 200n.28). Later, this understanding was challenged: it is likely that Chen here refers to a Chu dependency, a former state of Chen 陳 which was annexed by Chu in 534 BCE, regained independence in 529, and was annexed again in 478 BCE. Little is known of its management thereafter, but it is possible that the former Chen territory, which served as a springboard of dynastic coup in 529 BCE, played a similar role in attempts of the ousted Prince Ding to regain power in Chu. See also *Qinghua er*, 923–24.

91. This sentence shifts the narrative back to the moment before Chu's defeat at Wuyang.

92. *Qinghua 2*: 196.

93. The *ganzhi* 60-days cycle was unrelated to the month counting; and in any case in every month only a half of the *ganzhi* dates could occur. Without a month, the *ganzhi* date does not provide an adequate chronological information.

94. There are only very few instances of the *ganzhi* dating in the anecdotes from the Warring States and the Han period (a section of the *Guoyu* "Jin yu 4" is the major exception); and when the *ganzhi* do appear they may be a result of a careless incorporation of earlier annalistic materials. For instance, in one of the *Han Feizi* anecdotes, an otherwise meaningless *ganzhi* date appears due to its incorporation from the *Zuozhuan* (cf. *Han Feizi jijie* 韓非子集解, annotated by Wang Xianshen 王先慎 [Beijing: Zhonghua shuju, 1998], "Nan 難 4" 39: 384 vs. *Zuo*, Huan 17.8: 150 and discussion in Pines, *Foundations*, 29–30).

95. As mentioned in note 67 above, the precise dating of the Chu kings' reign periods from the late fifth–early fourth centuries BCE is still much disputed; hence

the dating of the events depicted in *Xinian* 23 remains approximate. It is possible, albeit not much probable, that the narrative "jumped" a few years without mentioning it; in this case, the last events, viz. the Wuyang campaign, should have taken place in 394 BCE and not in 396 BCE as in my estimate. See *Xinian er*, 917–21.

96. David Schaberg, "Functionary Speech: On the Work of *shi* 使 and *shi* 史," in *Facing the Monarch: Modes of Advice in the Early Chinese Court*, ed. Garret P.S. Olberding (Cambridge, MA: Harvard University Press, 2013), 40.

97. For a similar supposition, see also Huang Xinyong 黃梓勇, "Lun Qinghua jian *Xinian* de xingzhi" 論清華簡《繫年》的性質, *Qinghua jian yanjiu* 清華簡研究 2 (2015), 248–49.

98. I analyze some of these obvious distortions and the resultant loss of argumentative power of historical anecdotes in Pines, "Speeches." For the importance of the anecdotes in ideological debates of the Warring States Period see other chapters in this volume.

99. See Yuri Pines, "Political Mythology and Dynastic Legitimacy in the *Rong Cheng shi* manuscript," *Bulletin of the School of Oriental and Asian Studies*, 73, no. 3 (2010): 503–29.

9

Cultural Memory and Excavated Anecdotes in "Documentary" Narrative
Mediating Generic Tensions in the *Baoxun* Manuscript

Rens Krijgsman[1]

The immense importance of early Chinese manuscripts to the Chinese cultural heritage is evident from their increasingly lavish publications. As Martin Kern notes, the rich publications of these monumental artifacts are monuments in their own right, and can be seen to represent a re-appropriation of the Chinese heritage by Chinese academia.[2] The publishing of books such as *Zouchu yigu shidai* 走出疑古時代 (Walking out of the Age of Doubting Antiquity) underscores that for many scholars, manuscript-texts are regarded as tools to settle issues of dating, and to correct or corroborate historical narratives from the transmitted textual record.[3]

The recently acquired manuscripts from the Warring States Period 戰國 (453–221 BCE), held at Qinghua (Tsinghua) University 清華大學 for example, are hailed as being closely related to two collections of texts in the so-called documentary (*shu* 書) genre: the *Shangshu* 尚書 (Ancient Documents) and *Yi Zhou shu* 逸周書 (Remaining Zhou Documents).[4] Both collections contain material purported to hail from the much earlier Western Zhou 西周 (ca. 1045–771 BCE) period. Some Qinghua manuscripts are claimed to represent Warring States Period editions or even lost texts (*yiwen* 佚文) from these two collections.[5]

Texts classified as belonging to the "documentary" genre (more on this below), have historically and nowadays predominantly been read as if authentically preserving the *actual* actions and words of Zhou dynastic founders such as King Wen 文王 (r. 1099/56–1050 BCE),[6] or crucial regents such as the Duke of Zhou 周公 (r. 1042–1036 BCE).[7] These figures form part of what Assmann has styled the "foundational past."[8] They represent the founding fathers of a culture, and the stories that accrue to these figures are considered important narratives that represent a set of values and commonplaces upon which a shared cultural identity is grafted. Texts that provide information about these figures are thus considered culturally important and many of them have been canonized. These texts, their protagonists, and their stories therefore represent what a society wants to remember about its past. Accordingly, to many present-day Chinese scholars, excavated texts corroborating such narratives are automatically imbued with historical truth-value for the simple reason that they date from a time that was relatively close to the situation they describe.

If narratives such as these represent what groups from the Warring States wanted to remember about their past, we ought to ask what happens in these texts of a documentary type that make many modern and ancient readers alike believe they represent the *actual* and authoritative past, rather than a mere (un-authoritative) version of it. In what sense does the documentary representation of the past differ from anecdotes?[9] Are these ways of representing the past commensurable with each other, and to what extent do they interact? Compare, for example, the following two narratives about the consolidation of Zhou rule over their Shang 商 (ca. 1500–1045 BCE) predecessors. In the first narrative, an anecdote from the *Shuoyuan* 說苑 (Garden of Illustrative Examples), the Duke of Zhou is represented as providing the most persuasive advice to King Wu 武王 (r. 1049/45–1043 BCE) on how to best deal with the remaining Shang aristocracy:

> After King Wu had conquered the Yin [Shang], he summoned the Grand Duke and asked him, "How do we now deal with their officers and people?" The Grand Duke responded, "I heard that those who love a person, they even love the crows on their roof; those who detest a person, they even hate the four walls surrounding them; kill all your enemies, so that you will have obliterated all that remains, how about that?" The King said, "Not permissible." The Grand Duke left, and Duke Shao entered. The King asked, "How would you go about it?" Duke Shao responded, "Kill those who committed crimes, spare those who did not, how about that?" The King said, "Not permissible." Duke Shao left, and the Duke of Zhou entered. The King asked, "How would

you go about it?" The Duke of Zhou answered, "Let each live in their own residence, and farm their own fields. Do not upset the old for the new; only the humane are to be endeared. If the common people make mistakes, their offence lies only in you, the one man." King Wu said, "How broadminded, it will pacify the world! As a rule, officers and gentemen are prized for their humaneness and virtue!"

武王克殷，召太公而問曰：「將奈其士眾何？」太公對曰：「臣聞愛其人者, 兼屋上之烏; 憎其人者, 惡其餘胥; 咸劉厥敵，使靡有餘, 何如？」王曰：「不可.」太公出, 邵公入. 王曰：「為之奈何？」邵公對曰：「有罪者殺之, 無罪者活之, 何如？」王曰：「不可.」邵公出, 周公入. 王曰：「為之奈何？」周公曰：「使各居其宅, 田其田, 無變舊新, 唯仁是親, 百姓有過, 在予一人！」武王曰：「廣大乎, 平天下矣. 凡所以貴士君子者, 以其仁而有德也！」[10]

In typical anecdotal form, the clichéd moral advice of the Duke of Zhou is dramatically presented as trumping the other two suggestions, followed by the King spinning it into a generally applicable maxim on the art of good rulership. The language is accessible and littered with the moralistic vocabulary of Warring States and early imperial philosophical texts. Equally characteristic, the anecdote has a clear moral message, presented as the culmination of the argument. The message itself could easily have been divorced from the anecdotal situation, but it gains in strength by being attributed to foundational figures in a crucial episode of Western Zhou history.

Compare how the problem is treated in the opening lines of the *Shangshu* chapter "Duoshi" 多士 (Numerous Officers), purporting to be a record of the actual speech presented to the officers of the Shang. The single, solemn voice of authority relayed in the speech is presented without any dispute or mention of prior debate, and could not be more different from the anecdote's presence of multiple dissenting voices in a relatively open "question and answer" tone. Possible events preceding the speech such as the episode narrated in the anecdote above are not even mentioned, and the Duke of Zhou merely relates the words of King Wu in the voice of tradition and authority:

In the third month, at the commencement [of the government] of the Duke of Zhou in the new city of Luo, he announced [the royal will] to the officers of the Shang [king], saying, "The king speaks to this effect: 'Ye numerous officers who remain from the dynasty of Yin, great ruin came down on Yin from the cessation of forbearance in compassionate Heaven, and we, the lords of Zhou, received its favoring decree. We felt charged with its bright terrors, carried out the punishments which kings inflict, rightly disposed of the appointment of Yin, and finished (the work of) the Lord on High. Now, ye numerous officers, it was not our small state that dared to aim at the appointment belonging to Yin. But Heaven was not with (Yin), for indeed it would not strengthen its misrule. It (therefore) helped us; did we dare to seek the throne of ourselves? The lord on high was not for (Yin), as appeared from the mind and conduct of our inferior people, in which there is the brilliant dreadfulness of Heaven.'"[11]

惟三月, 周公初于新邑洛, 用告商王士. 王若曰: 「爾殷遺多士, 弗弔旻天, 大降喪于殷, 我有周佑命, 將天明威, 致王罰, 敕殷命終于帝. 肆爾多士! 非我小國敢弋殷命. 惟天不畀允罔固亂, 弼我, 我其敢求位? 惟帝不畀, 惟我下民秉為, 惟天明畏.」[12]

The tone and diction are typical for documentary-type narratives, and combined with its focus on the speech event rather than a competitive and intimate environment of persuasion, it differs in considerable degree from the anecdote. This chapter analyzes the differences between these two modes of portraying the foundational past. In what ways do the anecdotal mode and the documentary mode construct the past differently? What type of arguments about the past do these constructions enable? Are these two modes of argumentation mutually commensurable?

In this chapter, I explore these questions in light of the *Baoxun* 保訓 ("Treasured Instructions") manuscript-text from the Qinghua collection, which I translate in full.[13] The *Baoxun*, so titled by its present-day editors, narrates the transmission of King Wen's deathbed instructions to his son and heir prince Fa 發, the future King Wu. It does so in a highly unusual fashion by combining on the one hand the generic form and language of the documentary mode, while on the other hand featuring two anecdotes as the text's eponymous instruction.

In this chapter, I show how the use of anecdotal and documentary narratives during the Warring States Period evince different modes of constructing the foundational past. I briefly discuss what it means for the *Baoxun* to be classified as a documentary type text and how this structures its narration of the past. This mode of narration is juxtaposed with an anecdotal mode of narration. I argue that there is a fundamental tension between these two modes of representing the past due to the different types of claims they make in constructing cultural memory, the former predicative and the latter attributive. The *Baoxun* employs several textual strategies to mediate this tension, such as the use of formulas, framing, and structuring devices. I conclude by arguing that the incorporation of two distinct modes of narrating the past should be seen in light of the changes in textual culture during the Warring States Period.

The *Baoxun* and Its Modern Classification

The *Baoxun* has commonly been understood as a documentary-type text. In the publications accompanying the initial transcription, Li Xueqin describes the Qinghua strips as being closely related to the documentary texts from the *Shangshu* and *Yi Zhou shu*, pointing for instance to the *Baoxun*'s similarity to the "Guming" 顧命 (Testimonial Charge) chapter in the *Shangshu*.[14] The transcription and reconstruction by Li Shoukui likewise takes other documentary texts as its main point of comparison and primary reference for difficult readings, but he does not explicitly posit a connection.[15] The anecdotes within the text are referred to as historical legends (*lishi chuanshuo* 歷史傳說).[16] Accordingly, although some hesitation in defining the exact nature of the *Baoxun* is evident, the text is read as if it were a Document containing anecdotes.

In a recent article Sarah Allan also refers to the *Baoxun* as a "previously unknown *shu*," but she goes further and asks what this identification might mean.[17] In a nutshell, Allan argues that Documents can be described "as a form of literary composition, rather than as chapters of known historical compilations." Texts in this form, she continues: "were—or pretended to be—contemporaneous records" and "they include formal speeches by model kings and ministers from ancient times (Western Zhou or earlier)," and they are marked by a distinct vocabulary and use of formulaic phrases, for example "the king thus said" (*wang ruo yue* 王若曰).[18] I suggest we extend the last criterion to include other expressions similar to the language used in bronze inscriptions and note that Documents primarily deal with events of foundational importance in early historiography.[19] One of the merits of conceiving of Documents as a literary form is that it underscores that it is not important whether these Documents actually relate the words of the former kings and ministers verbatim, but rather that they *present* themselves as doing so. In Allan's words: "An important aspect of this literary form—a contemporaneous record of direct speech—is that the form itself demands an acceptance of historical authenticity: this is not a historical record or an interpretation. There is no intermediary: it is what kings and ministers actually said."[20]

Admittedly, both documentary narrative and anecdotal narrative relate a story about the past, but how are they different? While intuitively this difference seems fairly evident, it bears merit to analyze explicitly what this difference between types of text and argument means. Moreover, it is a question whether or not a documentary text can indeed make free use of different types of argument. To my understanding, this is a problem not clearly identified in the current discussion on Documents, or in definitions of anecdotes. At the basis of this problematic lies a simple observation. While anecdotes are freely used in certain types of philosophical and historical arguments, they would appear out of place in many of the texts later considered canonical, such as the *yi* 易 (Changes), *shi* 詩 (Odes), and as I will show, the *shu* 書 (Documents).[21] This incompatibility becomes apparent when we analyze the different modes of narration that characterize anecdotes and Documents.

Although both documentary and anecdotal narrative deal with the past, they do so in fundamentally different ways. As Allan's definition makes clear, Documents purport to present the words of former kings and ministers as they were actually said. Martin Kern has analyzed this language in light of their ritual context. He argues that, just as the official rituals during the Western Zhou meant to actualize and perpetuate a sense of ritual continuity and cultural stability, its language is likewise marked by a measure of redundancy and repetition, and by a focus on continuity. This ritualistic continuity in the language of the Documents, that ostensibly reflects the long past, is used to create, perpetuate, and instill narratives of cultural memory among its participants.[22] This way of dealing with cultural memory can be called a language of "remembrance and preservation." As in the example from the "Duoshi" chapter above, it is a language of implicit cultural authority that presents itself as unchanged and untainted by later developments. Epithetic descriptions of the ancients could, therefore be said to be presented as *predicative*, that is to say: "this is how the Duke of Zhou *actually was*."

Anecdotes similarly relate information about what is considered culturally significant (that is, the foundational past), but they do so in a fundamentally different mode. Instead of remembering and preserving, they explicitly "recollect and reflect" on the past. The language is *attributive*, and it adduces desirable qualities and actions to the already established predicates of these foundational characters, that is to say "this is *an example illustrating* how the Duke of Zhou was." In the above example, the anecdote attributes eloquence, moral superiority, and trustworthiness to the Duke of Zhou, but to do so, it employs a set of moral commonplaces in a clichéd representation of idealized debate. Thus, whereas Document-type texts through various literary techniques attempt to convey historical immediacy and actuality, anecdotal narrative as a form of argument relates general lessons *abstracted* from historical *commonplaces* that could reasonably be related to existing foundational narratives.

One of the consequences of this, as Schaberg notes, is the adaptable and retellable quality that characterizes early anecdotes.[23] Similarly, Sarah A. Queen emphasizes the "pithy, punchy illustration of some abstract principle [. . .] or some quality of a significant cultural icon," that is common to many anecdotes.[24] These aspects, and their general brevity, are what make anecdotes so memorable and enjoyable. However, these aspects also imbue the anecdote with a sense of distance and abstraction from the events they purport to present, and their often quite witty narrative turns make them less appropriate for inclusion in royal speeches. Often, this anecdotal mode of narration is marked by awareness, at least in texts dated to the late Warring States and early empires, of its malleable and attributive nature.[25] One of the consequences of the differences between the anecdotal and documentary modes of relating the past is therefore that the use of anecdotal narrative in Document-type texts is extremely rare, to say the least.[26]

In other words, the generic conventions of documentary texts seem to preclude the occurrence of anecdotes. When an anecdote does occur in such a text, it generates a fundamental tension between genre and argument, and between different modes of narrating the past. As I show below, the *Baoxun* employs a number of strategies to mediate this tension. It seems that the *Baoxun* tries to take advantage of both anecdotal argument and documentary genre qualities.

The Baoxun

The manuscript features eleven bamboo strips measuring 28.5 cm in length. They were originally bound by two threads and contain twenty-two to twenty-four graphs each. The other strips in the Qinghua collection measure roughly 44.4 to 45 cm and were bound with three threads. Li Xueqin writes that, due to the different physical characteristics of the *Baoxun* manuscript, the editors decided to organize, transcribe, and publish it first.[27] By and large the manuscript is well preserved. Only the top half of the second strip is broken off, and accordingly eleven to thirteen graphs are missing. The strips are written from the very top, and at the end of each strip a space with the size of roughly one graph is left blank. Other than the usual repetition marks, the manuscript does not come with any punctuation and its ending is marked by leaving the remainder of the last bamboo strip blank. The manuscript is written in a uniform calligraphy likely from a single hand, the style of which is markedly different from the other texts in the collection.[28] On the basis of the physical characteristics, it is uncertain whether the manuscript was bound before or after writing.[29] What is clear is that, unlike some other texts in the Qinghua collection, such as the *Jinteng* 金滕 (Metal Bound Coffer), the back of the strips are not numbered. The manuscript did not come with a title or other identifying features, and was named *Baoxun*, or "Treasured Instructions," by the modern editors.[30]

Because the bamboo strips were bought on the Hong Kong antique market, their provenance is unclear and their authenticity can be tested on material grounds alone. The preliminary report published in the journal *Wenwu* 文物 (Cultural Relics) describes this threefold testing. After review by outside experts from competing institutions,[31] paleographic analysis of the script was carried out pointing to the mid-late Warring States Period.[32] This analysis was corroborated by researchers from Peking University 北京大學 who carried out a calibrated C14 dating of samples of un-inscribed, broken bamboo strips which established a date of 305 BCE plus or minus thirty years.[33] These reports are not published, and no analysis of the ink has been made. Nevertheless, the general consensus is that the bamboo strips and their writing are authentic products of the late Warring States.

The text of the *Baoxun* can roughly be divided into three parts: it opens with a historical frame, followed by the primary narrative which in turn functions as narrative frame for the two anecdotes. These parts can be further subdivided as follows: the primary narrative is split into an opening and a concluding formula, and the sub-anecdotes are likewise composed in the structure of opening frame–body–conclusion. As such, the structure on the micro-level of the anecdotes mimics the macro-level of the text.

The Frame

A frame is a device that circumscribes the reading of a narrative. It limits the possible readings of a narrative, both temporally and spatially, and provides a recipient with background information against which the narrative develops. The frame of the *Baoxun* contains a number of opening formulas commonly seen in documentary narrative and bronze inscriptions, introducing a temporal setting, the main characters, and the general backdrop of the events:

> It was in the fiftieth year of our king, that he was not well. Our king thought about the many years that had passed, and feared that the "Treasured Instructions" would be lost. On day *wuzi*, our king washed his face. On day *jichou*, at the break of day [. . .]
>
> 1: 惟王五十年, 不豫, 王念日之多歷, 恐墜保³⁴訓. 戊子, 自 靧水. 己丑, 昧
>
> 2: [爽]☐☐☐☐☐☐☐☐☐³⁵

The frame introduces a narrative set during the fiftieth year of the king; the exceptionally long span of the reign allowing a recipient to conjecture that the monarch in question must be King Wen. The king is described as feeling not well (*bu yu* 不豫), generic terms also seen in the *Jinteng* manuscript and in the "Guming" chapter of the *Shangshu*, and it is implied that he is about to die. As a result, the recipient is cued to expect a narrative detailing the upcoming succession. By further specifying the king's fear of losing the "Treasured Instructions," later identified as a text crucial to the succession, the main theme of the story is introduced rather dramatically.

The opening frame is presented in a voice with some distance from the events in the narrative. It is presented from the perspective of the omniscient narrator, aware of everything from washing rituals to how the king feels. The information is presented in a formal, succinct manner, reminiscent of bronze inscriptions and terse court chronicles in the use of its temporal structuring devices following the ritual calendar day by day. If a voice is present, it is the voice of the official court scribe, who objectively narrates events of dynastic importance.³⁶ Other details, such as the washing of the face and the formula break of day (*meishuang* 昧爽) are commonly seen in the *Documents*, and bronzes, respectively.³⁷

These details in the frame lend the narrative a sense of immediacy and authenticity, and elliptically introduce King Wen as the main (type-) character. Accordingly, the opening frame supplies the context to interpret the text. It also places the narrative within the genre of Documents, which provides a hermeneutic context structuring the reception of the text.

Genre

The frame is characterized by a high level of intertextuality germane to the very definition of formulaic phrasing. It therefore presents a set of links to narratives of remembrance and preservation seen in other documentary texts and bronze inscriptions. These intertextual links connect the *Baoxun* to the interpretative framework that structures the reading of documentary narratives and this has several profound consequences for the reception of the text.

First, generic identification creates reception expectations.³⁸ It suggests to a recipient that similar generically coded stock phrases and formulas such as "our king thus said" (*wang ruo yue* 王若曰), are bound to occur in the text, and that these are also to be understood along the lines of generic convention. As such, the patterns of emergence for certain types of language and its rules of interpretation become predictable and understandable. The language used in the text is archaic, formulaic, and ritualistic. It is intimately related to the institutions responsible for the remembrance and preservation of cultural values, such as the temple, the court, and its scribes. Its language is structured by a different set of rules and should be interpreted along different lines than colloquial statements, or anecdotes for instance.³⁹

Second, a text signified as a Document allows the recipient to deduce some characteristics of the narrative. For example, that a foundational event such as a succession, a royal declaration, or the aftermath of an important victory is about to be discussed; that a royal scion will likely be presenting a speech, expounding an important cultural narrative; and that the development of the plot will be structured along lines familiar to its audience because it will share characteristics with similar narratives. The rite of succession, for example, is a familiar trope within Document texts, and it generally consists of a set number of events such as a set of important lessons for the heir. This set narrative structure is one of the assumptions triggered in a recipient when confronted with the generic formulas opening the *Baoxun*, and thus also helps fill in the blanks that are left in the narrative. In other words, generic expectations to a large extent inform the way a text is read, and structure the meanings that are culled from its content.

Third, the authority and historicity of the text is foregrounded by virtue of it being intertextually linked to other narratives that are deemed to be authoritative and foundational. This means that the text wants to be considered an authentic contemporaneous statement on events, and is therefore deemed worthy of remembrance and perpetuation. In other words, its language purports to relate predicative, stereotypical images that structure the cultural memory of the royal Zhou court, its kings, and its main events. These stereotypical statements serve as mnemonic pegs upon which a whole range of narratives, including anecdotes, can be grafted. It gains its authority by virtue of presenting itself as a primary, contemporary, and generically sanctioned statement. Any later statement in the stream of tradition cannot replace its predicates, unless it is similarly presented as a Document. It can merely elaborate by attributing other events and characteristics to these established foundations.

In sum, the *Baoxun* can be understood as presenting itself as a Document. It wants to be perceived as if it remembers and authentically relates the rock bed of cultural unity and the dominant frame of ritual discourse. It places the text in an intimate relation to the foundational period of wise kings and advisors known through tradition, and it purports to present a true, verbatim record of their discourse. However, the generic presentation of a text such as the *Baoxun* does not just provide a set of positive identifications structuring its reception. If, as I argue, the documentary and anecdotal mode are fundamentally different ways of narrating the past, the anecdotal is unlikely to occur in a documentary narrative. If it does occur, there is a tension that needs to be ironed out in order to remain an authoritative statement.[40] In what follows I describe how the text attempts to mediate the tension between purporting to be a Document and its inclusion of anecdotal narrative.

The Primary Narrative

The following segment introduces the narrative proper and provides a rationale for some of the irregularities in the *Baoxun*. The layout of the text and translation mimic the textual structure:

Our king thus said, "Fa, Our condition quickly deteriorates, and We fear We shall not have time to instruct you.

In times of yore, when the early kings passed on the "Treasured" [Instructions], these were to be received through recitation. However, because Our condition is truly severe, We fear that we will not be able to intone it to the end. You will receive it in writing [instead].

Revere it! Do not defile it!

2: . . . [王]若曰: "發, 朕疾漸[41]甚, 恐不汝及3: 訓.
昔前人傳保, 必受之以誦[42]. 今朕疾允病, 恐弗唸[43] 終, 汝以書4: 受之.
欽哉! 勿淫!

The mode of narration shifts from abstract documentation to direct speech of the king, as if witnessed by someone present on site. The king is presented as talking to his son and heir Fa, the future King Wu, who does not talk back but is a straw man for the argument. The impending death of the king and the fear of losing his instructions are raised twice more, not in the impersonal narration of the scribe but as a father-king talking to his son-heir. What follows is a highly self-reflexive statement on the practice of transmission.

The passage relates that, traditionally, the "Treasured Instructions" were transmitted through oral, and likely guided, recitation. Whether or not an actual written document was present as a basis for recitation is unclear, but the implied length required to complete the process of recitation suggests that in the transmission of the "Instructions" more than just a physical object was being relayed. Possibly, a particular reading mode, ways of pronunciation and pause, and extratextual information and explanation were included, and it is likely that the aim of transmission was correct memorization of the text and these features.[44]

However, due to his illness, the king fears he is not able to recite the passage in full and therefore breaches tradition and has the instructions passed on in writing without any further mediation. This passage is significant because it attempts to provide a pretext for irregularities in the occurrence and final form of the narrative. One such difference could be its inclusion of anecdotes. On the other hand, by repeatedly stressing the king's illness, it provides a rationale for the text's appearance in writing. This is important because it signals that, apparently, the author(s) of the text saw the need to justify its appearance within the stream of tradition, indicating that the *Baoxun*, despite the ancient pedigree it claims, was likely a newcomer to the Document-type texts in circulation during the Warring States.[45]

In a sense, a statement like this can be compared to the function of the short introductory formulas in the *Shangshu*. Its texts are preceded by a short statement (*xu* 序) describing their purported origins.[46] The *Shangshu* version of the *Jinteng* for instance, is preceded by the short line: "King Wu had an illness, the Duke of Zhou composed the *Jinteng*" 武王有疾, 周公作《金滕》.[47] Note that the *Jinteng* similarly uses illness as a pretext for the irregular appearance of a written document.[48] These headings provide a narrative describing the origination of the written text and its link to a certain author. In a sense, it presents a rather apologetic introduction of a text. This is necessary in the *Baoxun* for two reasons. As argued, the text needed to be rationalized as an authentic member of documentary texts. Moreover, any irregularities within the text such as its inclusion of anecdotes are likewise validated by its presentation as a written account from the time of King Wen that has only now resurfaced. The text premeditatedly responds to any doubts about its origination.

Anecdotes

Whereas Document-type texts employ the language of cultural memory to underscore cultural unity and stability, and claim to faithfully preserve the foundational past, anecdotes use these resources as an agent for change. They attribute new information to existing characters and narratives. Accordingly, anecdotes are ideally suited to introduce novel philosophical ideas, and can be adapted to serve numerous ends and philosophical agendas.[49] As a result, the occurrence of anecdotes within a textual genre purporting to represent continuity is rather out of place. While anecdotes reflect on the past, and thus attribute new, contemporaneous, elements to existing narratives, Documents present themselves as attempting to remember the past as it *was*. They purport to be the very resource to which anecdotes harken back. This is not to say that genres such as the Documents write a more objective history, rather, it is a fundamental difference in modes of *representing* the past, and of the time frame in which these modes operate. A documentary type of narrative operates in foundational time itself and its characters are purportedly present *at* the time of the events of the narrative. The events that frame the narrative are markers presented from a contemporaneous, and thus narrative-internal perspective rather than one step removed in time. Anecdotes can only *re*-present and reflect on foundational time. Commonly they do so through a narrative mode commenting on *back when* the events occurred and often explicitly marked temporally with formulas such as *xi* 昔 (in times of yore) or X *zhi shi* X 之時 (at the time of X).⁵⁰ In the case of the *Baoxun*, by having foundational figures reflect on even earlier foundational figures, it attempts to wed the mode of reflection to that of remembrance. To mediate this problem, the *Baoxun* uses the following structuring devices.

The anecdotes are structured in a similar way as the narrative at large. They open with a frame, specifying time, protagonist, and a location. The phrasing of this frame is similar to the primary narrative, thus structurally linking the two together. The body of the anecdote consists of a philosophical "payload" that centers around the unspecified but instrumental concept of *zhong* 中 (middle, center) which can be read as an object, type of behavior, or a form of knowledge that, once obtained by the protagonist, ensures successful rule.⁵¹ The anecdotes are closed by a formula specifying how diligent behavior has favorable consequences (obtaining the mandate) and an exhortation to respect its message. This formula likewise concludes the primary narrative. The use of similar opening and closing formulas establishes a unity of presentation and thus mediates possible discrepancies between narrative forms. The shared elements are underscored below:

> In times of yore, Shun was for a long time in the position of a petty man, he personally plowed (the slopes of) Mount Li and the uncultivated plains, and reverently sought *zhong*.
>
> He examined his own intent, and did not abandon the needs of the myriad people. He implemented this from the highest to the lowest, and from the nearest to the farthest. Thereupon, he ordered the entitlements and arranged the records, gave measure to the things of Yin and Yang, all followed and none opposed. Shun accordingly attained *zhong*: when speaking, he did not alter substance nor change name.
>
> In his person, he was faithful in following it, and reverent without laxity, and used it to make the 'Three descended virtues.'⁵² Emperor Yao lauded it, and therefore bestowed his charge on him.
>
> Oh! Revere it!

Cultural Memory and Excavated Anecdotes

4: . . . <u>昔舜久</u>⁵³<u>作小人，親耕于鬲茅</u>⁵⁴，恭求中.

自稽厥志, 5: 不違于庶萬姓之多欲, 厥有施于上下遠邇. 乃易位設稽, 測6:陰陽之物, 咸順不逆. 舜既得中, 言不易實變名.

<u>身茲服</u>⁵⁵<u>惟</u>7: 允, 翼翼不懈, 用作三降之德. 帝堯 嘉之, 用授厥緒.

嗚呼! 祇之8: 哉!

<u>In times of yore, (Shangjia) Wei appropriated *zhong* from He (Bo)</u>,⁵⁶ in order to get back at You Yi. You Yi met his punishment. Wei was unharmed and compensated *zhong* to He (Bo). Wei remembered it and did not forget, and handed it down to his sons and grandsons up to Cheng Tang.

<u>Reverently following it without laxity he thus received the Great Mandate.</u>

Oh Fa! Respect it!

8: . . . <u>昔微假中于河</u>, 以復有易, 有易服厥罪. 微無害, 乃追⁵⁷中于河. 9: 微志弗忘, 傳貽子孫, 至于成湯.

<u>祇服不懈, 用受大命.</u>

嗚呼! 發, 敬哉!

Both the anecdotes and the primary narrative open with a reference to historical lore using the language of recollection, such as: "In times of yore (when) the ancients . . ." 昔前人. As a result, a shared time formula is introduced: the unspecified past. This places the two distinct modes of dealing with the past on the same temporal plane and mediates the discrepancies between modes of narration. As such, the Document is brought in a mode of reflection while at the same time the vague reference to "the ancients" and the specific references to the foundational figures Shun and Shangjia Wei indicate that this temporal plane reflected upon is located in the foundational period. Because these figures are associated with a limited number of stereotypes, including typical behavior and moral character, they transform into type characters similar to generic markers in that they structure the expectations and cultural baggage that recipients bring to the anecdote.

Sarah Allan has previously analyzed the structural patterns that exist in the representation of many of these type characters. In Allan's analysis, Shun stands for the virtuous commoner who succeeded Yao on account of merit. Such a figure is thus ideally suited for a narrative on succession.[58] Indeed, his virtuous methods are described in the anecdote as the reason why Yao bestowed his charge on him. Shangjia Wei on the other hand conforms to the pattern observed by Allan signifying hereditary transfer of rule.[59] Although much less commonly seen in anecdotes, his figure is described as revenging the king of Yin, his (licentious) uncle, after which he himself becomes the ruler of Yin.[60] In this version of the anecdote, Shangjia Wei's revenge on Youyi is presented as justified because his uncle's debauchery is not mentioned, and because Wei's actions eventually lead to Yin's obtainment of the heavenly mandate.[61]

Accordingly, two different types of government are personified. Shun portrays the ideal of virtuous, civilized rule (*wen* 文), and Wei represents martial prowess (*wu* 武). Both are linked to obtaining "the middle" through which they secure the mandate. Possibly, the concept *zhong* bears on finding the middle ground between these two different aspects of rule. What is clear, though, is that while the concept is foregrounded as instrumental to the philosophical import of the two anecdotes, it is largely undefined. As a result, the politico-philosophical import of the anecdotes could have been steered in any number of directions by its proponent(s) and thus applied to a number of situations. Where the representation and significance of Shun and Shangjia Wei as type characters is based in the cultural memory of the Warring States at large, the specific import of these individual anecdotes needed a localized form of extratextual explanation and interpretation by a teacher or textual community. The local proponent(s) of this text thus interacted with a widely shared body of cultural memory as a frame of reference and a means to slot in new ideas, while simultaneously underdefining these new ideas. This underscores that the generic function of the *Baoxun* as a Document-type text merely provided the legitimating pretext and the structuring narrative of the argument while the interpretive power over its lessons remained to the respective proponent(s) of the text.

The closing formulas that follow reaffirm the legitimacy of the text and are comprised of varieties of: *zhifu bu xie, yong shou da ming* 祇服不懈, 用受大命 (to reverently follow without laxity, and accordingly obtain the Great Mandate). These are followed by a final exhortation demanding Prince Fa (and thus also the reader) *qin zai! wu yin* 欽哉! 勿淫 (to respect and not corrupt) the text's message, on bamboo strip 4 for example. Both formulas are repeated at the end of each anecdote, and the opening and the closing parts of the primary narrative:

We have not known this for long, the Mandate [of the Shang?] does not have much longer. Now if you reverently comply and are not lax, you will have your accomplishment. We will not see you personally receive the great mandate.

Respect it! Do not defile it!

Our days are numbered, and our nights do not last forever.

10: 朕聞茲不久, 命未有所延.
今汝祇服毋懈, 其有所修⁶²矣.
不11: 及爾身受大命. 敬哉! 毋淫! 日不足, 惟宿不羕."⁶³

The repetition of these structural devices establishes a patterned continuity, and accordingly mediates the occurrence of anecdotes within the documentary narrative of this particular text. As a result, the differences in the two modes of representing cultural memory are neutralized. A second, related element lies in the type of language of these recurring elements. Repeatedly the prince—and therefore, the recipient of the text who is placed in the same receptive position—is exhorted to respect and faithfully uphold the message in the different parts of the text. These elements of direct speech again bring the anecdote on the same time plane as the documentary narrative and likewise employ the diction associated with the perpetuation of tradition into the future. I would argue that the closing formulas ("respect and do not corrupt!" and "reverently follow without laxity in order to receive the great mandate"), shared by the primary narrative and the two anecdotes alike, similarly function to impress the necessity for upholding cultural continuity on account of the recipient. The formulas demand of the recipients, who are placed in the same passively receptive role as Prince Fa, to remain faithful to the text's content and not to change it. The assumption of this narrative is that the message is eternally valid and should be upheld in order to preserve cultural continuity. As a result, even though this text is presented in irregular fashion, these formulas attempt to stress that it is nonetheless a valid Document-type text, and that its inclusion of anecdotes should be regarded as a regular occurrence. In other words, the extensive repetition of these mediating formulas bespeaks an awareness of its irregularity.

Discussion and Conclusion

In this chapter I explored a fundamental tension between anecdotes and documentary narrative. I argued that this tension is predicated upon two different modes of dealing with cultural memory. Documents, like Odes and certain ritual texts, construct the past as a unified entity, whose lessons should be remembered and perpetuated. The past is presented in predicative terms: "this is how it was (and should still be)." Anecdotes treat the past as a resource with which philosophical arguments are articulated and substantiated. Their mode of narration is one of reflection, in which new elements can be added to existing foundational resources. The *Baoxun*, in its language, its formulaic expressions, and its narrative structure, purports to be a Document. It wants to be perceived as the actual instructions given by King Wen on his deathbed. These instructions are two fairly common anecdotes that have been adapted so that both Shun and Shangjia Wei are presented as having obtained something called *zhong*, which allowed them to receive the mandate. As a result, the *Baoxun* becomes a text that attempts to wed the use of anecdotes as carriers of novel ideas to a generic narrative structure purporting to present the pristine, unchanged past. This wedding of narratives represents changes in the conceptualization of textuality and cultural memory during the Warring States.

Assmann's theory of cultural memory proposes two distinct stages in dealing with the past as a means to create cultural identity and an interpretive framework for dealing with the present. The first is one of ritual continuity. In this stage, or rather mode,[64] identity is constructed through shared participation in ritualistic structures. Its language is that of continuity and preservation. In it, the same tropes and figures are recycled to meet daily needs of interpretation, but the basic structure of these figures remains the same.[65] Assmann connects this mode of identity formation with predominantly oral modes of discourse that revolve around easily memorable and oft repeated type figures and events. The second stage is that of textual continuity. The foundational narratives structuring the stage of ritual continuity have gradually gained fixed, canonical form, and the main mode of discourse is centered on interpreting these fixed artifacts through the use of commentary and exegesis. Change in society is grafted upon existing narratives in ways more lasting in that they are put in writing. Instead of ritual experts, like the court scribe mentioned above, the task of interpreting culture and the past is relegated to textual scholars that study the canon. Tradition is no longer a living entity but fixed and needs to be commented upon to suit contemporaneous needs.[66]

Indeed, many Chinese foundational texts were gradually dislodged from their ritual, performative contexts, and were finally canonized during the early empires.⁶⁷ Roughly around the Eastern Han 東漢 (25–220 CE), this period of canonization and the transition toward textual continuity and exegesis was well in place. This development saw the rise of extensive commentary, categorization and editing of classical texts, and hailed a fundamentally different perception of textuality and writing.⁶⁸ It can be argued that the late Warring States to Western Han 西漢 (202 BCE-9 CE) periods straddle these developments. While textual culture had not become fixed, new modes of reflecting on the past began to emerge. Commentarial frameworks on the *Odes* and the *Changes* started to appear, evident from texts such as the *Kongzi shilun* 孔子詩論 (Confucius's Discussion of the Odes) and the commentaries attached to the *Changes* in the Shanghai collections.⁶⁹ Similarly, a proliferation of argumentative texts creatively dealing with narratives of the past appeared, becoming increasingly separable from their ritual or lineage interpretative context.⁷⁰ However, many texts had not yet received their final, canonized form nor were they fixed in interpretive traditions.

In this transitional period, styled the transition from a manuscript culture to a text culture by Meyer, many different text types started to emerge and different forms of argument and dealing with the past proliferated.⁷¹ One of the most popular forms was the anecdote.⁷² Another development is the increasing stabilization in writing of foundational texts such as the Documents. This is not to say that these narratives were not in place earlier, and could not have been textualized at earlier stages. It rather means that the Warring States Period saw an unprecedented increase in the textualization of a variety of narratives serving different ends. I argue that the emergence of a text such as the *Baoxun* should be seen in light of these new developments in textuality, and emergent modes of dealing with the past. The observation that the *Baoxun* in its textual representation attempts to pass for a Document-type narrative illustrates that the formal characteristics associated with the literary genre of Document were settling in place, or at least emergent. In other words, the emulation of the dominant form of a genre argues for the prevalence, and accordingly, recognizability of the genre.⁷³ While texts in this form by all accounts were available centuries earlier than the late Warring States, it is in this period that we have the first evidence for the practice of quotation, reference, and emulation of the texts and forms associated with the genre.⁷⁴ The practice of identifying something as a Document, be that explicit or implicit,⁷⁵ testifies to the emergence of the wider spread and more general understanding of its characteristics. In short, it testifies to an emerging genre consciousness in understanding the genre as a category of *reception* rather than just a tradition of literary or ritual *production*.

The text of the *Baoxun*, conceived as an argument, thus attempts to tap into two widespread and popular strategies of argument construction. The rhetorical efficacy of anecdotes in presenting new ideas in light of established figures is amplified by their incorporation in a text that eschews the patina of cultural continuity. The foundational and symbolical authority of figures like Shun and Shangjia Wei is thus strengthened by presenting the anecdotes as if even King Wen made use of them in his instructions. The message presented by the *Baoxun* is thus that its anecdotes, unlike the result of creative argument construction of the Warring States they appear to be, are in fact to be seen as an age old and patented mode of presenting philosophical ideas. Any discrepancies in mode of representation this might entail are brushed under the carpet by the careful patterning of the argument in the *Baoxun*. At every possible turn, the *Baoxun* carefully frames the anecdotes in structures that are emphatic in their rhetoric of ritual continuity. The documentary nature of the argument, if you will, is underscored time and again, and in no way are the anecdotes passed off as creative instances of "counter-history."[76] Rather, by couching the novelty of the anecdotes in the rhetoric of continuity, their message is labeled with the stamp of ancient approval in much the same way as ascribing a maxim to Confucius 孔子, or framing a generic anecdote with the judgment of Laozi 老子 (Old Master) or the *Odes* works to establish its truth-value.[77] The last example is especially telling, as it similarly weds the use of anecdotes to the language of preservation and remembrance of foundational texts.

That the *Baoxun* is at least modestly successful in its attempt can be discerned from present-day comments, some of which exhibit the belief that with this text, we finally have *the* instructions that King Wen passed on to his son.[78] Interestingly, other Document-type texts—such as the "Wuyi" 無逸 (Against Luxurious Ease) from the *Shangshu*—likewise attempt to combine different forms of argumentation, including anecdotes, which shows that this kind of argument construction might have gained some currency during this period. Lastly, the *Baoxun* is a case in point for the recognition of the rhetorical power of anecdotes. By all (arguably later) accounts on the hierarchy of genres, the prestige of Documents was far greater than that of assorted sayings and anecdotes.[79] The fact that anecdotes were nonetheless incorporated in a text purporting to be a Document serves as testimony to their growing importance in the Warring States Period.

Notes

1. This chapter was first presented as a paper at the Anecdotes Workshop in Leiden (2013). I want to thank the conference organizer and participants, especially the discussant of my paper, Newell Ann Van Auken, for creating an atmosphere of constructive dialogue. In addition I would like to thank Dirk Meyer, Laurence Mann, Ulrich Schmiedel, Yegor Grebnyev, Barend ter Haar, and Peter Ditmanson for their critical readings and helpful suggestions during the preparation of this article. Moreover, Joachim Gentz, Jörn Grundmann, and other participants of a stimulating reading group in Edinburgh gave valuable feedback for rewriting portions of this article. Finally, I want to thank the volume's editors, Paul van Els and Sarah A. Queen, and the anonymous reviewers for their helpful comments and suggestions.

2. Martin Kern, "The 'Jinteng' Chapter of the Shangshu and its Newly Discovered Manuscript Version from ca. 300 BCE: Comparison and Methodological Considerations" (paper presented at the Workshop for Manuscript and Text Culture, The Queen's College, Oxford, January 30, 2013). Kern notes that the unwieldy and antiquarian quality of the publications should be interpreted as characteristic of this monumentality.

3. Li Xueqin 李學勤, *Zouchu yigu shidai* 走出疑古時代 (Jilin: Changchun Chubanshe 2007). This book has triggered an extensive debate on the authenticity of early source material within China, see Paul Fischer, "Authentication Studies (辨偽學) Methodology and the Polymorphous Text Paradigm," *Early China* 32 (2008–2009): 35.

4. Unless otherwise noted, all dates of source materials and historical periods are BCE. I use "Document" or "Documents" to refer to a genre of historiographical narratives in the documentary mode, and *Documents*, in italics, to the canonized collection of narratives of this type, the *Shangshu* 尚書 (Ancient Documents) and the later, sometimes considered apocryphal collection, *Yi Zhou shu* 逸周書 (Remaining Zhou Documents).

5. See for example Li Xueqin 李學勤, "Qinghua jian jiupian zongshu" 清華簡九篇綜述, *Wenwu* 文物 no. 5 (2010).

6. Dates for the Western Zhou are necessarily tentative; I follow Edward Shaughnessy, *Sources of Western Zhou History: Inscribed Bronze Vessels* (Berkeley, Los Angeles: University of California Press, 1991), xix.

7. See for example Li Xueqin, "Qinghua jian zongshu."

8. Jan Assmann, *Cultural Memory and Early Civilization: Writing, Remembrance, and Political Imagination* (Cambridge: Cambridge University Press, 2011), 38.

9. For a discussion of the term "anecdote," see below.

10. Lu Yuanjun 盧元駿, comm. and trans., *Shuoyuan jinzhu jinyi* 說苑今注今譯 (Taibei: Shangwu yinshuguan, 1979), 133–34.

11. Translation adapted from James Legge, *The Sacred Books of the East. Volume III. The Sacred Books of China. The Texts of Confucianism. Part 1. Shu King, Shih King, Hsiao King* (Oxford, Clarendon Press, 1879), 454–55.

12. Sun Xingyan 孫星衍, *Shangshu jinguwen zhushu* 尚書今古文註疏 (Beijing: Zhonghua shuju, 2004), 423–25.

13. Li Xueqin 李學勤, ed., *Qinghua daxue cang Zhanguo zhujian (1)* 清華大學藏戰國竹簡 (壹) (Shanghai: Zhongxi shuju, 2010), life-size pictures pp. 8–9, close-up pictures pp. 55–62, transcription and notes pp. 142–48.

14. Li Xueqin 李學勤, "Lun Qinghua jian Baoxun de jige wenti" 論清華簡保訓的幾個問題, *Wenwu* 文物 no. 6 (2009): 76; and Li Xueqin, "Qinghua jian zongshu," 53. See also Li Xueqin, ed., *Qinghua zhujian*, 1.

15. Li Xueqin, ed., *Qinghua zhujian*, 143–48.

16. Li Xueqin, "Baoxun," 77.

17. Sarah Allan, "On *Shu* (Documents) and the Origin of the *Shangshu* (Ancient Documents) in Light of Recently Discovered Bamboo Slip Manuscripts," *Bulletin of the School of Oriental and African Studies* 75, no. 3 (2012): 548n.1.

18. Allan, "On *Shu*," 552.

19. Of course, the question of genre is complex and requires more treatment than feasible within this chapter. The close relation between the *Shangshu*, *Yi Zhou shu* and bronze inscriptions has long been asserted. Bronze language is seen as setting the standards (both generically and philologically) against which narratives in the documentary mode are evaluated, see for example Jiang Shanguo 蔣善國, *Shangshu zongshu* 尚書綜述 (Shanghai: Shanghai guji chubanshe, 1988), and Chen Mengjia 陳夢家, *Shangshu tonglun* 尚書通論 (Beijing: Zhonghua shuju, 1985).

20. Allan, "On *Shu*," 556.

21. Note that this does not apply to their commentaries, compare for instance the anecdotes in the *Hanshi waizhuan* 韓詩外傳 (Han's Supplementary Commentary to the Odes), the three commentaries to the *Chunqiu* 春秋 (Spring and Autumn Annals), or the *Xicizhuan* 繫辭傳 (Appended Sayings). This is because, as I argue below, commentaries flesh out existing foundational frameworks and thus reflect on their respective traditions. Accordingly, while I agree with Pines's insightful contribution to this volume on the widespread occurrence and application of anecdotes in early historiography, I think their occurrence in texts that by the Warring States and early Han periods were perceived as culturally authoritative (or even proto-canonical) such as the *shi*, *shu*, and *yi* (as evinced, for instance, from quotation practices) is extremely limited and uncommon.

22. Martin Kern, "Shi jing Songs as Performance Texts: A Case Study of 'Chu ci' ('Thorny Caltrop')," *Early China* 25 (2000): 49–111. Martin Kern, "Bronze Inscriptions, the *Shangshu*, and the *Shijing*: The Evolution of the Ancestral Sacrifice During the Western Zhou," in *Early Chinese Religion, Part One: Shang Through Han (1250 BC to 220 AD)*, eds. John Lagerwey and Marc Kalinowski (Leiden: Brill, 2009), 179–82. Lothar von Falkenhausen, "Issues in Western Zhou Studies: A Review Article," *Early China* 18 (1993): 146–52.

23. David Schaberg, *A Patterned Past: Form and Thought in Early Chinese Historiography* (Cambridge, MA, and London: Harvard University Asia Center, 2001), 395.

24. Sarah A. Queen, "The Creation and Domestication of the Techniques of Lao-Zhuang: Anecdotal Narrative and Philosophical Argumentation in *Huainanzi* 12," *Asia Major* 21, no. 1 (2008): 201–02n.2.

25. See for instance the comments in *Han Feizi* 韓非子 on the use of anecdotes in the chapter "Nanyan" 難言 (Finding It Hard to Speak). Note also the discussion in David Schaberg, "Chinese History and Philosophy," in *The Oxford History of Historical Writing Volume 1: Beginnings to AD 600*, eds. Andrew Feldherr and Grant Hardy (Oxford: Oxford University Press, 2011), 410, on the explicit use of anecdotes and the demystification of the past.

26. This is particularly true for the core layer of the collection. To my knowledge, the narratives discussing the virtues of former kings in the *Shangshu* chapters "Wuyi" 無逸 (Against Luxurious Ease) and "Jun Shi" 君奭 (Prince Shi) are some of the few cases in which descriptions reminiscent of anecdotes are employed to illustrate a moral point. Even though the ancient kings in these texts are presented as exemplars of specific virtues, their descriptions do not comprise of specific events nor contain unexpected or judgmental punchlines. The language, however, is attributive and correlates the early kings with specific virtuous activities. Perhaps these descriptions should be understood in line with the use of epithets as a mode of attributing desirable qualities. In any case, its occurrence shows that multiple instances of experimenting with this form of argument construction were being practiced and that texts like the *Baoxun*, though rare, were not an isolated phenomenon.

27. Li Xueqin, "Baoxun," 76.

29. The calligraphic style in the other texts in the volume is characterized by thin, cursive strokes close to some of the script in Guodian 郭店 as opposed to the *Baoxun*'s thicker, leveled, and squared style that seems more reminiscent of bronze inscriptions.

29. While there is no clear sign of the threads overlapping the graphs of the manuscript, there are equally no clear signs of deliberate graph spacing to avoid the binding threads.

30. Li Xueqin, ed., *Qinghua zhujian*, 142. For the distinction between the physical manuscript (i.e., the material carrier and other physical characteristics such as calligraphy, titles, punctuation) and the verbal text see Dirk Meyer, *Philosophy on Bamboo: Text and the Production of Meaning in Early China* (Leiden: Brill, 2012), and Matthias L. Richter, "Textual Identity and the Role of Literacy in the Transmission of Early Chinese Literature," in *Writing & Literacy in Early China*, eds. Li Feng and David Prager Branner (Seattle: University of Washington Press, 2011), 206–36.

31. Note that because of competitive funding allocation, the other manuscript holding institutions that verified the manuscripts, such as for instance Peking University and the Shanghai Museum, have an interest in critically evaluating the finds.

32. Noteworthy in the argument over the authenticity of the manuscript is the fact that the component halves of the graphs on the split bamboo strip end of strip 10 match up when joined together again. This shows that the graphs on the strip where written before the strip split, rather than being added later on by modern forgers using ancient strips as in the case of the Zhejiang manuscripts. See the articles by Xing Wen, "Zheda cangjian bianwei" 浙大藏簡辨偽, *Guangming ribao* 光明日報, May 28, June 4, June 25, and July 2, 2012, accessed April 24, 2013.

33. Li Xueqin, "Baoxun," 76.

34. Note that *bao* pˤuʔ 保 (preserve, protect) is read as the cognate *bao* pˤuʔ 寶 (treasure). Phonological reconstructions in this chapter where possible follow William H. Baxter and Laurent Sagart, "Baxter-Sagart Old Chinese reconstruction, version of 20 February 2011," http://crlao.ehess.fr/document.php?id=1217, accessed April 24, 2013.

35. The edition used in this chapter is based on Li Xueqin, ed., *Qinghua zhujian* with emendations drawing on the substantial discussion in the secondary literature. Philological explanations deviating from Li Xueqin, ed., *Qinghua zhujian* are provided in the footnotes but commonly accepted loans such as *wei* 惟 for *zhui* 隹 are incorporated without further comment. Numbers followed by a colon represent the strip numbers; reconstructions are presented in square brackets and □ indicates a missing graph. For an extensive overview of the different graph readings and reconstructions up to June 20, 2011, see Chen Minzhen 陳民鎮, ed., "Qinghua jian Baoxun jishi" 清華簡保訓集釋, in *Yantai daxue Zhongguo xueshu yanjiusuo yanjiusheng dushuhui* Qinghua jian (yi) *jishi 3* 煙臺大學中國學術研究所研究生讀書會《清華簡 (壹) 集釋》, ed. Chen Minzhen 陳民鎮, *Guwenzi Wang* 古文字網, http://www.gwz.fudan.edu.cn/SrcShow.asp?Src_ID=1654, accessed April 12, 2013. For an excellent, different analysis of the structure of the *Baoxun* as seen in the light of the "Guming," see Dirk Meyer, "The Gù mìng 顧命 (Testimonial Charge): The Construction of Memory in Warring States Politico-philosophical Debate," in *The Classic of Documents and the Origins of Chinese Political Philosophy*, eds. Martin Kern and Dirk Meyer (Leiden: Brill, forthcoming).

36. Martin Kern, "The Performance of Writing in Western Zhou China," in *The Poetics of Grammar and the Metaphysics of Sound and Sign*, eds. Sergio La Porta and David Shulman (Leiden: Brill, 2007), 109–75; von Falkenhausen, "Issues," 162–63.

37. The dating formula "*wei wang* 惟王 [time formula]" is ubiquitous in bronze inscriptions, occurring over 240 times in the Zhongguo shehui kexue yuan kaogu yanjiusuo 中國社會科學院考古研究所, ed., *Yin Zhou jinwen jicheng* 殷周金文集成 (Beijing: Zhonghua shuju, 1984) concordance; *meishuang* 昧爽 occurs twenty times, mostly in bronzes from the Spring and Autumn Period.

38. The following discussion draws on genre theory in John Frow, *Genre* (London: Routledge, 2006) and the collection of essays in David Duff, *Modern Genre Theory* (Harlow: Longman, 2000).

39. This idea is informed by the Bahktinian notion of "speech genres," see Duff, *Genre Theory*, 82–95. For similar considerations see von Falkenhausen, "Issues," 148–52 and Kern, "Ancestral Sacrifice," 179–82.

40. Or this is deliberately done in order to create dramatic irony, compare the iconoclastic reworking of Confucius sayings in *Mozi* and *Zhuangzi*. See Michael J. Hunter, "Sayings of Confucius: Deselected" (PhD Diss., Princeton University, 2012), 94–98.

41. This graph has proven difficult to decipher and many solutions have been advanced. Li Xueqin, ed., *Qinghua zhujian*, 144 suggests to read it as *jie* dzap 捷, meaning "speedy, quick." The other strongly argued position is that of Meng Pengshen 孟蓬生, "Baoxun 'Jishen' shijie" 保訓'疾甚'試解, *Guwenzi wang* 古文字網, http://www.guwenzi.com/SrcShow.asp?Src_ID=844, accessed April 12, 2013. He reads this graph as a loan for *jian* dzam? 漸. Meng's reading is phonologically complex but valid. The difference between the two readings lies in their transcription, hinging on a "single, short, horizontal stroke." A transcription of either *di* 遆 tˤek-s, or *shi* s-tek 適 (as in the first published transcription, Qinghua daxue chutu wenxian yanjiu yu baohu zhongxin 清華大學出土文獻研究與保護中心,"Qinghua daxue cang Zhanguo zhujian Baoxun shiwen" 清華大學藏戰國竹簡保訓釋文, *Wenwu* 文物 no. 6 (2009): 73–75) that contain the *di* tˤek-s 帝 phonophore in combination with the *zhi* 止 signific is more sensible (compare He Linyi 何琳儀, *Zhanguo guwen zidian: Zhanguo wenzi shengxi* 戰國古文字典: 戰國文字聲系 (Beijing: Zhonghua shuju, 1998), 477–79). Because those transcriptions do not offer a satisfactory reading, I tentatively follow Meng's reading of *jian* 漸 as he cites similar occurrences in a number of *Shangshu* chapters. For a completer discussion see Chen Minzhen, ed., "Baoxun jishi," 27–30.

42. The two main readings of the graph *tong* doŋʔ 詷 revolve around different strategies presented in Li Xueqin, ed., *Qinghua zhujian*, 144–45. The first, advanced by Li Shoukui 李守奎, "Baoxun erti" 保訓二題, *Chutu wenxian* 出土文獻 1 (Shanghai: Zhongxi shuju, 2010), 81, argues for reading this graph in light of *Shangshu* "Guming" and its commentaries that suggest reception of *tong* by an heir in a ritual ceremony; *tong* is then variously interpreted as a wine vessel, a young boy (akin to a pupil) or a set of instructions; compare Chen Minzhen, ed., "Baoxun jishi," 34–36. The other suggestion is to read as *song* sə-loŋ-s 誦 (recitation), because it presents a contrast to "writing" mentioned on strip 3. Both options are phonologically sound. As such I follow Li Ling 李零 "Du Qinghua jian Baoxun shiwen" 讀清華簡保訓釋文, *Zhongguo wenwu bao* 中國文物報 (August 21, 2009), who argues that in light of the parallel *song* 誦 is the better option. See also Chen Wei 陳偉, "Baoxun ziju shidu" 保訓字句試讀, *Chutu wenxian* 出土文獻 1 (Shanghai: Zhongxi shuju, 2010), 60, who offers a similar reading based on different arguments.

43. Two solutions are regularly advanced for the reading of *nian* nəms (nˤim-s) 念 here. One option, as chosen in Li Xueqin, ed., *Qinghua zhujian*, 145 and Zhao Ping'an 趙平安, "Baoxun de xingzhi he jiegou" 保訓的性質和結構, *Guangming*

ribao 光明日報 (April 13, 2009), suggests to read the graph as a loan for *kan khum* (k^{hˤ}əm) 堪 (be able to), which suggest it operating as a co-verb to the main verb *zhong* 終 (end), both of which a quick search of the transmitted corpus reveal to be rather irregular occurrences. The more straightforward solution is to read 念 as either *nian* təms 唸 (recite) or *shen* hjəm? 諗 (recite, subvocalize, remonstrate), as argued Lin Zhipeng 林志鵬, "Qinghua daxue cang Zhanguo zhushu Baoxun jiaoshi" 清華大學藏戰國竹書保訓校釋, *Jianbo Yanjiu* 簡帛研究, http://www.bsm.org.cn/show_article.php?id=1241, accessed April 12, 2013.

44. As was common for secret instructions, see Donald Harper, "The Sexual Arts of Ancient China as described in a Manuscript of the Second Century B.C.," *Harvard Journal of Asiatic Studies* 47, no. 2 (1987): 563–64. Note that written texts without oral teaching accompaniment were in fact long seen as less trustworthy; see for instance Rosalind Thomas, *Literacy and Orality in Ancient Greece* (Cambridge: Cambridge University Press, 1992) on Ancient Greece. One of the main reasons for this distrust being that transmission could not be controlled easily, as can be seen from our example. On the semantics of *song* 誦 and *nian* 唸 from the perspective of reading, see the excellent article by Wolfgang Behr and Bernard Führer, "Einführende Notizen zum Lesen in China mit besonderer Berücksichtigung der Frühzeit," in *Aspekte des Lesens in China in Vergangenheit und Gegenwart*, ed. Bernard Führer (Bochum: Project Verlag, 2005), 1–42. As became clear from a stimulating discussion with Joachim Gentz and his reading group, the dichotomy raised here in the text calls for a further investigation in the range of possibilities beyond the oral–written distinction in determining the possible connotations of *song*, *nian*, and *shu* for instance.

45. Note that the language and content of the *Baoxun* would likewise place it firmly in the Warring States. Moreover, it has no transmitted counterparts or citations in other texts, and is the only text dealing with King Wen's instructions to his son, although this does not necessarily mean that it was not in circulation during the period. For a similar point see Dirk Meyer, "The Gù mìng."

46. On these prefaces see Edward L. Shaughnessy, "*Shang shu* 尚書 (*Shu ching*書經)," in Michael Loewe, ed., *Early Chinese Texts*, 376.

47. Sun Xingyan 孫星衍, ed., *Shangshu jinguwen zhushu* 尚書今古文注疏 (Beijing: Zhonghua shuju, 1986), 323.

48. An important element of the *Jinteng* centers on the irregular presentation of its text: it is explicit about being put into writing so that it could be stored and later rediscovered, so as to absolve the Duke of Zhou of any blame.

49. Paul van Els, "Tilting Vessels and Collapsing Walls—On the Rhetorical Function of Anecdotes in Early Chinese Texts," *Extrême-Orient, Extrême-Occident* 34 (2012): 141–66; Sarah Allan, *The Heir and the Sage: Dynastic Legend in Early China* (San Francisco: Chinese Materials Center, 1981); Queen, "Anecdotal Narrative;" Schaberg, "Chinese History."

50. Note that such formulas do often occur in the prefaces to individual Documents because these prefaces equally reflect on previous times from a contemporaneous point of view.

51. A discussion of the meaning of *zhong* lies beyond the scope of the present chapter. The text does not clearly define it and likely needed extra explanation. This aspect is taken up further below. For a decent summary of the discussion on *zhong* to date, see Chen Minzhen 陳民鎮, "Qinghua jian Baoxun 'zhong' zi jiedu zhushuo pingyi" 清華簡保訓"中"字解讀諸說平議, *Guwenzi Wang* 古文字網 (2011), http://www.gwz.fudan.edu.cn/SrcShow.asp?Src_ID=1655, accessed April 12, 2013.

52. For different suggestions on how to interpret the "Three Descended Virtues," as a text or doctrine for example, see Chen Minzhen, "Baoxun jishi," 76–79.

53. Consensus reads *jiu* N-kwə?-s 舊 as *jiu* kwə? 久, a common loan in Chu script. See Chen Minzhen, "Baoxun Jishi," 44–45.

54. Li Xueqin, *Qinghua zhujian*, 145, chooses to read *limao* 鬲茅 as *liqiu* 歷丘 citing many parallels for this story, which use this name for the mountain. However, there are many similar excavated anecdotes, such as in the recent *Qiongda yishi* 窮達以時 (Success and Failure Come at Their Respective Times) manuscript from Guodian and the *Rongchengshi* 容成氏 in the Shanghai collection describing Shun as working in the *caomao* 草茅 (grasslands). Likely, as Zhao Ping'an, "Baoxun de xingzhi," and Chen Minzhen, ed., "Baoxun jishi," 50, point out, this anecdote rather combines two references to different locations where Shun worked the land.

55. Reading *bei* brək-s 備 as a loan for *fu* bək 服 as is common in Chu manuscripts. Also note the suggestion in Huang Rener 黃人二, "Qinghua daxue cang Zhanguo zhujian Baoxun jiaodu" 清華大學藏戰國竹簡寶訓校讀, *Kaogu yu wenwu* 考古與文物 no. 6 (2009): 75–81, to read *zi* tsjə 茲 as a loan for *zhi* dzjə 祇 which would enhance the parallelism of the two lines.

56. Interestingly, the river deity He 河 is anthropomorphically represented in the anecdote and here functions to explain mythological narratives in a historicized mode. This process of "reverse euhemerization" [*sic*] (in fact: euhemerization) has been discussed in William Boltz, "Kung-kung and the Flood: Reverse Euhemerization in the Yao Tien," *T'oung Pao* 67, no. 3 (1981): 141–53.

57. This graph, composed of *zhui* 追 with a *shan* 山 signific on top is taken as a variant for *zhui* truj 追, which according to Li Xueqin, *Qinghua zhujian*, 147 can be used as a loan for *gui* kʷəj 歸 (to return). Although this would accord nicely with the earlier *jia* 假 (to borrow), the phonology is problematic (different main vowel and initial). I thus follow Huang Ren'er, *Baoxun jiaodu* who reads *zhui* 追 in the meaning of to "compensate for earlier deeds" which structurally fulfills a similar function as reading *gui* 歸 would.

58. Allan, *Heir and Sage*, 37, 44–45. See also other transmitted versions of this anecdote in Sima Qian 司馬遷, *Shiji* 史記 (Beijing: Zhonghua shuju, 1959), 1.31; Li Xiangfeng 黎翔鳳, ed., *Guanzi jiaozhu* 管子校注, Xinbian zhuzi jicheng 新編諸子集成, ed. (Beijing: Zhonghua shuju, 2004), 66.1205; Sun Yirang 孫詒讓, ed., *Mozi jiangu* 墨子間詁, Xinbian zhuzi jicheng 新編諸子集成, ed., (Beijing: Zhonghua shuju, 2001), 9.57–8, 10.68; Wang Xianshen 王先慎, ed., *Han Feizi*

jijie 韓非子集解, *Xinbian zhuzi jicheng* 新編諸子集成, ed. (Beijing: Zhonghua shuju, 2003), 36.349.

59. Allan, *Heir and Sage*, 33.

60. See the note on a *Zhushu jinian* 竹書紀年 (Bamboo Annals) passage in Guo Pu 郭璞, ed., *Shanhaijing* 山海經, Sibu Congkan Chubian, ed., 四部叢刊初編, vol. 46 (Shanghai: Shangwu yinshuguan, 1919–1922), 14.130 for the other rendition of this anecdote: "The king of Yin, Zihai, was hosted at You Yi and misbehaved there. You Yi's lord, Mian Chen killed him and dumped his body. Because of this, the (new) ruler of Yin, Shangjia Wei borrowed an army from He Bo in order to attack You Yi. He conquered him and then killed his lord Mian Chen." 殷王子亥賓于有易而淫焉, 有易之君綿臣殺而放之, 是故殷主甲微假師于河伯, 以伐有易, 克之, 遂殺其君綿臣也.

61. Compare Allan, *Heir and Sage*, 78–80, 131–33.

62. Many different options are phonologically viable for this problematic graph; see Chen Minzhen, ed., "Baoxun jishi," 111–14. I favor the reading of *xiu* s-liw 修 (adornment, accomplishment) in Liao Mingchun 廖名春, "Qinghua daxue cang Zhanguo zhujian Baoxun shiwen chudu" 清華大學藏戰國竹簡保訓釋文初讀, *Chutu wenxian* 出土文獻 1 (Shanghai: Zhongxi shuju, 2010), 63–75, because it similarly follows the effort-reward structure repeatedly seen in the text.

63. Variants of this line are a common formula in documentary mode language, see Chen Minzhen, ed., "Baoxun jishi," 115–16, Li Xueqin, "Baoxun," Li Xueqin, "Qinghua jian zongshu," 53. Li Ling, "Du Qinghua jian" makes a convincing case that *yang* ɢaŋʔ-s 養 here should be interpreted as *yong* ɢʷraŋʔ 永 (eternal, lasting) corresponding to *ri buzu* 日不足 (our days are limited) thus forming a paralleled couplet; it has been suggested that this graph, through similar form corruption has led to *xi* 悉 in the other occurrences of the formula, see the discussion in Chen Minzhen, ed., "Baoxun jishi," 118–19.

64. Assmann, *Cultural Memory*, 52–53, rightly argues that the two need not be seen as distinct stages per se, but can be conceptualized as two modes of dealing with the past, present in different degrees in societies up to today.

65. Assmann, *Cultural Memory*, 70–76.

66. Assmann, *Cultural Memory*, 78–83. John B. Henderson, *Scripture, Canon, and Commentary: A Comparison of Confucian and Western Exegesis* (Princeton, NJ: Princeton University Press, 1991).

67. Kern, "Ancestral Sacrifice."

68. Michael Nylan, "On Libraries and Manuscript Culture in Western Han Chang'an and Alexandria" (paper presented at the Comparing Ancient Worlds: Greece and China conference, Cambridge, January 24, 2013).

69. Martin Kern, "The Odes in Excavated Manuscripts," in *Text and Ritual in Early China*, ed. Martin Kern (Seattle and London: University of Washington Press, 2005), 149–93. Edward Shaughnessy, "A First Reading of the Shanghai Museum Bamboo-Strip Manuscript of the *Zhou Yi*," *Early China* 30 (2005–2006): 1–26.

70. Meyer, *Philosophy on Bamboo*, 227–28.

71. Meyer, *Philosophy on Bamboo*, 239–43.

72. On the historical development of the anecdote see Schaberg, "Chinese History."

73. As such, while my understanding of Allan's description of the genre at the beginning of this chapter will not cover all aspects of what was considered to be a documentary type text, a text with these characteristics would be recognized as belonging to the genre.

74. See for instance Chen Mengjia, *Shangshu tonglun*.

75. Compare the early general descriptions of generic categories, for instance in the *Xunzi* 荀子 "Ruxiao" 儒校 (Emulating the Ru), and Guodian *Yucong* 語叢 (Thicket of Sayings) 1, strips 36–44, where unfortunately the strip with the description of Documents is missing. See the succinct comparison of these lists of genres in Li Ling 李零, *Guodian Chu jian jiaoduji* 郭店楚簡校讀記 (增訂本), rev. ed. (Beijing: Renmin daxue chubanshe, 2007), 217–19.

76. Lionel Gossman, "Anecdote and History," *History and Theory* 42 (2003), 154.

77. Compare Hunter, *Sayings of Confucius*; van Els, "Tilting Vessels," and the chapter by Queen in this volume.

78. Li Xueqin, "Baoxun."

79. Note the order in the Han imperial library catalogue with its distinction between *jing* 經 (classic) and *za* 雜 (eclectic).

10

Old Stories No Longer Told
The End of the Anecdotes Tradition of Early China

Paul van Els[1]

Anecdotes were of paramount importance in the written culture of early China, the period from the Zhou Dynasty 周 (ca. 1045–256 BCE) to the former half of the Han Dynasty 漢 (202 BCE–220 CE). The short, freestanding accounts of particular events—"true" or invented—in Chinese history occur in large quantities in a wide range of texts and genres.[2] Most texts contain at least a few anecdotes, while some texts consist almost entirely of anecdotes. Several early Chinese anecdotes feature unnamed protagonists that are vaguely identified as "someone who was plowing the fields" (*geng tian zhe* 耕田者), "someone who waded through a river in winter" (*dong she shui zhe* 冬涉水者), and so on, with the name of the state where they hailed from casually (and possibly fictitiously) added to give readers at least some background of these persons. The vast majority of early Chinese anecdotes, by contrast, feature actual historical people mentioned by name, such as famous rulers, noblemen, statesmen, archers, officers, inventors, philosophers, teachers, recluses, cooks, and concubines. The most illustrious of these persons each generated an abundance of anecdotes, some of which occur in more than one text. The wording of the anecdotes may differ from text to text, and they may be used for different rhetorical purposes in each new context, but the basic events remain the same. Given the abundance of anecdotes in early Chinese texts, and their importance in these texts, it seems that authors felt compelled to display their knowledge of China's past and spice up their writings with appropriate anecdotes. In this cultural tradition, they kept on referring to some of the same historical figures, and

331

telling some of the same stories involving them, thereby creating what could be loosely termed a "corpus" of early Chinese historical anecdotes. The rich and lively tradition of drawing on this corpus of historical anecdotes lasted until the end of the Western Han Dynasty 西漢 (202 BCE–9 CE), and appears to have faded from the Eastern Han Dynasty 東漢 (25–220 CE) onwards, only to make way for new storytelling traditions. It thus seems that as the Western Han Dynasty came to an end, so did a long tradition of discussing and arguing through that particular corpus of historical anecdotes. At the dawn of the Eastern Han Dynasty, a new history was created, with little room for the ancient anecdotes.

This chapter analyzes the anecdotes tradition of early China. It contains three parts. Part 1 is a case study of a single anecdote, which serves as a typical example of the thriving anecdotal tradition of early China, from the earliest Chinese narrative histories to the end of the Western Han Dynasty. Part 2 continues the case study by analyzing what happened to that single anecdote in texts from the Eastern Han Dynasty onwards, thereby illustrating the rapid decline of the anecdotes tradition of early China. Part 3 offers tentative explanations for the decline.

Part 1: A Thriving Tradition

The main protagonist of the anecdote that is central to our case study is the illustrious Duke Wen of Jin 晉文公 (r. 636–628 BCE), whose given name was Chong'er 重耳 (Double Ears), and who was a son of Duke Xian of Jin 晉獻公 (r. 676–651 BCE). In 656 BCE, as Chong'er was in his early forties, a conflict over his father's succession arose when Li Ji 驪姬, his father's favorite concubine, schemed to have the crown prince replaced by her son. She succeeded through a series of intrigues, a tumultuous episode in Jin history known as "the Li Ji Unrest" (*Li Ji zhi luan* 驪姬之亂). The upheaval led the original crown prince to commit suicide and forced Duke Xian's other sons, including Chong'er, to flee. With a small group of loyal and able retainers, such as Zhao Cui 趙衰 and Hu Yan 狐偃, Chong'er traveled from state to state, spending a total of nineteen years in exile. In 636 BCE, supported by his retainers and backed by the army of Qin 秦, the state where he resided at the time and whose ruler he had befriended, Chong'er returned to Jin where he successfully claimed the rulership. Once in power, he implemented major reforms that strengthened Jin, and he formed strategic alliances that fortified Jin's position among the other states. Two important events solidified his reign. In 635 BCE, he helped the recently ousted King Xiang of Zhou 周襄王 (r. 651–619 BCE) to regain the throne, and for his support he was enfeoffed with Wen 溫, Yuan 原, and other city-states in the royal domain of the Zhou monarchy. In 632 BCE, his army crushed that of Chu 楚 in the epic Battle of Chengpu 城濮, thereby defeating the only state powerful enough to challenge his hegemony.³ This victory effectively made him a hegemon (*ba* 霸), a ruler who, despite lip service allegiance to the house of Zhou above him, reigned supreme as de facto ruler of "all under heaven" (*tianxia* 天下), or the whole world as known to the Chinese at the time. Following his demise in 628 BCE, Chong'er received the posthumous name of Wen 文, and so he is known to history as Duke Wen of Jin.⁴

As with any prominent personality, there is a cornucopia of stories about Duke Wen. In this chapter, I shall focus on one anecdote in particular. The anecdote relates an event that supposedly took place in the winter of 635 BCE, the year after Duke Wen was installed as the new ruler of Jin. In broad strokes, the story goes as follows: Earlier in the year 635 BCE, King Xiang bestows the city of Yuan upon Duke Wen, but the inhabitants of Yuan refuse to give Duke Wen their allegiance. Duke Wen's army thereupon lays siege to Yuan, and he vows to take the city within a specified number of days. At the end of that period Yuan still stands, but just as Duke Wen is giving up the siege, news arrives that the city will not hold out much longer. Duke Wen nevertheless refuses to extend the siege beyond the period that he had promised earlier, for it would mean losing his trustworthiness, which is more dear to him than winning Yuan. Hearing these noble thoughts, the inhabitants of Yuan readily surrender to him.

There are no fewer than six distinct versions of the anecdote in the extant literature from early China. In this chapter I present these versions in what may be the chronological order of the texts in which they appear. These texts are: *Zuozhuan* 左傳 (Zuo Commentary), *Guoyu* 國語 (Discourses of the States), *Lüshi chunqiu* 呂氏春秋 (Spring and Autumn Annals of Mr. Lü), *Han Feizi* 韓非子 (Master Han Fei), *Huainanzi* 淮南子 (The Master of Huainan), and *Xinxu* 新序 (Newly Arranged [Anecdotes]). Note that for my argument the sequential order of these texts is of little relevance, as I am more interested in how the distinct versions of the anecdote are used in their relative contexts, than when precisely they were put to writing.

Version 1: *Zuozhuan*

The *Zuozhuan*, traditionally attributed to a historian named Zuo Qiuming 左丘明 (fl. 6th–5th c. BCE), is one of the earliest Chinese narrative histories.[5] It describes events that took place between 722 and 463 BCE. In its current form the text serves as a commentary to the *Chunqiu* 春秋 (Spring and Autumn Annals), the influential chronicle compiled in the state of Lu 魯. In the *Zuozhuan*, the following event is associated with the 25th year of the reign of Duke Xi of Lu 魯僖公 (r. 659–627 BCE), which corresponds to the year 635 BCE in the Gregorian calendar:

> In winter, when the Marquis of Jin [i.e., Duke Wen] laid siege to Yuan, he commanded [his troops to capture the city with] three days worth of provisions. When [three days passed and] Yuan did not surrender, he gave the command to quit the place. A spy then emerged [from within Yuan] and exclaimed, "Yuan is about to surrender!" The commanding officers of his army entreated their lord to wait for this, but he replied, "Trust is the precious jewel of a state. It is what the people rely on. If obtaining Yuan means losing my trustworthiness, what would they have to rely on? My loss would be greater [than my gain.]" After his troops retreated a mere one day's march, Yuan surrendered. He then removed Guan, the Earl of Yuan, to Ji; made Zhao Cui governor of Yuan; and Hu Zhen governor of Wen.[6]

> 冬, 晉侯圍原, 命三日之糧. 原不降, 命去之. 諜出, 曰:「原將降矣!」軍吏曰:「請待之.」公曰:「信, 國之寶也, 民之所庇也. 得原失信, 何以庇之. 所亡滋多.」退一舍而原降. 遷原伯貫于冀, 趙衰為原大夫, 狐溱為溫大夫.[7]

This passage offers a number of specific elements that set this version of the anecdote apart from other renderings. To begin, the main protagonist is here referred to both as *hou* 侯, marquis, the hereditary title he carried, and as *gong* 公, "duke," a term often used in early Chinese texts to refer more broadly to a "lord."[8] Other versions of the anecdote, discussed below, exclusively use the latter appellation, *gong*, to refer to him. Also, by providing his troops with provisions for three days, Duke Wen here implicitly vows to take Yuan within that period. In other versions, as we shall see below, the deadline is set at three, five, seven, or even ten days. Finally, Duke Wen here refers to trustworthiness as "the precious jewel of a state" (*guo zhi bao* 國之寶), an element we find in some other versions of the anecdote, but not all. These are fairly trivial variations between this version of the anecdote and other versions. More telling differences occur at the beginning and end of the passage.

In my understanding, the passage consists of three parts: an introductory phrase ("In winter"), the anecdote proper, and a closing comment ("He then removed . . .").

The *Zuozhuan* introduces the anecdote by noting that the siege of Yuan took place in winter, and it is the only text to do so. This is, of course, because the *Zuozhuan* is a chronicle that—much like the *Chunqiu* to which it is appended as a commentary—presents events chronologically. The introductory phrase "in winter" connects this anecdote to anecdotes immediately preceding it, which describe events that took place in the spring, summer, and fall of the same year. In other words, the mention of the word "winter" puts the encirclement of Yuan at its correct place within the sequence of events in the year 635 BCE.

The *Zuozhuan* ends this passage by describing the reshuffling of official positions following the surrender of Yuan, and again it is the only text to do so. That the text mentions the removal of the earl of Yuan, who at first refused to give allegiance to Duke Wen, is understandable even without further context. Other elements are less clear. Who is Zhao Cui? Why was he made governor of Yuan? Who is Hu Zhen? Why was he made governor of Wen? How is the governor of Wen related to the siege of Yuan? The answers to these questions lie elsewhere in the *Zuozhuan*. In that text, Zhao Cui is repeatedly mentioned as an early follower of Duke Wen, whom he accompanied from the very beginning of his exile from Jin. Zhao Cui's governorship of Yuan must be understood as a reward for his many years of loyal service to Duke Wen.[9] Hu Zhen was a son of Hu Mao 狐毛, who is also described in the *Zuozhuan* as one of Duke Wen's close confidants. Hu Zhen's governorship is probably also best understood as a token of appreciation for loyalty. In all likelihood it is mentioned here because the city of Wen was recently bestowed upon Duke Wen by King Xiang, as part of a set of gifts that also included the city of Yuan. In sum, the concluding remarks of the passage do make sense, but only within the larger context of the *Zuozhuan*. They firmly link the account of the siege of Yuan to the larger narrative on Duke Wen and his retainers in the *Zuozhuan*.

Duke Wen receives exceptional coverage in the *Zuozhuan*, as evidenced by "the amount of attention paid to his early years, to his distinctive physical features, and to the assortment of wives that he acquired in the course of his odyssey," as the translator Burton Watson points out.¹⁰ The *Zuozhuan* is clearly intrigued by this historical figure. The account of his peaceful seizure of Yuan enriches the text's biographical portrayal of Duke Wen, by narrating an event that occurred in his life and calling attention to one of his supposed character traits: trustworthiness.

In my understanding, the anecdote serves three main functions in the *Zuozhuan*: historical, biographical, and moral. (1) As a commentary to the *Chunqiu*, a highly terse text, the *Zuozhuan* fleshes out the concise entries of that text. With a meager seven brief entries, the year 635 BCE is only sketchily outlined in the *Chunqiu*, and so as part of the *Zuozhuan* commentary, the anecdote adds detail to the history of the year that witnessed the siege of Yuan. (2) Within the context of the *Zuozhuan*, a text fascinated with the illustrious Duke Wen, the anecdote adds biographical detail to his life. (3) Still, perhaps the most important function of the anecdote is moral. As Watson points out, the aim of the *Zuozhuan* is to edify, and as a result "its lessons are overwhelmingly political and moral in nature."¹¹ This also holds true for lessons involving Duke Wen, and the account of the siege of Yuan is no exception. The *Zuozhuan* generally paints a positive picture of Duke Wen, namely that of a ruler whose years in exile made him humble and well-suited to become a hegemon.¹² One of his fine qualities was trustworthiness, for which the anecdote serves as an apposite example, as it suggests that trustworthiness on the part of the lord creates loyalty by the subjects. This moral significance of the anecdote is made explicit elsewhere in the *Zuozhuan*. When Duke Wen was about to mobilize his people for battle, an advisor warned him that "the people do not yet understand trustworthiness" (*min wei zhi xin* 民未知信), and it is said that in response to this Duke Wen "attacked Yuan to show them trustworthiness" (*fa Yuan yi shi zhi xin* 伐原以示之信).¹³ In sum, in the *Zuozhuan* the anecdote serves to highlight the values of trustworthiness and loyalty which ideally bind the lord and his people.

Version 2: *Guoyu*

The *Guoyu* is another early Chinese narrative history.¹⁴ Although the text is demonstrably written by several hands, Zuo Qiuming is nevertheless traditionally seen as its author. This is because the *Guoyu* and the *Zuozhuan*, also ascribed to him, largely overlap in scope and content. A major difference between the two texts is that the emphasis in the *Guoyu* is more on the sayings, rather than the doings, of rulers and other dignitaries. Also, the *Guoyu* organizes material per state, and chronologically only within each state. There are one or more chapters devoted to each of these states: Zhou 周, Lu 魯, Qi 齊, Jin 晉, Zheng 鄭, Chu 楚, Wu 吳, and Yue 越. Occupying nine chapters out of a total of twenty-one, Jin receives more attention than any other state in the *Guoyu*. In the fourth chapter on Jin, we find this version of the anecdote:

> When Duke Wen attacked Yuan, he ordered [his troops to capture the city] with three days worth of provisions. When three days passed and Yuan did not surrender, the duke gave orders to withdraw his army and quit the place. A spy then emerged [from within Yuan] and exclaimed, "Yuan will not last more than one or two days!" The commanding officers of his army reported this to the duke, who replied, "If obtaining Yuan means I will lose my trustworthiness, with what would I lead my people? You see, trustworthiness is what the people rely on. It must not be lost." And so they quit the place, but as soon as they reached Mengmen, Yuan asked to surrender.
>
> 文公伐原，令以三日之糧. 三日而原不降，公令疏軍而去之. 諜出，曰：「原不過一二日矣！」軍吏以告，公曰：「得原而失信，何以使人？夫信，民之所庇也，不可失.」乃去之，及孟門，而原請降.¹⁵

There are some minor variations between this version of the anecdote and the one in the *Zuozhuan* quoted above. For starters, this passage contains no more than the anecdote proper: it has no phrases at the beginning and end informing the reader that the siege took place in winter and that several officials found new jobs after the surrender of Yuan. Also, this passage does not refer to trustworthiness as "the precious jewel of a state," as does the *Zuozhuan*. Finally, this passage does not measure the retreat of Duke Wen's army as a one-day march, but more specifically mentions that they had reached the nearby mountain pass of Mengmen 孟門 when Yuan surrendered.¹⁶

In the *Guoyu*, the fourth chapter on the state of Jin consists in its entirety of chronologically arranged passages narrating the words and deeds of Duke Wen. The passage immediately preceding the account of the attack on Yuan describes how Duke Wen and his army besieged another walled fortification in the spring of 635 BCE, half a year before they encircled Yuan. He initially planned to take that fortification by military means, but won the population over by his outstanding character—as was the case with Yuan. The passage immediately following the siege of Yuan describes how Duke Wen in 632 BCE defeated the state of Chu in the famous Battle of Chengpu that effectively made him the most powerful ruler of his day and age.

In sum, the *Guoyu* resembles the *Zuozhuan* in that the purposes of the anecdote are historical, biographical, and moral, as both texts place the siege of Yuan in the larger context of Duke Wen's actions and highlight his virtuous conduct. This is hardly surprising because, as Kierman notes, "the Chinese chroniclers compiled their record moralistically, narrating battles in a way to prove that those who won deserved to do so."[17]

Version 3: *Lüshi chunqiu*

The *Lüshi chunqiu* is a voluminous and well-organized work compiled around 239 BCE under the patronage of Lü Buwei 呂不韋 (d. 235 BCE), chancellor of the state of Qin. The encyclopedic text contains three major parts—"Almanacs" (*ji* 紀), "Examinations" (*lan* 覽), "Discussions" (*lun* 論)—each subdivided into an apparently auspicious number of books, chapters, and sections. Broadly speaking, the Almanacs discuss human activities in correspondence with the workings of the seasons, the Examinations focus on governance, and the Discussions are somewhat incoherent passages on the exemplary behavior of worthy rulers.[18] In Book 19 of the *Lüshi chunqiu*, which is part of the Examinations, we find this version of the anecdote:

> When Duke Wen of Jin attacked Yuan, he agreed with his officers on a period of seven days [to capture the city]. When seven days passed and Yuan did not capitulate, he gave the command to quit the place. A collaborating officer then exclaimed, "Yuan is about to capitulate."[19] The officers in command of his army entreated the duke to wait for this, but he replied, "Trust is the precious jewel of the state. If obtaining Yuan means losing this treasure, I will not do it." Thereupon they quit the place. The next year he again attacked Yuan. This time he agreed with his officers that they would return home only after they had

obtained Yuan. When the inhabitants of Yuan heard about this, they surrendered. When the inhabitants of Wei heard about this, they regarded Duke Wen as the epitome of trustworthiness and therefore also gave their allegiance to him.[20]

Hence, the saying "obtaining Wei by launching an offensive against Yuan" refers to this episode. It is not that Duke Wen did not desire to obtain Yuan. Rather, he thought it best not to obtain Yuan if obtaining it meant being untrustworthy. Because he insisted on obtaining Yuan through sincere trustworthiness, it was not merely Wei that gave him allegiance. Duke Wen may properly be termed a man who "knew how to seek what he desired!"[21]

晉文公伐原，與士期七日，七日而原不下，命去之. 謀士言曰：「原將下矣！」師吏請待之. 公曰：「信，國之寶也. 得原失寶，吾不為也.」遂去之. 明年復伐之，與士期必得原然後反，原人聞之乃下. 衛人聞之，以文公之信為至矣，乃歸文公. 故曰「攻原得衛」者，此之謂也. 文公非不欲得原也，以不信得原，不若勿得也. 必誠信以得之，歸之者非獨衛也. 文公可謂知求欲矣.[22]

Lü Buwei and his team clearly had a liking for drama. In their version, the deadline for defeating Yuan is seven days, not just three. Also, Duke Wen does not retreat a mere one-day's march but a full year, only to come back with an emboldened promise the next year. Finally, in this rendering of the story Duke Wen does not win just one city, but two, a double victory that inspired the early Chinese equivalent of the saying of two birds with one stone.

In my understanding, the anecdote proper runs from the opening line "When Duke Wen of Jin attacked Yuan" to "also gave their allegiance to him." The remainder of this passage, from "Hence, the saying" to the end, evaluates the anecdote and embeds it within the larger textual unit, which is chapter 6 in book 19 in the *Lüshi chunqiu*. Book 19 is "concerned with the techniques by which a ruler can 'employ the people,' that is, make them willing to die for his causes," as the translators Knoblock and Riegel point out.[23] Chapter 6, titled "Using Desire" (*wei yu* 為欲), highlights the importance of desires from the perspective of the ruler. If the people are without desires, they will have no incentive to work, making it difficult for the ruler to employ them. The more they desire, the easier it will be for the ruler to manipulate them into working for him. Now, the anecdote about the siege of Yuan comes at the very end of the chapter. It is related to the chapter's central theme because Duke Wen desired Yuan but not at all costs. He is therefore explicitly identified as someone who "knew how to seek what he desired" (*zhi qiu yu* 知求欲).

This is the only anecdotal example in the otherwise essayistic chapter. It is perhaps somewhat strange that Lü Buwei and his team selected this particular anecdote. Whereas the chapter focuses on how rulers can make use of the desires of their people, the anecdote shows the benefits for rulers if they temper their own desires. Perhaps the idea is that, for the system of "using the people's desires" to work, it is of utmost importance that the ruler himself knows how to control his own desires. Duke Wen serves as an apposite example of such a ruler. He desired Yuan, but not at all costs, and by patiently displaying his trustworthiness, in the end he effortlessly gained even more than what he initially desired. Incidentally, the next chapter in the *Lüshi chunqiu* is titled "Valuing Trustworthiness" (*gui xin* 貴信), and the anecdote of Duke Wen could have easily—and perhaps more appropriately—served as an example there as well. Quite possibly the anecdote serves to bridge the two chapters.

In the *Zuozhuan* and the *Guoyu*, the anecdote forms part of historical narratives—chronological descriptions of events in the life of Duke Wen, in the state of Jin, and in the year 635 BCE—but both texts also deploy the anecdote to articulate a didactic message about trustworthiness. In the *Lüshi chunqiu*, by contrast, the anecdote is detached from its historical context, and used instead as an example in an expository essay on "using desires" as a specific technique of rulership. The emphasis in the *Lüshi chunqiu* appears to be on knowing how to get what one desires, which can easily be misconstrued as an argument in favor of endless greed. It is perhaps for this reason that the text specifically adds the quality of sincere trustworthiness (*cheng xin* 誠信), as if it wants to make clear that Duke Wen was truly trustworthy and not just feigning trustworthiness to gain territory.

It seems that the *Zuozhuan*, *Guoyu*, and *Lüshi chunqiu* all use the story to exemplify or illustrate an aspect of Duke Wen's character but they make different claims about what should be highlighted about him. The *Zuozhuan* and the *Guoyu* emphasize the importance of trustworthiness, whereas in the *Lüshi chunqiu* the moral value of trustworthiness is subordinated to the art of "knowing how to go after what you desire," which is probably why the text has to emphasize that Duke Wen's trustworthiness was sincere. This shows how different didactic points might be drawn from the same anecdote. Below we will see how other texts draw their didactic points from this anecdote.

Version 4: *Han Feizi*

The *Han Feizi* is named after Han Fei 韓非 (ca. 280–233 BCE) who, being born into the ruling family of the state of Han 韓, was the only early Chinese thinker of noble descent. The text, probably largely written by himself, contains essays on law, power, and other aspects of statecraft.[24] The *Han Feizi* contains six chapters, all titled "Chushuo" 儲說 (Collection of Illustrative Examples), in which anecdotes illustrate the point the author is trying to make. In one of the chapters, we find this version of the anecdote:

> When Duke Wen of Jin launched an offensive against Yuan, he [made his troops] bundle ten days of provisions and accordingly agreed with his grandees on a period of ten days [to capture the city]. When ten days had passed since their arrival and Yuan did not capitulate, he sounded the bells of retreat, put an end to the military operation and quit the place. One of his officers then emerged from within Yuan and exclaimed, "In three days, Yuan will capitulate!" His entire cabinet and all his confidants remonstrated, saying, "Look, Yuan's food supplies are depleted and their morale is exhausted. Would you not wait a little for this?" He replied, "I had agreed with my troops on a period of ten days. If we do not quit, I will loose my trustworthiness. If obtaining Yuan means losing my trustworthiness, I will not do it." Thereupon he put an end to the military operation and left. When the inhabitants of Yuan heard this, they said, "How can we not give our allegiance to a lord as trustworthy as this one?!" Thereupon they surrendered to the duke. When the inhabitants of Wei heard this, they said, "How can we not follow a lord as trustworthy as this one?!" Thereupon they surrendered to the duke.
>
> When Confucius heard about this, he made the following note, "Trustworthiness is what causes someone to obtain Wei by attacking Yuan."

晉文公攻原，裹十日糧，遂與大夫期十日，至原十日而原不下，擊金而退，罷兵而去. 士有從原中出者曰：「原三日即下矣!」群臣左右諫曰：「夫原之食竭力盡矣, 君姑待之?」

公曰:「吾與士期十日. 不去, 是亡吾信也. 得原失信, 吾不
為也.」遂罷兵而去. 原人聞曰:「有君如彼其信也, 可無歸
乎?」乃降公. 衛人聞曰:「有君如彼其信也, 可無
從乎?」乃降公. 孔子聞而記之曰:「攻原得衛者信也.」[25]

This reading of the anecdote is more discursive than the ones we saw earlier. Here, Duke Wen's advisors are allowed to explain why they oppose a troop withdrawal, and the inhabitants of Yuan and Wei similarly explain their reasons for surrendering to Duke Wen—all in direct speech. Similar to the version in the *Lüshi chunqiu*, this version maintains that the surrender of Yuan was followed by the spontaneous surrender of Wei. A major difference between the two versions, however, is that the "two cities with one siege" saying, whose origin is not specified in the *Lüshi chunqiu*, is here attributed to Confucius. As Michael Hunter notes, why Confucius "was felt to be an appropriate mouthpiece for the one comment but not the other is an open question."[26]

The "Chushuo" chapters in the *Han Feizi* start with a series of political "guidelines" (*jing* 經) that are explained through what the text calls "illustrative examples" (*shuo* 說). The guideline for which the Siege of Yuan anecdote serves as an illustrative example is this:

> Once small trust is completed, large trust is established. That is why the enlightened ruler gradually builds up trust. If penalties and punishments are not trusted, instructions and prohibitions will not be carried out. For illustrative examples, see "Duke Wen's offensive against Yuan" and "Ji Zheng saves people from starvation."

> 小信成則大信立, 故明主積於信. 賞罰不信, 則禁令不行. 說在文公之攻原與箕鄭救餓也.[27]

Readers who wish to know about the gradual accumulation of trust may follow Han Fei's directions and read the anecdotes (further on in the text) about Duke Wen who, having gained the trust of Yuan also gained the trust of Wei, and Ji Zheng, who explains how three different kinds of trust may prevent starvation among the population.

In the *Han Feizi*, similar to the *Lüshi chunqiu* discussed above, the anecdote is detached from its historical context and used instead to illustrate a political principle. The main difference between the two texts is that in the former, the anecdote shows rulers the best way to go after what they desire, whereas in the latter it shows how a ruler can gradually accumulate trust. By showing the inhabitants of Yuan he is a man of his word, he ensures that both Yuan and Wei pledge their allegiance to him—a small act of trust on the part of the ruler inspiring a large act of trust on the part of the people, as the "guideline" in the *Han Feizi* puts it.

Version 5: *Huainanzi*

The *Huainanzi* is a voluminous work written under the auspices of Liu An 劉安 (ca. 179–122 BCE), the King of Huainan 淮南王. It was supposedly finalized around 139 BCE, for in that year it was presented to Liu An's nephew, Emperor Wu of the Han Dynasty 漢武帝 (r. 141–87 BCE). In twenty-one chapters, the *Huainanzi* discusses a range of topics (cosmology, military, and so on), a thorough understanding of which can lead one to become an exemplary ruler.[28] In one chapter we find this version of the anecdote:

> When Duke Wen of Jin attacked Yuan, he agreed with his grandees on a period of three days [to capture the city]. When three days passed and Yuan did not surrender, Duke Wen gave the command to quit the place. The commanding officers then exclaimed, "Yuan will surely surrender in another day or two!" Their lord replied, "When I agreed with my grandees on three days, I did not realize Yuan could not be made to capitulate in this period. If I do not put an end to this military operation now that the three days are over, it would mean obtaining Yuan by losing my trustworthiness. I will not do it." When the inhabitants of Yuan heard about this, they said, "How could we refuse to surrender to a lord like this?" They promptly surrendered. When the people of Wen heard about this, they also asked to surrender.
>
> As Laozi puts it, "Dark, dim, inside it lies the essence. The essence is quite genuine, inside it lies trust." Also, "fine words can buy honor, fine deeds can add people."[29]

晉文公伐原, 與大夫期三日. 三日而原不降, 文公令去之. 軍吏曰:「原不過一, 二日將降矣.」君曰:「吾不知原三日而不可得下也, 以與大夫期, 盡而不罷, 失信得原, 吾弗為也.」原人聞之曰：「有君若此，可弗降也.」遂降. 溫人聞，亦請降. 故《老子》曰：「窈兮冥兮，其中有精，其精甚真，其中有信.」故「美言可以市尊，美行可以加人.」[30]

This passage occurs in *Huainanzi* chapter 12, titled "Daoying" 道應 (Responses of the Way). The chapter contains over fifty anecdotes, each coupled with one or more sayings attributed to Laozi 老子 (trad. 6th c. BCE), the mythical founder of Daoism. The anecdotes relate the abstruse teachings of Laozi to the real world. In this particular case, the anecdote of the siege of Yuan illustrates teachings that can be found in chapters 21 and 62 of the received *Laozi*.

Chapter 21 of the *Laozi* contains the following passage that paints a poetic image of the Way (*dao* 道), the guiding principle of the universe:

> The Way is something elusive and evasive. Evasive, elusive, inside it lies an image. Elusive, evasive, inside it lies something substantial. Dark, dim, inside it lies the essence. The essence is quite genuine, inside it lies trust.[31]

> 道之為物，惟恍惟惚. 惚兮恍兮，其中有象；恍兮惚兮，其中有物. 窈兮冥兮，其中有精；其精甚真，其中有信.[32]

This *Laozi* passage is almost as unfathomable as the Way itself. Interpretations differ widely. For instance, the last word, *xin* 信, is variously translated as "evidences" (Chan), "truth" (Cleary), "true genuineness" (Lafargue), and "something that can be tested" (Lau). It is this word, which also means "trust" or "trustworthiness," that links the *Laozi* passage to the Duke Wen anecdote in the *Huainanzi*. By linking the two, Liu An and his team appear to say that by attributing more value to "trust" than to military gain, Duke Wen values the very essence of the Way. It is therefore no surprise that the inhabitants of Yuan and Wen, upon realizing this, gladly surrender to him.

Chapter 62 of the *Laozi* contains a statement that can be translated as "fine words can buy, honorable deeds can add people" (美言可以市，尊行可以加人).[33] The last two words of the Chinese sentence, *jia ren* 加人, are often translated as "raise [someone] above others." In the context of the *Huainanzi*, I would translate these words more literally as "add people" in the sense of "attracting people to oneself." By linking the *Laozi* statement to the anecdote, Liu An and his team present Duke Wen as someone whose fine words bought him honor and whose fine deeds caused the people of Yuan and Wen to pledge allegiance to him.

In sum, in the *Huainanzi* the anecdote serves to illustrate the teachings of Laozi, as it occurs in a chapter that consists in its entirety of similar combinations of historical anecdotes and *Laozi* quotes.³⁴

Version 6: *Xinxu*

The *Xinxu* is a collection of anecdotes compiled under the auspices of the imperial librarian Liu Xiang 劉向 (ca. 79–8 BCE). A prolific writer, Liu Xiang is also responsible for the compilation of the *Bielu* 別錄 (Separate Records), *Zhanguoce* 戰國策 (Stratagems of the Warring States), *Shuoyuan* 說苑 (Garden of Illustrative Examples), *Lienüzhuan* 列女傳 (Biographies of Exemplary Women), and other texts. The received text of the *Xinxu* contains 165 anecdotes, arranged in ten chapters. The first five chapters all carry the unimaginative title "Zashi" 雜事 (Miscellaneous Affairs). One of these affairs is this version of the anecdote:

> When Duke Wen of Jin attacked Yuan, he agreed with his grandees on a period of five days [to capture the city]. When five days passed and Yuan did not surrender, Duke Wen gave the command to quit the place. His officers then exclaimed, "Yuan will surely surrender in another three days; you may want to wait for that." Their lord replied, "If obtaining Yuan means losing my trustworthiness, I will not do it." When the inhabitants of Yuan heard about this, they said, "It is impossible not to surrender to a lord as righteous as this." So they promptly surrendered. When the inhabitants of Wen heard about this, they also asked to surrender. Hence, the saying "Wen surrenders by attacking Yuan" refers to this episode. Thereupon many regional lords gave their allegiance to him. Next, he invaded Cao and attacked Wei, gathered heads of state at Jiantu, and after the pact with Wen he crushed the southern state of Chu. He then paid respect to the royal house of Zhou, which completed his achievements as a hegemon, making him the second hegemon after Duke Huan of Qi. His basic trustworthiness comes from his attack on Yuan.

> 晉文公伐原，與大夫期五日，五日而原不降，文公令去之．吏曰：「原不過三日，將降矣，君不如待之．」君曰：「得原失信，吾不為也．」原人聞之曰：「有君義若此，不可不降．」遂降，溫人聞之，亦請降．故曰：「伐原而溫降．」此之謂也．

於是諸侯歸之, 遂侵曹, 伐衛, 為踐土之會, 溫之盟, 後南破強楚, 尊事周室, 遂成霸功, 上次齊桓. 本信, 由伐原也.³⁵

The title of the text in which this passage appears, *Xinxu*, translates as "Newly Arranged [Anecdotes]." The stories it contains are not new, but borrowed from earlier texts, edited, and placed in a new sequential order. The chapter in which this passage appears is full of anecdotes involving a wide range of historical figures. These anecdotes are not arranged chronologically, but more or less thematically. Overall, they illustrate how rulers may win over the population by their virtue. The anecdote immediately preceding the account of the siege of Yuan describes how trustworthiness played a major role in the process by which Duke Huan of Qi 齊桓公 (r. 685–643 BCE) became a hegemon. In sum, it seems that within this *Xinxu* chapter, the two anecdotes form a mini-cluster that highlights the importance of trustworthiness for a ruler, with two powerful hegemons as an example.

This case study analyzed one anecdote in six distinct versions, each with a unique purpose depending on the context in which it appears. The anecdote may serve a historical purpose by showing what happened in 635 BCE, or by fleshing out the history of the state of Jin. It may serve a biographical purpose, by adding detail to the eventful life of Duke Wen. It may also serve as a vivid illustration in an essay about getting what one desires, or about the importance of trustworthiness. Finally, when combined with quotations from the *Laozi*, it may serve to show the essence and importance of that foundational scripture. Early Chinese texts readily incorporated the account of the Siege of Yuan, and many other anecdotes for that matter, because they could be molded to suit a range of rhetorical purposes and hence served as powerful building blocks in arguments. Taken together, the anecdotes seem to have constituted a pool of material that anyone in those days could—and may even have been expected to—draw upon to ornament and illustrate their writings. In fact, one will be hard pressed to find a narrative text that does not contain a single anecdote.³⁶ In sum, this pool of anecdotes formed an integral part of the intellectual framework of writers and readers in those days, which is why they occur in such large numbers, for so many different purposes, in such a wide range of texts.

Part 2: A Fading Tradition

Until the end of the Western Han Dynasty, it was apparently a must in almost any text to draw upon the large "corpus" of historical anecdotes, that is, anecdotes about actual historical figures, such as Duke Wen of Jin. Soon afterwards, however, the corpus seems to have lost its appeal, as the tradition of incorporating these particular anecdotes in texts gradually faded. By way of an example, let us return to our case study, the Siege of Yuan, and examine how it is received after the end of the Western Han.

In the two-thousand years following the fall of the Western Han, only a handful of essays, commentaries, and encyclopedias refer to the Siege of Yuan. Here are a few examples:

The *Shuijingzhu* 水經注 (Commentary on the Waterways Classic), compiled by Li Daoyuan 酈道元 (d. 527), provides a wealth of information regarding the courses of rivers in China. The commentary to the chapter on the Ji River 濟水 explains that one source of this river is located northeast of Yuan 原. The commentary then goes on to say that "It is this city that, long ago, surrendered to Duke Wen of Jin when he attacked it with trustworthiness" (昔晉文公伐原以信, 而原降, 即此城也).[37] The commentator does not provide the anecdote in full, as the authors of texts discussed above did. That said, he is obviously well-informed of Duke Wen's military endeavor, its geographical location, and the moral lesson it teaches, and by briefly and casually referring to the anecdote, even without quoting it in full, he obviously expects his readers to be familiar with the story as well.

The *Liuzi xinlun* 劉子新論 (Master Liu's New Discussions), a text that also dates from the sixth century, contains a chapter titled "Lüxin" 履信 (Treading on the Topic of Trustworthiness). The chapter identifies human activity as the essence of being human, and trust as the foundation of all activities. It presents four historical figures as beacons of trustworthiness:

> Duke Huan [of Qi] did not violate his pact with Cao Gui; [Duke] Wen of Jin did not break his promise when attacking Yuan; Wu Qi did not hold back the reward he promised for moving the shafts of his carriage; Marquis [Wen of] Wei did not skip the appointment he made with his game warden.
>
> 齊桓不背曹劌之盟, 晉文不棄伐原之誓, 吳起不虧移轅之賞, 魏侯不乖虞人之期.[38]

The Siege of Yuan is here part of a series of historical maxims, brief references to episodes in history that are narrated in with more detail in the *Zuozhuan*, *Han Feizi*, *Zhanguoce*, and other early Chinese texts. The casual references require knowledge of the historical events to be fully appreciated as examples of trustworthiness. This passage in *Liuzi xinlun* obviously expects its audience to possess this historical knowledge, which suggests that at the time the Siege of Yuan was well-known.

The *Zizhi tongjian* 資治通鑒 (Comprehensive Mirror in Aid of Governance), compiled and published in 1084 under the leadership of the historian Sima Guang 司馬光 (1019–1086), is a chronological narrative of the history of China. To one historical event Sima Guang adds a comment in which he dilates on trustworthiness, a quality he familiarly refers to as "the greatest precious jewel of the people's lord" (人君之大寶). Using the same four historical examples of trustworthiness as the *Liuzi xinlun*, he notes that "Duke Wen of Jin did not covet the gains of an attack on Yuan" (晉文公不貪伐原之利).[39]

The *Taiping yulan* 太平御覽 (Imperial Readings of the Taiping Era), a voluminous encyclopedia created under the auspices of Li Fang 李昉 (925–996), quotes line for line the Siege of Yuan version as it occurs in the *Lüshi chunqiu*, including the comment that Duke Wen was a man who "knew how to seek what he desired."[40] Whereas the *Lüshi chunqiu* passage serves as an example of "using desires," the *Taiping yulan* incorporates the passage in a chapter on trustworthiness.

The *Kongzi jiyu* 孔子集語 (Collected Sayings of Confucius), compiled by Sun Xingyan 孫星衍 (1753–1818), collects sayings ascribed to Confucius. It includes the Siege of Yuan anecdote in the version of the *Han Feizi*, which as we have seen attributes the saying "obtaining Wei by attacking Yuan" to Confucius.

These examples suffice to show that after the Western Han Dynasty, texts either briefly referred to the Siege of Yuan, expecting readers to be familiar with the historical event and its moral lesson, or they quote in full one of the earlier versions of the anecdote, including any comment the earlier authors attached to the anecdote. What authors after the Western Han do not do, however, is create new versions of the anecdote and embed these as illustrative examples in their essays. In other words, to authors from the Eastern Han onwards, the Siege of Yuan may still be known, and what it signifies (the importance of trustworthiness) may still be understood, but the anecdote itself is no longer actively used.

This case study of just one anecdote is suggestive of a much broader trend. Until the end of the Western Han, writers strongly felt a need to draw upon a corpus of historical anecdotes to strengthen their arguments by molding the anecdotes in certain ways. From the beginning of the Eastern Han, we no longer see that strong urge in the surviving literature, even though some authors still referred—often through brief maxims—to some of the more famous early Chinese historical anecdotes.

Part 3: Musings on the End of a Tradition

Why did the corpus of early Chinese anecdotes lose its appeal? Why did authors grow less inclined to draw from the pool of early Chinese anecdotes to reinforce their writings? It is not easy to pinpoint the cause of the decline of tradition, and there might not even be one single cause for the decline. More likely, several concurrent trends combined to bring about the decline. Here are my musings on several of those trends.

If we wish to find out why the early Chinese anecdotes lost their appeal, we should ask ourselves what caused their appeal in the first place. After all, it is quite remarkable that writers over a span of several centuries, from the Warring States to the Han, and in various literary genres, mention some of the same historical figures and draw upon the same pool of anecdotes for their writings. It seems that these historical figures, and the events they were involved in, and the lessons to be learned from those events, were part of the intellectual framework of the literate classes in early China. When expressing their thoughts in writing, authors reinforced the very framework from within they wrote. This self-perpetuating system among the cultural elites of early China not only led scholars to sprinkle their writings with anecdotes, but also to create entire collections of anecdotes. The most prominent person in this regard is the prodigious imperial librarian Liu Xiang, who lived at the end of the Western Han and was responsible for several influential collections of anecdotes. For example, he is said to have compiled the *Xinxu*, *Shuoyuan*, *Zhanguoce*, and *Lienüzhuan*. With all these collections of anecdotes occurring around the same time, mainly through the efforts of one man, it is hard to imagine how that achievement could be topped. Of course, one could rearrange the anecdotes in yet another collection, but that would add little new to what had already been done so many times before. So it seems that by the end of the Western Han Dynasty, the intensive usage of anecdotes had reached its natural peak, and that the massive interest in anecdotes by Liu Xiang and his peers paradoxically also led to the decline of the tradition, as there was little new that could be done with the old stories.

Little over a decade after Liu Xiang passed away, Wang Mang 王莽 (45 BCE–23 CE) seized the throne and founded a new dynasty. It was short-lived and followed by what is generally termed the "restoration" of the Han dynasty. Traditional historiography divides the Han dynasty in two, with Wang Mang's interregnum as an uncomfortable anomaly in between. Still, his aptly named Xin 新 ("New") Dynasty was a something of a watershed in Chinese history. For one thing, it enabled scholars to take a critical look at their tradition, and see where it had gone wrong. To be sure, earlier scholars had also viewed history with a critical eye. As David Schaberg notes:

> Only with Sima Qian does a theme of historical verification become at all prominent, and even his *Shiji* includes much anecdotal material that is acknowledged to be unverifiable, legendary, and useful more for its lessons than for its historical truth.[41]

The same could be said for some of the scholars who lived after Liu Xiang. They, too, appreciated the early Chinese anecdotes more for the lessons that can be drawn from them, than for their historical truth.

One of the first truly critical minds is Wang Chong 王充 (27–100 CE), who lived right after the Xin at the beginning of the Eastern Han. Tradition has it that he was born into a family of humble origins, and that he enjoyed reading books in bookstalls in the capital city, with no financial means to actually buy the books he read. As an autodidact, Wang Chong grew to become one of the most critical thinkers of his time. He was highly skeptical of many beliefs, theories, and practices of his contemporaries. In his *Lunheng* 論衡 (Balanced Discourses), a voluminous book completed around 50 CE, anecdotes play a significantly less prominent role than in the texts produced in previous centuries. For example, although his book consists of more than 200,000 words, Wang Chong mentions the Siege of Yuan not even once, and Duke Wen only twice.[42] By contrast, the *Huainanzi*, which was compiled almost two centuries earlier and is half the *Lunheng* in size, does mention the Siege of Yuan anecdote and it brings up Duke Wen in no fewer than seven chapters. Similarly, the *Lüshi chunqiu*, compiled almost three centuries before the *Lunheng* and also roughly half its size, likewise contains the Siege of Yuan anecdote and it mentions Duke Wen over a dozen times. Duke Wen clearly does not hold the same appeal for Wang Chong as he did for Lü Buwei and Liu An. Other historical figures can count on Wang Chong's attention, but he views the anecdotes that involve them with a critical eye. For example, Duke Huan of Qi, the first of the so-called hegemons, is said to have married his seven cousins, which would have been a major faux pas even in early China—that is, if it were true. Wang Chong for one does not think it was true. In a chapter titled "Shuxu" 書虛 (Falsehoods in Books), we find this passage:

> It has been recorded that Duke Huan of Qi married his seven cousins. That cannot be true, for it would be incest and a violation of the laws of consanguinity. [. . .] Had Duke Huan married

his seven cousins, his viciousness would have left behind that of [the tyrants] Jie and Zhòu. [. . .] The *Chunqiu* commends the smallest merit and condemns the slightest wrong. For what reason then did it not condemn the great crime of Duke Huan? [. . .] Why was the *Chunqiu* so hard upon Duke Xiang, recording his lewdness, and why so lenient to Duke Huan, concealing his crime and having no word of reproof for it? [. . .] The fault of Duke Huan consisted in his too great condescension towards the ladies of his harem. Six concubines enjoyed his special favor, and five princes contended to become his heirs. [. . .] People hearing of these six favorites, and that no distinction was made between the sons of his wife and his concubines, then said that he misbehaved himself with seven cousins.[43]

傳書言: 齊桓公妻姑姊妹七人. 此言虛也. 夫亂骨肉, 犯親戚 [. . .] 桓公妻姑姊妹七人, 惡浮於桀, 紂 [. . .] 《春秋》采毫毛之美, 貶纖芥之惡, 桓公惡大, 不貶何哉? [. . .] 《春秋》何尤於襄公, 而書其奸? 何宥於桓公, 隱而不譏? [. . .] 案桓公之過, 多內寵, 內嬖如夫人者六. 有五公子爭立 [. . .] 世聞內嬖六人, 嫡庶無別, 則言亂於姑姊妹七人矣.[44]

Wang Chong is one of the first persons to treat anecdotes about historical figures with a grain of salt. As Schilling and Ptak point out in their study of stories involving Duke Huan, Wang Chong rectifies some crazy stories and "admonishes the reader to be critical with literary works."[45] What we are witnessing here with Wang Chong is the beginning of a critical look at the historical veracity of anecdotes. Up to that point this was hardly the case, as Schaberg points out:

> Historicity mattered to the users of anecdotes, but as a complement to rhetorical aims rather than as a goal in its own right. The details of events often drifted and changed as an anecdote was retold over the centuries, and there is little to suggest that discrepancies of this kind troubled Warring States and early Han writers. Facts were not entirely open to manipulation, but it is significant that, in all the debates of the era, writers so rarely saw fit to question the details of each other's accounts.[46]

Wang Chong is one of the first to question the details of earlier accounts. And once the details are being questioned, the account itself loses some of its authority, and hence some of its appeal. This is not to say that people stopped producing anecdotes or that people lost interest in history, but the large corpus of early Chinese anecdotes that includes the account of the Siege of Yuan was no longer a must for Wang Chong and the writers after him.

Conclusion

The point of this chapter is not to argue that authors from the Eastern Han onwards no longer used anecdotes in their writings, or even that the specific corpus of early Chinese historical anecdotes fell into oblivion after the Western Han. To the contrary, we often find brief references to early Chinese historical anecdotes in later texts, which suggests that to the authors and their readers the stories were still known and relevant. I merely want to point out that the intensive and almost compulsory use of a specific set of anecdotes—a tradition that led no fewer than six texts to include a variant of the Siege of Yuan story—until the end of the Western Han, stands in marked contrast to the modest use of the corpus after the Western Han. To be sure, anecdotes continued to be important, but the fall of the Western Han was the start of a new period that created its own anecdotes. The culmination of this process is the *Shishuo xinyu* 世說新語 (A New Account of the Tales of the World), compiled and edited by Liu Yiqing 劉義慶 (403–444), which contains over a thousand anecdotes about historical figures from the Han Dynasty and beyond. It seems that by that time, anecdotes about earlier Chinese historical figures had gone past their expiration date.

Notes

1. This chapter was written under the financial support of an Innovational Research Incentives Scheme grant from the Netherlands Organisation for Scientific Research (NWO), for which I am most grateful. I am also grateful for helpful comments by participants and audience members at the venues where I delivered earlier versions of this piece. My collaborator on this book, Sarah A. Queen, carefully read a draft of the chapter and offered helpful corrections and suggestions, for which I cannot thank her enough. Thanks also to the anonymous reviewers for their feedback.

2. This definition of the word *anecdote* is based on Lionel Gossman, "Anecdote and History," *History and Theory* 42 (2003): 143.

3. For more on this battle, see Frank A. Kierman, Jr., "Phases and Modes of Combat in Early China," in *Chinese Ways in Warfare*, eds. Frank A. Kierman, Jr., and John K. Fairbank (Cambridge, MA: Harvard University Press, 1974), 47–56.

4. For an extensive study of early narrative accounts of Duke Wen, see Jeff Bissell, "Literary Studies of Historical Texts: Early Narrative Accounts of Chonger, Duke Wen of Jin" (PhD Diss., University of Wisconsin, 1996). For a study of historical accounts of Duke Wen's ascendancy, see David W. Pankenier, "Applied Field-Allocation Astrology in Zhou China: Duke Wen of Jin and the Battle of Chengpu (632 B.C.)," *Journal of the American Oriental Society* 119, no. 2 (1999): 261–79. For a translation of select *Zuozhuan* stories on Duke Wen, see Burton Watson, *The Tso Chuan: Selections From China's Oldest Narrative History* (New York: Columbia University Press, 1989), chapters 11–14.

5. For more on the *Zuozhuan*, see for instance Bernhard Karlgren, *On the Authenticity and Nature of the Tso Chuan* (Göteborg: Elanders boktryckeri aktiebolag, 1926); Ronald C. Egan, "Narratives in the *Tso Chuan*," *Harvard Journal of Asiatic Studies* 37, no. 2 (1977): 323–52; John C. Y. Wang, "Early Chinese Narrative: The *Tso-chuan* as Example," in *Chinese Narrative: Critical and Theoretical Essays*, ed. Andrew H. Plaks (Princeton, NJ: Princeton University Press, 1977), 3–20; and Anne Cheng, "Ch'un ch'iu 春秋, Kung yang 公羊, Ku liang 穀梁 and Tso chuan 左傳," in *Early Chinese Texts: A Bibliographical Guide*, ed. Michael Loewe, Early China Special Monograph Series 2 (Berkeley: The Society for the Study of Early China and The Institute of East Asian Studies, University of California, 1993), 67–76.

6. Cf. James Legge, *The Chinese Classics, Vol. 5: The Ch'un Ts'ew with The Tso Chuen* (Taipei: SMC Publishing Inc, 1994), 196; Watson, *Tso Chuan*, 53n.8.

7. *Zuozhuan*, Xi 25.4. *Chunqiu Zuozhuan zhu* 春秋左傳注, ed. Yang Bojun 楊伯峻 (Beijing: Zhonghua shuju, 1981), 1:435–436.

8. As the ruler of Jin, he carried the hereditary title of *hou* 侯, which is conventionally translated as "marquis." Following his demise, he was often referred to as *gong* 公, a title customarily translated as "duke," but which often translates more loosely as "ruler," "prince," or "lord." It would probably be more appropriate to refer to him in English as Lord Wen, but for the sake of consistency across the present volume, and in correspondence with the many other publications in which he is referred to as Duke Wen, I will opt for that as well. For more on the problematic translation of *gong* as "duke," see C. N. Tay, "On the Interpretation of *Kung* (Duke?) in the *Tso-chuan*," *Journal of the American Oriental Society* 93, no. 4 (1973): 550–55.

9. A related passage in the *Zuozhuan* explicitly mentions Zhao Cui's loyalty as the reason for making him governor of Yuan. In that passage, when Duke Wen wonders whom he should put in charge of Yuan, he is reminded that: "Formerly, Zhao Cui followed you on your peregrinations with a pot of food, and never ate

from it even when he was starving." 昔趙衰以壺飱從徑, 餒而弗食 (*Zuozhuan*, Xi 25.6; *Chunqiu Zuozhuan zhu* 1:436; cf. Legge, *Tso Chuen*, 196).

10. Watson, *Tso Chuan*, xix.

11. Watson, *Tso Chuan*, xx.

12. This picture differs from other texts, such as the *Lunyu* 論語 (Analects). In that text, Confucius denounces Duke Wen as "crafty and lacking integrity" (*jue er bu zheng* 譎而不正). *Lunyu* 14.15; cf. D. C. Lau, *The Analects* (London: Penguin Books, 1979), 126.

13. *Zuozhuan*, Xi 27.4 (*Chunqiu Zuozhuan zhu* 1:447; cf. Legge, *Tso Chuen*, 201–02; Watson, *Tso Chuan*, 53). This passage suggests that Duke Wen, when preparing his people for the Battle of Chengpu, besieged Yuan to show them what it means to be trustworthy. Chronologically this would only work if Duke Wen started preparing his masses for the Battle of Chengpu (632 BCE) at least three years prior to the Siege of Yuan (635 BCE).

14. For more on the *Guoyu*, see I-jen Chang, William G. Boltz, and Michael Loewe, "Kuo yü," in *Early Chinese Texts*, 263–68.

15. *Guoyu*, Jinyu 4; *Guoyu* 國語, 2 vols. (Shanghai: Shanghai guji chubanshe, 1978), 376–77.

16. Yang Bojun (*Chunqiu Zuozhuan zhu*, 435–36) identifies Mengmen as a mountain pass in present-day Henan 河南 province. He adds that Mengmen indeed would have been a mere one-day march from Yuan but, oddly, not in a direction the Jin army would take to return home.

17. Kierman, "Phases and Modes of Combat in Early China," 48.

18. For more on the *Lüshi Chunqiu*, see: Michael Carson and Michael Loewe, "Lü shih ch'un ch'iu," in *Early Chinese Texts*, 324–30. For a complete annotated translation of the text, see: John Knoblock and Jeffrey Riegel, *The Annals of Lü Buwei: A Complete Translation and Study* (Stanford, CA: Stanford University Press, 2000).

19. I suspect that *mou* 謀 "to collaborate" is probably a slip of the brush, as other versions have the graphically similar but semantically superior word *die* 諜 "spy." If this is the case, Lü Buwei and his team may have added the word *shi* 士 "officer" to create a noun phrase ("collaborating officer"), because *mou* on its own normally functions as a verb.

20. The *Lüshi chunqiu* claims that Wei 衛 followed the example of Yuan in surrendering to Duke Wen. The *Zuozhuan* makes no mention of this, and claims instead that Wei continued to exist as an independent state. The *Zuozhuan* does, as we have seen, mention new governors for the cities of Yuan and Wen 溫, and the *Huainanzi* and the *Xinxu*, as we will see, also mention that Wen surrendered after the fall of Yuan. Hence, it seems that the *Lüshi chunqiu* mixed up the geographical locations of Wei and Wen.

21. Cf. Knoblock and Riegel, *The Annals of Lü Buwei*, 499–500.

22. *Lüshi chunqiu*, "Li su lan" 離俗覽, "Wei yu" 為欲. *Lüshi chunqiu zhushu* 呂氏春秋註疏, ed., Wang Liqi 王利器 (Chengdu: Ba-Shu shushe, 2002), 2383–85.

23. Knoblock and Riegel, *The Annals of Lü Buwei*, 473.

24. Relevant studies of the *Han Feizi* include: Hsiao-po Wang and Leo S. Chang, *The Philosophical Foundations of Han Fei's Political Theory* (Honolulu: University of Hawai'i Press, 1986); Bertil Lundahl, *Han Fei Zi: The Man and the Work* (Stockholm: Institute of Oriental Languages, 1992); Michael Andrew Hall Reeve, "Demonstrating the World: Mind and Society in the Shuo Lin Chapters of the *Han Fei Zi*." (PhD Diss., Princeton University, 2003); and Paul R. Goldin, ed. *Dao Companion to the Philosophy of Han Fei* (Dordrecht: Springer, 2013). Translations include: W. K. Liao, trans., *The Complete Works of Han Fei Tzu, Vol. I–II* (London: Arthur Probsthain, 1939); Burton Watson, trans., *Han Fei Tzu: Basic Writings* (New York: Columbia University Press, 1964); and Jean Lévi, trans., *Han Fei-tse ou le Tao du prince: la stratégie de la domination absolue* (Paris: Seuil, 1999).

25. *Han Feizi jijie* 韓非子集解, ed. Wang Xianshen 王先慎, Xinbian zhuzi jicheng 新編諸子集成 edition (Beijing: Zhonghua shuju, 2003), chap. 32, 285–86.

26. Michael J. Hunter, "Sayings of Confucius: Deselected" (PhD Diss., Princeton University, 2012), 50.

27. *Han Feizi jijie*, chap. 32, 265.

28. For more on the *Huainanzi*, see: Charles Le Blanc, "Huai nan tzu," in *Early Chinese Texts*, 189–95. For a translation, see: John S. Major, Sarah A. Queen, Andrew Seth Meyer, and Harold D. Roth, trans. and eds., *The Huainanzi: A Guide to the Theory and Practice of Government in Early Han China* (New York: Columbia University Press, 2010).

29. Cf. Major et al., *The Huainanzi*, 463.

30. *Huainanzi jishi* 淮南子集釋, ed. He Ning 何寧, Xinbian zhuzi jicheng 新編諸子集成 edition (Beijing: Zhonghua shuju, 2003), chap. 12, 869.

31. My translation is a mere amalgamation of existing translations, including: Arthur Waley, trans., *The Way and Its Power: A Study of the Tao Tê Ching and its Place in Chinese Thought* (London: George Allen & Unwin Ltd., 1934); Wing-tsit Chan, trans., *The Way of Lao Tzu (Tao-te ching)* (Indianapolis, IN: The Bobbs-Merrill Company, 1963); D. C. Lau, trans., *Lao Tzu: Tao Te Ching* (London: Penguin Books, 1963); Ku-ying Ch'en, *Lao Tzu: Text, Notes, and Comments*, trans. Rhett Y. W. Young and Roger T. Ames (San Francisco: Chinese Materials Center, 1981); D. C. Lau, trans., *Tao Te Ching*, Chinese Classics edition (Hong Kong: Chinese University Press, 1989); Michael LaFargue, trans., *The Tao of the Tao Te Ching: A Translation and Commentary* (Albany, NY: State University of New York Press, 1992).

32. *Laozi* 21.

33. *Laozi* 62. This statement feels incomplete (the two sentences are not perfectly parallel), and many translators—based on the *Huainanzi* parallel—add an extra word "fine" (*mei* 美), creating the sentence "fine words can buy honor, fine deeds can add people." Other translations include: "There is a traffic in speakers of fine words; Persons of grave demeanour are accepted as gifts" (Waley, *The Way and Its Power*, 218); "Beautiful words when offered will win high rank in return. Beautiful deeds can raise a man above others" (Lau, *Lao Tzu*, 69); "Beautiful words

can be used for bartering; Honoured behaviour can put a man above others" (Lau, *Tao Te Ching*, 229); "Fine words can buy honor, and fine deeds can gain respect from others" (Chan, *Lao Tzu*, 210); "The fine words [of the adept man] can win him respect, and the fine behavior can cause him to be admired by others" (Ch'en, *Lao Tzu*, 264); "Elegant words can buy and sell; fine conduct gets people promoted" (LaFargue, *Tao*, 104).

34. For more on this chapter in the *Huainanzi*, see: Sarah A. Queen, "The Creation and Domestication of the Techniques of Lao-Zhuang: Anecdotal Narrative and Philosophical Argumentation in *Huainanzi* 12," *Asia Major* 21, no. 1 (2008): 201–47; Paul van Els, "Tilting Vessels and Collapsing Walls: On the Rhetorical Function of Anecdotes in Early Chinese Texts," *Extrême-Orient, Extrême-Occident* 34 (2012): 141–66.

35. *Xinxu jiaoshi* 新序校釋, ed. Shi Guangying 石光瑛, 2 vols. (Beijing: Zhonghua shuju, 2001), chap. 4, 505–09.

36. Yuri Pines did; see his contribution to the present volume.

37. *Shuijingzhu* 水經注, comp. Li Daoyuan 酈道元 (Changchun: Shidai wenyi chubanshe, 2001), *juan* 7, "Ji shui," 54.

38. *Xinbian Liuzi xinlun* 新編劉子新論, ed. Jiang Jianjun 江建俊 (Taipei: Taiwan guji chubanshe, 2001), chap. 8, "Lüxin," 101.

39. *Zizhi tongjian* 資治通鑑, 20 vols., ed. Sima Guang 司馬光 (Beijing: Zhonghua shuju, [1956] 1976), chap. 2, "Zhou ji, er," 48–49.

40. *Taiping yulan* 太平御覽, 4 vols., ed. Li Fang 李昉 (Beijing: Zhonghua shuju, [1960] 1995), vol. 2, chap. 430, "Xin," 1981.

41. David Schaberg, "Chinese History and Philosophy," in *The Oxford History of Historical Writing, Volume 1: Beginnings to AD 600*, eds. Andrew Feldherr and Grant Hardy (Oxford: Oxford University Press, 2011), 398n.12.

42. In one passage (*Lunheng* 3), Wang Chong claims that people's fate can be easily known by the structure of their bones, adding that "Chong'er, the Prince of Jin, became a hegemon over the regional lords because his ribs were grown together" (晉公子重耳仳脅, 為諸侯霸). In another passage (*Lunheng* 20), he describes how Duke Wen, in exile and begging for food, angrily refused a piece of soil offered by a plowman, which was explained by his retainers as inappropriate behavior for a prince who may one day be presented with the land of Jin.

43. Translation by Alfred Forke, *Lun-Hêng, Part II: Miscellaneous Essays of Wang Ch'ung* (Berlin: Georg Reimer, 1911), 253–55.

44. *Lunheng jiaoshi* 論衡校釋, ed. Huang Hui 黃暉 (Beijing: Zhonghua shuju, 1990), 16.190–91.

45. Dennis Schilling and Roderich Ptak, "The Ulcers of Duke Huan of Ch'i," *Journal of the American Oriental Society* 118, no. 2 (1998): 223.

46. Schaberg, "Chinese History and Philosophy," 398.

Contributors

Heng Du (MA, University of Colorado, 2010) is a PhD student at the Department of East Asian Languages and Civilizations, Harvard University. She is currently writing a dissertation on the collection and rhetorical usage of anecdotes in "master texts" from the Warring States Period and in compilations from the Han Dynasty.

Paul R. Goldin (PhD, Harvard University, 1996) is Professor of East Asian Languages and Civilizations at the University of Pennsylvania. His publications include *Rituals of the Way: The Philosophy of Xunzi* (Open Court, 1999), *The Culture of Sex in Ancient China* (University of Hawai'i Press, 2002), *After Confucius: Studies in Early Chinese Philosophy* (University of Hawai'i Press, 2005), and *Confucianism* (University of California Press, 2011). In addition, he has edited the *Dao Companion to the Philosophy of Han Fei* (Springer, 2011), as well as the revised edition of Robert van Gulik's classic *Sexual Life in Ancient China* (Brill, 2003), and has co-edited with Victor H. Mair and Nancy S. Steinhardt, *Hawai'i Reader in Traditional Chinese Culture* (University of Hawai'i Press, 2002), and with Yuri Pines and Martin Kern, *Ideology of Power and Power of Ideology in Early China* (Brill, 2015).

Rens Krijgsman (DPhil, Oxford University, 2016) read a DPhil in Oriental Studies at Pembroke College, Oxford University, where he taught Classical Chinese language tutorials, as well as courses on topics ranging from the philosophy of the *Zhuangzi* to manuscript culture in early China. His dissertation, titled "The Rise of a Manuscript Culture and the Textualization of Discourse in Early China," discusses the shift in the use and perception of the written word and manuscripts in the Warring States Period. His publications include "Traveling Sayings as Carriers of Philosophical Debate: From the Intertextuality of the *Yucong 語叢 to the Dynamics of Cultural

Memory and Authorship in Early China" (*Asiatische Studien/Études Asiatiques* 68, no. 1). He is currently preparing a manuscript on historical changes of reading and manuscript materiality.

Ting-mien Lee (PhD, University of Leuven, 2015) is Assistant Professor in the Department of Philosophy at Tunghai University (Taichung, Taiwan). She specializes in Early Chinese thought, with a focus on the aspect of language use in philosophical and political discourses. In a recent publication—"When 'Ru-Mo' may not be 'Confucians and Mohists': The Meaning of 'Ru-Mo' and Early Intellectual Taxonomy" (*Oriens Extremus* 53)—she argues that "ru-mo" in texts from the Warring States Period and Han Dynasty is sometimes used as a pejorative term carrying the connotation of "moral hypocrites" or "abusers of moral language." She is currently writing an article on the pragmatic use of "ren-yi" (traditionally rendered as "humaneness and righteousness") in classical strategic manuals and its implications for the interpretation of the philosophies of Mengzi and Zhuangzi.

Wai-yee Li (PhD, Princeton University, 1988) is Professor of Chinese Literature at Harvard University. Her publications include *Enchantment and Disenchantment: Love and Illusion in Chinese Literature* (Princeton University Press, 1993); *The Readability of the Past in Early Chinese Historiography* (Harvard University Press, 2007); and *Women and National Trauma in Late Imperial Chinese Literature* (Harvard University Press, 2014). She wrote chapters for and co-edited with Wilt Idema and Ellen Widmer, *Trauma and Transcendence in Early Qing Literature* (Harvard University Press, 2006); and co-authored with Stephen Durrant, Michael Nylan, and Hans Van Ess, *The Letter to Ren An and Sima Qian's Legacy* (University of Washington Press, 2016). She is a contributing translator and co-editor, with C. T. Hsia and George Kao, of *The Columbia Anthology of Yuan Drama* (Columbia University Press, 2014). She is also the translator, with Stephen Durrant and David Schaberg, of *Zuo Tradition (Zuozhuan): Commentary on the "Spring and Autumn Annals"* (University of Washington Press, 2016).

Andrew Seth Meyer (PhD, Harvard University, 1999) is Associate Professor of History at Brooklyn College, the City University of New York. He specializes in early Chinese intellectual history, and is a co-translator of *The Huainanzi: A Guide to the Theory and Practice of Government in Early Han China* (Columbia University Press, 2010) and author of *The Dao of the Military: Liu An's Art of War* (Columbia University Press, 2012).

Yuri Pines (PhD, The Hebrew University of Jerusalem, 1998) is Michael W. Lipson Professor of Asian Studies, the Hebrew University of Jerusalem; visiting professor at Beijing Normal University, China; and guest professor at Nankai University, Tianjin, China. His publications include *Foundations of Confucian Thought: Intellectual Life in the Chunqiu Period, 722–453 B.C.E.* (University of Hawai'i Press, 2002); *Envisioning Eternal Empire: Chinese Political Thought of the Warring States Era* (University of Hawai'i Press, 2009); and *The Everlasting Empire: Traditional Chinese Political Culture and Its Enduring Legacy* (Princeton University Press, 2012). With Gideon Shelach, Yitzhak Shichor, and Michal Biran he co-authored, in Hebrew, the three-volume *All-under-Heaven: Imperial China* (Open University Press, 2011, 2013, and forthcoming); with Lothar von Falkenhausen, Gideon Shelach, and Robin D. S. Yates he co-edited *Birth of an Empire: The State of Qin Revisited* (University of California Press, 2014), and with Paul R. Goldin and Martin Kern, *Ideology of Power and Power of Ideology in Early China* (Brill, 2015).

Sarah A. Queen (PhD, Harvard University, 1991) is Professor of History at Connecticut College. She is the author of *From Chronicle to Canon: The Hermeneutics of the Spring and Autumn Annals according to Tung Chung-shu* (Cambridge University Press, 1996). She co-edited with John Major, Andrew Seth Meyer, and Harold Roth, *The Huainanzi: A Guide to the Theory and Practice of Government in Early Han China* (Columbia University Press, 2010); with Michael Puett, *The Huainanzi and Textual Production in Early China* (Brill, 2014), and with John Major, *The Luxuriant Gems of the Spring and Autumn* (Columbia University Press, 2015).

Christian Schwermann (PhD, University of Bonn, 2005), is University Lecturer of Classical Chinese at the University of Bonn, and works mainly on early Chinese literature. He has published a monograph on the concept of stupidity in ancient texts, *"Dummheit" in altchinesischen Texten* (Harrassowitz, 2011), and he co-edited with Raji C. Steineck a conference volume on authorship in East Asian literatures from the beginnings to the seventeenth century, *That Wonderful Composite Called Author* (Brill, 2014).

Paul van Els (PhD, Leiden University, 2006), is University Lecturer of China Studies at Leiden University, where he teaches Classical Chinese language tutorials and courses on a wide range op topics, including Chinese culture, history, philosophy, and religion. His publications include a monograph on a perplexing Daoist text, *The Wenzi: Creation, Manipulation, and Reception of a Chinese Philosophical Text* (Brill, forthcoming), and a two-volume Dutch-language textbook of Classical Chinese, *Van orakelbot tot weblog* (Leiden University Press, 2011, 2015).

Index

Adams, Ansel, 6, 7
Ai, Duke of Lu, 74–75, 213, 242
Ai, Marquis of Cai, 274–75, 276
Allan, Sarah, 18–19, 305, 306,
    315–16, 329n73
Aloff, Mindy, 34n27
An, Battle of, 259n56
analogy, 43, 44–46, 93, 96, 187n87,
    210, 216
anecdotes
    declining use of, 21, 31, 332,
        346–52
    definitions of, 5, 8, 331
    in early Chinese texts, 7–24
    features of, 4–7, 9–10, 74
    as illustrative examples, 12–13, 17
    protagonists of, 6–10, 19, 331–32,
        347, 349, 352
    rhetorical functions of, 3, 4, 16, 18,
        24, 27–29, 31
    stock, 93
    studies of, 3–4
    terms for, 4, 33n7
    variations in, 11–12, 26, 31
aphorisms, 23, 42
argumentation (dispute, debate; *bian*),
    4, 28, 43, 168, 173n17, 304, 306
    in *Baoxun*, 320
    barbarians and, 114
    commentaries and, 319

deductive vs. non-deductive, 25,
    41–62, 82
in *Han Feizi*, 29, 194–96, 199–201,
    204–6, 211, 214, 216, 218, 220–21
oral, 65, 84
philosophical, 22, 24–27, 31, 86,
    90n34
in *Shuoyuan*, 147–92
Aristotle, 41–42, 56nn5–6, 148
Assmann, Jan, 302, 318
authorship
    of *Gongyangzhuan*, 254n4, 260n67
    of *Han Feizi*, 193, 217–18, 220
    individual, 150, 168, 169, 174n23,
        176n30
    of *Shuoyuan*, 148–53, 167, 168–69

Baihutong (Comprehensive Discussions
    in the White Tiger Hall), 46,
    159, 184n72
Baijia (Accounts of the Hundred
    Thinkers), 150, 151, 152,
    179n41, 183n61
Ban Gu, 21, 137, 171n11, 173n19
    See also *Hanshu*
Bao Shuya (Bao Shu), 31, 161, 164,
    188n93
Baoxun (Treasured Instructions;
    Qinghua University manuscript),
    30–31, 301–29

Baoxun (continued)
  anecdotes in, 308–9, 311, 312, 313–17, 318, 320
  authenticity of, 324n32
  dating of, 308
  as documentary vs. anecdotal text, 305–7, 310–11, 318
  physical description of, 308
  structure of, 308–9
  transmitted texts and, 301–2
barbarians, 27, 113–44
  acculturation of, 129, 133, 135
  boundaries with, 127–34
  definition of, 113–14
  diplomacy and, 114, 129–34
  in "You Yu" anecdote, 114–21
Bentham, Jeremy, 46
Bi, Battle of, 252
bian. *See* argumentation; expediency
Biannianji (Record of Sequential Years), 20
Bickford, Maggie, 166
Bielu (Separate Records), 345
Bigan, Prince, 68, 88n14, 161–62
biographies (*zhuan*), 20–21
  See also *Lienüzhuan*
"Blue Flies" (ode; *Shijing*), 131–33
Boji, Lady (Song Boji), 10, 230, 250, 251, 259n57
Bonaventura, S., 169, 170n8
bronze inscriptions, 306, 309, 310, 322n19, 323n29, 324n37

Cai, state of, 276
  See also "Chen and Cai, frontier between"
Cao, state of, 248, 265, 345
Cao Gui, 347
Cao Ji (Xi Fuji), 158, 159, 167, 185n74, 190n110
Chao Gongwu, 154, 170n11, 182n50
Chen, Jack W., 3

Chen, state of, 280, 298n90
"Chen and Cai, frontier between" ("sojourner" anecdote), 26, 63–91
  contradictory versions of, 74–80
  as philosophical reasoning, 65–74
Chen Hao, 285
Chen Jimu, 285
Chen Minzhen, 293n35
Chen Nong, 181n50
Chen Qi, 259n47
Chen Qiyou, 224n32, 225n46, 226n49, 226n64, 228n79
Chen Wei, 293n35
Cheng, Emperor (Han; Liu Ao), 154, 155, 181n50
Cheng, King of Chu, 275
Cheng, Prince of Zhao, 123, 127
Cheng Xuanying, 90n38
Chengpu, Battle of, 333, 338, 354n13
Chin, Tamara, 138, 141n18
Chong'er, Prince. *See* Wen, Duke of Jin
Chu, state of, 129, 137, 252, 265
  Duke Wen of Jin and, 333
  in *Guoyu*, 337, 338
  in *Hanshi waizhuan*, 133
  historiography of, 281–87
  in *Mozi*, 94–96, 99–101, 108n8
  in *Shuoyuan*, 165–66
  in *Xinian*, 271–74, 276–77, 281–87, 288
  in *Xinxu*, 345
  in *Zuozhuan*, 280
Chuju (Qinghua University manuscript), 293n32
Chunqiu (Spring and Autumn Annals), 3, 18, 19–20, 264, 270
  commentaries to, 322n21
  Gongyangzhuan and, 29, 30, 231, 241, 242, 245, 246, 250, 251, 253, 260n67
  on remonstrance, 158, 159

Wang Chong on, 351
worthies in, 233, 234, 235, 236
Xinian and, 276, 283, 284
Zuozhuan and, 265, 280, 334, 335, 336
Chunqiu fanlu (Luxuriant Gems of the Spring and Autumn), 217, 250, 258n43
Chunyu Kun, 91n57
Confucianism (*rujia*; Ruism)
  appeal to example and, 46–47
  in *Han Feizi*, 194–95, 214, 217, 219, 222n8, 223n13
  vs. Mohism, 69, 71, 73–80, 88n18, 195, 201–4, 211
Confucius (Kongzi), 7, 25, 159, 348
  barbarians and, 127, 133, 135
  deductive reasoning and, 41, 42, 43, 55
  in documentary texts, 320
  on Duke Wen, 354n12
  in *Gongyangzhuan*, 230–31, 241, 252, 253
  Han Fei and, 208
  in *Han Feizi*, 28, 193–228, 222n6, 341, 342
  Mo Di and, 94, 104, 106, 107
  in *Mozi*, 102, 104, 325n40
  music and, 118
  on *Odes*, 132, 319
  on remonstrance, 157, 159, 160
  in "sojourner" anecdote, 26, 63–91
  in *Zhuangzi*, 325n40
Crump, James I., 180n47
cultural identity, 302, 318
  barbarians and, 113–14, 127–34, 136
  sharing of, 131–33, 137, 138, 168
cultural memory, 306, 310, 311, 313, 316–18
cultural relativism, 115, 133, 144n61

Dai, state of, 126–27
Danses et légendes de la Chine ancienne (Granet), 149–50
dao (the Way), 44, 72, 344
Dao (Daozhe), King of Chu, 273, 282, 283, 297n79
Daoism, 15, 120
  in *Han Feizi*, 223n11
  Huainanzi and, 111n37
  Mohism and, 93–112
  Mozi and, 26–27, 102, 103, 105, 106
  See also *Laozi*; *Zhuangzi*
Daowu, Lord of Pingye, 284, 285, 297n84
Daozang (Daoist Canon), 108n5
de (virtue), 44
  barbarians and, 119, 122–23, 125
  in governance, 14, 50, 154, 210, 215, 231, 303, 316, 346
  reputation and, 98–99, 101, 103, 104, 106, 110nn24–25, 112n49
  in "soujourner" anecdote, 67, 69–71, 80
  See also morality
Di tribes, 113, 115, 122, 126, 133, 136
Ding, Prince of Chu, 282, 283, 285–86
Dingzhou (Hebei) manuscripts, 171n13
documentary texts (*shu*), 18–20, 30–31, 301, 321n4, 329n75
  vs. anecdotes, 302–7, 318
  Baoxun as, 305–7, 310–11, 318
  expectations of, 310–11, 315
  historicity of, 19, 306, 311
  language in, 310, 317, 318
  text culture and, 319–20
  vocabulary of, 305–6
  See also *Shangshu*
Du Heng, 28–29

Du Jiaqi, 148, 154, 164, 167, 171n13
Du Zhi, 125, 126
Duo Jiao, 293n35
Duoshiwei (Subtleties of Mr. Duo), 293n35

Euthyphro (Plato), 81–85
example, appeal to, 43, 46–51, 60n65, 148, 167, 194, 207
  in anecdotes, 12–13, 17
  See also *shuo/shui*
expediency (*bian*), 123–24, 159, 160, 164, 168
expedient assessment (*quan*), 240–41, 257n27

fa (standards, laws), 196–201, 204–12, 207, 216, 218–19
  See also Legalism
Fadiman, Clifton, 5
Fan Xuanzi, 129–33, 132
Fang Shouchu, 97
Fayan (Exemplary Sayings), 173n19
Fei Wuji, 279
Fei Yi, 122–23, 127, 138
"Feigong" (Lu Xun), 98
Feng Choufu, 240
Fielding, Henry, 147
Fineman, Joel, 6
First Emperor of China, 2
framing, 4, 12–16, 21, 24, 64
  in *Baoxun*, 31, 305, 308, 309–10, 314, 320
  in *Shuoyuan*, 161, 165, 166, 167
frugality, 114–18, 134, 154
Fu Yu of Jin, 282
Fuchai, King of Wu, 7, 88n16, 89n23
Fuchai, Prince of Cao, 248
Fuxi, 124

Galvany, Albert, 3
Gan Long, 125, 126

Gao Heng, 184n70, 226n64, 227n64
Gao Shiqi, 290n9
Gaozi (Master Gao), 45
genres, 4, 16–24, 230
  annalistic, 19–20, 29
  in *Gongyangzhuan*, 255n5
  historical, 16–21, 27, 30
  narrative, 16–17, 26, 176n34, 263, 264–70, 287, 288, 302–7
  philosophical, 21–24, 25, 27, 63–64
  in *Xinian*, 273–74, 289, 293n35
  See also documentary texts; historiography; philosophy
gentleman (*junzi*), 85, 240, 267
  in "sojourner" anecdotes, 66–67, 79–80, 81
Goldin, Paul R., 14, 25, 82, 193, 200, 220
Gong, Earl of, 71
"Gongshu" anecdote (*Mozi* 50), 93–112
  body of, 95–96, 106–7
  discourse circles in, 99–106, 106–7
  ending of, 96–97, 106–7
  tensions in, 94–99, 106–7
Gongshu Ban, 95, 96, 100, 102
Gongsun Yang. See Shang Yang
Gongyangzhuan (Gongyang Commentary), 3, 19, 20, 27, 29, 229–60
  authorship of, 254n4, 260n67
  themes of, 30, 231–32
  worthies in, 232–52
Gossman, Lionel, 4, 16, 32n6
Goujian, King of Yue, 7, 70, 71, 88n16, 89n23, 133–34
governance
  abdication and, 52–53, 55
  Baoxun on, 316
  barbarians and, 138
  framing of anecdotes on, 12–13
  Gongyangzhuan on, 231–32, 245–49

Han Feizi on, 28, 196–97, 215, 216, 218
Lüshi chunqiu on, 338, 339, 340
Shuoyuan on, 154, 160, 302–3
in "sojourner" anecdote, 73
succession and, 310, 312, 316, 332
Graham, A. C., 217
Granet, Marcel, 149–50
Guan Longfeng, 68, 88n15, 161–62
Guan Zhong, 50, 51
Guanzi (Master Guan), 111n44, 152
Guliangzhuan (Guliang Commentary), 20, 255n13
Guo Yongbing, 292n31
Guodian Tomb (Hubei), 271, 327n54, 329n75
Guoyu (Discourses of the States), 3, 31, 64, 263, 296n66, 340
dates in, 298n94
"Siege of Yuan" anecdote in, 333, 336–38
vs. *Zuozhuan*, 267, 290n14, 337, 338, 340

Han, state of, 283
Han dynasty
barbarians and, 113, 136–37
decline of anecdotes in, 31, 346–47, 348, 349, 352
Eastern (Later), 31, 319, 332, 348, 350, 352
textual culture in, 319–20
vs. Warring States period, 195
Western (Former), 2, 21, 154, 331–32
Han Fei, 2, 193, 203–4, 341
in *Han Feizi*, 219, 220, 228n87
Han Feizi (Master Han Fei), 21, 27, 31, 63, 65, 193–228, 263
appeal to example in, 48, 49–50, 51
authorship of, 193, 217–18, 220
on barbarians, 142n35

"Chushuo" chapters of, 194, 205–7, 209, 213–14, 216, 221, 222n6, 225n46, 341, 342
Cluster B in, 195, 205–16, 217, 218
Clusters A and C in, 195, 196–204, 205, 217, 218
expositions vs. anecdotes in, 194, 195–96, 217–21
formation of, 28–29
framing techniques in, 12–15
inconsistencies in, 193, 204, 218
"Jade Disk of Mr. He" in, 82
"jade earrings" anecdote in, 1–2, 8–15, 23
"Nan" chapters of, 205, 206, 207, 214–16, 221, 222n6, 323n25
shuo/shui in, 22, 23, 197–208, 216–21, 222n6, 224n27, 225n43, 226n49, 342
Shuoyuan and, 155, 207
"Siege of Yuan" anecdote in, 333, 341–43, 347, 348, 354n20
"spear and shield" anecdote in, 215, 216
"You Yu" anecdote in, 116–18
Han Qu (Marquis Lie of Han), 285, 298n88
Han Ying, 143n54
Hanshi waizhuan (Han's Supplementary Commentary to the Odes), 3, 21, 31, 155, 227n77, 230, 322n21
"Lian Ji" anecdote in, 133–34
"mantis" anecdote in, 166
"You Yu" anecdote in, 116, 140n14
Hanshu (History of the Former Han Dynasty), 3, 18, 21, 137, 152
on Liu Xiang, 154–55, 168, 171n11
Hay, Peter, 34n24
He Bo, 315
He Shegu, 259n56
Heaven (*tian*), 69, 81, 88n20, 89n22

Heaven's Mandate (*tian ming*), 164, 316, 318
Heaven's will (*tianzhi*), 69, 70
Hegel, G. W. F., 56n3
Heguanzi (Pheasant Cap Master), 112n44
Heiyao, 277
Helu, King of Wu, 248–49, 279
historicity, 4, 6, 7, 10, 16
  of appeals to example, 50–51
  decline of anecdotes and, 350–52
  of documentary texts, 19, 306, 311
  of "sojourner" anecdote, 64, 87n4
historiography, 29–31
  of Chu, 281–87
  European vs. Chinese, 16–17, 18
  evolutionary, 210–11
  of *Gongyangzhuan*, 253
  informative, 264, 288
  later forms of, 20–21
  non-anecdotal, 263–99
  non-didactic, 264, 270
  vs. philosophy, 21, 63, 80–81
  praise and blame, 235, 253, 270
  role of anecdotes in, 17–18, 63–64, 229–30
Hong, Battle of, 252
Hou Hanshu (History of the Later Han Dynasty), 161, 188n91
"Hu clothing" anecdote, 121–27, 138
Hu Mao, 335
Hu Sanxing, 293n37
Hu Shih, 41
Hu Yan, 332
Hu Zhen, 334, 335
Hua Du of Song, 233–35, 256n13
Hua Feisui, 266, 267
Hua Yuan of Song, 252
Huainanzi (The Master of Huainan), 3, 9, 17, 21, 23, 31, 112n44, 230
  on barbarians, 134–35
  Confucius in, 193

  framing in, 14–15
  Han Feizi and, 217–18, 227n77
  Laozi and, 111n37, 343–46, 355n33
  Mozi 50 and, 94, 99–104, 106
  "Siege of Yuan" anecdote in, 333, 343–45, 350, 354n20
Huan, Duke of Lu, 245–47, 255n8
Huan, Duke of Qi (Xiaobai), 230, 272
  in *Han Feizi*, 50, 212
  in *Shuoyuan*, 161, 188nn93–95
  in "soujourner" anecdote, 70, 71, 89n23
  trustworthiness of, 250–51, 346, 347
  Wang Chong on, 350–51
Huanding, Lord of Yangcheng, 282, 285
Huangdi sijing (Four Canons of the Yellow Emperor), 112n44
Hui, Duke of Jin, 129–31
Hui, Duke of Lu, 245
Hui, King of Chu, 94–96, 99–101, 108n8
Hui Shi, 43
humaneness (*ren*)
  in "Gongshu" anecdote, 95
  in *Han Feizi*, 203, 215, 216
  in "Hu clothing" anecdote, 125
  in "sojourner" anecdote, 78
  in "You Yu" anecdote, 119
Hunter, Michael, 198, 342

Idle Talk: Gossip and Anecdote in Traditional China (Chen and Schaberg), 3

"Jade Disk of Mr. He," 82, 84, 91n52, 198
"jade earrings" anecdote, 1–2, 8–15, 23
Jamieson, Dale, 74
Ji Huanzi, 118, 140n12

Ji Wuzi, 132, 143n53
Ji You of Lu (Jizi), 242, 243–44
Ji Zheng, 342
jia (intellectual schools), 219, 220
Jia of Jing (Jing Jia), 282
Jia Yi, 48
Jian, Duke of Zheng, 211, 227n64
jian bai (hard and white), 199, 201, 224n29
jian'ai (impartial care), 51–52
Jianshu (Qin minister), 140n14
jiao (teaching), 134–35
Jie (tyrant), 47, 88n15, 161–62
Jin, state of, 252, 265, 267
  barbarians and, 129–33, 142n43
  Duke Wen and, 332–56
  in *Xinian*, 271–74, 277, 282–85, 288
  in *Zuozhuan*, 277–78
jing (guidelines, propositions)
  in *Han Feizi*, 205–7, 209, 211, 213, 222n6, 342, 343
  in *Shuoyuan*, 148, 155, 156, 157, 167, 168, 184n67
Jing, Duke of Qi, 161–62, 211, 227n66, 251–52, 259n47
Jingping, King of Chu, 279
Jinteng (Metal Bound Coffer; Qinghua University manuscript), 308, 309, 313, 326n48
Jiu Fan, 160–61, 188n90, 188n91
Jueyou, Prince of Wu, 278–79
Junzhai dushu (Chao Gongwu), 154
justice, statist vs. familial, 231, 241, 242, 245, 250, 253, 254
Justinian I (Byzantine emperor), 5, 6
Juzhi (Rong chieftan), 129–33, 134, 137, 138

Kern, Martin, 301, 306
Kierman, Frank A., 338
Knoblock, John, 339

Kong Yingda, 132
Kongfu Jia of Song, 233–35, 256n13
Kongzi jiayu (School Sayings of Confucius), 159
Kongzi jiyu (Collected Sayings of Confucius), 348
Kongzi shilun (Confucius's Discussion of the Odes), 319
Krijgsman, Rens, 19, 29, 30–31

Laozi, 15, 111n37, 223n11, 320, 343, 344, 345
Laozi (Old Master), 15, 44, 46
  Han Feizi and, 203, 205, 223n11
  Huainanzi and, 111n37, 343–46, 355n33
  Mozi and, 27, 103, 106
Lee, Ting-mien, 26–27, 86, 221, 223n13
Legalism (*fajia*), 194, 219, 220, 223n11
Lewis, Mark Edward, 173n17, 174n23
Li (tyrant), 47
Li, Duke of Zheng, 257n28
Li Ci, 142n35
Li Daoyuan, 347
Li Fang, 348
Li Ji, 238–39
Li Ji Unrest, 332
Li Ke, 237–39
Li Shoukui, 305
Li Wai-yee, 3, 27, 197, 266, 270, 295n63
Li Xueqin, 273, 293n35, 305, 308
Lian Ji, 133, 134, 137, 138, 143n55
Liang Qichao, 97, 108n9
Liao of Wu, 247, 248–49
Lienüzhuan (Biographies of Exemplary Women), 3, 149, 161, 172n14, 345, 349
  Xinian and, 276, 277
Liezi (Master Lie), 152, 175n27

Liezi xinshu (New Documents by Master Lie), 152
Liji (Records of Ritual), 136, 179n39, 186n77
Ling, Duke of Chen, 158, 277, 278
Ling, Duke of Jin, 242, 243, 244, 259n56
Ling, King of Chu, 278–79
Liu An, King of Huainan, 14–15, 344, 345, 350
Liu Ao. *See* Cheng, Emperor
Liu Wendian, 143n59
Liu Xiang, 23, 28, 65, 345, 349
  as author of *Shuoyuan*, 148–53, 167, 168–69
  memorial of, 150–51, 153, 167, 168, 171n12
  See also *Shuoyuan*
Liu Xiaogan, 217
Liu Xin, 183n61
Liu Yiqing, 352
Liuzi xinlun (Master Liu's New Discussions), 347–48
Lloyd, G. E. R., 220–21
Lu, state of, 19–20, 132, 232, 272, 274, 337
Lü Buwei, 21–22, 338, 339, 340, 350
Lu Xun, 98
Lunheng (Balanced Discourses), 350
Lunyu (Analects), 49, 85, 214
  barbarians and, 127, 134
  deductive reasoning and, 42–43
  Duke Wen in, 354n12
  on "pine and cypress," 42, 55, 82
  "sojourner" anecdotes and, 26, 66–67, 70, 72, 73, 76–78, 80, 89n27
Luo Genze, 148
Lüshi chunqiu (Spring and Autumn Annals of Mr. Lü), 21–22, 31, 65, 162, 263
  on barbarians, 140n14

  Greek philosophy and, 83–84
  Guoyu and, 340
  Han Feizi and, 342–43
  Mozi and, 94, 99–103, 104, 106
  shen and *ming* in, 112n44
  "Siege of Yuan" anecdote in, 333, 338–41, 348, 350, 354n20
  "sojourner" anecdote in, 26, 71–72, 73, 75, 76, 78, 79–80, 89n27
  Xinian and, 277
  "You Yu" anecdote in, 116
  Zuozhuan and, 340

Ma Zong, 182n50
Major, John, 217
Makeham, John, 89n27
Man tribes, 113, 136
"mantis" anecdote, 165–66
Masters (*zi*)
  Han Feizi and, 200, 217, 219–20, 221, 225n36
  "sojourner" anecdote and, 63–65, 66, 72, 74, 80, 82
  texts of (*zishu*), 194, 263
Mengzi (Mencius), 20, 45, 49
Mengzi (Mencius), 45, 76, 284
metaphors, 42–43, 178n35, 180n46
Meyer, Andrew Seth, 25–26, 42, 217, 221, 319
Mian Chen, 328n60
Miao tribes, 113, 123, 134, 140n8
Miao Wenyuan, 125
Min, Duke of Lu, 242, 243, 244
Min, Duke of Song, 236–37
ming (visible), 94, 97–99, 101, 103–6, 109n22, 111nn41–44, 112nn44–47
Miu, Duke of Song, 259n47
Mohism
  appeal to example and, 46–47
  Daoism and, 93–112
  deductive reasoning in, 51–52

in *Han Feizi*, 219
paradox and, 44
reputation and merit in, 98–99, 101, 103, 104, 106, 110nn24–25, 112n49
vs. Ruism, 69, 71, 73–80, 88n18, 195, 201–4, 211
"sojourner" anecdotes and, 69
See also *Mozi*
morality, 7, 10, 12, 14, 26, 45, 93
appeal to example and, 60n65
in documentary texts, 307
in *Gongyangzhuan*, 30, 240, 242, 249, 253, 254, 257n27
in *Guoyu*, 338
in historical narratives, 17, 263, 264, 266, 270, 287, 288
Shuoyuan on, 303
in "Siege of Yuan" anecdote, 336, 340–41
in "sojourner" anecdotes, 69, 70, 73, 75–76, 78, 80, 81
in *Xinian*, 274, 276, 281, 287, 289
in *Zuozhuan*, 268, 269–70
See also humaneness; righteousness; trustworthiness
Mozi (Master Mo), 3, 82, 115
Confucius in, 102, 104, 325n40
Daoism and, 26–27, 102, 103, 105, 106
dialogue chapters of, 98
"Gongshu" anecdote in, 93–112
Lüshi chunqiu and, 94, 99–103, 104, 106
shuo/shui and, 179n45
Shuoyuan and, 183n65
"sojourner" anecdote in, 26, 69, 70, 73–78
Xinian and, 296n66
vs. *Xunzi*, 89n22
Mozi (Mo Di), 46, 47, 88n18, 140n9, 201, 209

as Daoist, 26–27
on ritual, 114–15
Mu, Duke of Qin, 116, 117, 119, 120
Mu, Duke of Zheng, 277
"Mushi" (The Oath at Mu), 45–46
music
remonstrance against, 160–61
Shuoyuan on, 154, 155
in "sojourner" anecdotes, 73
in "You Yu" anecdote, 116–18, 119, 120
Muyi, Prince of Song, 245

Nangong Changwan of Song, 235–37
narrative. See *under* genres
Niu Zan, 125

oral tradition, 64, 65, 113, 281, 312, 318, 326n44
Ōta Hō, 225n46
Ouyue, state of, 123, 141n25

paradox, 43–44, 69, 224n30
Pascal's wager, 83, 91n52
Petersen, Jens Østergård, 3, 179n41
philosophy, 21–27, 41, 63–65, 318
in *Baoxun*, 313, 316
Greco-Roman, 24–25, 37n70, 41–42, 56nn5–6, 65, 80–85, 86, 220–21
in Masters texts, 194
schools (*jia*) of, 219, 220
See also Confucianism; Daoism; Legalism
"pine and cypress" (poplar) anecdote, 42, 55, 82, 85
Pines, Yuri, 3, 20, 29, 30, 115, 127, 210–11, 322n21
Ping, Duke of Jin, 160–61
Ping, King of Zhou, 128
Plato, 73–74, 81–82, 84, 85
Procopius of Caesarea, 5, 6

proverbs, 10, 48–49, 149, 230
Ptak, Roderich, 351
Puett, Michael, 85

Qi, state of, 13, 211, 265, 337
  in *Xinian*, 272, 277, 283, 286
qiang (strength), 103, 106
Qiang tribes, 113, 134
Qin, state of, 126, 129–31, 292n27
  Duke Wen of Jin and, 332
  in *Xinian*, 272, 277, 282, 288
  "You Yu" anecdote and, 120–21
Qin dynasty, 2, 113, 136–37, 263
Qing Fu of Lu, 242, 244
Qinghua University manuscripts, 18, 264, 271, 280, 293n32, 301, 308
  Chuju, 293n32
  Jinteng, 308, 309, 313, 326n48
  See also *Baoxun*
Qiongda yishi (Success and Failure Come at Their Respective Times; Guodian manuscript), 327n54
Qiu Mu, 233, 256n16
Qu Wu (Duke of Shen), 277, 278, 280
Queen, Sarah A., 3, 20, 29, 30, 193, 307
  on *Han Feizi*, 203, 225n47
  on *Huainanzi*, 193, 217
  on *shuo/shui*, 22, 274n27
Qunshu zhiyao, 110n26

Regan, Tom, 74
remonstrance
  direct, 170n7, 184n72
  indirect, 155, 157, 159–60, 163, 164, 166, 168, 184n72, 186n79, 187n87
  in *Shuoyuan*, 154–68
Republic (Plato), 73–74, 84–85
Rhetoric (Aristotle), 148
rhyme, 166, 168, 184n69, 191n118

riddles, 57n16, 160, 165
Riegel, Jeffrey, 339
Riffaterre, Michael, 174n25
righteousness (*yi*), 45, 83
  barbarians and, 135, 137
  in "Gongshu" anecdote, 95
  in *Gongyangzhuan*, 233, 234
  in *Han Feizi*, 203, 214
  in "Hu clothing" anecdote, 125
  in *Shuoyuan*, 152
  in "sojourner" anecdote, 67, 71, 73, 75–76, 78, 83
  in "You Yu" anecdote, 119
ritual (*li*)
  in *Baoxun*, 306, 309, 318, 320
  barbarians and, 128, 135, 137
  in *Gongyangzhuan*, 231, 250–52
  in *Han Feizi*, 214
  in "Hu clothing" anecdote, 123–24
  Mohist criticism of, 114–15
  Shuoyuan on, 152, 154, 179n39
  in "You Yu" anecdote, 121
  See also *Liji*
Rong tribes, 113, 115, 134, 136, 137, 138
  state of Jin and, 129–33
  in "You Yu" anecdote, 114–21
  Zhou dynasty and, 128–29
Roth, Harold, 217

sage kings (Former Kings), 52–53, 115
  in *Han Feizi*, 202–4, 209–10, 211, 216, 218
  See also Shun; Tang; Wen, King of Zhou; Wu, King of Zhou; Yao; Yu
sages, 47–48, 87n6
  See also Masters
Schaberg, David, 3, 17, 63–64, 65, 66, 69, 80, 81, 263, 264, 268, 269, 281, 287–88, 307, 350, 351
Schilling, Dennis, 351

Schwermann, Christian, 28, 29, 65, 194, 207, 225n43
Shang, Duke of Song (Yuyi), 233–35, 259n47
Shang dynasty, 116, 206, 207, 209, 302, 316
Shang Yang (Gongsun Yang), 125, 126, 127
  in *Han Feizi*, 194, 206, 208–9, 219–20, 228n87
Shanghai Museum manuscripts, 263, 271, 289, 319
Shangjia Wei, 315, 316, 318, 320, 328n60
Shangjunshu (Book of Lord Shang), 121, 125–26, 211
Shangshu (*Shujing*; Book of Documents), 18, 181n47, 301, 323n26
  Baoxun and, 30–31, 305, 310, 313, 320
  bronze inscriptions and, 322n19
  documentary genre and, 303–4, 321n4
  in "You Yu" anecdote, 119
Shao Kong (Xia Ji), 277–78, 280, 294n44, 295n63
Shao Ruzi, 165–66
Shejian, Duke of Teng, 284
shen (invisible), 94, 97–99, 101, 103–6, 109n22, 111nn41–44, 112nn44–47
Shen, Protector, 162
Shen Baoxu, 280
Shen Buhai, 219, 220, 228n87
Shen Dao, 219, 228n87
Shen Qinhan, 171n12
Shen Sheng of Jin, 238–39
Sheng (Shenghuan), King of Chu, 282, 283, 286
Shennong, 124
shenren (numinous man), 105, 106, 112n47

shi (historical account, narrative), 176n34
Shi Kuang, 188n91
Shiji (Records of the Historian), 3, 18, 21, 86n4, 350
  on barbarians, 122, 126, 137, 138, 139
  Han Feizi and, 223n11, 225n36
  Shuoyuan and, 176n30, 177n34
  Xinian and, 296n70
  "You Yu" anecdote in, 116, 118–21
Shijing (Book of Odes), 59n40, 131–33
  commentaries on, 132, 230, 319
  documentary texts and, 306, 318, 320
  Han Feizi and, 211, 212, 227n70
  in "You Yu" anecdote, 119
Shishuo xinyu (A New Account of the Tales of the World), 352
Shizi (Master Shi), 94, 99–101, 103–5, 111n41, 112n47
Shou, King of Shang, 46
Shu Wu of Wei, 247
Shu Ya of Lu, 242, 243
Shuijingzhu (Commentary on the Waterways Classic), 347
Shun (sage-king), 47, 53, 64, 140n8, 161
  in *Baoxun*, 314, 315, 316, 318, 320
  barbarians and, 115, 123, 124, 127
  in *Han Feizi*, 202, 203, 215
  in "You Yu" anecdote, 116
shuo/shui (illustrative examples; persuasion), 22–24, 148, 153, 155, 167, 179n44
  in *Han Feizi*, 22, 23, 197–208, 216–21, 222n6, 224n27, 225n43, 226n49, 342
Shuoyuan (*Shuiyuan*; Garden of Illustrative Examples/Persuasions), 3, 27, 28, 31, 345, 349

Shuoyuan (continued)
  argumentation in, 147–92
  authorship of, 148–53, 167, 168–69
  on barbarians, 135, 140n14
  chapter 9 ("Zhengjian") of, 153, 155–66, 167, 168, 189n99
  chapter 11 ("Shanshui") of, 153, 167
  chapter titles of, 152
  on Duke of Zhou, 302–3
  as explanation vs. persuasion, 65, 153–56
  graphs in title of, 22, 23, 148, 167, 178n35, 180n46
  Han Feizi and, 155, 207
  introductions in, 149, 152, 154, 155, 156–57, 167, 181n48
  "mantis" anecdote in, 165–66
  structuring devices in, 156–57, 167
  "You Yu" anecdote in, 116
Shushu of Zhulou, 248
Shuzhong Hui, 255n8, 259n47
Shuzi Gong, 282
"Siege of Yuan" anecdote, 333–46, 352
  in *Guoyu*, 333, 336–38
  in *Han Feizi*, 333, 341–43, 347, 354n20
  in *Huainanzi*, 333, 343–45
  in *Lüshi chunqiu*, 333, 338–41, 348, 350, 354n20
  in *Xinxu*, 333, 345–46, 354n20
  in *Zuozhuan*, 333, 334–36, 347, 354n20
Sima Guang, 120, 348
Sima Qian, 21, 86n4, 263, 288, 289nn4–5
  authorship and, 169
  on barbarians, 137, 138
  historicity and, 350
  "You Yu" anecdote and, 121
  See also *Shiji*
Sima Zifan of Chu, 252

Smith, Kidder, 202
Socrates, 81, 82, 83, 84–85
"sojourner" anecdote. See "Chen and Cai, frontier between"
Song, state of, 94–95, 96, 100, 252
  in *Xinian*, 283, 284
  in *Zuozhuan*, 265–67, 269
"spear and shield" anecdote, 215–16
Sui, Prince of Lu, 255n8
Sun Qing xinshu (New Documents by Sun Qing), 152
Sun Xingyan, 348
Sun Yirang, 97, 125
Sunshu Ao, 31
Sunzi (Sun Tzu), 7
syllogisms, 41–42, 52, 61n78

Tai, Earl of Zheng, 282
Taigong Ren, 77, 78, 90n38
Taiping yulan (Imperial Readings of the Taiping Era), 348
Taixuan (Supreme Mystery), 173n19
Takigawa Kametarō, 125
Tang (sage-king), 47, 48
Teng, state of, 297n85
text culture, 31, 305, 319–20
text formation, 27–29
  collage-like, 149, 150, 174n21, 174n25, 184n69
  of *Shuoyuan*, 149–53
  structuring devices for, 156–57, 167
  wandering anecdotes in, 164–65, 168
Theodora (Byzantine empress), 5
thought experiments, 65, 73–74, 76, 81–83, 90n31, 90n34, 91n54
Tian, Duke of Song, 282
Tian Chengzi, 189n99
Tian Ying. See Xue, Duke of
time frame, 7, 8, 313–14, 315
tradition, 114, 121–27, 134
Trauzettel, Rolf, 168

trustworthiness (*xin*), 348, 354n13
  Duke Wen of Jin and, 333, 334–36
  in *Gongyangzhuan*, 238–39, 250–52, 253
  in *Guoyu*, 337–38
  in *Han Feizi*, 341–43
  in *Huainanzi*, 343–45
  in *Lüshi chunqiu*, 339, 340
  in "Siege of Yuan" anecdote, 347
  in *Xinxu*, 345–46

van Els, Paul, 3, 21, 31, 227n77
Vogelsang, Kai, 3

Wan (Nangong Changwan) of Song, 235–37
Wang Chong, 127, 140n8, 169, 350–52, 356n42
Wang Mang, 349
Wang Shou, 31
Wang Wei, 120
Wang Xianshen, 227n64, 228n79
Wang Yinglin, 182n50, 208
Wangsun Xie, 123
Warring States period, 2, 11, 14
  barbarians in, 113, 136–37
  vs. Han, 195, 255n4
  ministerial class in, 232
  philosophical debate in, 80–83, 194, 200, 220, 270, 288
  texts from, 18, 82, 86, 194, 211, 229, 263–64, 271, 289, 301–3
  textual culture in, 21, 150, 207, 220, 305, 319–20
  See also particular texts
Watson, Burton, 336
Wei, King of Qi (Tian Yinqi), 1–2, 8
Wei, state of, 122, 247, 265, 266, 354n20
  in *Han Feizi*, 341, 342, 343
  in *Lüshi chunqiu*, 339

  in *Xinian*, 283
  in *Xinxu*, 345
Wei Choufu, 53–54
Wei Ji (Marquis Wu of Wei), 285, 298n88
wen (cultural refinement), 114–21, 134
Wen, city of, 343, 344, 345–46, 354n20
Wen, Duke of Jin (Prince Chong'er), 7, 64, 70–71, 89n23, 185n74, 188n90, 332–56
  Confucius on, 354n12
  decline of anecdotes and, 350
  in *Guoyu*, 336–38
  in *Han Feizi*, 341–43
  in *Huainanzi*, 343–45
  in *Lüshi chunqiu*, 338–41
  Wang Chong on, 356n42
  in *Xinxu*, 345–46
  in *Zuozhuan*, 334–36
Wen, Emperor (Han), 138, 144n64
Wen, King of Chu, 275, 276
Wen, King of Jing, 162
Wen, King of Zhou (sage-king), 47, 302
  in *Baoxun*, 304, 309, 310, 313, 318, 320
  in *Gongyangzhuan*, 231, 232, 241, 253
  in *Han Feizi*, 203, 204
Wen, Marquis of Wei, 347
Wen Jiang, 255n8
wenxue (textual learning), 200–201, 216, 224n29
Wenzi (Master Wen), 112n44
worthies (*xian*)
  abdicators, 247–50
  avengers, 241–45
  moral conflicts of, 240, 242, 249, 253, 254, 257n27
  of propriety and trustworthiness, 250–52

worthies *(continued)*
  protectors, 232–41
  regents, 245–47, 248
Wu, Duke of Zheng, 9
Wu, Emperor (Han), 121, 288, 345
Wu, king of, 165–66
Wu, King of Zhou (sage-king), 46, 47, 48, 302–3
  in *Baoxun*, 304, 312, 313
  in *Han Feizi*, 203
Wu, state of, 137, 265, 277–78, 280, 337
Wu Ji (Ji of Wu), 279, 280, 281
Wu Qi, 347
Wu Zixu (Wu Yun), 68, 88n16, 242, 279, 280, 295n54
Wuling, King of Zhao, 121–27, 138, 142n35, 210

Xi, Duke of Qi, 188n95
Xi, Duke of Zheng, 255n8
Xi Fuji. *See* Cao Ji
Xi Gui, 274–75, 276
Xi Ke, 240, 259n56
Xi Qi of Jin, 238–39
Xia dynasty, 48, 53, 88n15, 116, 137
Xia Ji (Shao Kong), 277–78, 280, 294n44, 295n63
Xia Zhengshu, 278, 280
Xiafu of Zhulou, 248
Xian, Duke of Jin, 238–39, 257n23, 332
Xiang, Duke of Qi, 242
Xiang, Duke of Song, 211, 227n64, 245, 252
Xiang, Duke of Zhao, 122
Xiang, King of Zhou, 333, 335
Xiang Zonglu, 170n7, 188n91
Xianyun tribes, 113
Xiao, Duke of Qin, 125
Xicizhuan (Appended Sayings), 322n21
Xie Mingren, 148, 167, 171n13, 181n50

Xie Ye, 158, 159, 185n74
Xin dynasty (Wang Mang), 349
Xin You, 128
Xinian (Sequence of Years), 20, 271–74
  audience for, 264, 287–88
  dates in, 286, 298n95
  dating of, 273, 292n31
  language in, 271–72, 297n78
  sources of, 272, 274, 280–81
  structure of, 273–74
  vs. *Zuozhuan*, 30, 272–81, 283, 286, 287, 296n66
Xinxu (Newly Arranged Anecdotes), 3, 31, 171n13, 178n38, 182n50
  author of, 151, 152, 349
  as compilation, 148–49
  as remonstrance, 154
  "Siege of Yuan" anecdote in, 333, 345–46, 354n20
Xinyuan (New Collection), 150, 153
Xiongnu tribes, 113, 121
  Han dynasty and, 136–37, 144n64
  "Hu clothing" anecdote and, 121
  Zhonghang Yue and, 137–38
Xishi, Prince, 247
Xiu, Duke of Song, 283, 297n79
Xu, Duke of Zheng, 283, 297n79
Xu Fuguan, 148, 167
Xu You, 71
Xu Zi Tuo (Tuo of Xu), 292n27
Xuan, Duke of Lu (Prince Sui), 255n8, 259n47
Xuan, Duke of Song, 259n47
Xuan, Emperor (Han; Liu Bingyi), 181n50
Xuan, Queen Dowager of Qin, 53–54
Xue, Duke of (Tian Ying; Lord Jingguo), 1–2, 8, 13
Xun Xi of Jin, 233, 237–39, 256n16, 257n23
Xunzi, 44, 134–35
  deductive reasoning by, 52–53, 55

Xunzi (Master Xun), 63, 82, 111n44, 329n75
  Han Feizi and, 212
  vs. *Mozi*, 89n22
  Shuoyuan and, 152, 189n102
  "sojourner" anecdote in, 26, 67–70, 75–78, 89n20, 89n27

Yan Hui, 71, 76–77, 79–80
Yan Kejun, 150
Yan Ying, 88n12, 160
Yan Zhuoju, 189n99
Yan Zhuqu, 161–62
Yang Chufu, 259n56
Yang Sheng of Qi, 259n47
Yang Xiong, 169, 173n19
Yanzi chunqiu (Spring and Autumn Annals of Master Yan), 3, 21, 88n12, 152, 175n27, 263
Yao (sage-king), 47, 48, 64, 161
  in *Baoxun*, 314, 316
  barbarians and, 115, 116, 124
  in *Han Feizi*, 202, 203, 215
Yellow Emperor, 124, 137
Yi Gao of Jin, 258n43
Yi Mei of Wu, 248
Yi tribes, 113, 115, 119, 127, 128, 133, 136
Yi Zhou shu (Remaining Zhou Documents), 18, 301, 305, 321n4, 322n19
Yijing (Book of Changes; *I Ching*), 157, 158, 184n70, 306, 319
Yin, Duke of Lu, 241, 245–47, 255n8
"Yiwenzhi" (Treatise on Arts and Letters), 219
Yong Ji, 257n28
Yong Rui, 54
Yoshimoto Michimasa, 292n31
You (tyrant), 47
You, Prince of Lu (Ji You), 242, 243–44
You Yi, 316, 328n60

"You Yu" anecdote, 115–21, 137, 138
Yu (sage-king), 47, 48, 53
  barbarians and, 115, 116, 123, 127, 137
Yu Ji of Wu, 248
Yuan. *See* "Siege of Yuan" anecdote
Yuan, Duke of Song, 265–67, 269
Yuan Shu, 293n35
Yucong (Thicket of Sayings; Guodian manuscript), 329n75
Yue, state of, 137, 277, 283, 297n85, 337
Yue Shifu, 88n12
Yue tribes, 135
Yuyi of Song, 233–35, 259n47

Zai Yu, 71
Zangsun Xu, 259n56
Zeng Gong, 170n11
Zeno, 5, 6
Zha, Prince of Wu (Jizi, Ji Zha), 247, 248–49
Zhaizhong of Zheng, 240–41, 257n28
Zhanguoce (Stratagems of the Warring States), 3, 14, 31, 48, 263, 345, 349
  on barbarians, 127, 142n35
  "Hu clothing" anecdote in, 121, 122, 125–26
  "jade earrings" anecdote in, 11
  Shuoyuan and, 154, 177n34
  "Siege of Yuan" anecdote in, 347
Zhao, Duke of Lu, 251–52, 266
Zhao, King of Chu, 86n4, 279
Zhao, King of Qin, 210
Zhao, King of Wei, 211
Zhao, Prince of Zhou, 267, 269
Zhao, state of, 121–27, 142n35, 283
Zhao Chuan, 242, 244, 258n43
Zhao Cui, 332, 334, 335, 353n9
Zhao Dun of Jin, 242, 243, 244, 250, 258n43
Zhao Jianzi, 31

Zhao Si, 285, 298n89
Zhao Wen, 124
Zhao Yan, 125
Zhao Zao, 124
Zhen, Prince of Wu, 279
Zheng, state of, 130, 266, 283, 284, 286–87, 337
Zheng Liangshu, 225n46
Zheng Xuan, 132
Zhengshu, Prince of Chen, 277, 294n44
zhong (middle, center), concept of, 314–15, 316, 327n51
zhongguo (central domains; China)
   vs. barbarians, 113–34
   defined, 113–14
Zhonghang Yue, 121, 137–38, 139
Zhongshan, state of, 123, 126, 142n35
Zhòu (tyrant), 47, 88n14, 161–62
Zhou, Duke of, 7, 302–4, 307, 313
Zhou dynasty, 2, 302, 311
   barbarians and, 113, 142n43
   capital of, 128
   Gongyangzhuan and, 254
   in *Guoyu*, 337
   in *Xinian*, 271, 273, 283
   in *Xinxu*, 345
   in *Zuozhuan*, 267, 269
Zhou Shao, 125
Zhu Xi, 132
Zhuang, Duke of Lu, 188n95, 235–37, 250
Zhuang, Duke of Zheng, 257n28
Zhuang, King of Chu, 128–29, 162–64, 252, 277
Zhuangping, Lord of Liang, 284
Zhuangzi (Master Zhuang), 3, 8, 10, 31, 33n7, 230
   appeals to example in, 50–51
   Confucius in, 325n40
   Han Feizi and, 217, 223n13
   "mantis" anecdote in, 166
   Mozi and, 27, 103, 105, 106
   reasoning in, 82

   shen and *ming* in, 112n47
   "sojourner" anecdote in, 26, 76–78, 79, 80
Zhuozi of Jin, 237–39
Zhushu jinian (Bamboo Annals), 122, 264, 273, 293n35, 296n66
Zhuyu Ji, 162–64, 190n107
Zi Ban, 242, 243
Zi Chi, Prince of Lu, 255n8, 259n47
Zifan, 277
Zigong, 71, 72, 87n4, 207
Ziju, 280
Zilu, 66–75, 135
Zishu Qizi, 132, 143n53
Zisi, 201, 255n8
Ziyang of Zheng, 284, 297n82
Zizhang, 201
Zizhi tongjian (Comprehensive Mirror in Aid of Governance), 293n35, 348
Zouchu yigu shidai (Walking out of the Age of Doubting Antiquity), 301
Zuo Qiuming, 334, 336–37
Zuo Songchao, 152, 167
Zuozhuan (Zuo Commentary), 3, 20, 31, 63, 64, 80, 263
   audience for, 268–70
   barbarians and, 128, 131, 132
   Chunqiu and, 265, 280, 334, 335, 336
   dating of, 290n19
   vs. *Gongyangzhuan*, 230–32, 252, 255n13, 256n18, 257n28, 257nn22–25, 259n57
   Guoyu and, 267, 290n14, 337, 338, 340
   language use in, 291n25
   non-anecdotal narratives in, 264–70, 288
   "Siege of Yuan" anecdote in, 333, 334–36, 347, 354n20
   "sojourner" anecdote in, 66
   sources of, 274, 280–81
   vs. *Xinian*, 30, 272–81, 283, 286, 287, 296n66

www.ingramcontent.com/pod-product-compliance
Ingram Content Group UK Ltd.
Pitfield, Milton Keynes, MK11 3LW, UK
UKHW042223130825
461842UK00011B/121